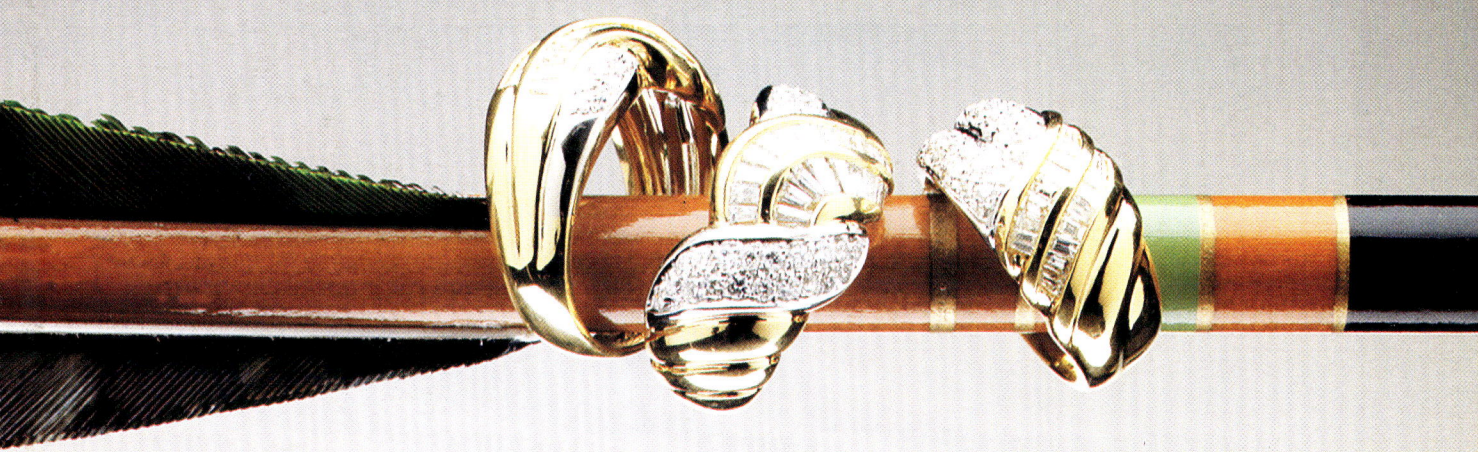

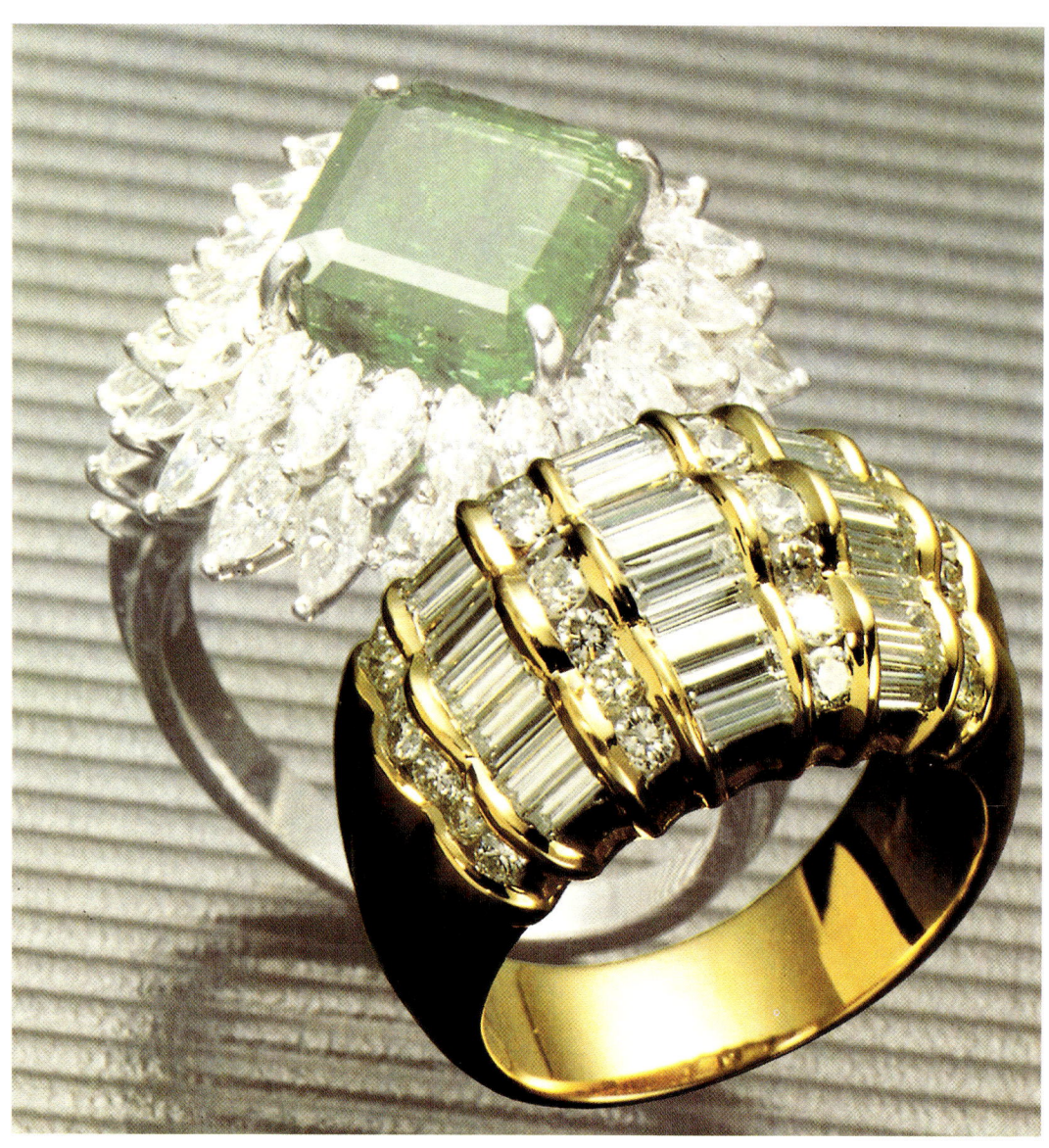

Time passes, jewels endure
Moraglione, goldsmith artisans since 1922

DESIGNER JEWELLERY

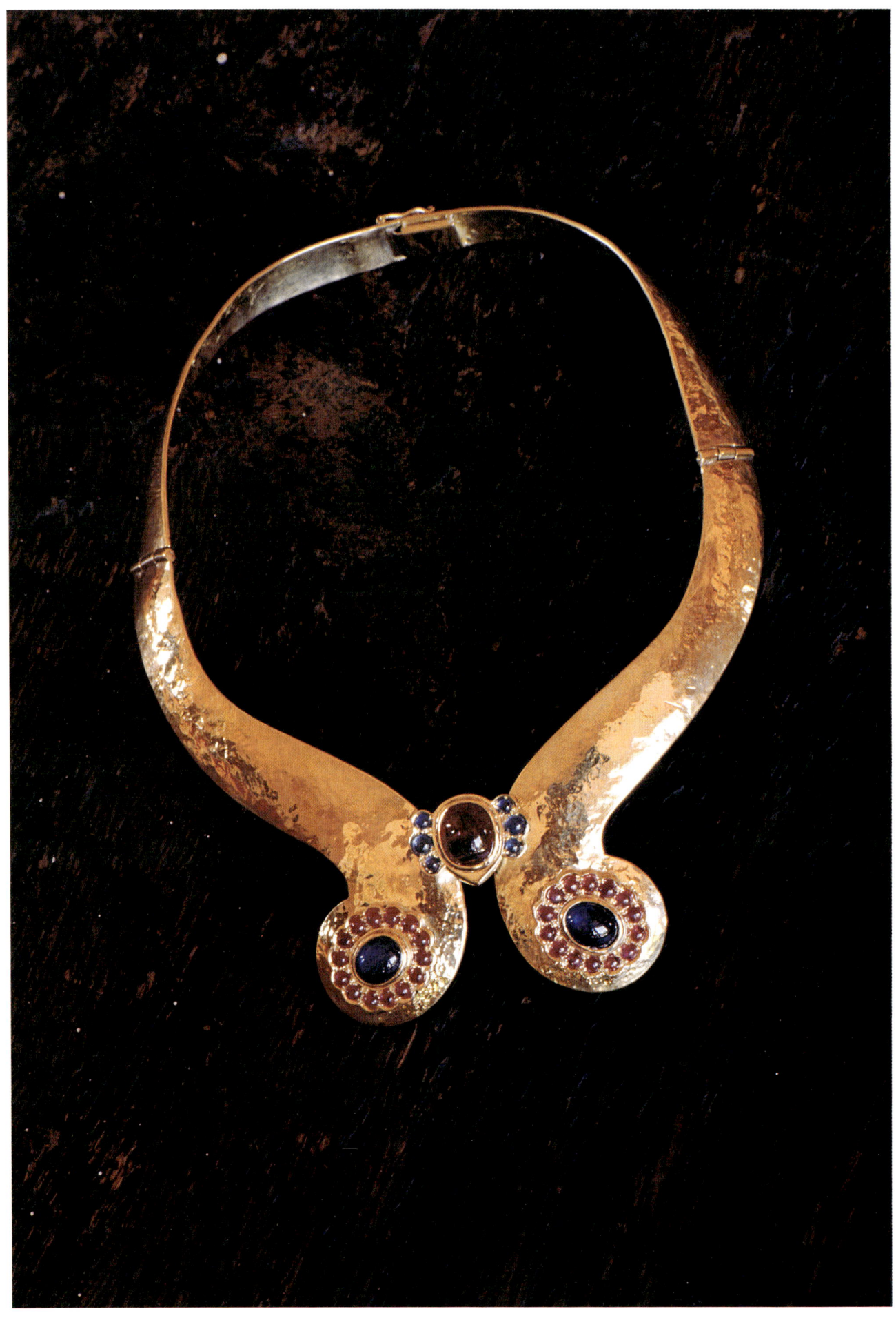

'Michèle', choker in gold, rubies and sapphires. Design by Claude Mazloum carried out in collaboration with Marcello Pizzari.

CLAUDE MAZLOUM

DESIGNER JEWELLERY

THE WORLD'S TOP ARTISTS

In collaboration with:

Jean VENDOME
Gabriel TOLKOWSKY
Bernd MUNSTEINER
Vincent De JAEGHER
Hubert MINNEBO
Caroline PORTAIL

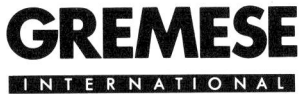

GREMESE
INTERNATIONAL

Thanks

The author would like to thank the following for their help: Dario BINA, Elena BONAPACE, Dorine BUNNIK, Gordon BURROWS, Inmee CHOI, Melissa COGHLAN, Chris COLEMONT, Rosanna COMI, Lut CONINCKX, Marianne CSERHATI, Mimi CZERNIN, Mia De DOOY, Christine DIETZ, Emile DUFOUR, Paola FANTINI, Susan FARMER, Guido GIOVANNINI-TORELLI, Marie-Christine HEEREN, Vincent De JAEGHER, Beth KULICK, Jean-Yves LE MIGNOT, Annie MALDANT, Atiyanee MATHAYOMCHAN, Hubert MINNEBO, Marina MORINI, Angeles MOYA, Jochen MULLER, Bernd MUNSTEINER, Wiltraut OPFERMANN, Alfred PETH, Caroline PORTAIL, Lynn RAMSEY, Aida SANTIAGO, Jye SHIOW, Teresa SICUPIRA, Cri-Cri SOLAK-EASTIN, Diane TAYLOR, Sophie TERNHEIM, Nicole TIXIER, Gabriel TOLKOWSKY, Jean VENDOME, Thierry VENDOME, Hans WINS and Hee YANG.

Cover: *Casa Damiani, ring in diamonds and gold.*
Fly-leaf: *MORAGLIONE, 3 rings in diamonds and gold.*
Back-cover: *J.P. de Saedeleer, necklace in gold and black pearls.*

French texts translated by: *Joyce Dall'Acqua Peterson*

Layout: *Fortunato Romani*

Jacket design by: *Antonio Dojmi*

Phototypeset and Photolithography: *Grafica Internazionale - Rome*

Printed and Bound by: *Conti Tipocolor - Calenzano (FI) - ITALY*

ISBN 88-7301-021-0
©1993 Gremese International s.r.l., Rome
Casella postale 14335
00149 Rome

CONTENTS

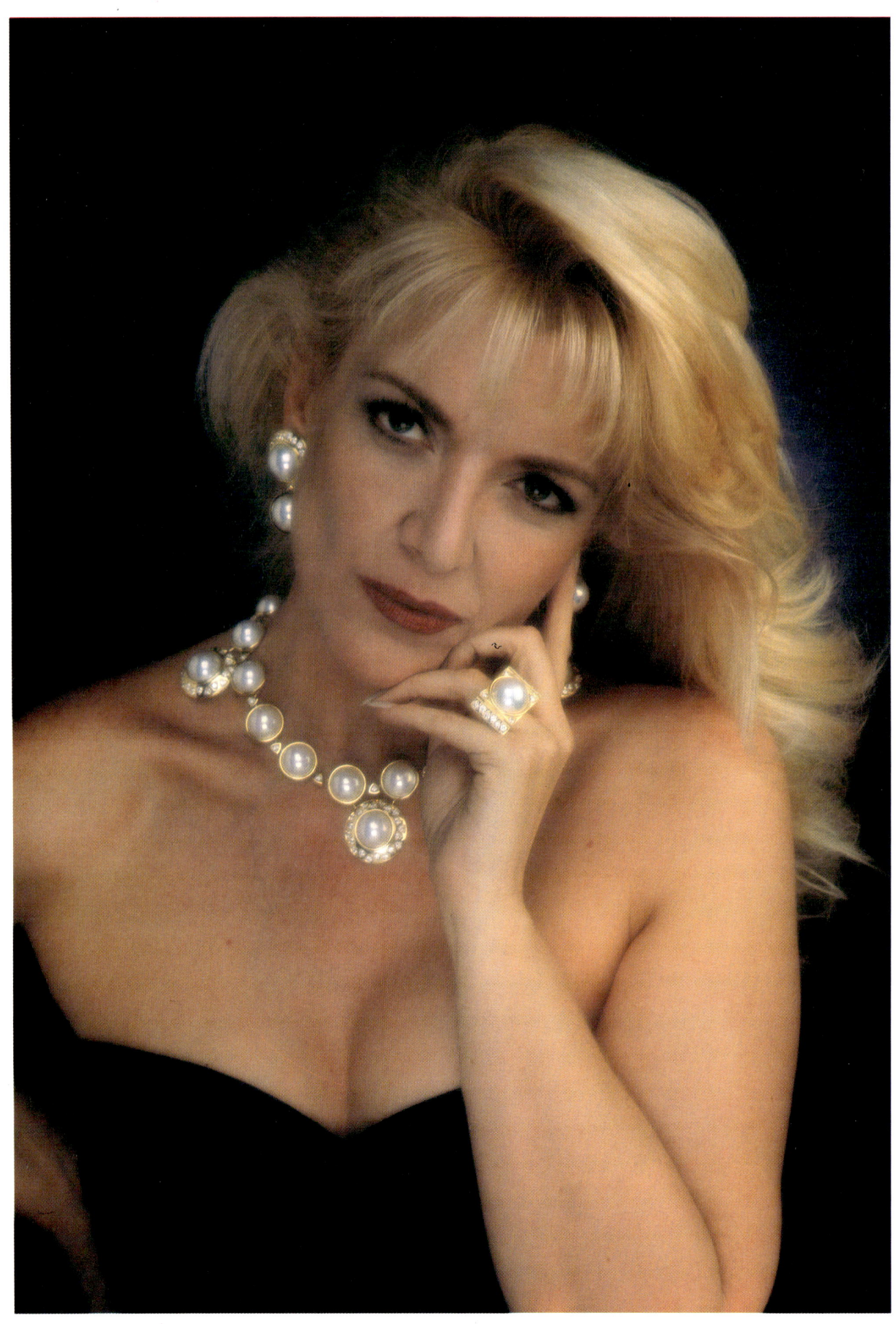

10 *Ring, necklace and earrings in gold with 29 mabé pearls and 22 carats of diamonds created by Jussara Caracante.*

PREFACE
by Jean Vendome, Paris Jeweller

To preface Claude Mazloum's book, I cannot help thinking of the phrase coined by the journalist Hélène François: 'A jewel is an encounter between this metal, this woman, this stone'. To that truth I may add that this book is simply a vehicle for encouraging the sparkling and magical encounter between precious materials and those who use them.

In this work, the collaboration of highly specialised individuals gives the reader a well defined idea of what art-jewellery really is. For my part, in the first chapter, I hope to communicate my philosophy of creation to the public, because, as a matter of fact, when I think of someone, I am already imagining the precious object that he should have, conceiving the jewel as a work of art, a mobile mini-sculpture that he can wear and bring alive at any moment of the day, and moreover, this piece will be perfectly at home in a living room display cabinet where it will shine ceaselessly.

The author is a creator himself who knew how to group together, under a single cover, all the hidden rays of light that these artists wish us to discover through their jewels. In this work, Claude Mazloum, the lapidary, shows us – as in a stone – all the facets of contemporary jewellery, with all its fire and all its brilliance.

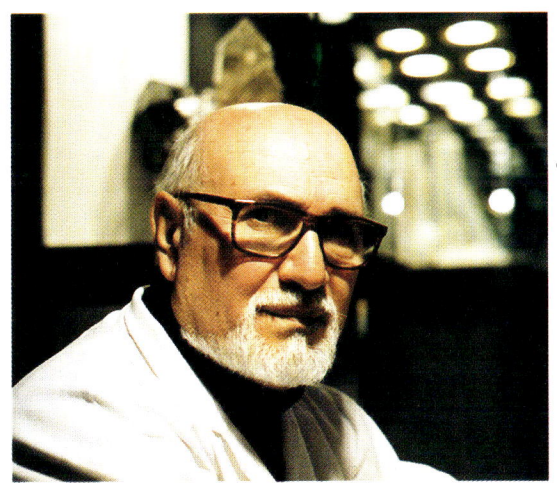

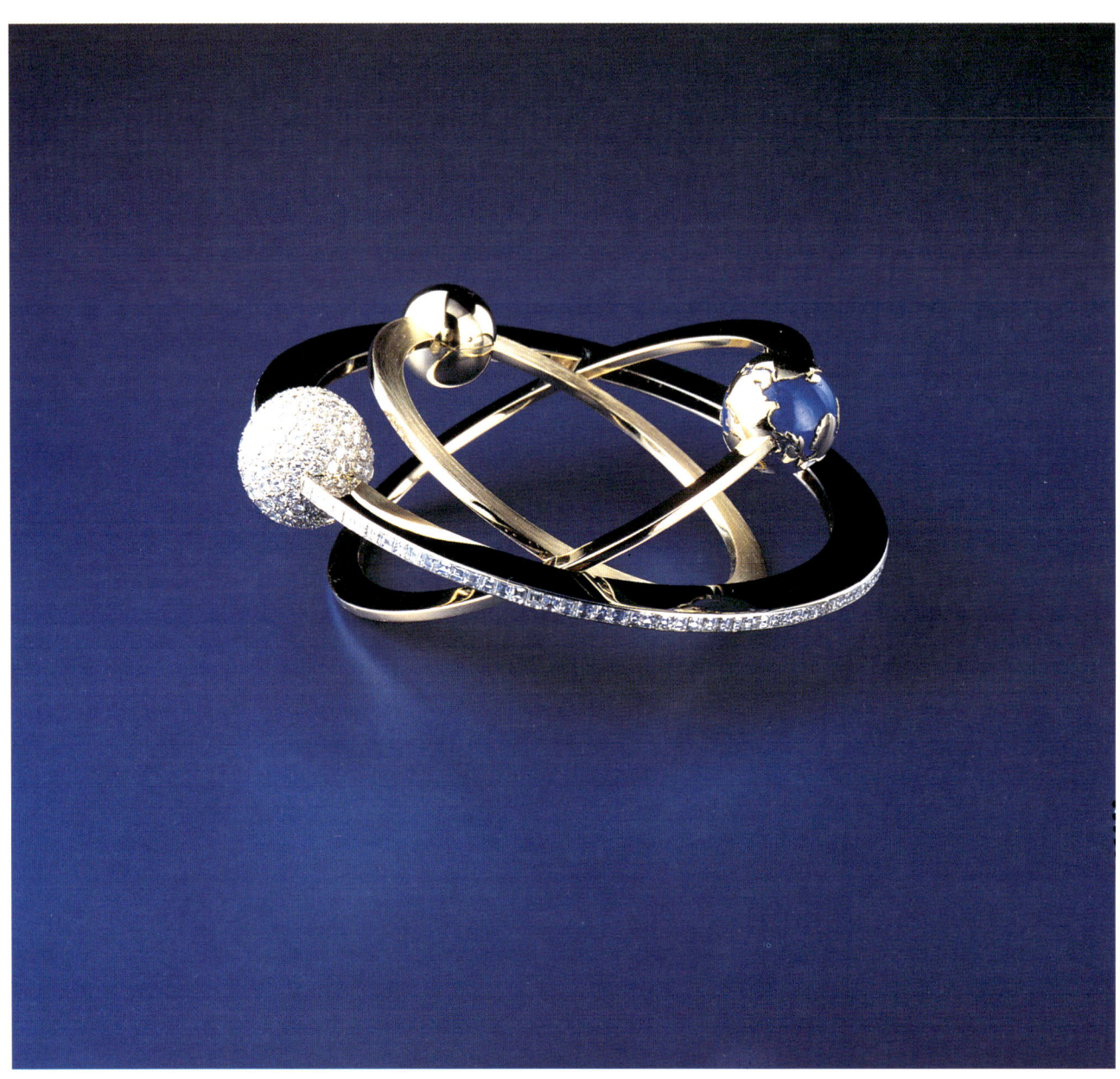

Bracelet in gold, lapis lazuli and diamonds, created by Jean Mouclier.

INTRODUCTION

'Creation' or 'jewel creator' are pretentious-looking terms. Even the greatest of artists has never had the right to the titles of 'creator of paintings' or 'creator of sculptures'. At the very most, someone now and then throws them a flattering 'maestro'.

The somewhat divine term 'jewel creator' was born to differentiate the artisan-jeweller from the artist-jeweller, the first being a specialised technician or simple shopkeeper, the second a 'maître d'art' who invents and realises objects of which he alone is the creator.

The principal aim of this book is to point out this difference. It is utterly pointless to describe commercial or manufactured jewels: they are so thoroughly advertised that all humanity recognises the medallions, chains and other products. But there exist on earth rare pieces of which a very few specimens are made and which thus can never be owned by all the word. These are sentimental jewels, the fruits of skill, intelligence and the dream of a single person, he who created them.

As you shall see, this book contains very little text and many images, as the most precious information must be presented above all through forms, colours and contrasts. To complete this message, I have asked some of my friends, whom I esteem for their excellence, to collaborate with me according to their specialisations. Each of these individuals has dedicated practically all his or her life in search of beauty. They are enthusiasts, linked by a common denominator: the art of creating.

Claude Mazloum

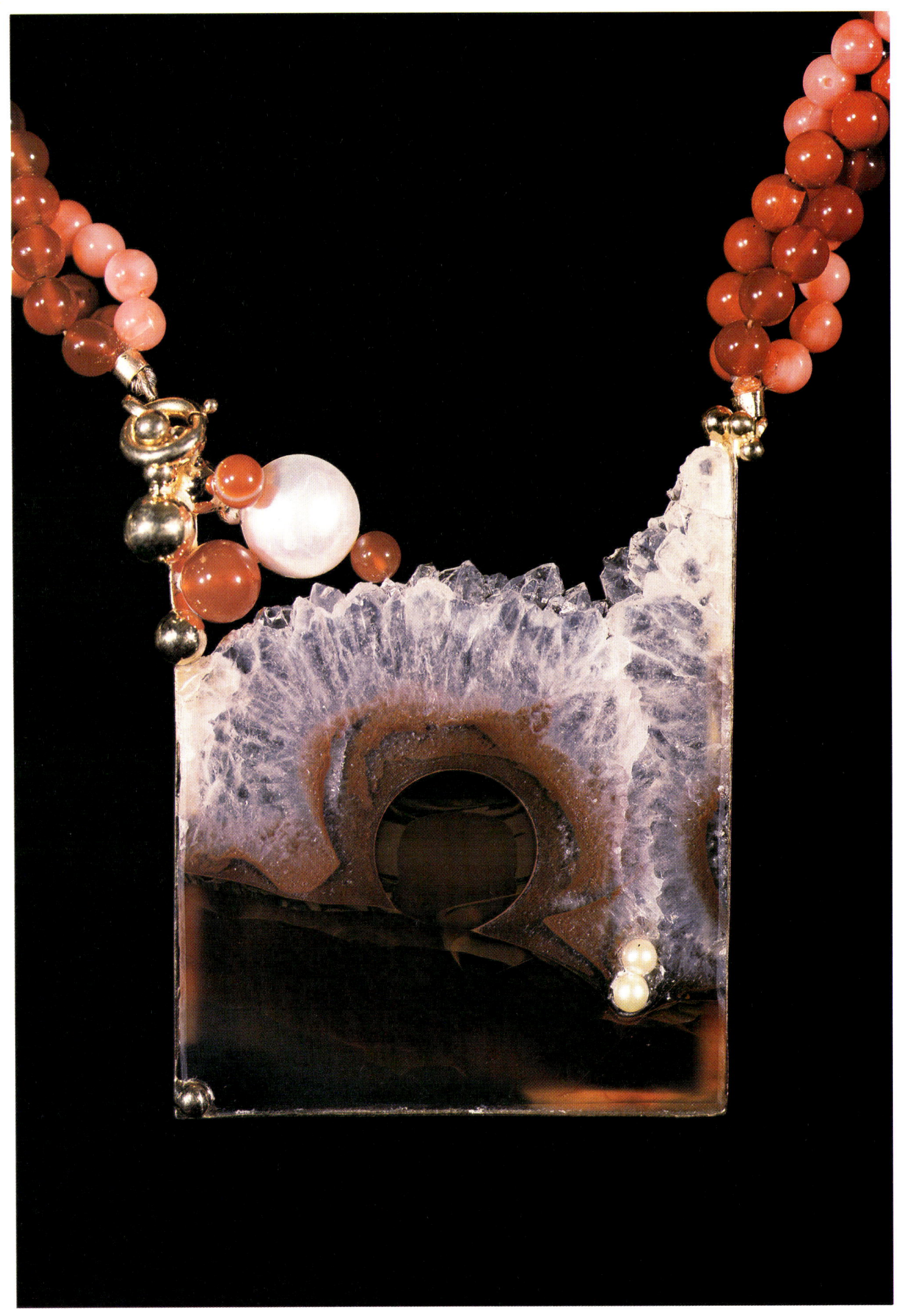

14 *Necklace in gold, pearls, coral, cornelians and amethyst crystal flower by Jean Vendome.*

CHAPTER I

THE ART OF CREATING JEWELS

In collaboration with Jean Vendome

It is no longer necessary to introduce the name of Jean Vendome; it is quite simply the very symbol of pure creativity in the sphere of jewellery-making. Moreover, there is good reason that most books and other encyclopaedias cite his name as the very symbol of contemporary designer jewellery. For this reason, it is the 'Great Master' himself who here shares his philosophy of jewel creation. 'At the age of 20, when I thought I had succeeded in creating a good piece, I would be so proud of myself. With time, I have learned that I have certain advantages in my chromosomes that set me apart from others, a heritage of my father who was also a creator – in another domain, certainly, but a creative one nevertheless. Later on I came to understand, with a great deal of respect, the importance of training and the history of jewels. Thanks to Monsieur Lalique, whom I thank sincerely, I have learned to depart from the beaten track. But wisdom and experience in themselves are not enough; there is surely a help that comes to us from without, because in the greater scheme of things one connot create anything by oneself alone.

The jewel and the artist

The artist can create only in complete freedom, without worrying about the commercial side of things; this is the primary handicap of fashion-jewellery manufacturers. The artist has the freedom to choose any materials and substances, he can browse through the styles that inspire him and choose lines that are sober, mathematical, kinetic, romantic, surreal, baroque, sensual, etc.

Jewellery is the indispensable frivolity

It answers a yearning in each of us, whether for the art of fine living, a symbol, a dream; for passion, beauty, ornament, display; investment, security, etc. No civilisation has ever managed to do without it. It has marked the great moments of history and continues to do so. To anoint an emperor there must be a crown; to seal a marriage vow there must be a wedding-ring.

Gold and jewels are eternally linked

Many materials have been used to make jewels, but thanks to its incomparable physical qualities, gold has always been and always will be the most highly prized of metals. Besides affecting the entire world with its market value, it is a fascinating metal: its lustre never tarnishes, and when polished it reflects one's image like a mirror. The Incas thought it was a sliver of sun fallen to earth; they worshipped it as a god. Gold also had its priests in Mesopotamia (Mithra) as well as Egypt, where it symbolised Râ, the sun-god. Among Christians, gold symbolises the supernatural light that emanates from the Holy Spirit.

Creating a successful jewel

It is important to proceed quickly from inspiration to actual creation, because if too

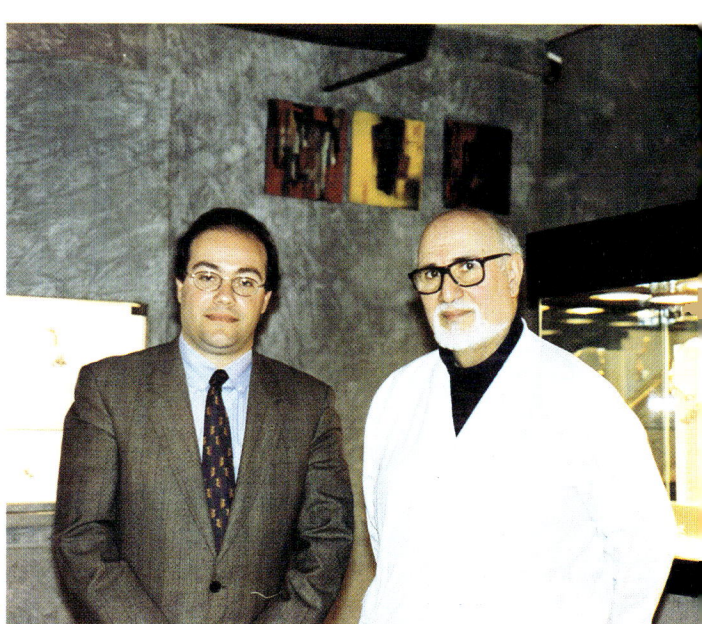

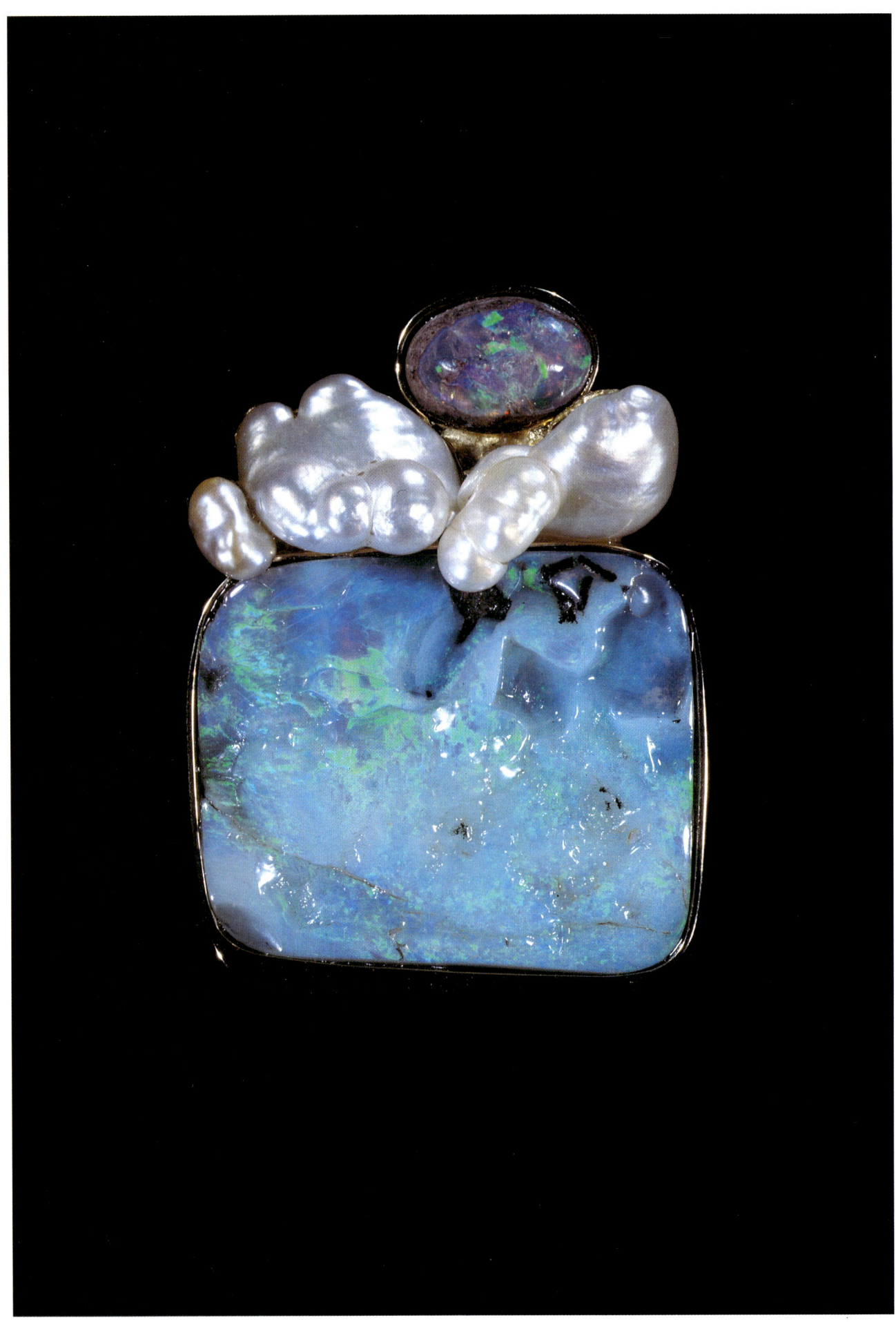

16   *Brooch in gold, baroque pearls and harlequin opals by Jean Vendome.*

much time passes, the same design could be interpreted differently, depending on the creator's state of mind. During Benvenuto Cellini's era, artisans worked for years on the same object. It has been some time since one could spend several months on a single piece; art patrons, who once supported artists as they spent a year on an object, have unfortunately disappeared. Today, a contemporary jewel must be made at the pace of modern life; it must reflect the everyday environment.

Any material can inspire the creator

We are naturally attracted by precious stones, by their brilliance and colour, by their transparency or iridescence, and also by the graphic forms that nature presents in its minerals, crystals and gems. But the creator may be inspired just as much by the texture of any granite, sandstone, slate, concrete, brick, wood, feather, leather or fur, or for example such sea-products as pearls, mother of pearl, shells, corals, scales and even driftwood polished by the sea and wind, which made up the principal theme of Thierry Vendome's collections in 1990, '91 and '92. It is not only the rarity of the materials that attracts the creator, but also their beauty and above all their personality, through which he is able to express his passion. I would like to take this opportunity to clarify a prejudice against an exceptionally beautiful stone: the opal, and the old saying 'opals bring bad luck'. It is easier to repeat a false rumour than to forget it. In the last century, the stone-setter who broke a stone was obliged to pay for it. Whenever a jeweller would ask an artisan to set an opal, the latter would reply, 'Here comes more bad luck.' This stone is, in fact, fragile, because it lacks a crystalline structure that would make it more compact. It is not very resistant to impacts; despite this, other countries, such as the United States, England, Germany, Japan and Australia, have made the opal their favourite stone. In addition, many French creators continue to use it to embellish their pieces, its beauty having overcome superstition and the fear of bad luck. Hopefully, this explanation will help stop the false rumours. In any case, it is strange that a stone should bring bad luck only in France!

A timeless jewel is created, not made

While manufactured jewels go out of date, or a piece of fashion jewellery is outmoded the year after it is made, the artist's jewel continues its way parallel to painting, sculpture, architecture or music. This art of original jewellery creation evolves along with other forms of expression, because in effect it is a major art-form linked to the history of humanity: a witness of its times. Today we know the history of the Hittite peoples, who lived five thousand years before Jesus Christ, thanks to the jewels found in excavations. Through these pieces, archaeologists have been able to describe to us their way of life and culture.'

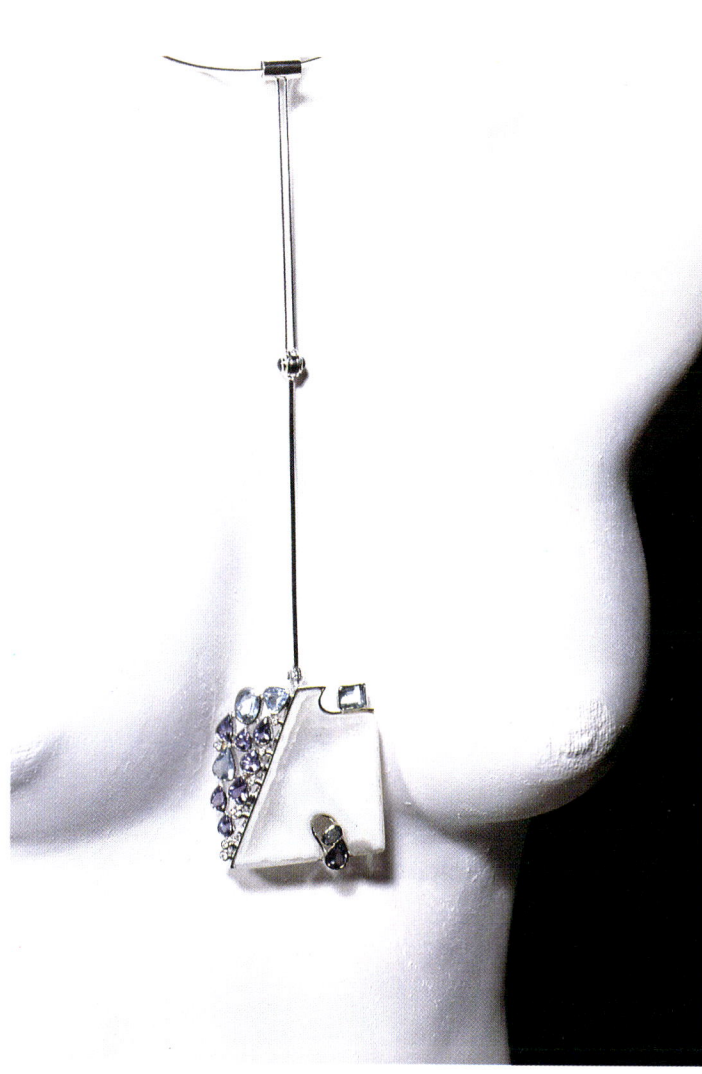

Pendant by Jean Vendome: 'No civilisation has managed to do without jewels.'

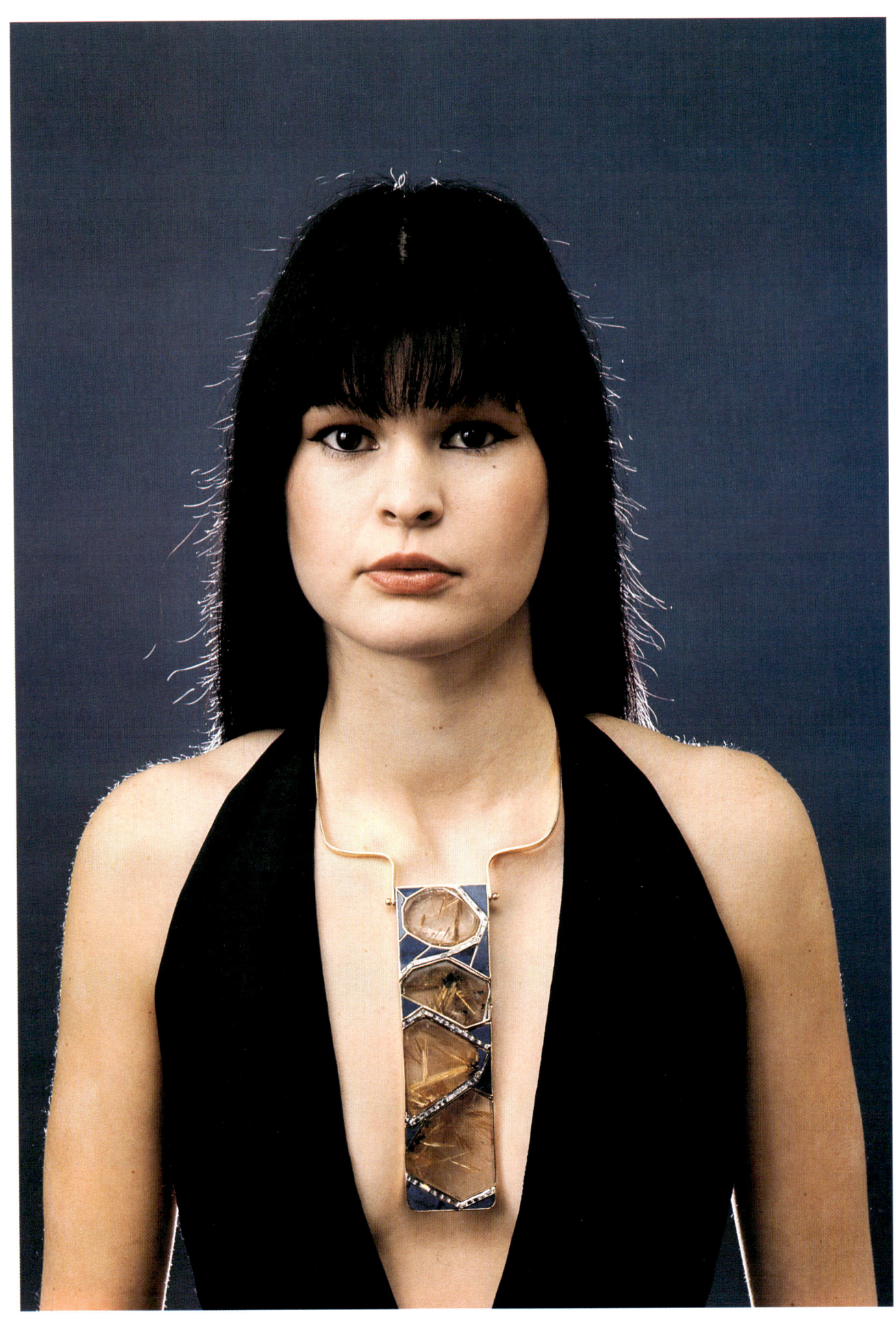

18   *Jean Vendome: necklace in gold, lapis lazuli, diamonds and angel-hair (rutile quartz).*

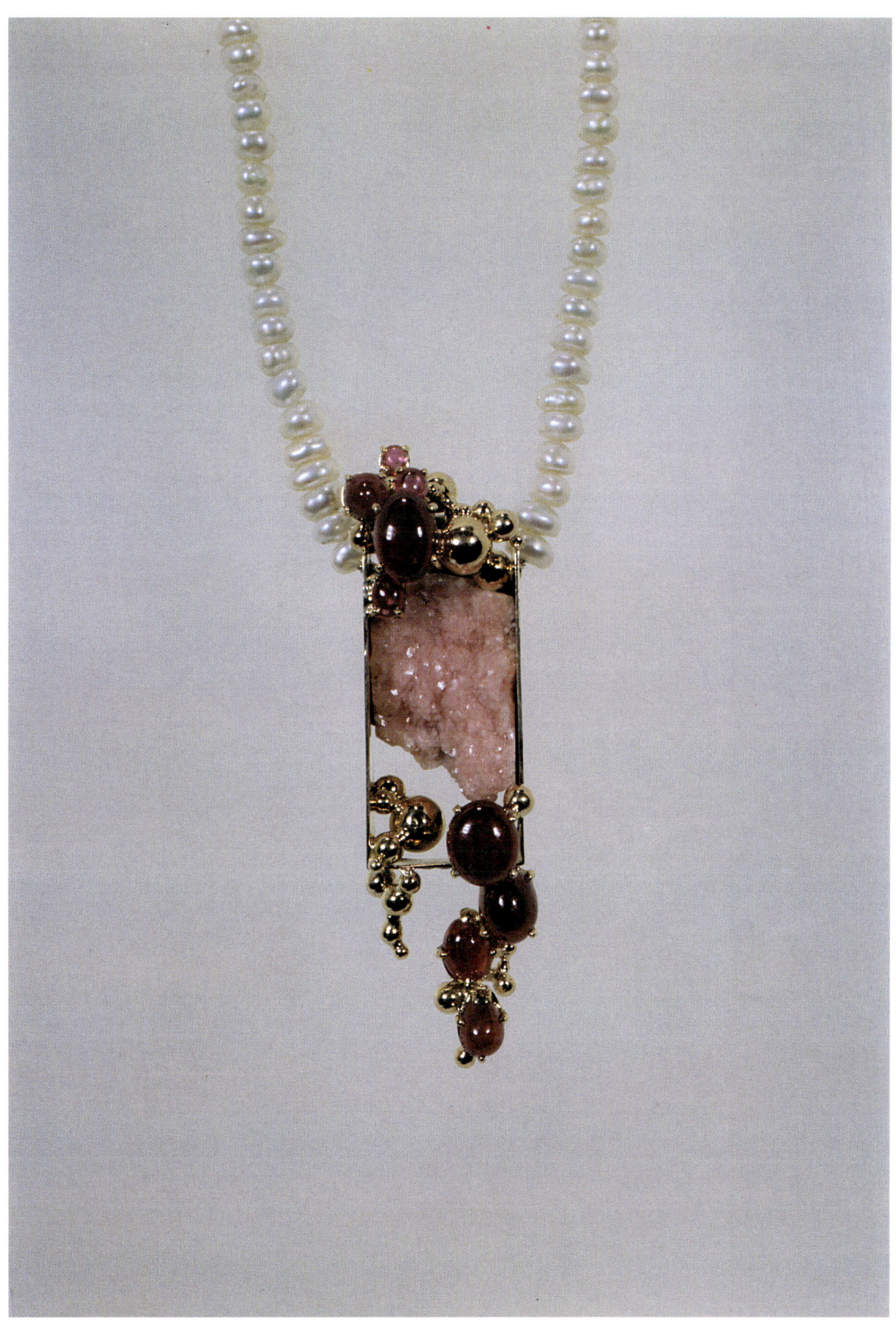

Jean Vendome: pendant in gold, pearls, rubies, rubelites, cornelian and rhodocrosite.

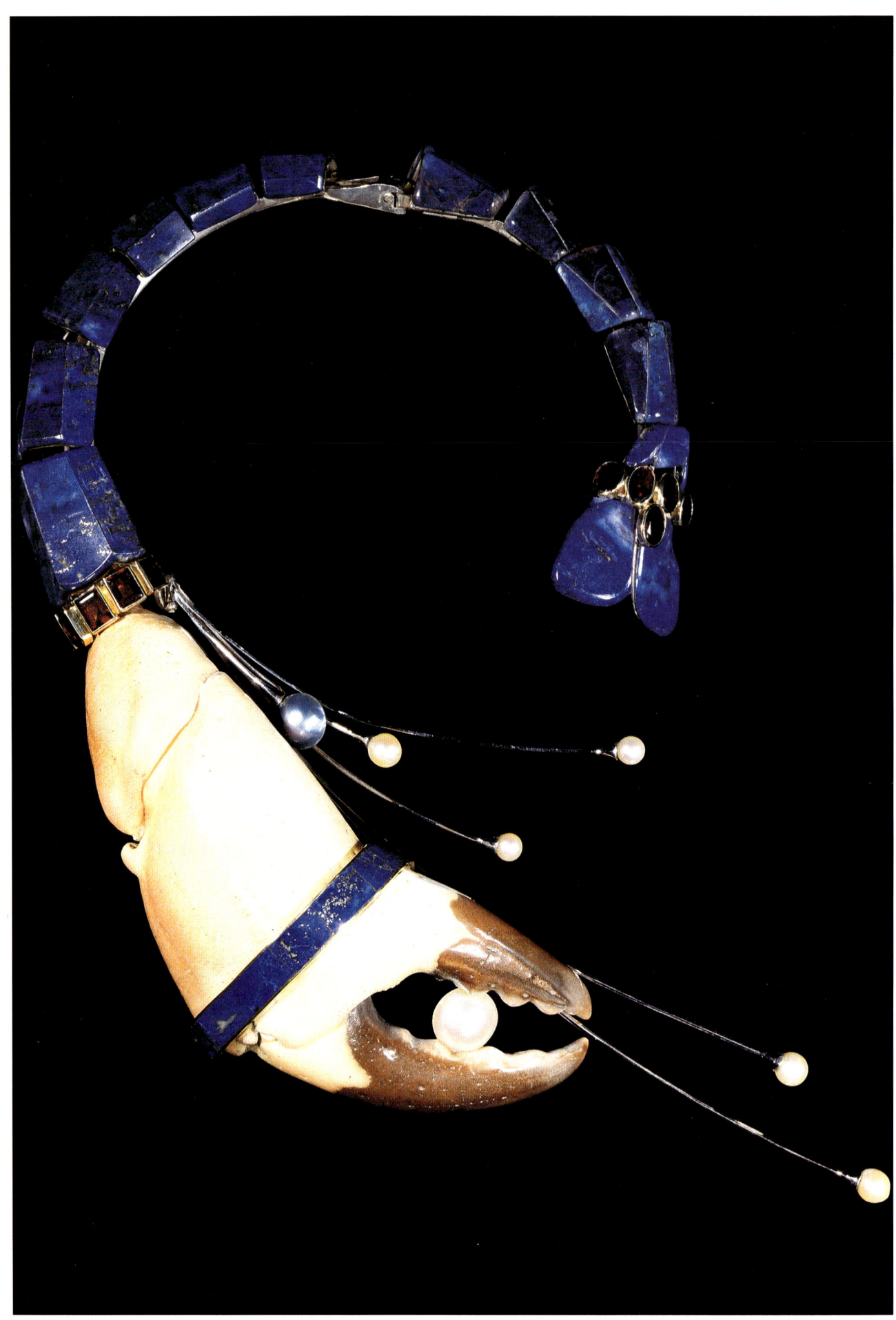

20 *Jean Vendome: necklace in lapis lazuli, gold, pearls, grenats and crab-claw.*

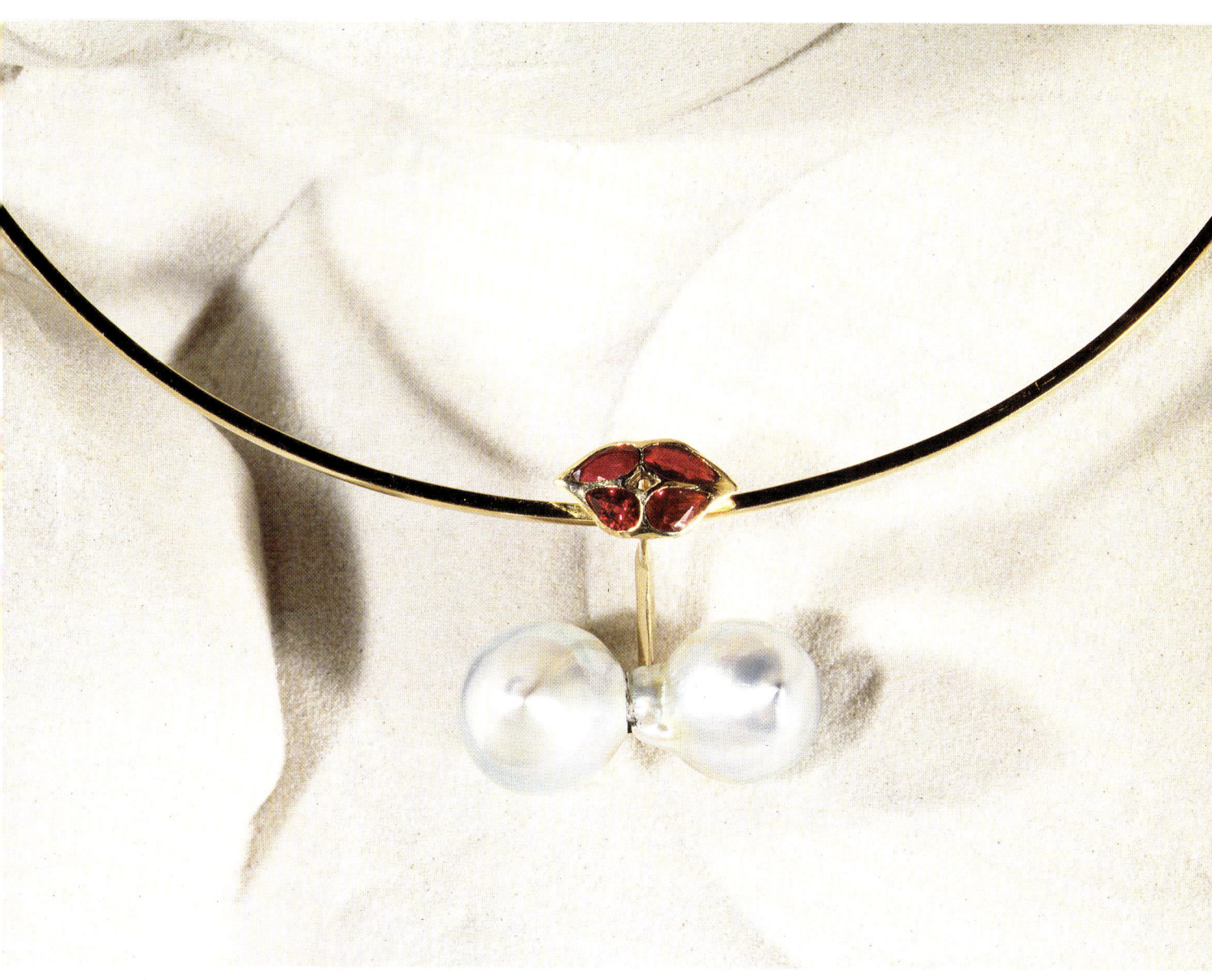

Jean Vendome: necklace in gold, pearls and rubies.

MICHEL WATTEBLED

Originally a Parisian, student of the École de la Rue de Louvre, Michel Wattebled worked and lived in Paris until 1966. At the age of 31, he left that city and moved to the Grand-Duchy of Luxembourg, where he creates and displays his jewels to the great pleasure of the Luxembourgers. His wife Christiane Wattebled, his principal collaborator, tells us her thoughts about jewels: 'In earlier times, emotion was more visual: a jewel must seduce the eye with its beauty.

'And then, at a touch, it must invoke a feeling of sensual pleasure.

'This can only be achieved by the use of precious materials, judiciously combined by workmanship in which technicality and complexity are completely subordinated to balance and comfort. As such a work of art, the jewel must command respect and admiration: one does not alter a quality jewel, one preserves it as it is.

'To achieve these qualities, the jewel must be freed from the petty concerns of social position and fashion, and moreover, the rarity of the object must be preserved. A jewel is made by hand. The manufactured object is to the jewel as lithography is to painting: the mere evocation of a work of art. Regarding creation (properly so called), one must not seek to astonish at all costs; originality and quality astonish on their own. As to originality, it is always enriched by new approaches to form and new techniques.'

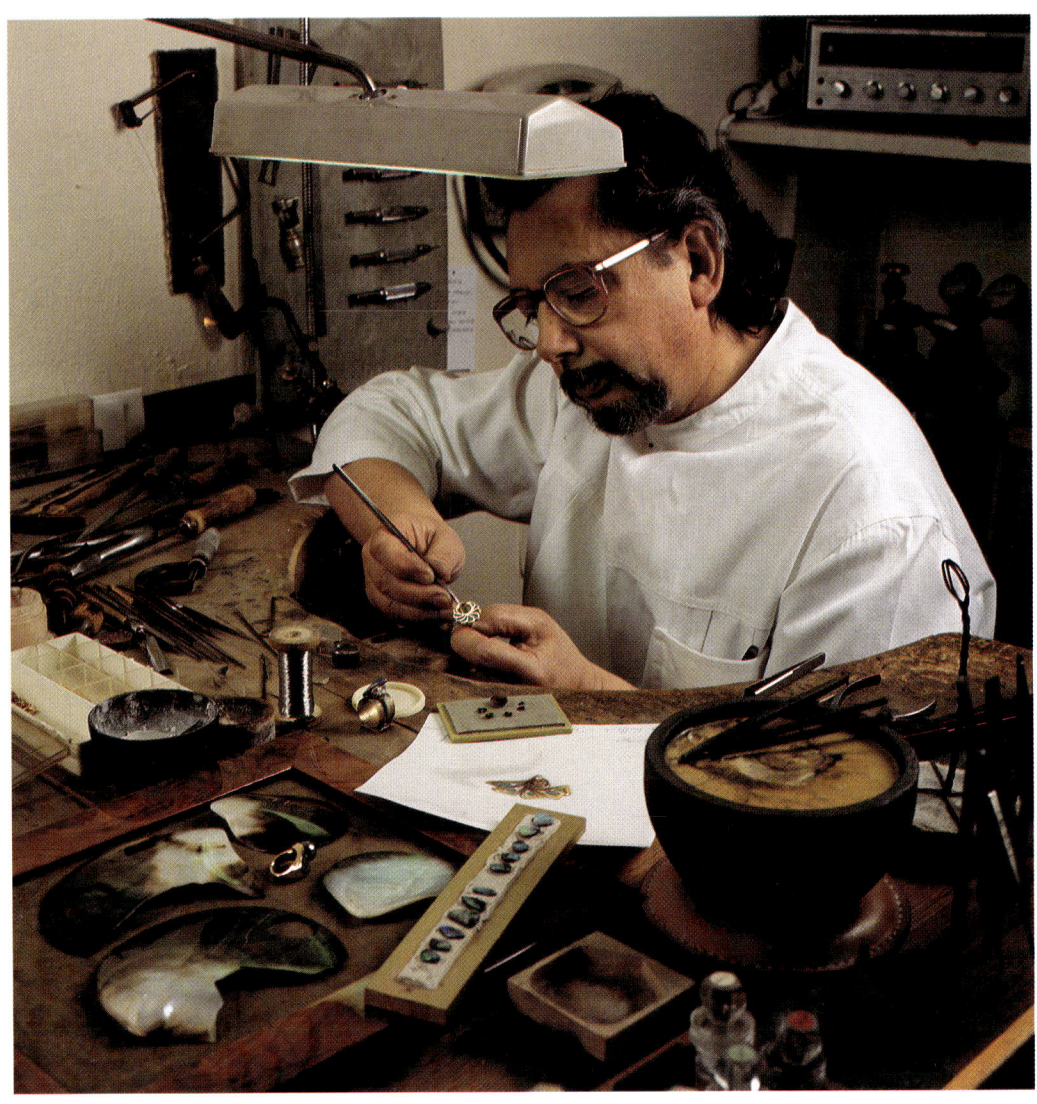

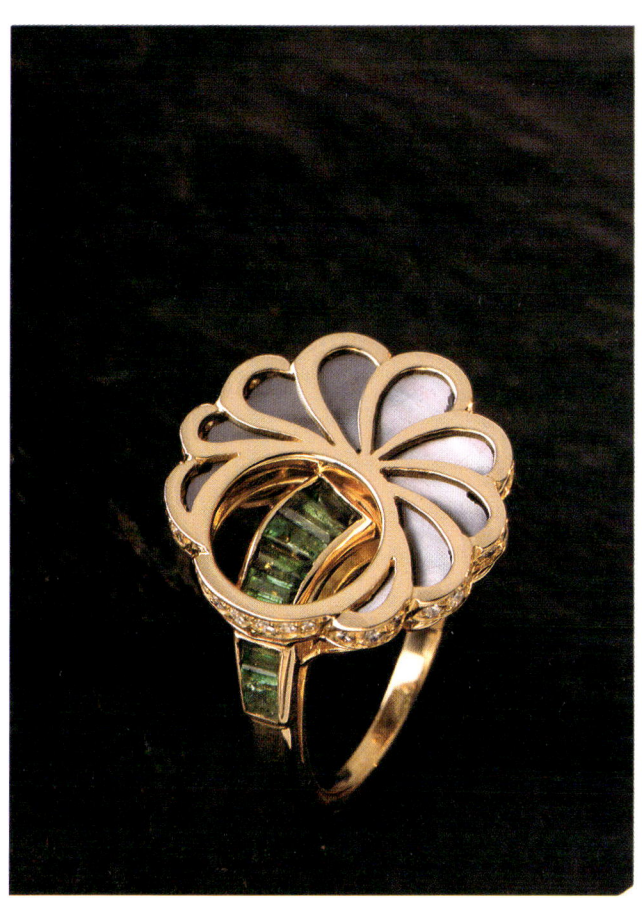

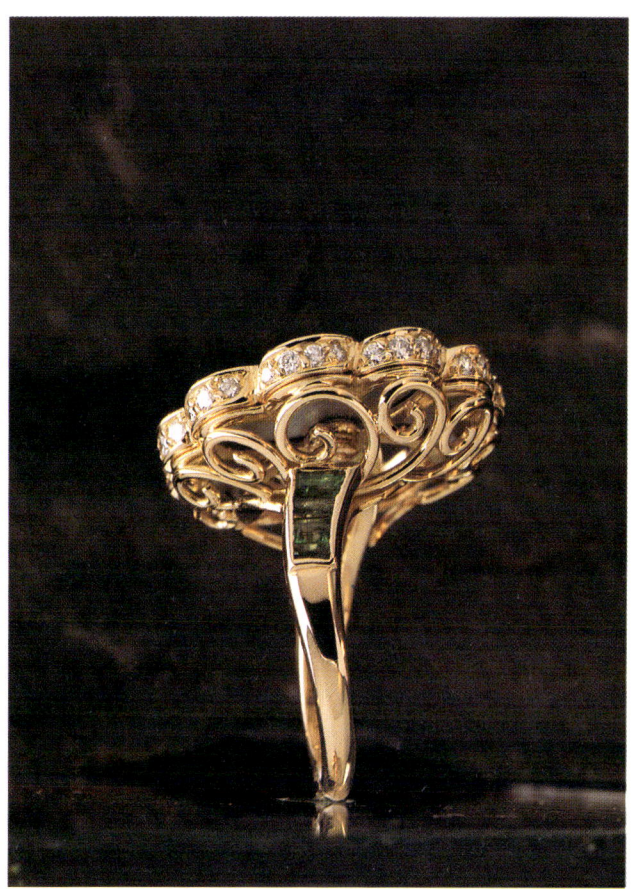

Ring in yellow gold, mother of pearl, emeralds and brilliants.

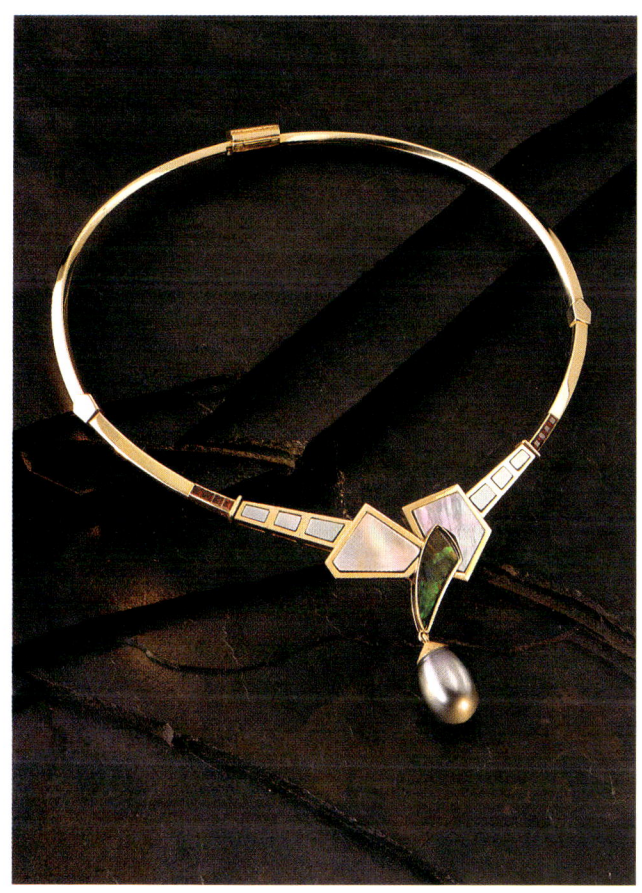

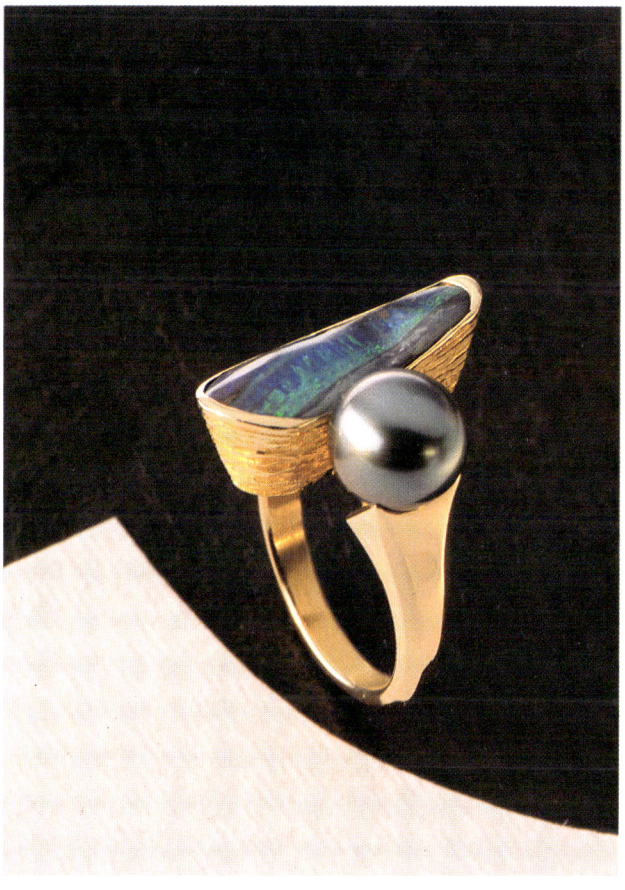

Necklace in yellow gold, mother of pearl, rubies, 'Boulder' opal and black Tahiti pearl.

Ring in yellow gold, 'Boulder' opal and black Tahiti pearl.

HANS SCHULLIN

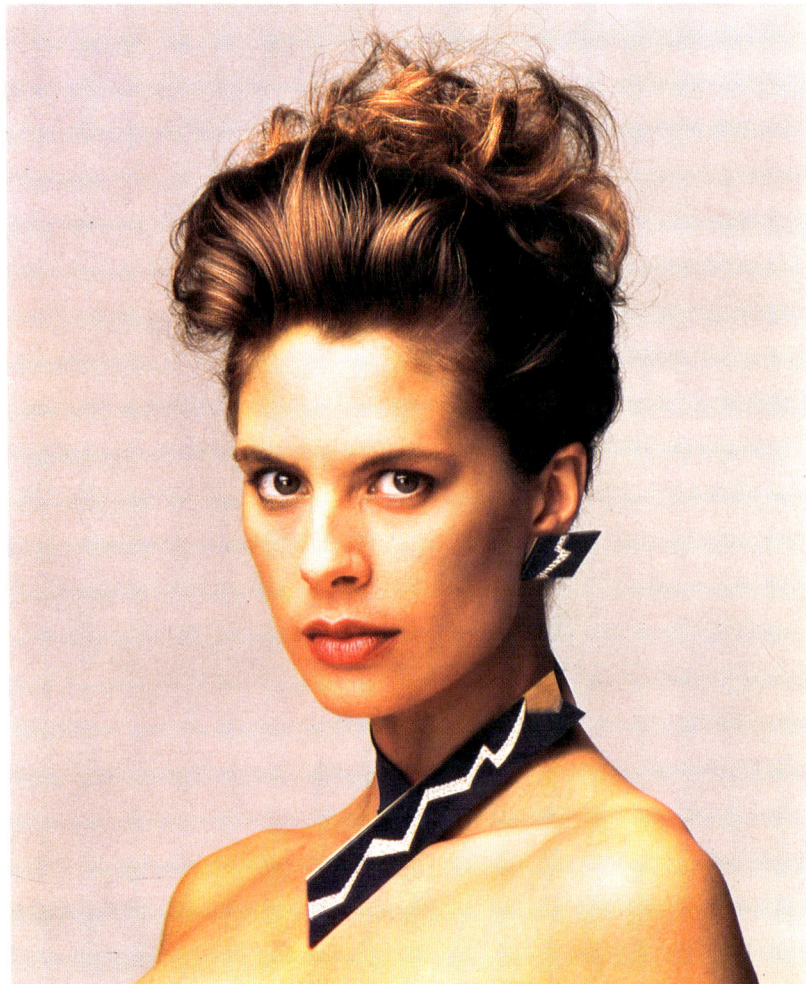

'Water', necklace and earrings in gold, platinum, lapis lazuli and diamond.

'A balance between provocation and conservation: in his designs, Hans Schullin adds a different and surprising element to the finest level of the goldsmith's craft. "High quality of workmanship is of prime importance, because the jewel is destined to distinguish, to enhance a person – it must be special. When a jewel is made with passion, its provocative, refined forms strongly emphasise the magnetism of the personality."'

'Maf', ring in gold with two square diamonds and emerald-cut canary diamond.

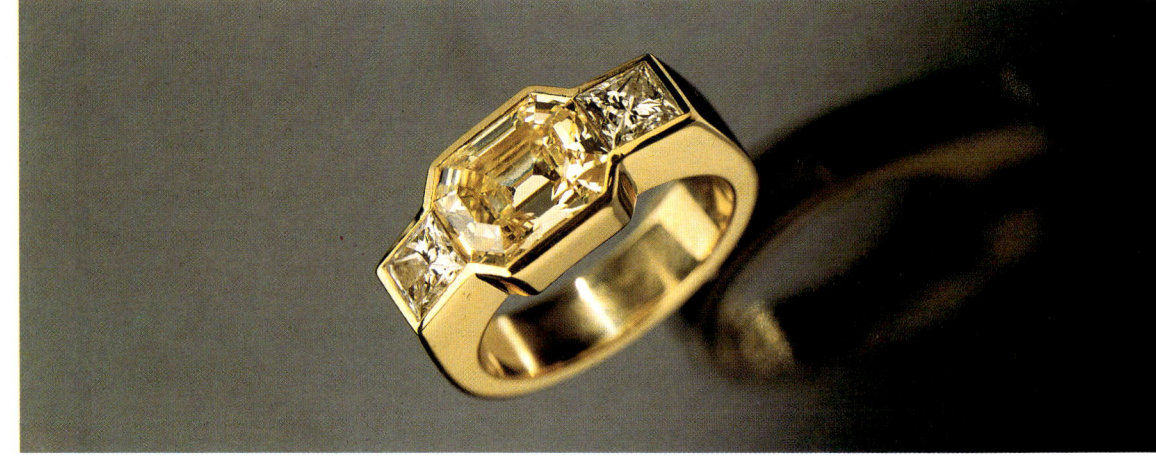

ULI GLASER

From Helsinki to Tokyo — by way of Hamburg, of course — Uri Glaser's works never cease to please the many enthusiasts who follow his career in the realm of design. His mixture of diverse materials and his use of ebony are his strong points.

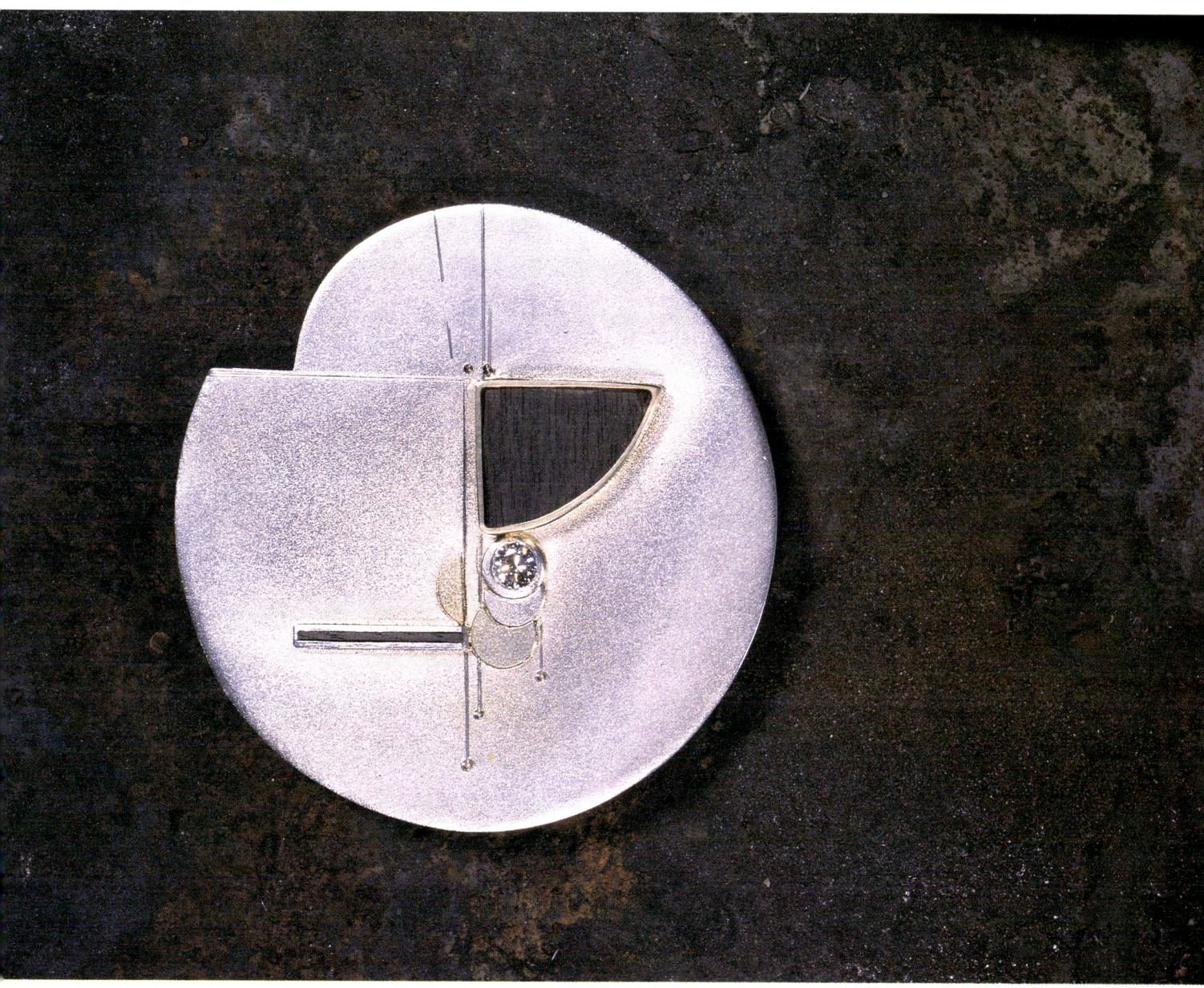

Brooch in silver and gold with diamond and ebony.

JEAN MOUCLIER

Scorpion ascending scorpion: Jean Mouclier was clearly born fascinated by fire. Rather like the moth, the creature that can be found flying around lamps in the summer and which, by a stroke of a magic wand, he has transformed into a ring. For this talented and eclectic creator of jewels, who has kept a childlike, wonder-filled view of the world and who endows his creations with his reminiscences, a diamond is above all fire, brilliance, magnificence.

Having come to jewellery by way of crystal-making, this multitalented artist has won the 'Diamonds International Awards'. He goes through life with an insatiable hunger to learn, unafraid of brushing aside things too well established to make way for his dreams. 'Jewellery is a voyage through the precious and the spiritual. To come close to the latter, one must make as little use of reality as possible. The essence of a jewel is in its conception, in the eye, the heart, the hand of the jeweller, and not in the geometrical dimensions of the object.

'Dreams remain in the memory; they bring meaning to the realities of the day.

'Every creation is a narcissistic reminiscence; this is my innermost need.'

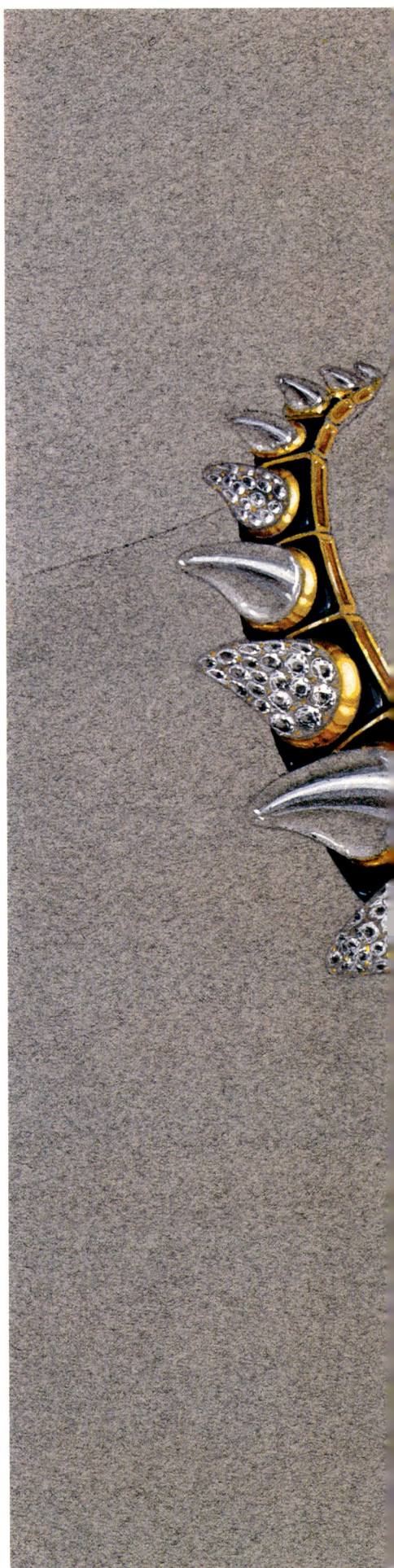

'The Feline or Catwoman', sketch for a necklace in gold, platinum, enamel, rock crystal and diamonds

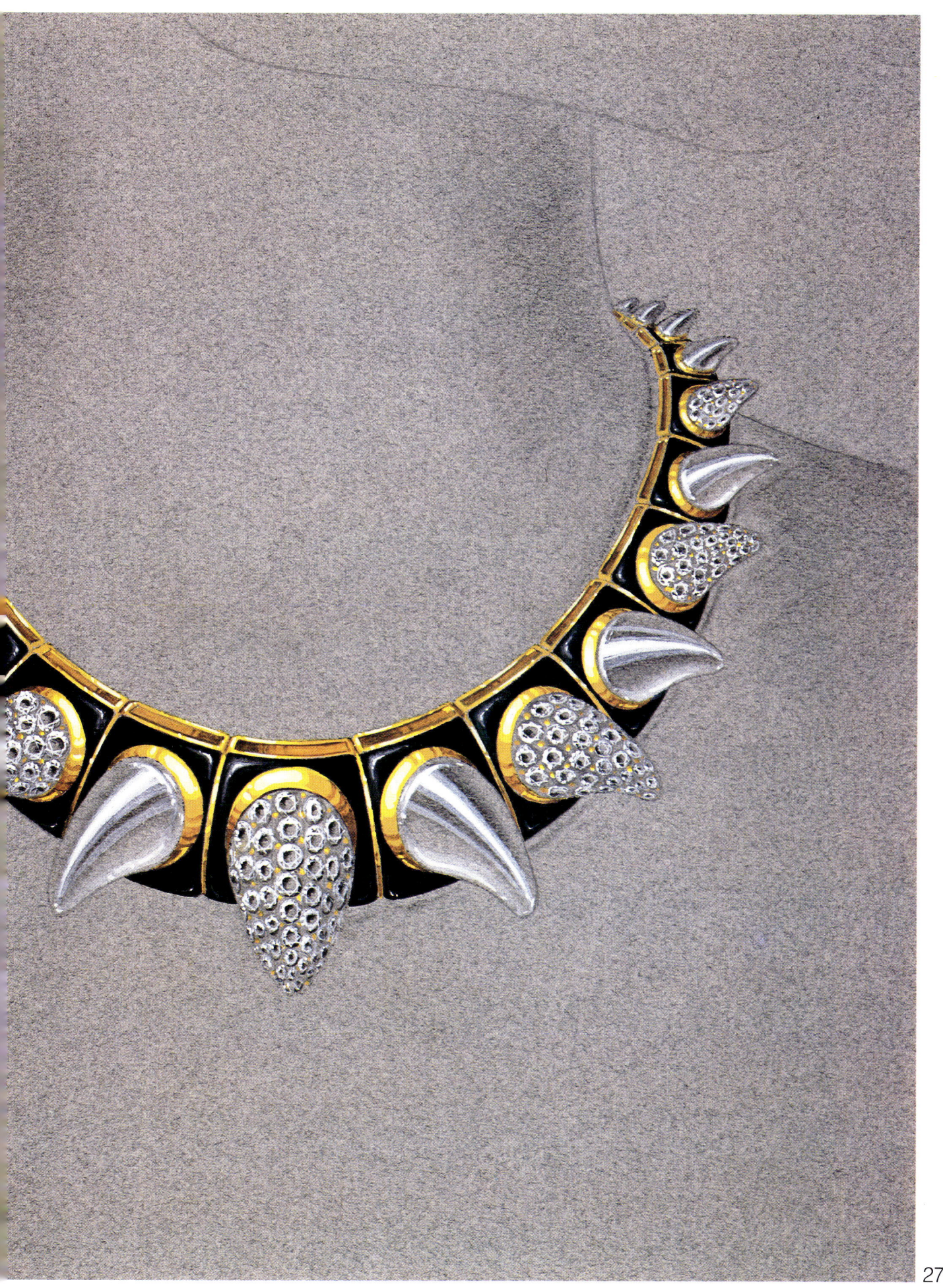

JEAN-PIERRE DE SAEDELEER

'The most beautiful jewels have always been the reflection of a civilisation, an era, an art. But to my way of thinking, they should not fall into the category of fashion. A jewel must endure through time. Above all, it must be wearable, be a sort of extension of the body and make the materials vibrate in harmony. The most thrilling thing is creating a 'custom' jewel, an expression of the personality of the woman who will wear it, of her complexion, of the colour of her eyes.

'The goal of the creator is not to produce great numbers of objects, but rather to have a personal and artistic output. In working with the noblest materials on earth, the creator sees himself in the role of a modern-day alchemist. The created object will vibrate with all its energy and will stimulate the person wearing it.

'My favourite materials are pearls, because they symbolise the passage between two states: animal and mineral. Their varied forms, their special colours are an inexhaustible font for the quest for forms. Sapphires, especially those from Sri-Lanka, give one a palette of rare colours. Diamonds inspire the same enchantment as musical notes well placed on a stave.'

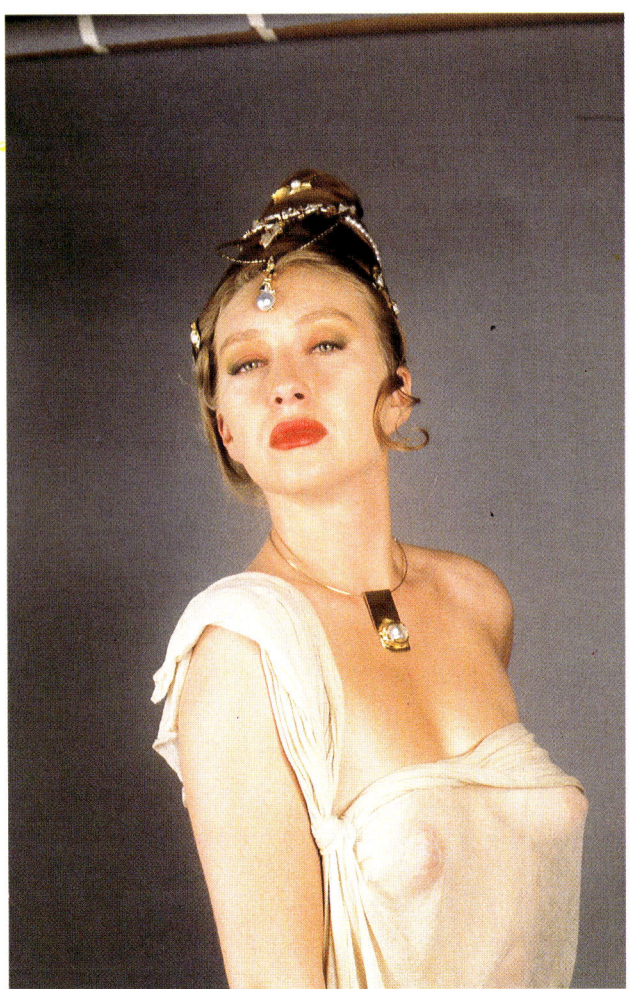 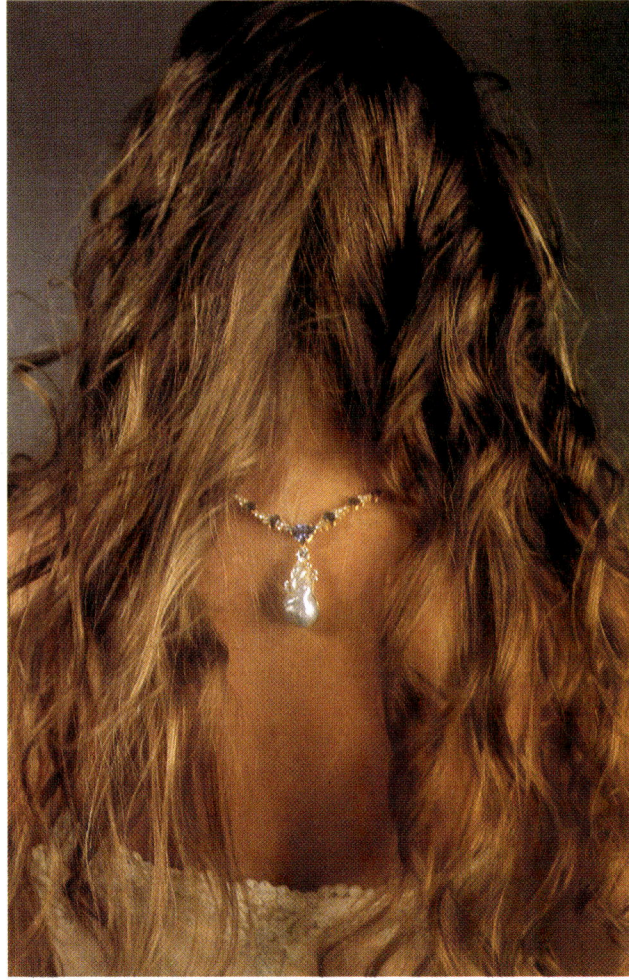

Femininity and sensuality emanate from Jean-Pierre De Saedeleer's jewels.

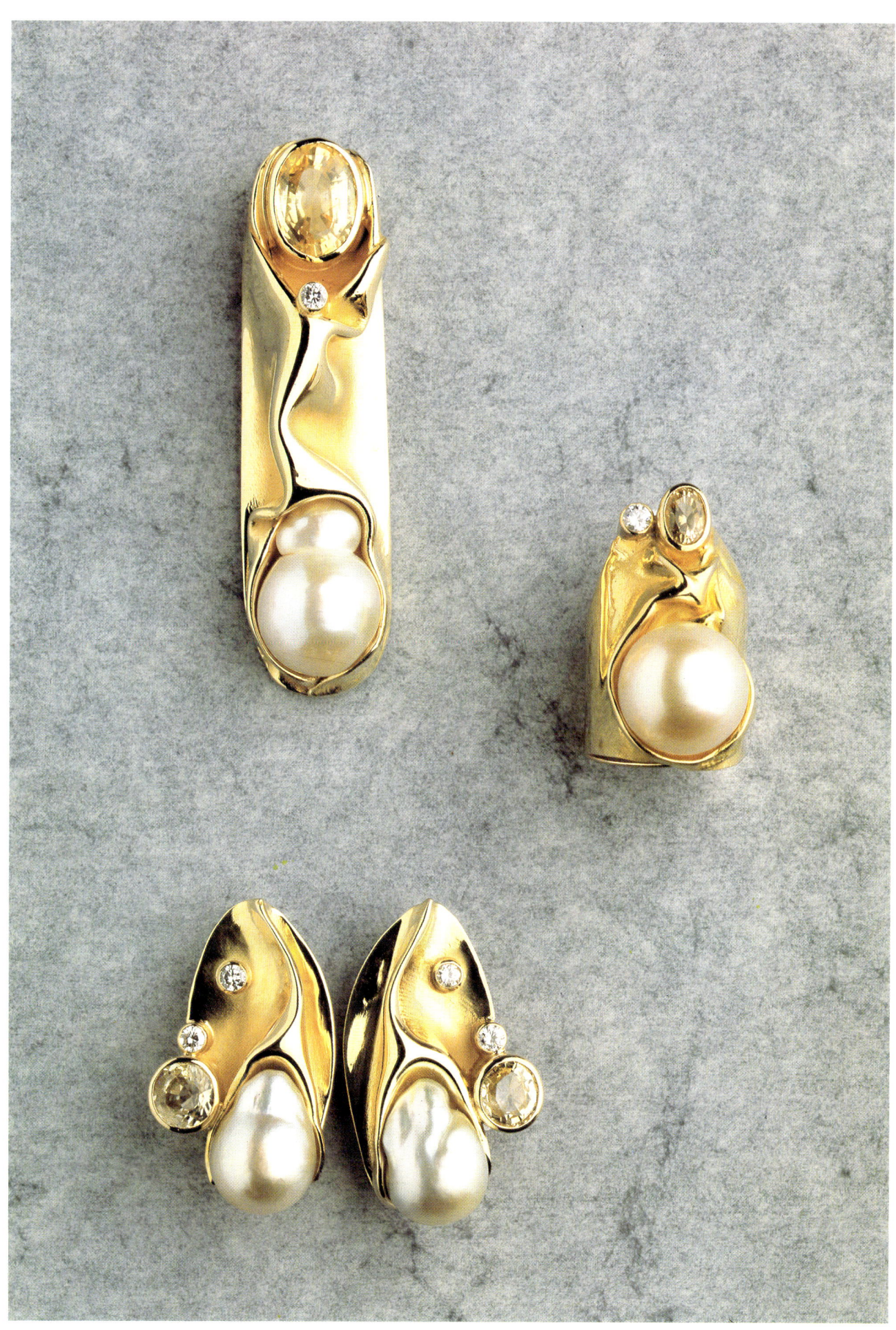

Set in yellow gold, pearls, stones and brilliants.

CAROLINE PORTAIL

It was through sculpture that Caroline Portail landed on the shore of jewellery-making. A sensitive artist, she knows how to take nature and reinvent it in the form of jewels. Her two rings "Ecume" and "Granit" symbolise the immutable power of movement that is both eternal and fleeting, and the miraculous combination of strength and fragility that she succeeds in balancing. In Chapter VI, Caroline Portail will explain her point of view on the creation of jewellery more fully, especially the contrasts that result from mixing precious materials and ordinary ones.

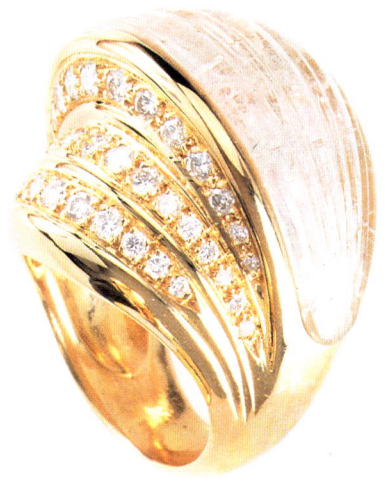

Ring in yellow gold, rock crystal and brilliants.

Ring in yellow gold, blue granite and 'Troïdia'-cut diamond.

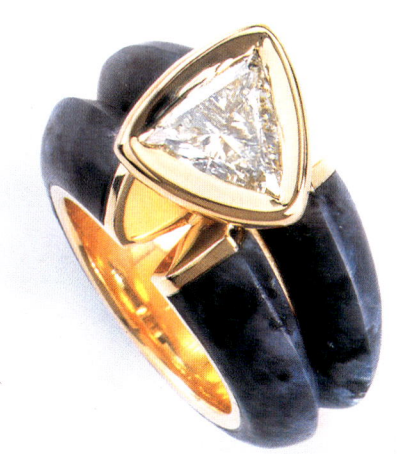

NICOLE THIENPONT

With a degree and license in chemistry, a former student of the Academie Royale des Beaux-Arts d'Anvers, Nicole Thienpont creates her jewels in Ghent. She talks to us about jewels from prehistory to the present day:

'Let me start with this quotation from F. Mathey (Paris): For as long as man has existed, he has loved objects. Objects are a vehicle of friendship, of love.

'Man has always wanted to show off through his personal ornaments. He began by finding shells and the teeth of ferocious animals, which he wore around his neck and arms. It is not always easy to "choose" an object, and for contemporary jewellery I like to be involved in presenting new forms before the choice is made.

'Nothing is tranquil, everything is vibrating: this is the idea that lives behind all my creations. This idea necessarily results in pieces that are light and dynamic.'

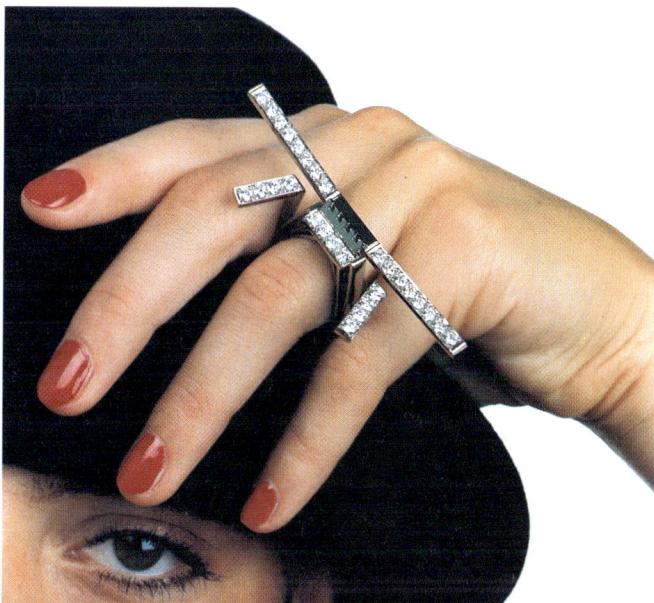

Ring in white gold and brilliants. Diamond Awards winner. This ring is composed of three different pieces that may be worn separately, in twos or all three together.

Ring in yellow gold. This is 'metal vibration' worn on a finger.

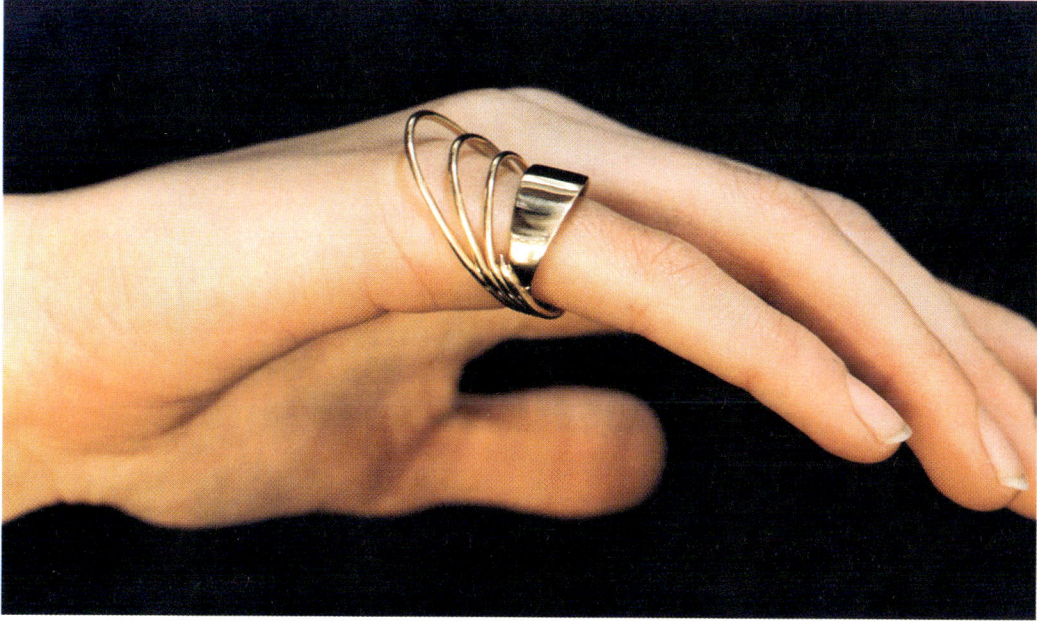

DANIELLE GOFFA

In introducing Danielle Goffa, it will suffice me to present these quotations from the international press:

– 'One can describe her jewels as being like a fine pearl. You have to know her work in order to understand why she has already won several prizes, and all her expositions demonstrate her talent and her obvious mastery of the art of creating.'

– 'Danielle Goffa won a prize for a jewel composed of a daring combination of plastic and precious metals of high technical quality.'

– 'The exhibitor creates jewels in which there is no lack of virtuosity of new techniques. With Danielle, jewels maintain their ability to delight.'

– 'Danielle uses different materials to create combinations that are daring, unique and original. A unique finesse emanates from the collection. With her experience, she takes risks in making her jewels that lead to exceptional results.'

I myself shall add that Danielle Goffa's jewels make me think, quite simply, of bits of nature ready to take flight from her work-bench and land on the body, which keeps them in perpetual motion.

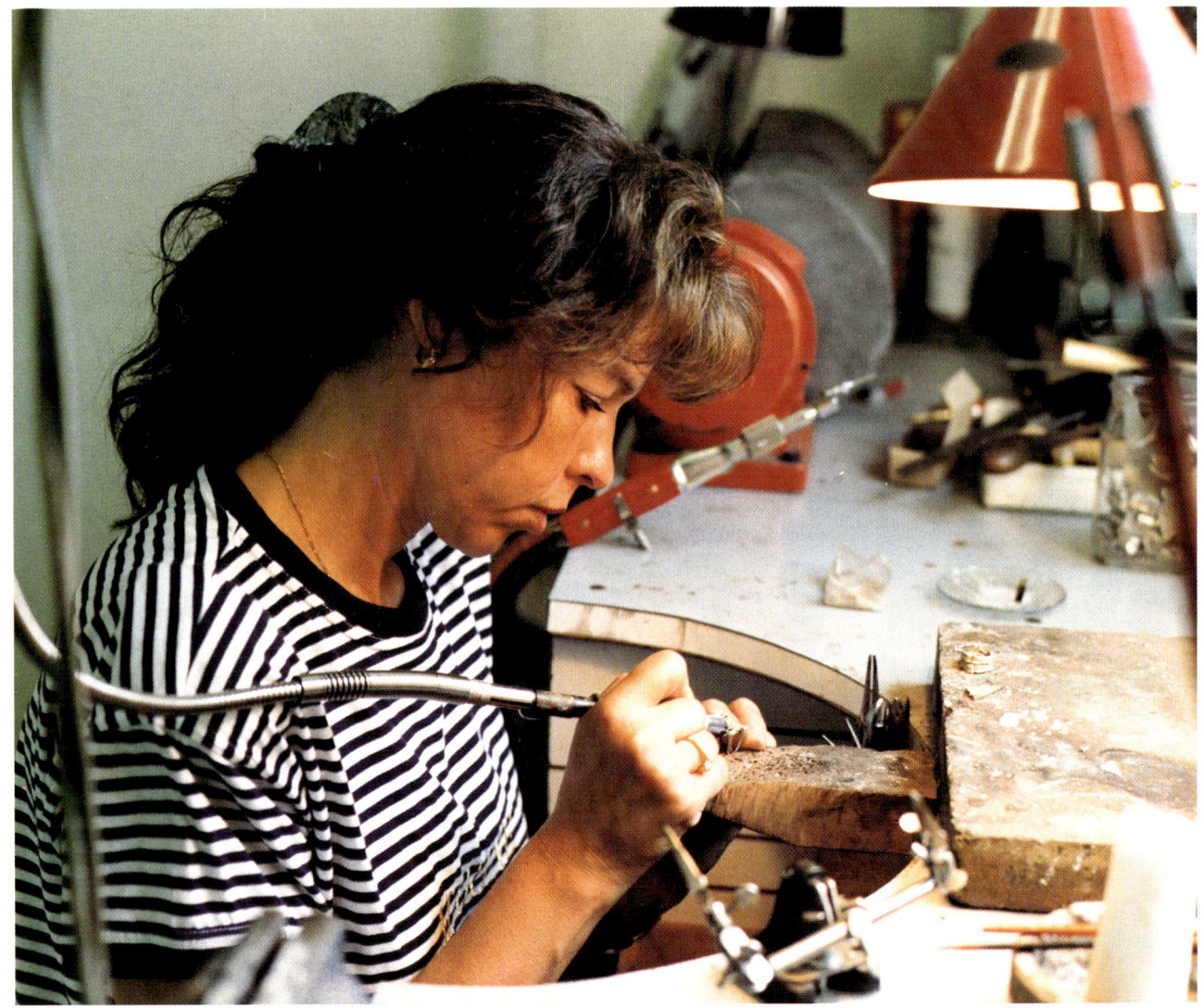

*Ring in silver and haematite.
The stone joins with the
metal and lets itself be
engulfed by it.*

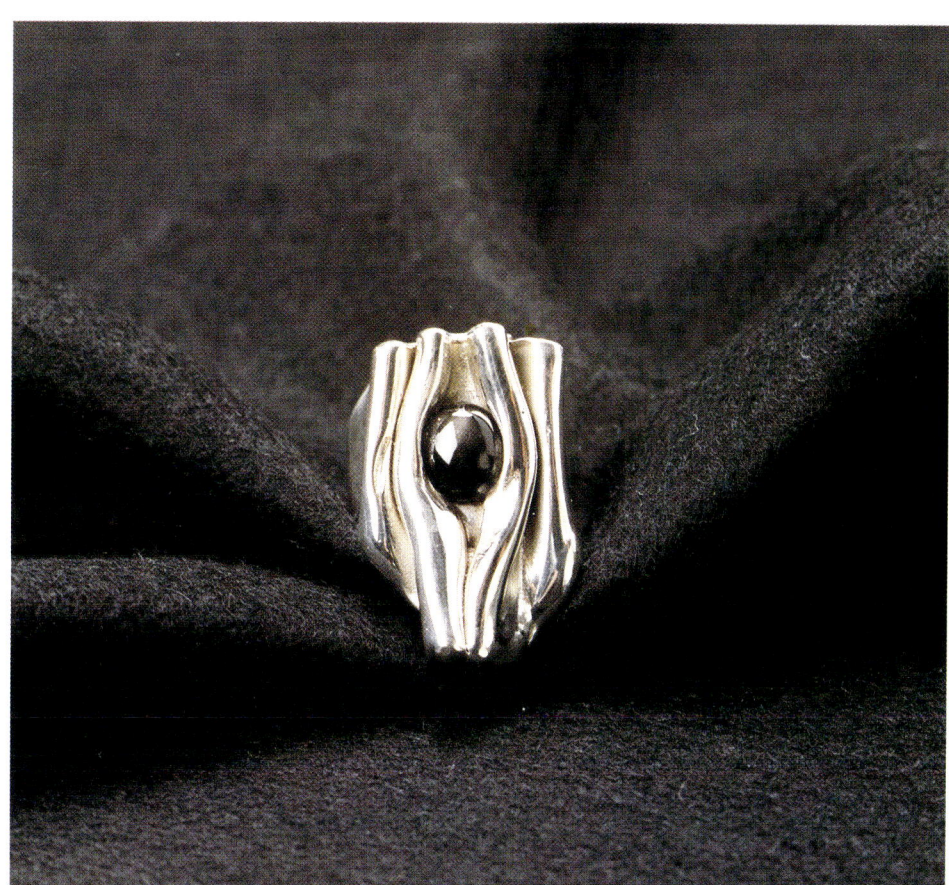

*Is it a fish or a hedgehog?
Is it a bird or a flower?
It is simply a brooch made of
silver, feathers and fur.*

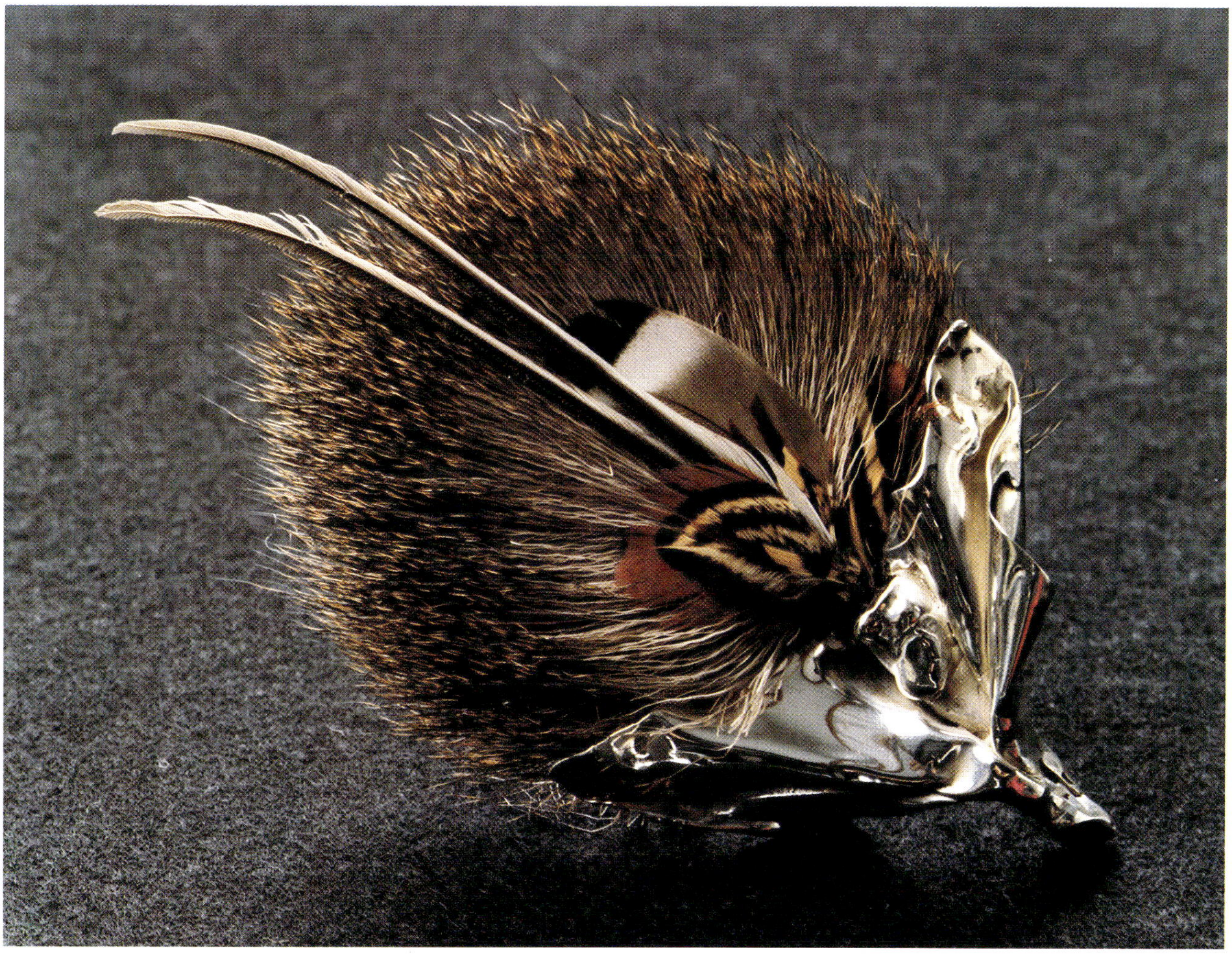

KERINA TROICOVICH

If someone were moved by curiosity to examine the works of the greatest painters of the Italian Renaissance in detail, he would be astonished to discover jewels of incomparable beauty and of a delicacy that inspires dreams. Unfortunately, these pieces themselves have disappeared, leaving us without their eloquent testimonial to the taste and refinement of an entire era. Karina Troicovich let herself be bewitched by these painted images, and her imagination inspired her to recapture the designs of some of these pieces to give them form and substance, while remaining faithful to the original designs and to the purpose for which they were originally conceived: to enhance a woman's beauty, provoking admiration and desire.

Five hundred years later, Piero della Francesca, Botticelli, Ghirlandaio, Leonardo da Vinci and Perugino once again show us, through their creations, that they were capable of conceiving a truly universal and timeless ideal of beauty.

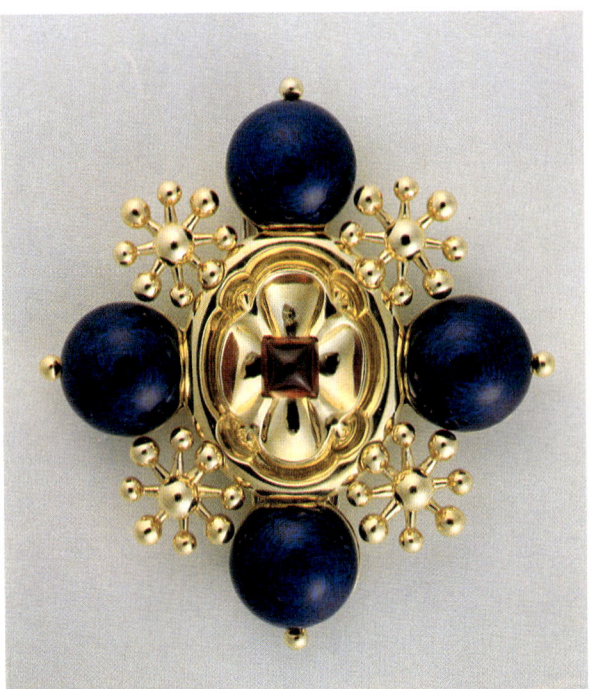

After Perugino, brooch/pendant in gold, enamel and rhodolite.

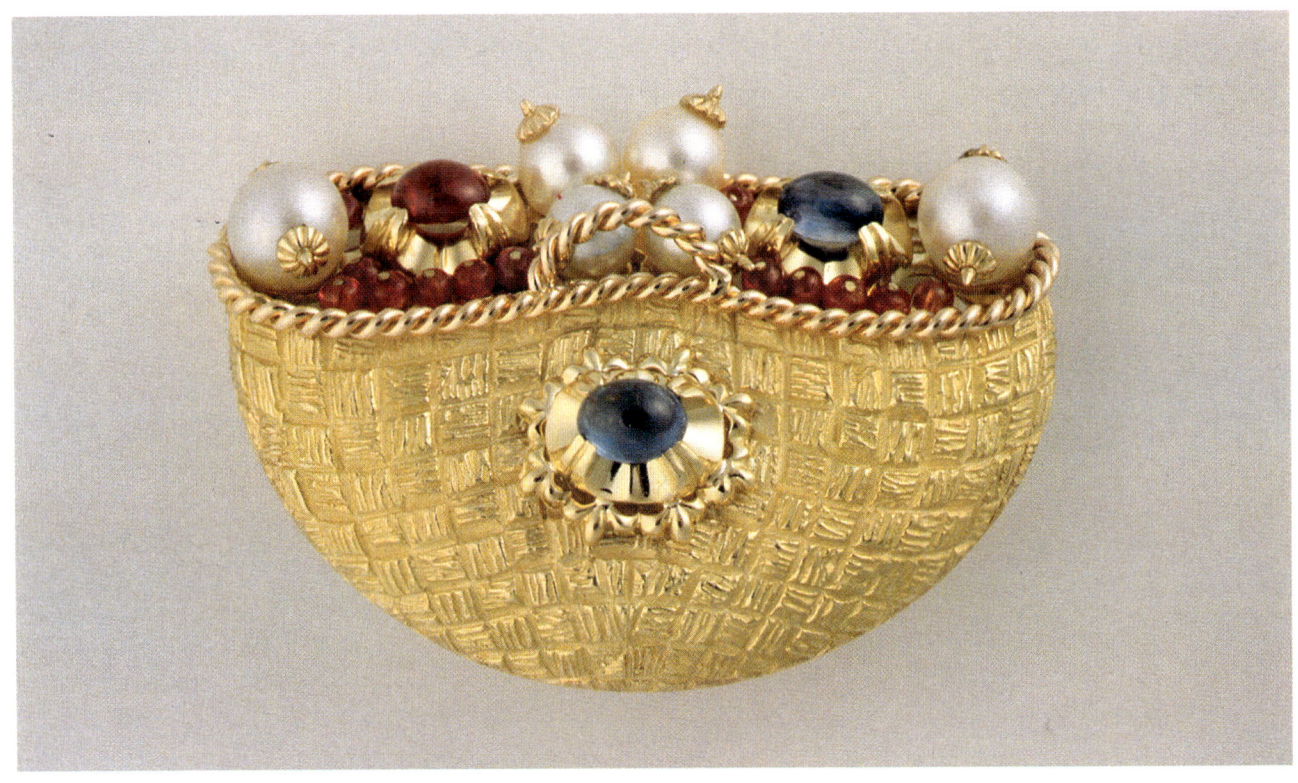

After Ghirlandaio, brooch in gold, pearls, cabochon rubies, spherical rubies and cabochon sapphires.

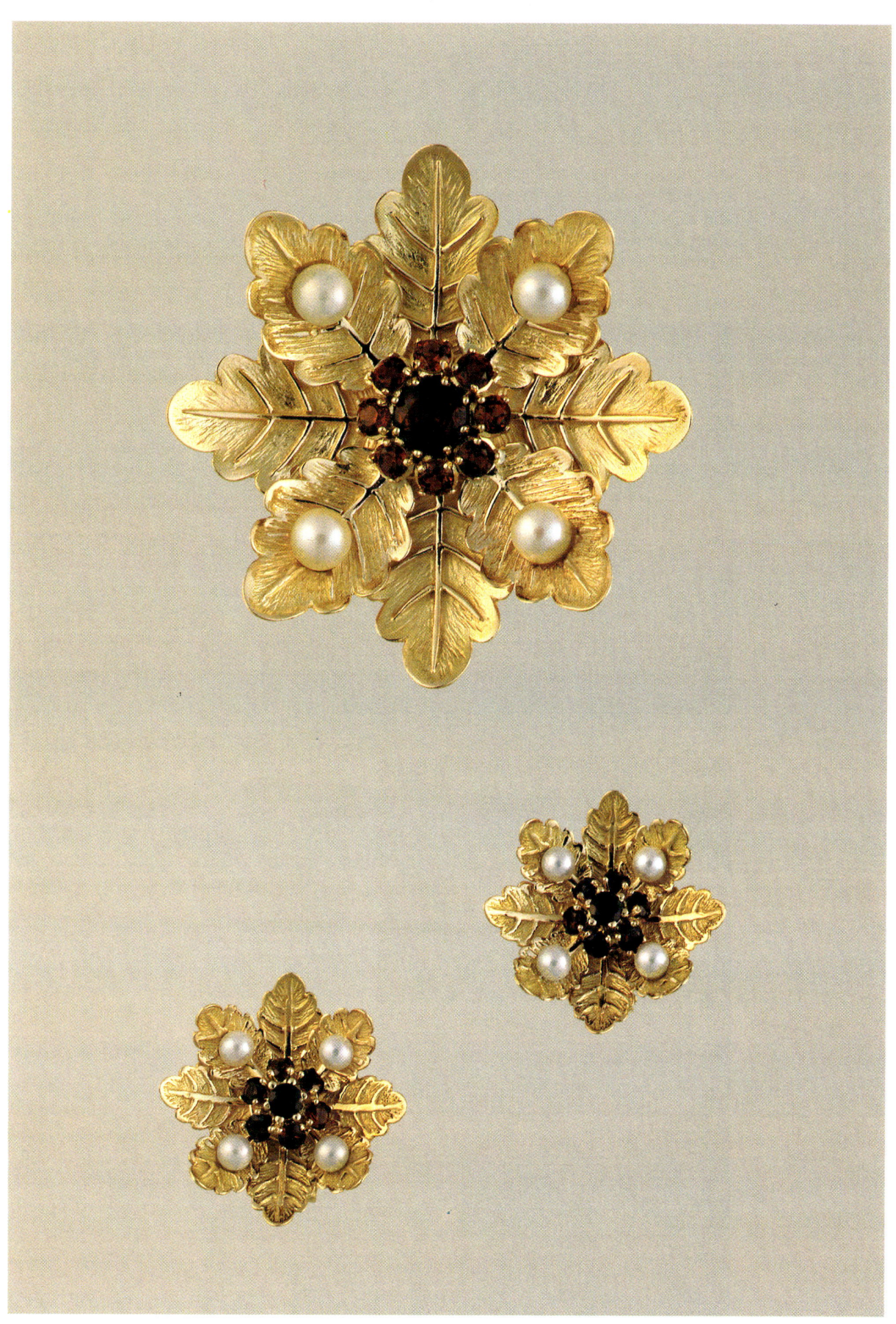

After Botticelli, brooch/pendant in gold, pearls and garnets.

DANIEL VAN NUFFEL

B y family tradition, Daniel Van Nuffel was destined to be a gemologist and jeweller, having learned the profession from his father. More than a jeweller, he is a technician of gold and stones. His moveable or transformable jewels adapt themselves to the personality of each wearer, according to form, position and colour.

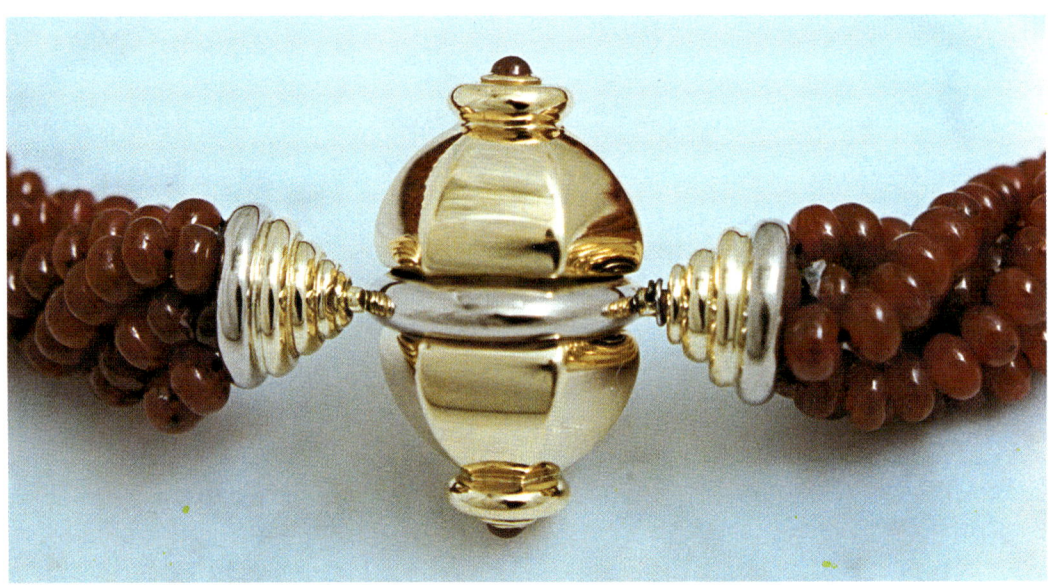

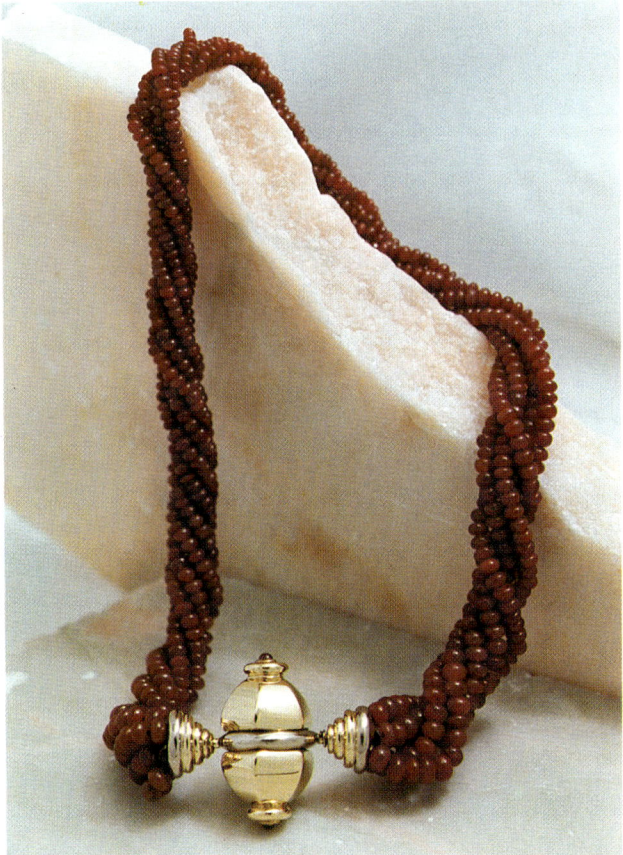

This piece is entirely moveable in every direction. The corals and ruby cabochons may be replaced by pearls and other stones, giving this model a multitude of wearing possibilities.

ROBERTA

Her ideas, transformed into jewels, have covered the hands and necks of tens of thousands of Italian women. I dislike speaking of fashion with regard to jewellery, but in this case I can use the term 'style', the Roberta style; she has made jewels from everyday objects that are gay and easy to wear. This gold stylist has succeeded in creating models that are truly original yet so wearable that all of Italy applauds her creations.

She is the worthy heiress of a family tradition that began in the last century. In fact, the Apa family has been established in Torre del Greco since 1848.

'Vigna', necklace in gold and coral.

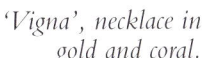

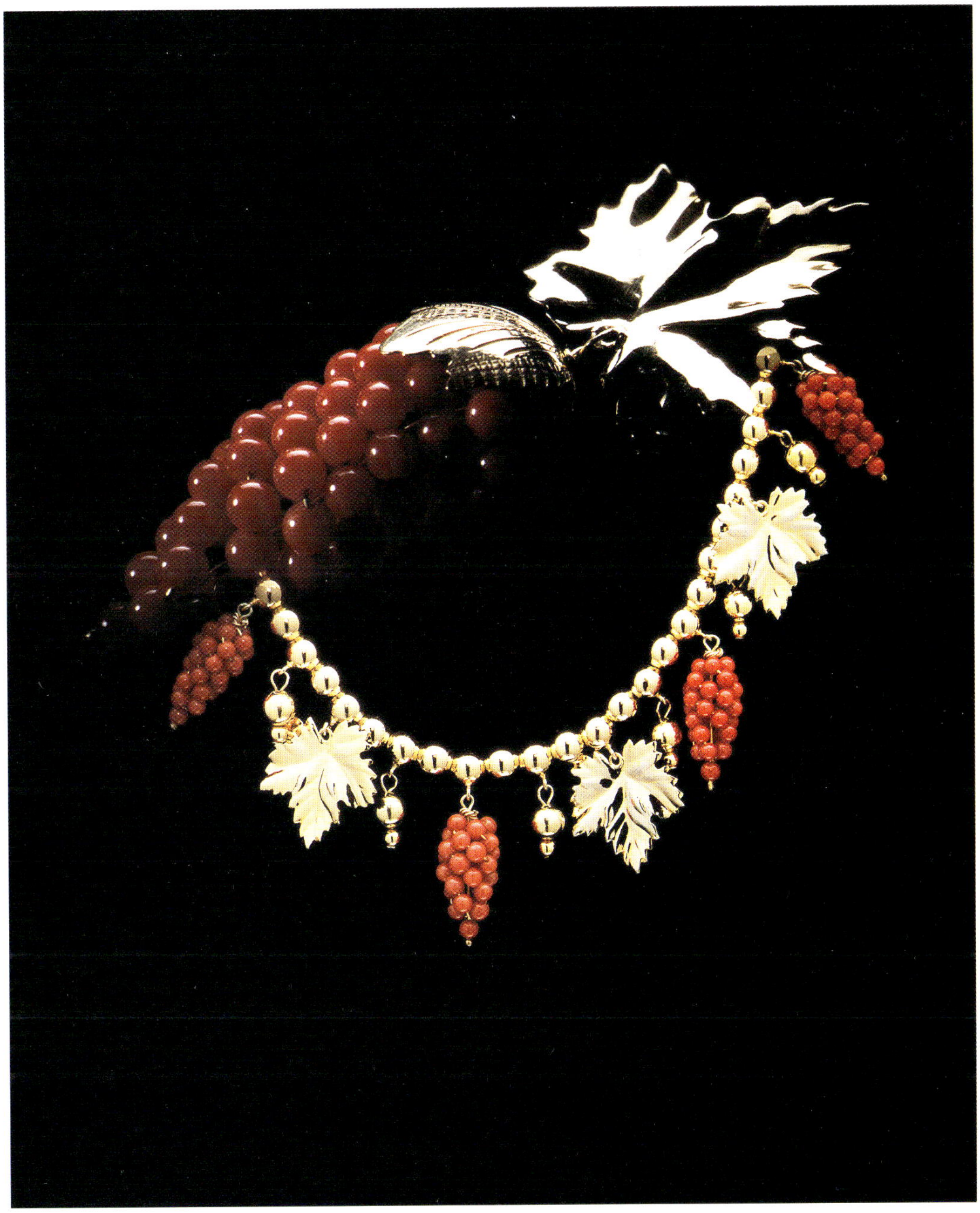

GUY BADOUX

He likes precious metals, stones and pearls. He likes putting them together in a harmonious way so that they transmit a message through their brilliance, their colour and their volume. Guy Badoux is a passionate artist who is practically obsessed with working to perfection.

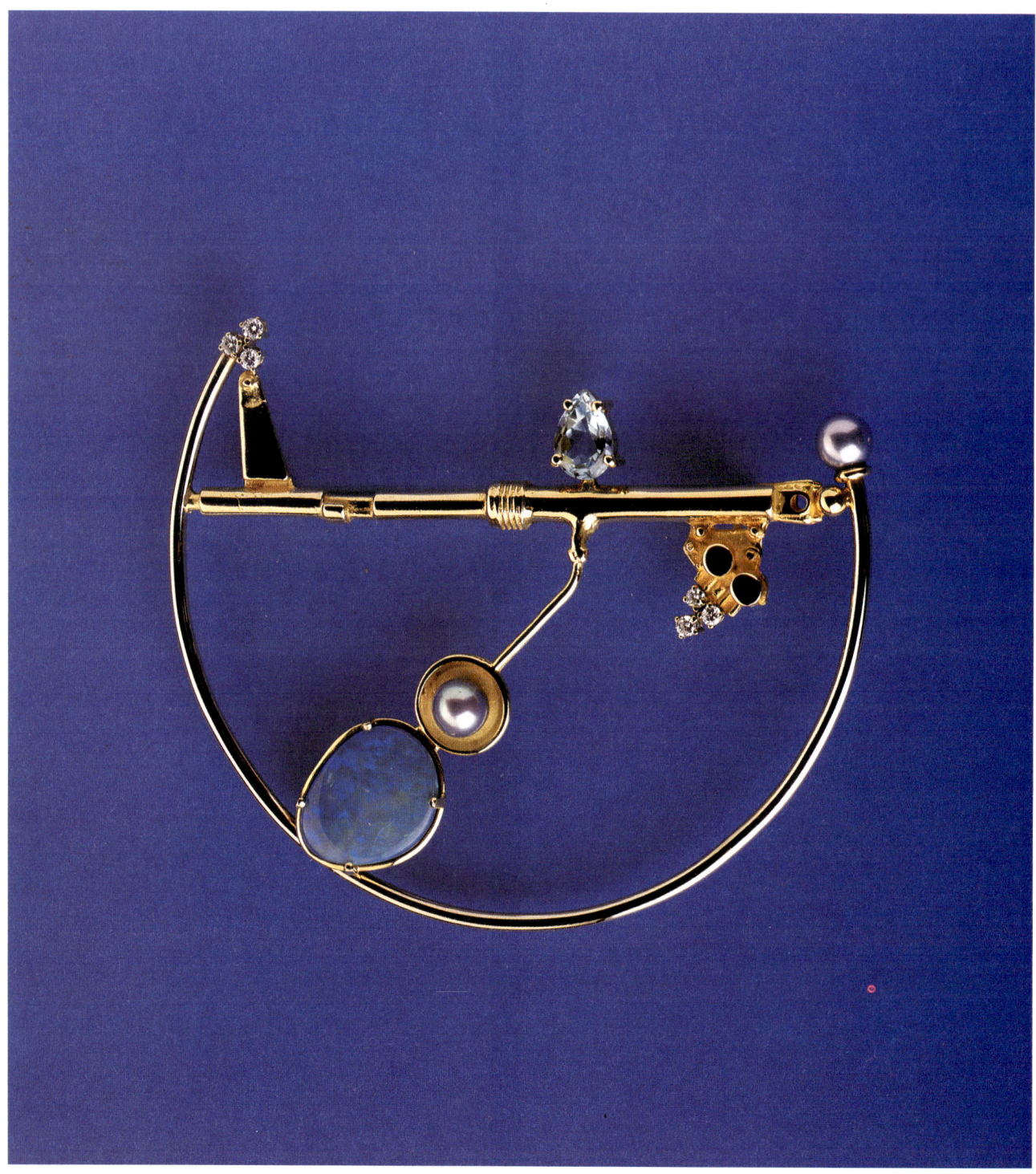

38 *Brooch in yellow gold, 'Boulder' opal, aquamarine, diamonds and pearls.*

JEAN-PIERRE LALOUX

Purity of line and carefully orchestrated harmony of volumes and colours give Jean-Pierre Laloux's pieces, irrespective of their size, the solidity of real sculptures. This rigour — and it is in this, without a doubt, that one can discern his very singular talent — does not exclude the fervour of the 'baroque'. A contemporary, timeless baroque that makes no explicit allusions to the conventions of the past, and that suits those irregular pearls that are referred to as 'baroque'. The choice of stones or pearls is determinant; they speak to the imagination, this one by its lovely curves, that one by its bluish brilliance, setting in motion the process that will integrate them into an original creation. Many and secret are the ways of this marriage between noble metal and the most beautiful products of rock or sea. The object is born of wax, its lines assert themselves and become pure, through subtle manipulations interspersed with periods of contemplation. When this alchemist's work comes to term, the piece will emerge from the broken mold still rough but full of all the promise of purest gold. With infinite patience, the artisan-artist leans over his workbench once again for the final touches. Stones and pearls take the places reserved for them. Jean-Pierre Laloux has before him his dream in material form, and soon, somewhere, another dream will be fulfilled in a marvellous encounter.

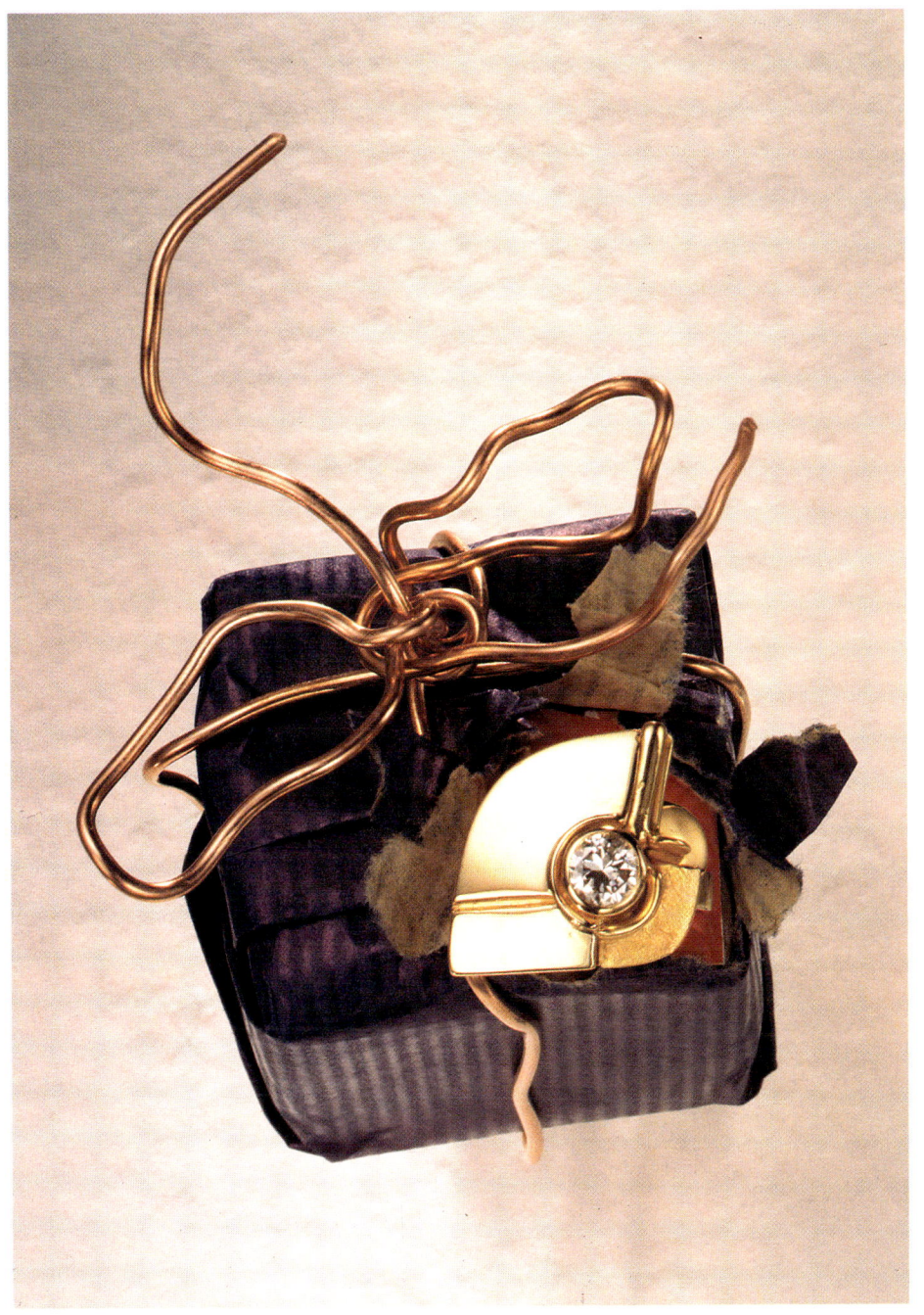

Ring in yellow gold and brilliant.

ZARKHANE

Winner of many special prizes, Zarkhane presents us with his philosophy for the creation of jewels:

'A jewel must above all correspond perfectly to the personality of the individual who wears it; otherwise, he or she will not feel at ease wearing it or quite simply will not like it.

'The work of the creator is being able to precisely discern this personality and create a jewel that relates to it. Accentuating, emphasising the personality.

'In creating a jewel, I am always seeking a harmony and a balance in its form; I also aim to keep it simple, while using new forms that are not shocking.'

Diamond brooch in yellow gold.

Ring in yellow gold, diamonds and black Tahiti pearl.

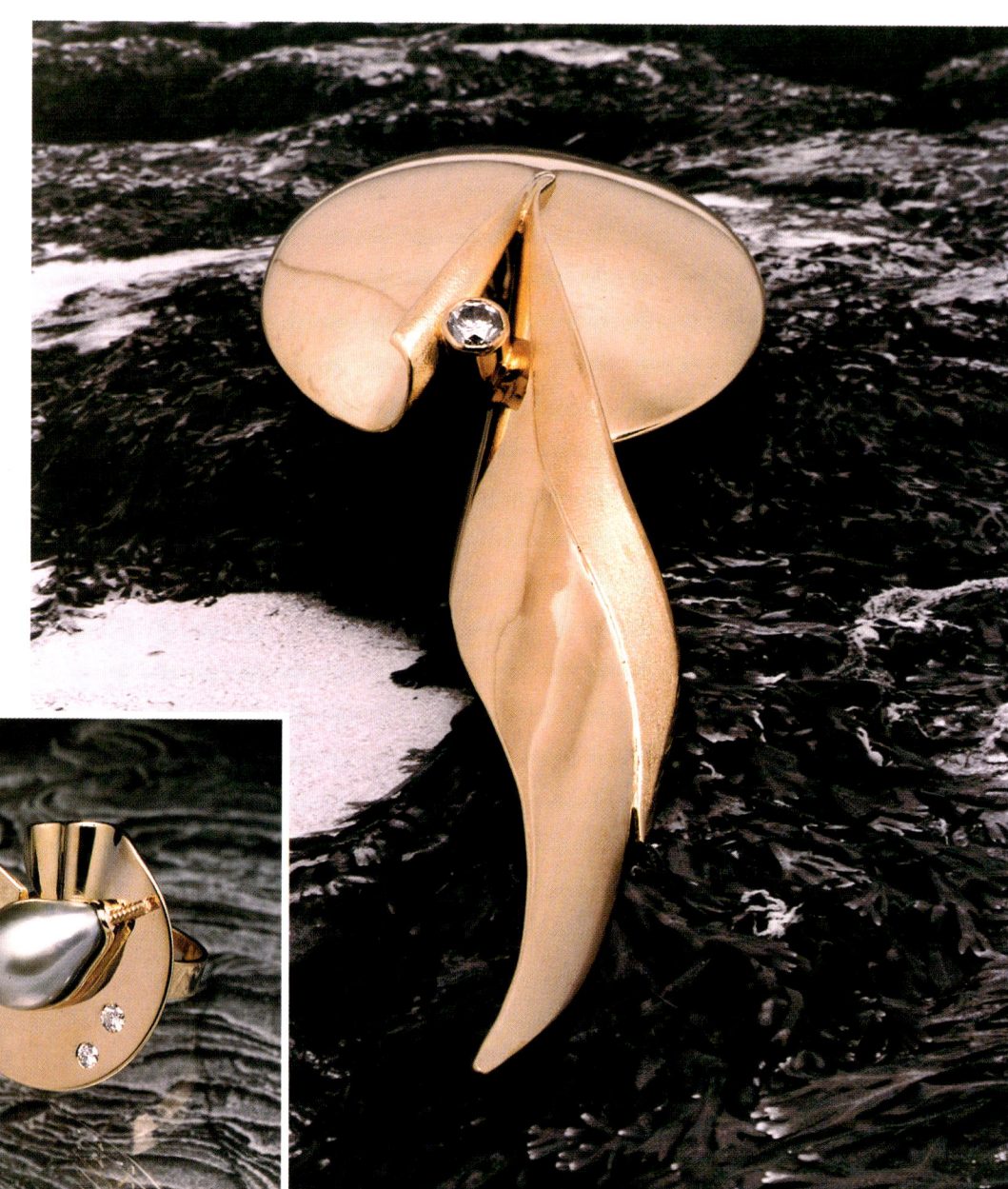

ALFREDO GROSSO

'**M**y interest in creating jewels was born by accident. I set to work right after reading an article entitled, "How to Make Jewellery Yourself".'

An art critic declares, 'Alfredo Grosso is the youngest and most lyrical of Brazilian jewel creators; his technique is highly recognisable. But the principal attraction of his pieces are the mixtures of metals he uses to obtain forms and colours that are identical to those found in nature'. Since 1991 he has been established in Italy – in Merano, to be precise.

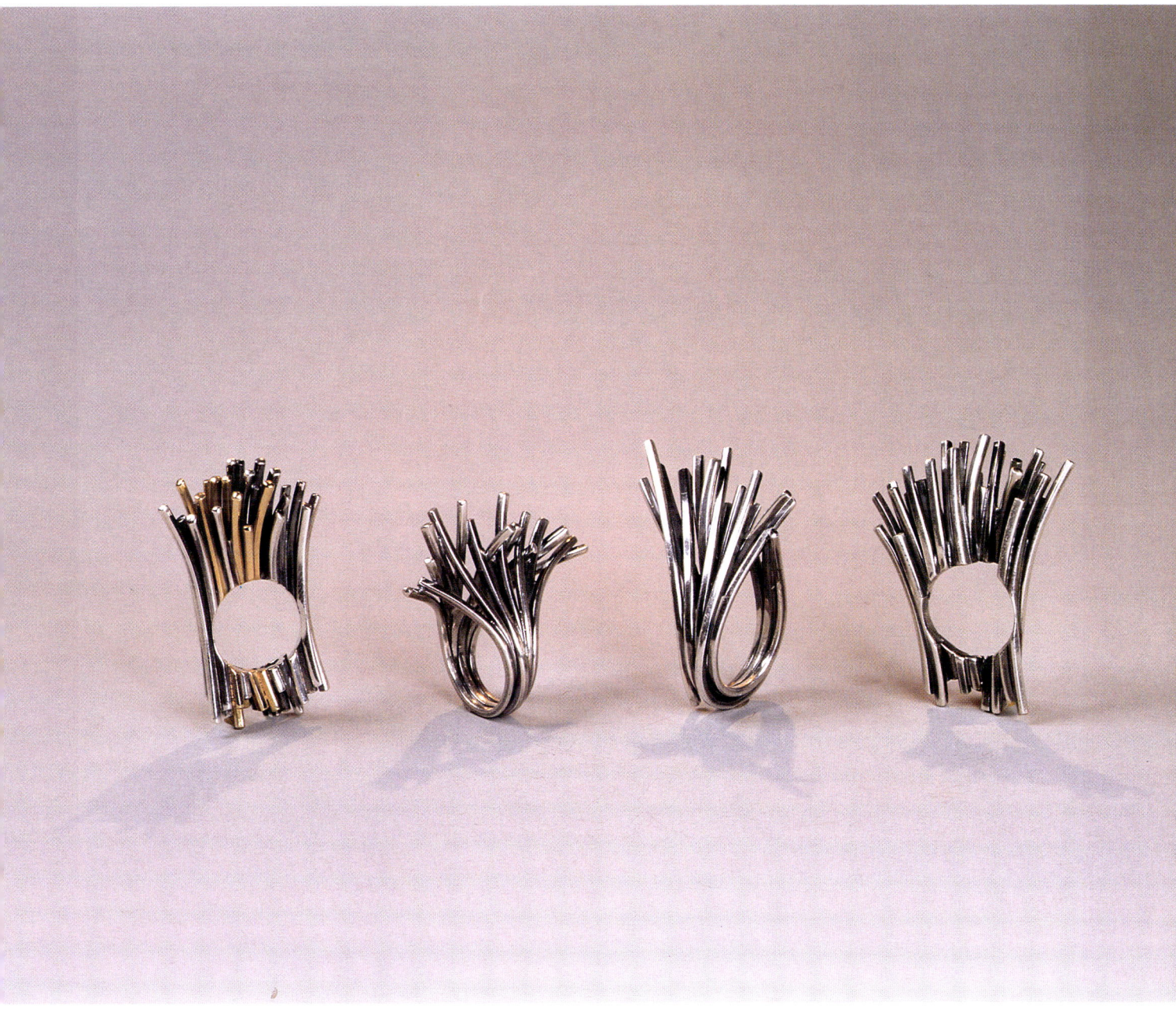

Series of 'bundle' rings in gold and silver.

CHRISTIGUEY

'Creating a jewel or a sculpture is a human adventure, and the finished work is a response that encloses the mystery of material and colour, the harmony of technique and inspiration, which the precious stone releases by its mysterious and fascinating brilliance. Rarity and preciousness are forgotten in the presence of timelessness.

'When I hold a stone in my hands, it produces a shock, a sympathetic magic that does not subside until I have translated this emotion into the realisation of a piece.

'Giving form to the imaginary is a sublime moment.'

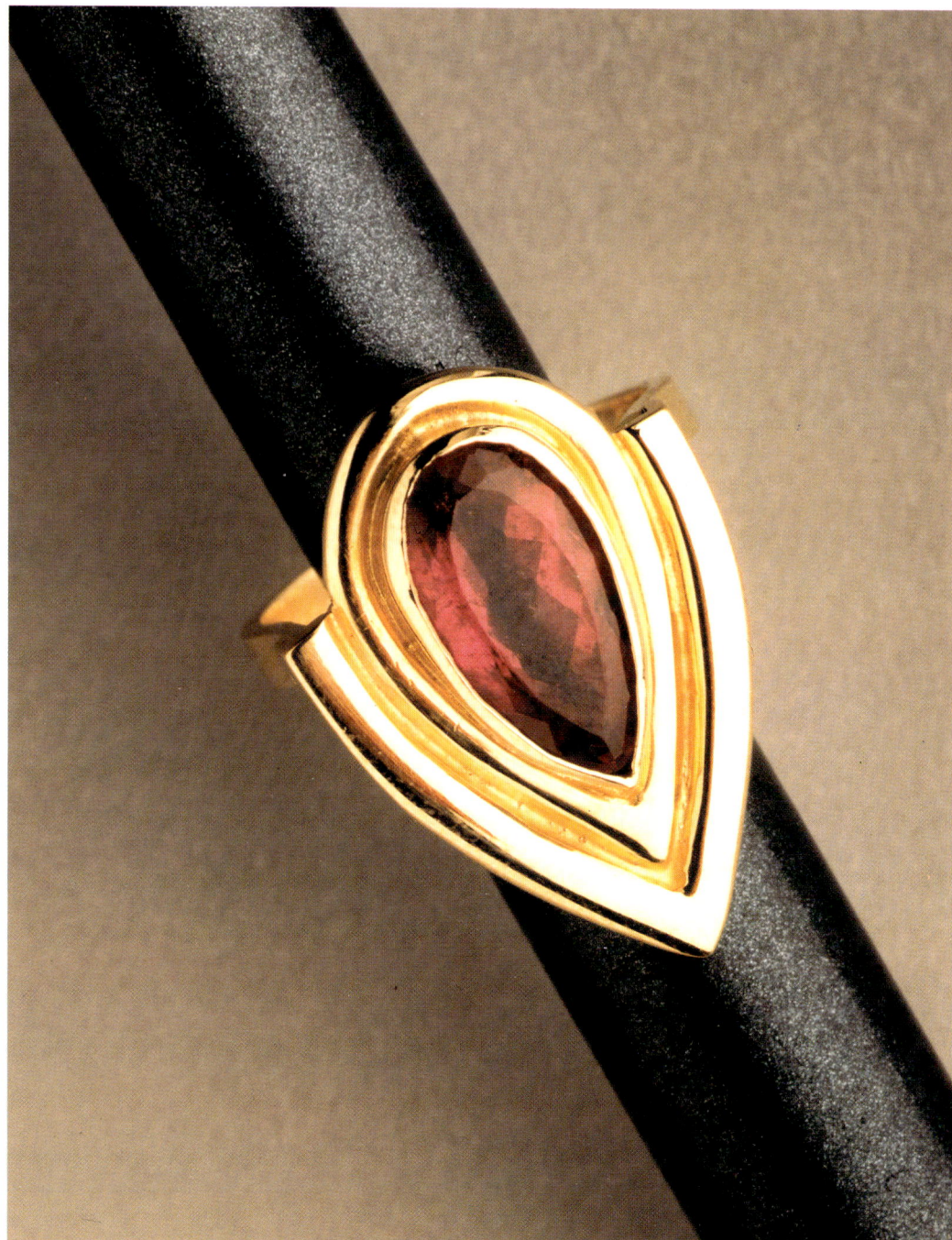

Ring/pendant in gold and rubelite (pink tourmaline) in the shape of a pear.

BARBARA ROMANO

Despite her youth, her pieces are of an appreciable maturity. From her first years of study, Barbara Romano has received prestigious prizes and awards. In 1973, she earned the exceptional mark of 110/110 for her thesis 'Reflexion', which was based on the evolution of Bauhaus architecture in the United States. Within this theme, she developed a series of jewels and objects wholly inspired by that movement of the 1930s.

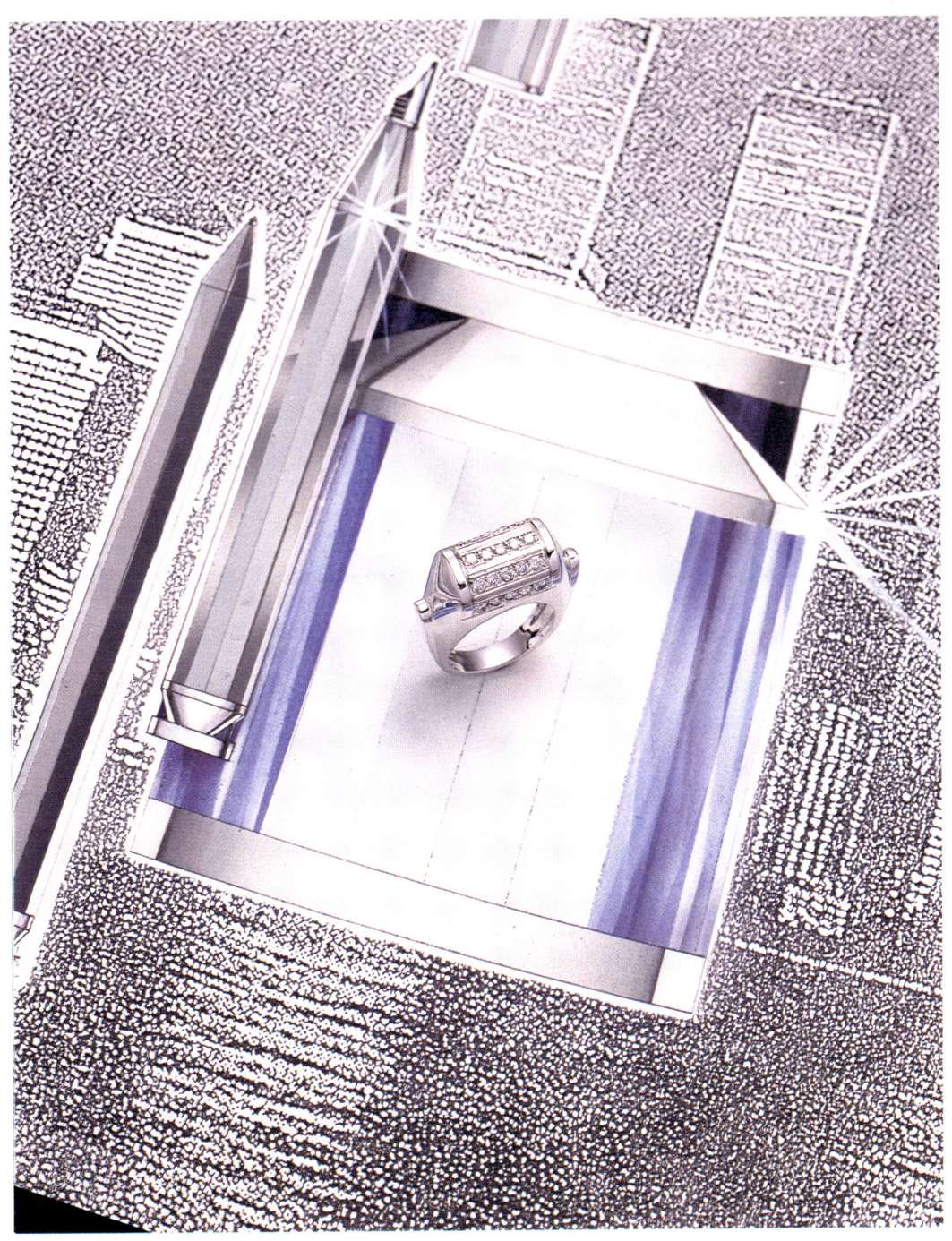

From the 'Reflexion' collection, a ring in white gold and diamonds.

IAIN WOOD

This Englishman working in Namour (Belgium) was a specialist in antique watches before becoming a jewel creator. It is his love of mechanical perfection and his study of history that have made him an artist unique in his personal genre. One of his most remarkable works is a miniaturisation of the historic landscape of Namur, a town he is madly in love with. His showroom is open to the public in Namur under the name Wood-MacArthur.

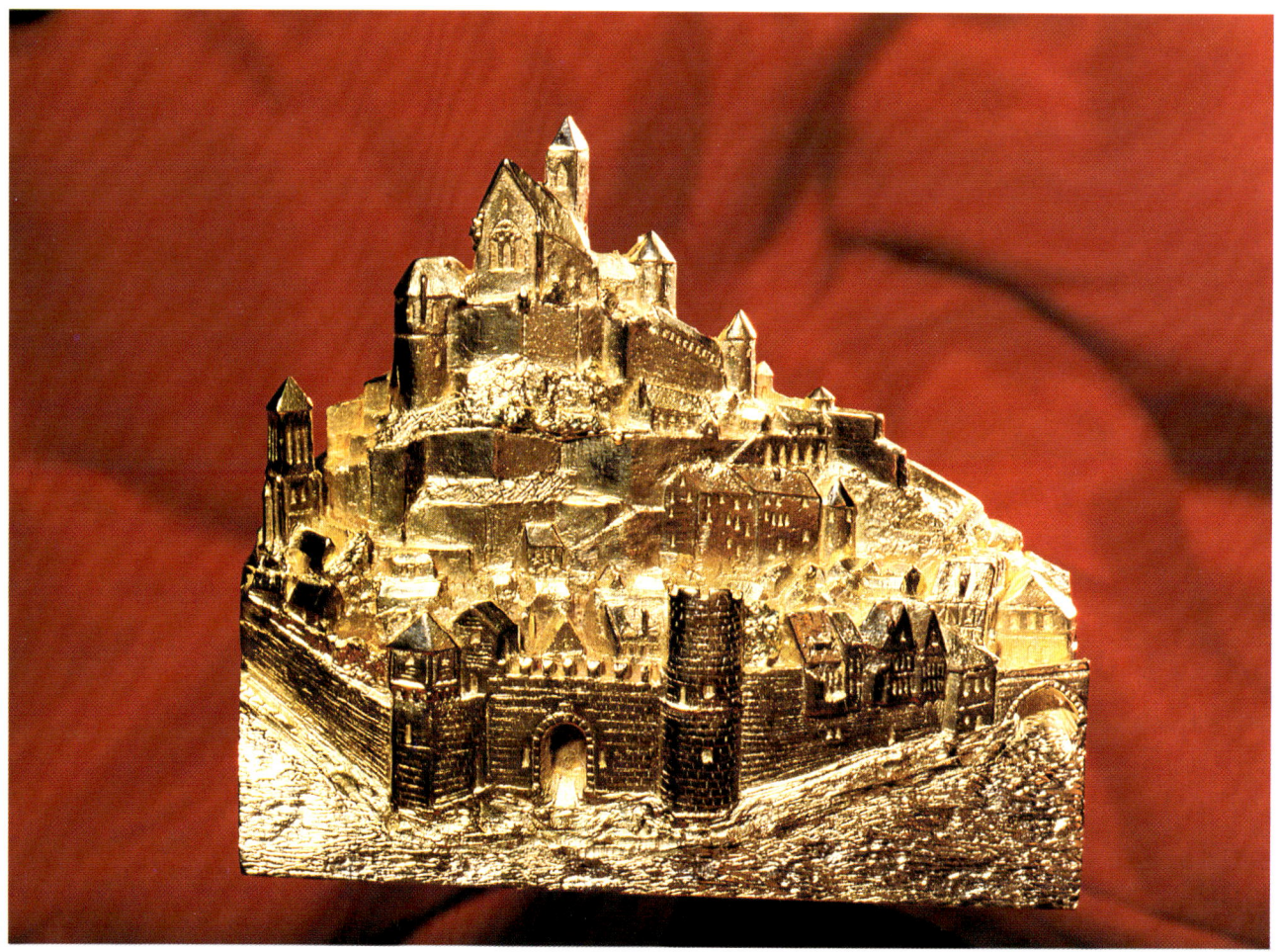

Brooch after Kegeljam, in white, yellow and green gold. It depicts the citadel of Namur in the 17th century, with the Nôtre-Dame and Saint-Pierre collegiate churches in relief (the Saint-Pierre tower was nicknamed 'l'oubliette', the secret dungeon).

ALBERTO ZORZI

A professor at the 'Pietro Selvatico' Institute of Art in Padua, Alberto Zorzi 'hunts' through the art world, capturing cubism and futurism to create pieces full of dynamic allure.

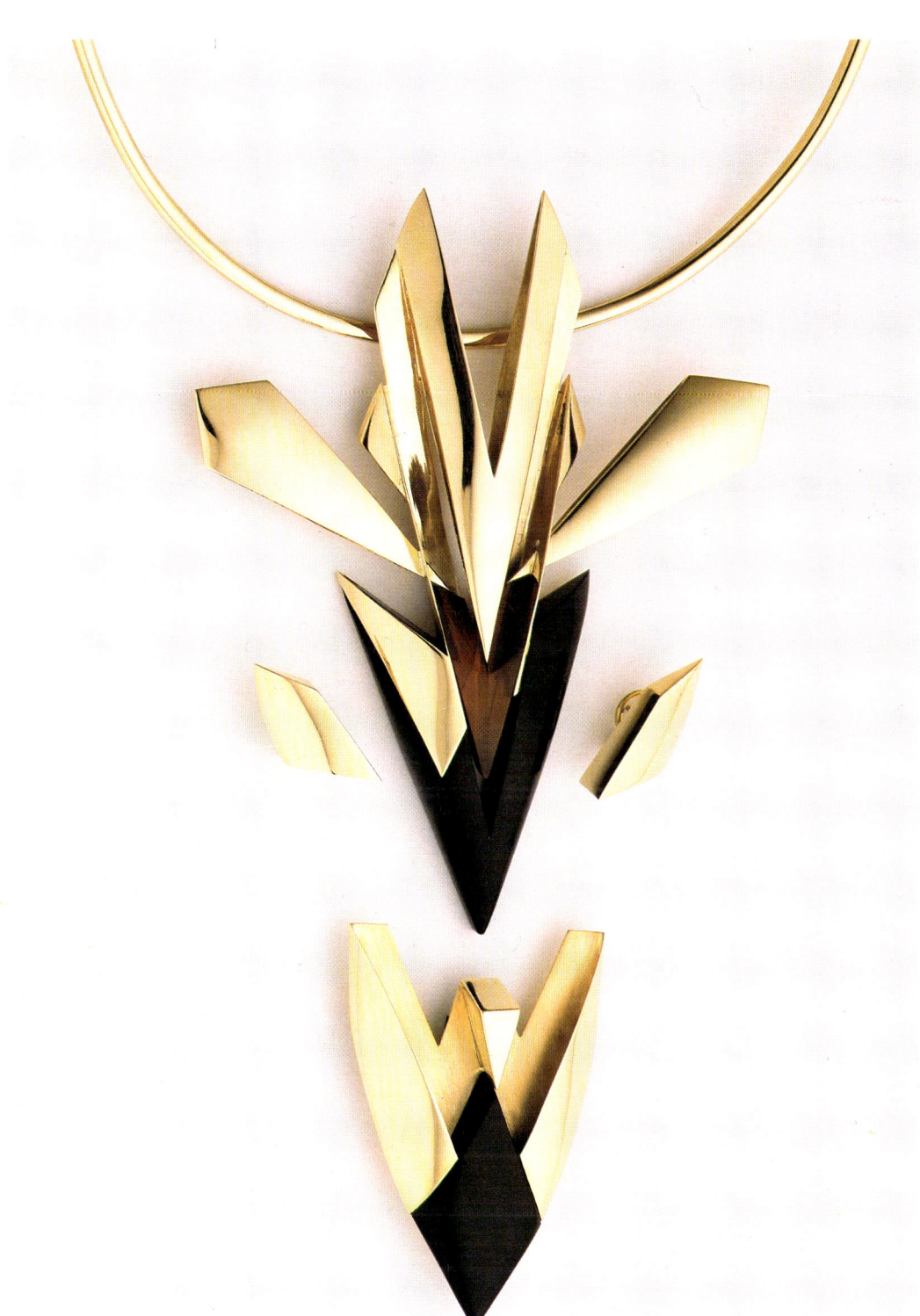

'Scarabeus' set, in black agate, Madeira quartz and yellow gold. Alberto Zorzi's jewels are handsome individually and often form another work of art when they are combined. Necklace, brooch and earrings.

AGATHE SAINT GIRONS

A fiery temperament, to match her red head of hair, Agathe Saint Girons is a young lightning-bolt of a woman. She creates with her heart. When she likes something, she commits herself to it. All her passion is engaged the moment she begins to create: sculpture, theatre sets, clothing and of course jewels — 'whimsical treasures or treasured whimsies', she calls them humorously. Her creations, her unique pieces, reveal all her fire, all her soul.

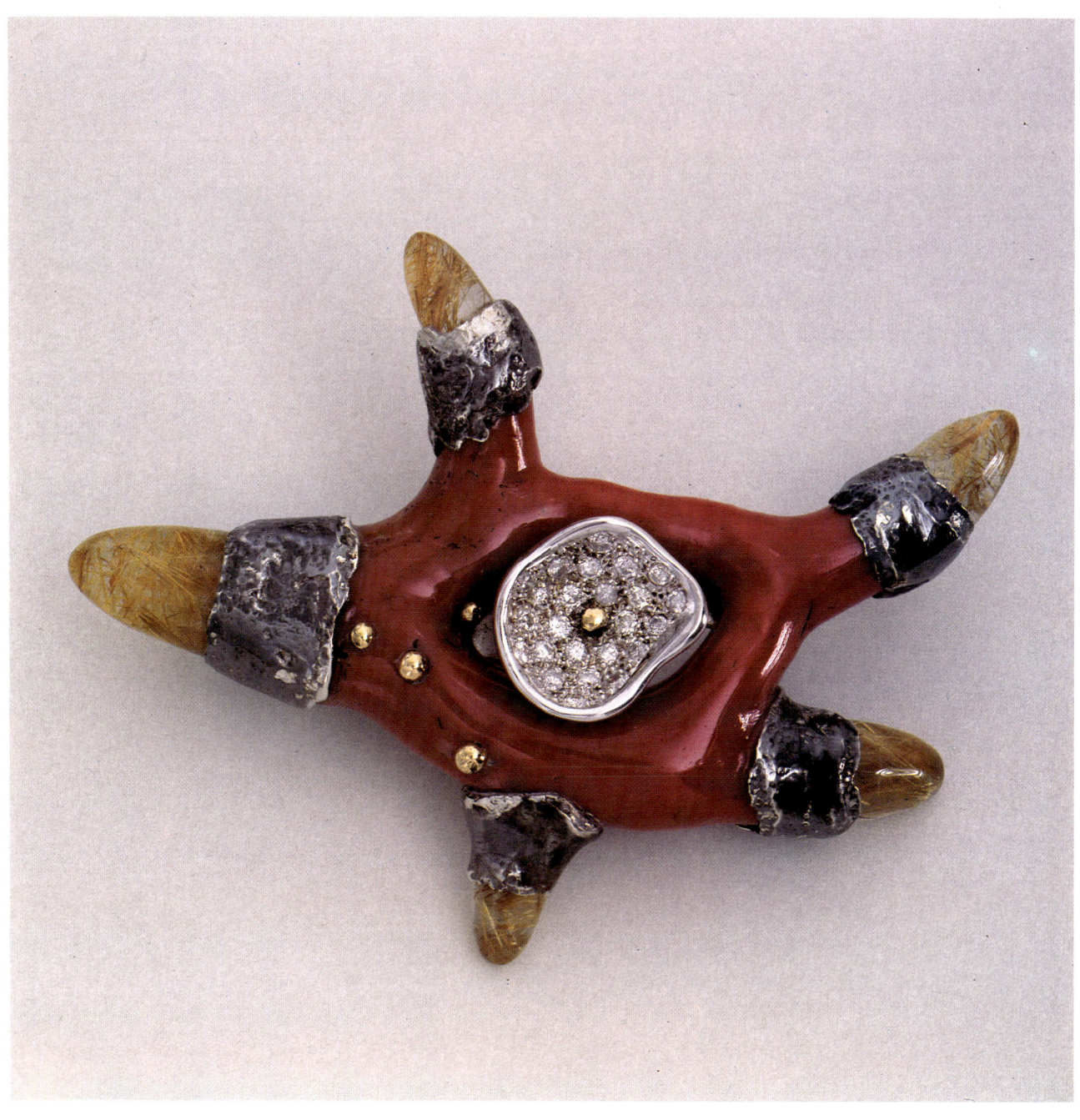

46 'Méditerranée' brooch in coral, gold, silver, diamond and angel-hair (rutile quartz).

STEFANO MICHELANGELI-POLIMENI

His hobby is creating in general, jewels in particular. Although he was a student of mine for some time, I consider him to be an authentic self-taught artist. Once his idea is in place, the technique that he applies to realise the piece simply comes from logic. Making a sculpture, a bas-relief or a jewel is an act of creation; the result and the dimensions depend on the quality of the raw material and the person who will use the object.

In jewellery, Stefano Michaelangeli-Polimeni has launched a style of jewel, called 'le volage' ('flight of fancy'), that is very symbolic, romantic and sensual.

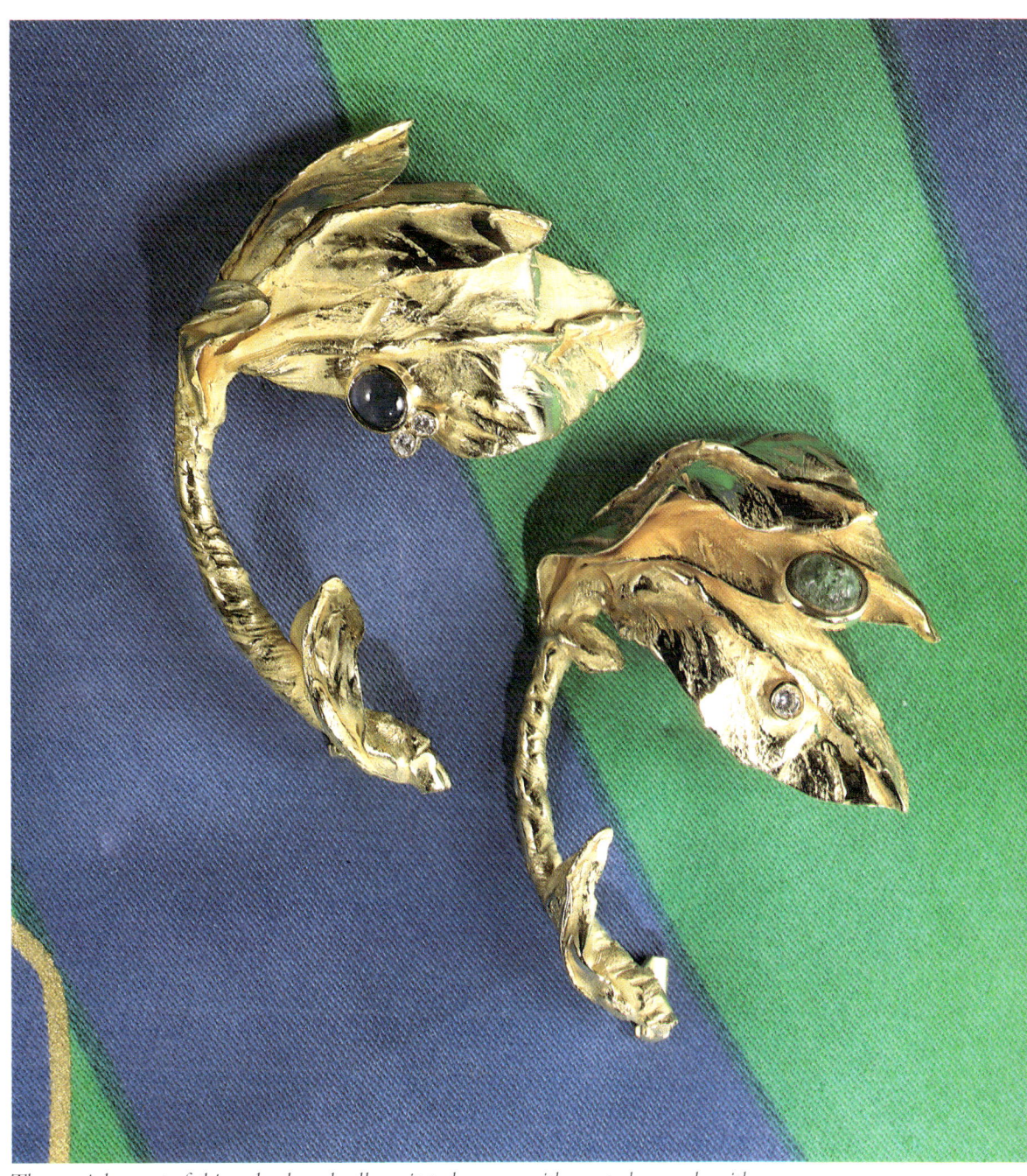

The special aspect of this palm-brooch allows it to be worn with great elegance by either a woman or a man. Stefano Michelangeli-Polimeni wanted to present the ideas of dreams and freedom with his 'flight of fancy' style. Gold, emerald, sapphire and diamonds.

47

SIMONNE
MUYLAERT HOFMAN

Her name is legendary in Belgium. When she works, she is already imagining the person who will wear her jewel, and she outdoes herself when she meets the man or woman who will own the object in advance. Simonne Muylaert Hofman combines and marries metals and stones with a poetry that inspires dreams; she is fascinated by smoothness of line contrasted by aggressive colours.

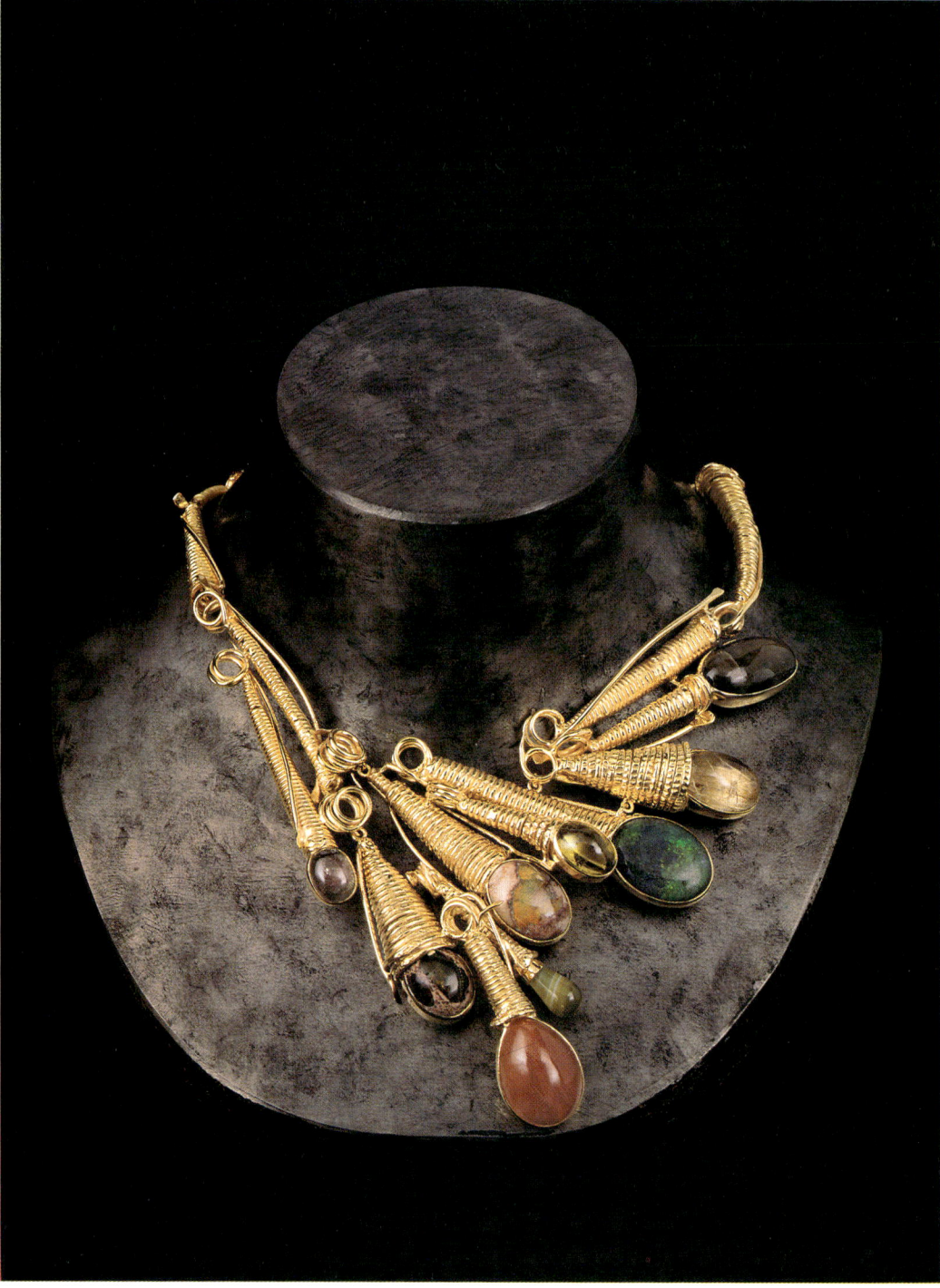

Necklace of gold and stones in all the colours of opals.

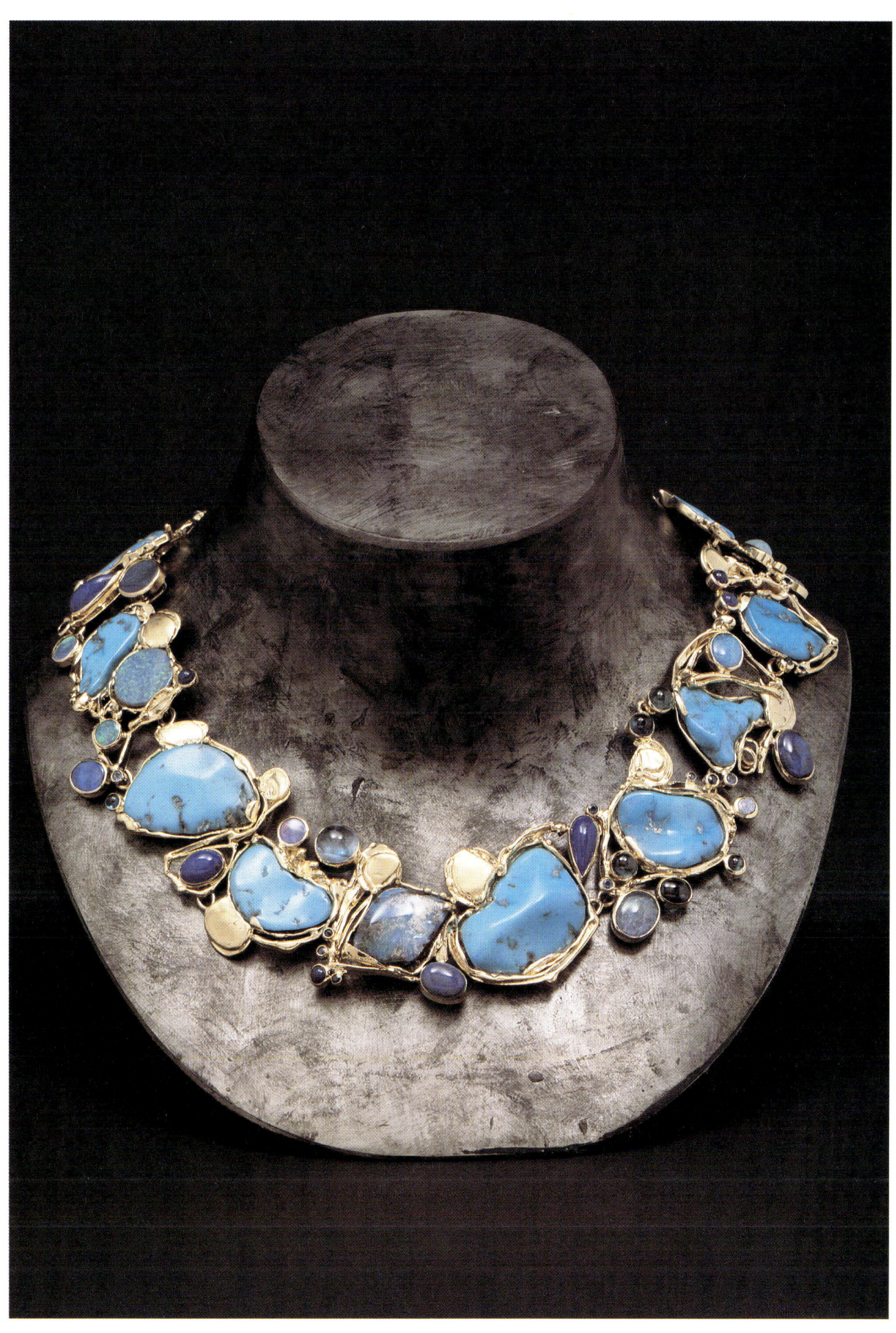

Collar in gold, turquoise, lapis lazuli, aquamarine, sapphires, opals, chalcedony and blue aventurines. An exceptionally successful marriage of forms and bluish tints.

49

GUIDO PERSICO

Guido Persico is actually one of the two designers that make up the 'AR-DUO' tandem, specialising in all levels of jewellery design projects. He works permanently in Milan; the other partner, Paola Valentini, is in Paris. This "duo" works for the major international jewellery companies, and they design not only jewels but also everything that surrounds them: jewel-cases, display cabinets, shops and even professional show-rooms. They are very fond of new and unusual materials.

Two rings in yellow and white gold with petrified wood.

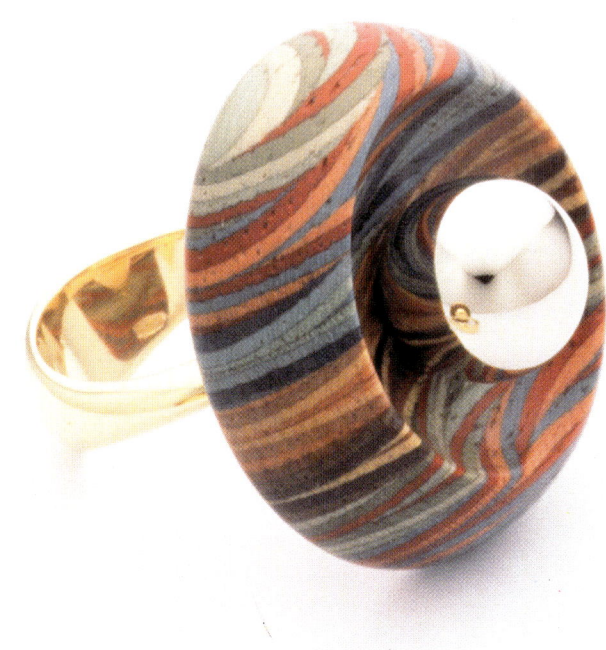

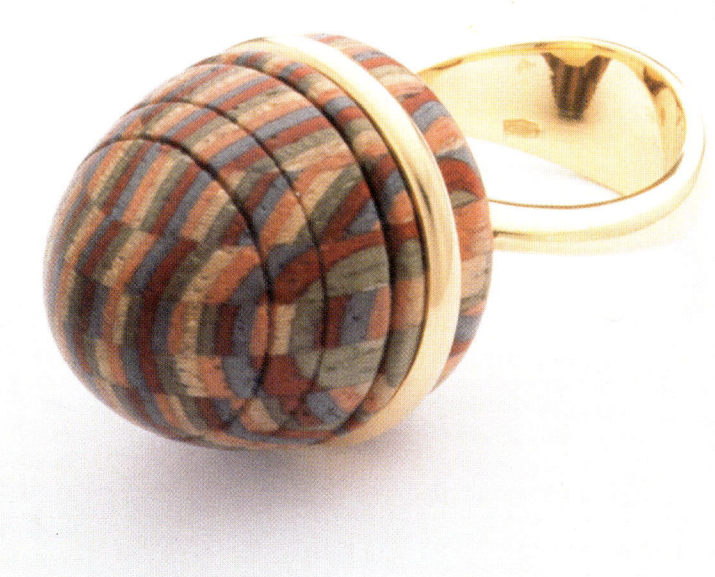

GEORG SPRENG

He is established in Schwäbisch Gmünd with the charming Sabine Loeckle, who collaborates with him in creating the jewels that I consider to be the wildest in the world. An unlimited gigantism is matched with a freedom of expression that is founded on irreproachably solid artistic bases. Using stones of 50 or 100 carats each to make a brassiere is a current form of Georg Spreng's. A ring the size of an egg is ridiculously small compared to his parameters. Each of his inventions is a work of art; he makes only a few of them a year. Platinum is hammer-wrought for days until the 'maestro' attains the curve he desires; time, dimension and value have no importance compared with the ultimate beauty.

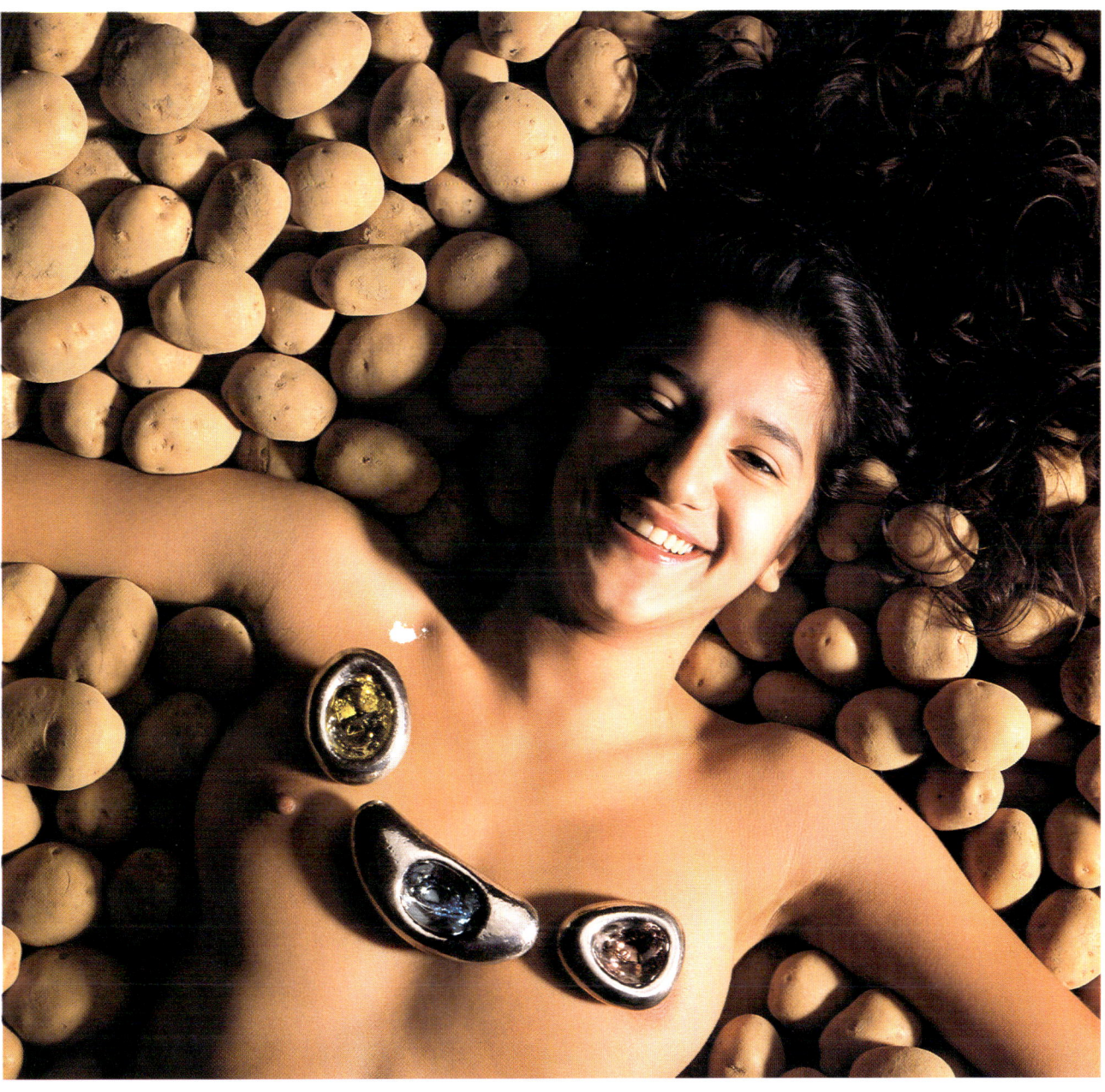

'Roasted Potatoes' is the title of this work of Georg Spreng's. Each potato, made of platinum set with a stone of more than 50 carats, may be worn alone or en groupe. It is not out of the question for this neck-lace to be worn as a breast-covering 'garment'.

BULGARI

The creation of a Bulgari jewel is the result of work that is very similar to that of Renaissance workshops.

Paolo Bulgari, who with his brother Nicola continues his family's tradition of art and style, develops each new idea in collaboration with a group of innovative designers and artisans with whom he works constantly, establishing a relationship of deep respect, intimacy, understanding and friendship.

These ideas may bring forth a single combination of different stones, or they may well be the result of an intensive study of a characteristic, of a particular artistic theme. The theme may relate to a specific historical era, analysed in its most essential elements and reinterpreted in jewels or silver objects.

The creative idea takes shape through a sketch that is worked out in water-colours or distemper. This sketch, thanks to the expert use of shades and colours, gives depth to the jewel and brings it alive, thus foreshadowing the emotion it will evoke once made up.

Starting from this sketch, the idea is then explored creatively, in order to see how it could be made up in different materials and colours, to see how the jewel will be worn, its consonance with history and the Bulgari style. This work may take months and, when it is finished, only a few designs will be deemed suitable for new jewels.

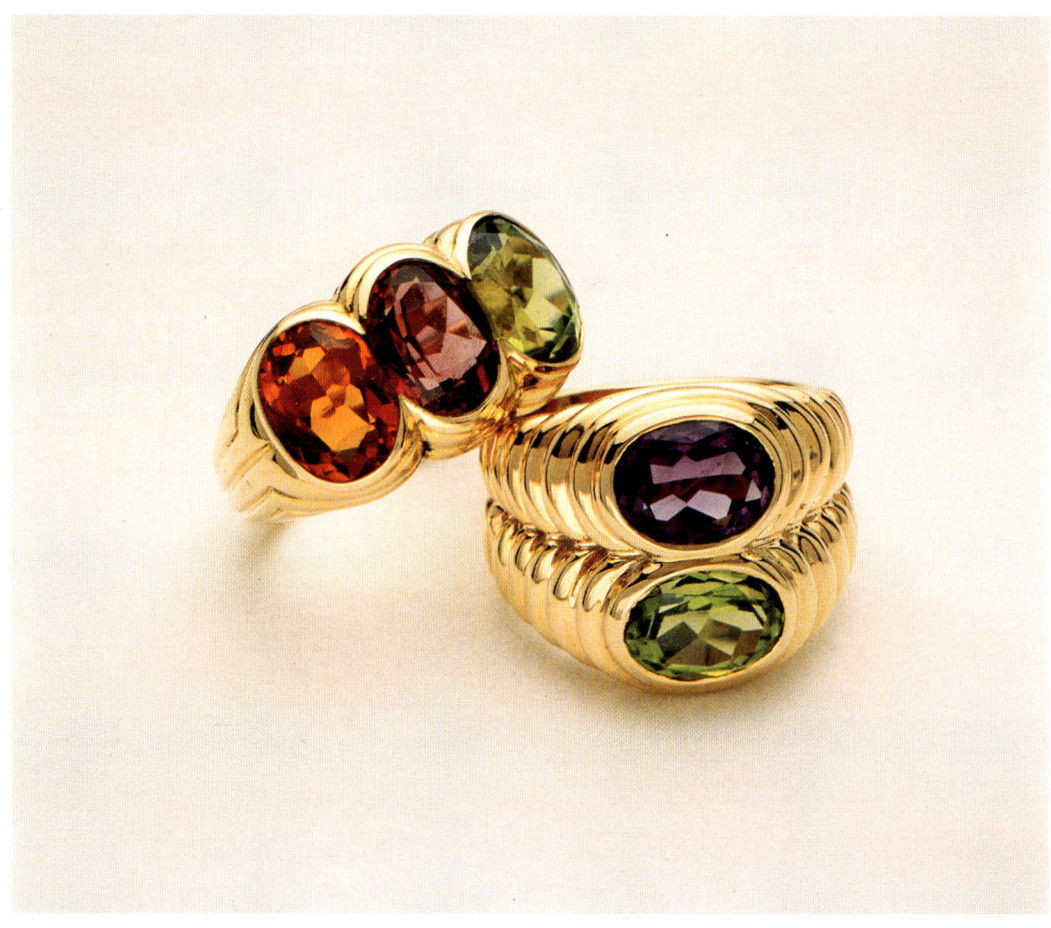

LAURENCE TUFENKDJIAN

There are in fact three brothers who work together, each in his own specialty. There is no doubt that the Tufenkdjian family directs the most important workshop for the creation and fabrication of jewels in the entire Middle East. For years they were the principal purveyors to Arabian princes. Today they address their collections more towards the West and Japan. I could define their creations as 'neoclassical jewellery' — they allow the stone to uphold its leading role.

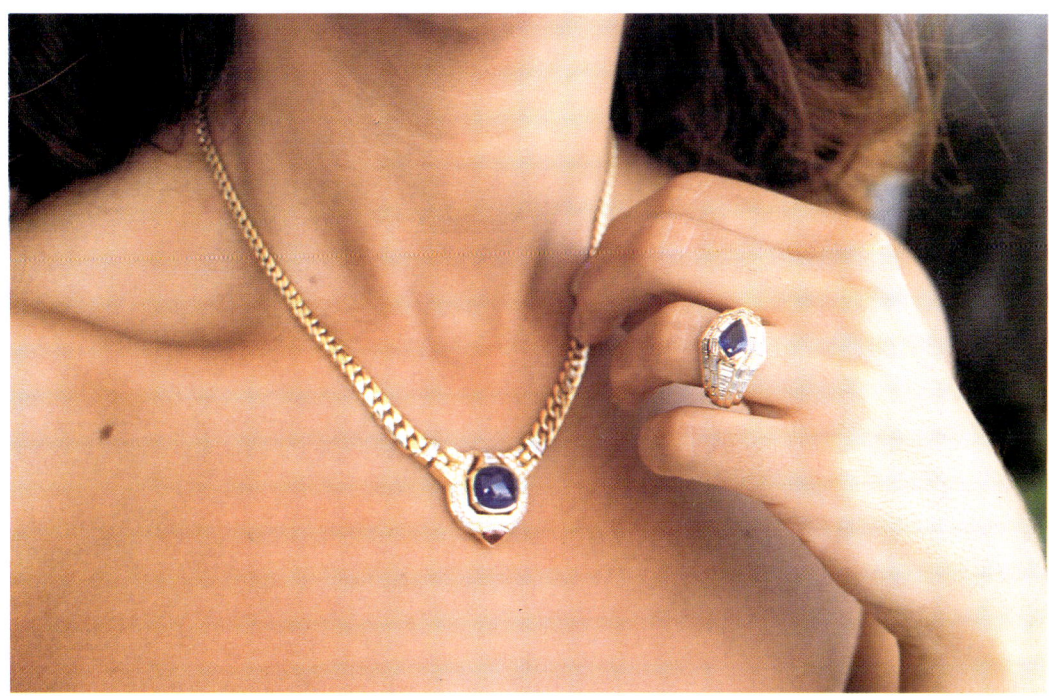

Gold necklace and ring with diamonds, rubies and sapphires.

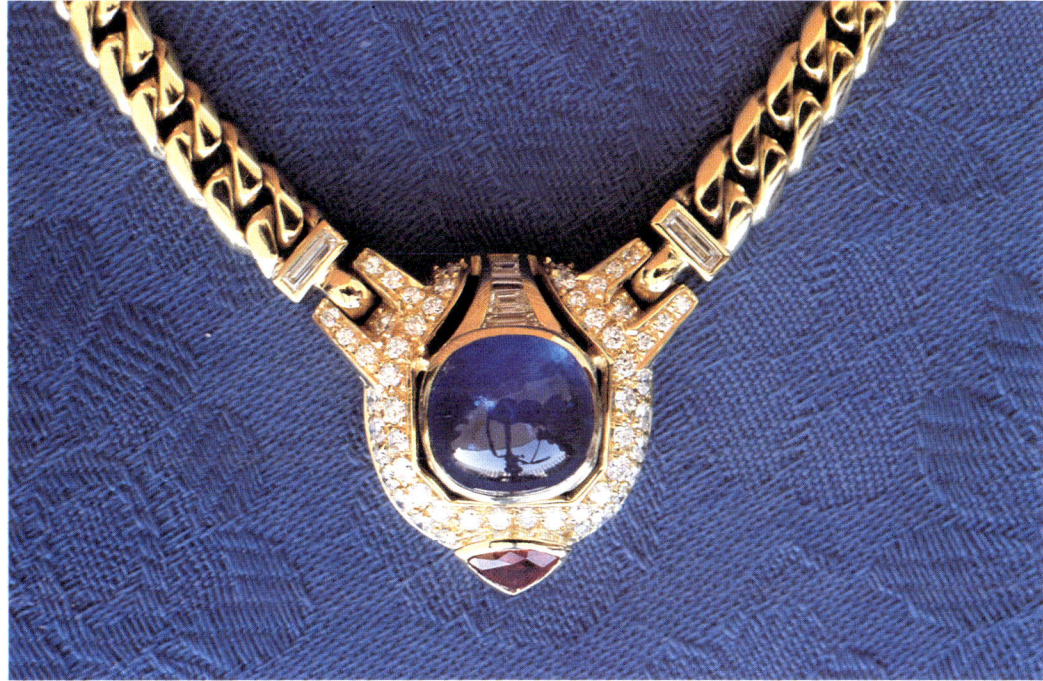

Centre of necklace enlarged.

53

ROBERTO VIOLA

Viola is an architect, sculptor and designer. He creates jewels in which traditional materials are mixed with those that he discovers in his continual explorations, such as luminous electronic circuits. Thus from his hands, unique pieces — small, portable sculptures — are born, pieces that skirt the border of informal art with his original language, in which colours and shapes play freely with the magic of unusual and fascinating stones.

'My expressive exploration aims to give form to the incessant dialogue between two different principles, for the dialectical and vital contrast between two opposing forces:

- light/darkness
- full/empty
- black/white
- presence/absence
- force/yielding
- surface/depth

'Because of this, the forms of my jewels are in a certain sense dynamic and in another sense changeable according to the perspective and feelings of the person looking at and wearing them'.

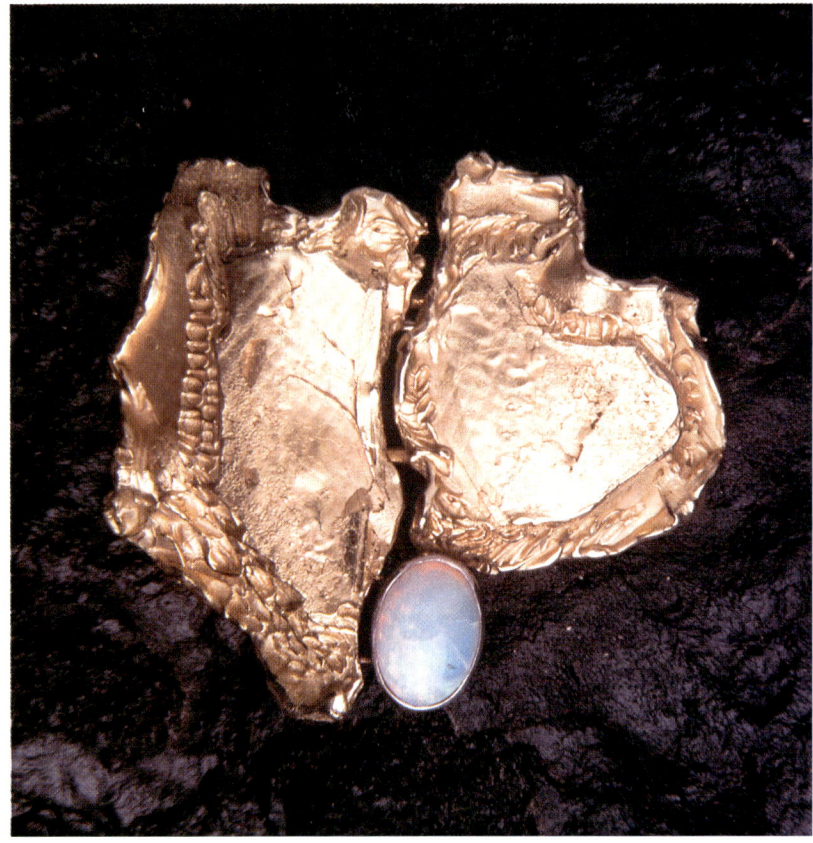

Gold and opal brooch/pendant. This piece is entitled 'The Talisman'.

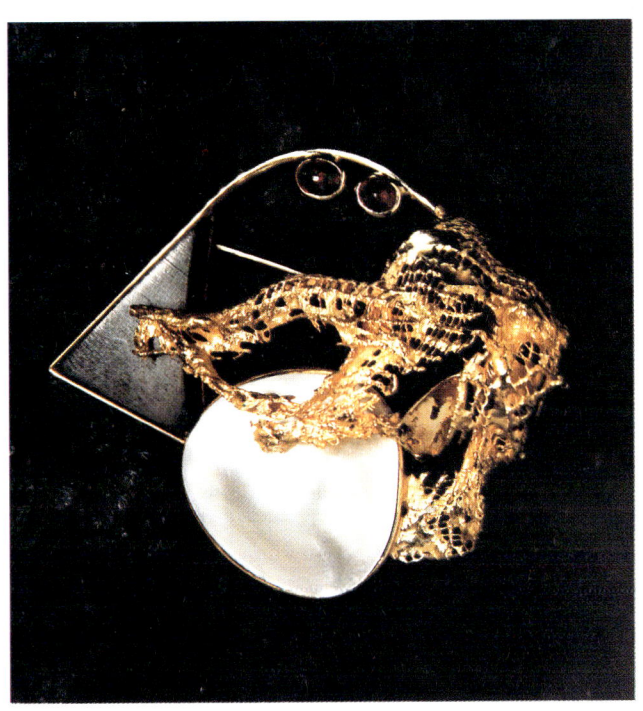

'Hearts in the Net' is a brooch in gold, ebony, mabé pearl and two cabochon rubies.

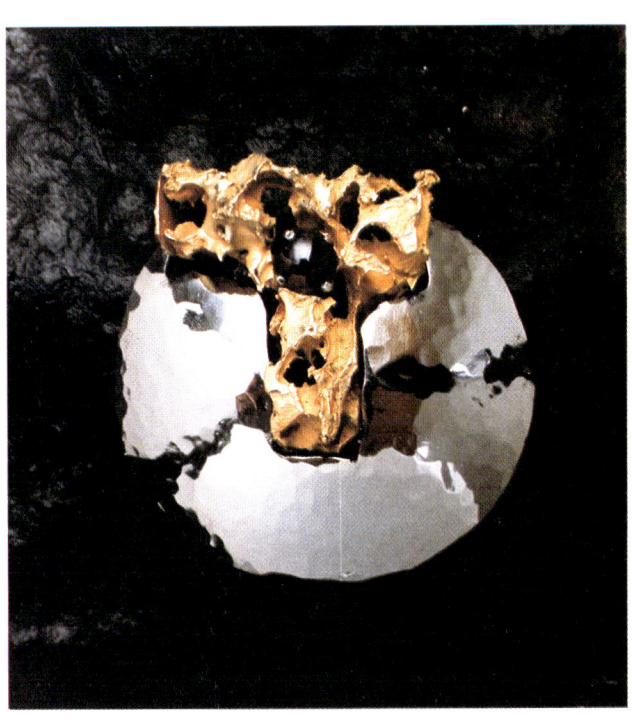

'The Shield of Time No. 2', brooch in gold, platinum and cabochon-cut garnet.

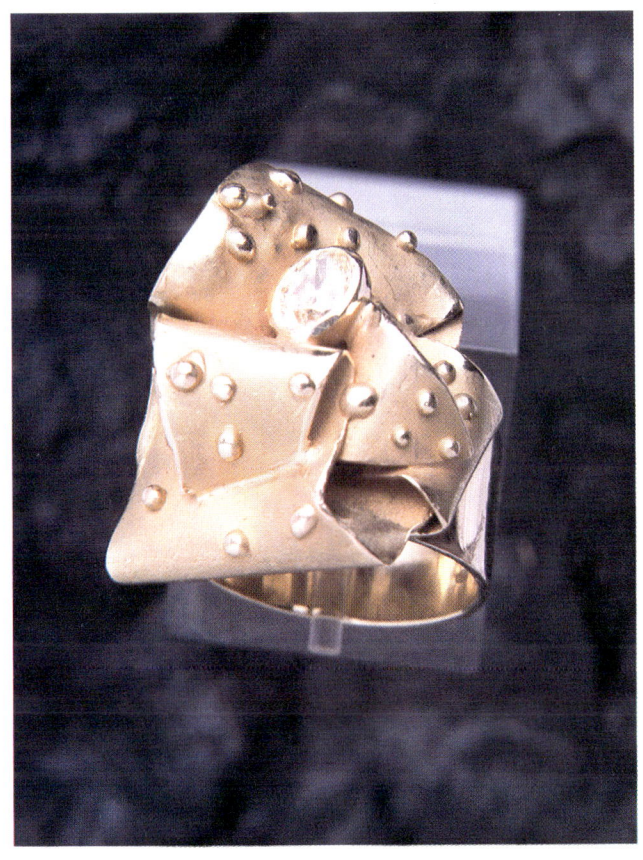

'Get to the Bottom of Things No. 1', brooch in pure gold (24 carats), ebony and opal.

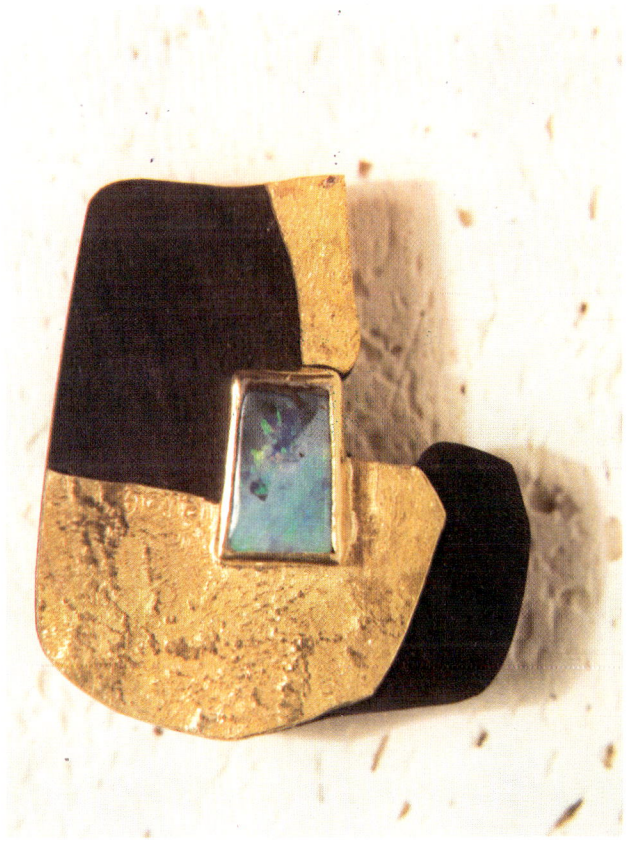

'Promises', gold ring with champagne-colour diamond. Each of these five pieces is one of a kind.

KATHY HANUISE

She defines her works as 'a global synthesis of the different aspects of gold.' An alchemist of precious metals, Kathy Hanvise has the knack of juggling with the reflections that result from mixing various polishing techniques. 'With one metal one can obtain an infinity of contrasts and special effects; it is very complex and simple at the same time.'

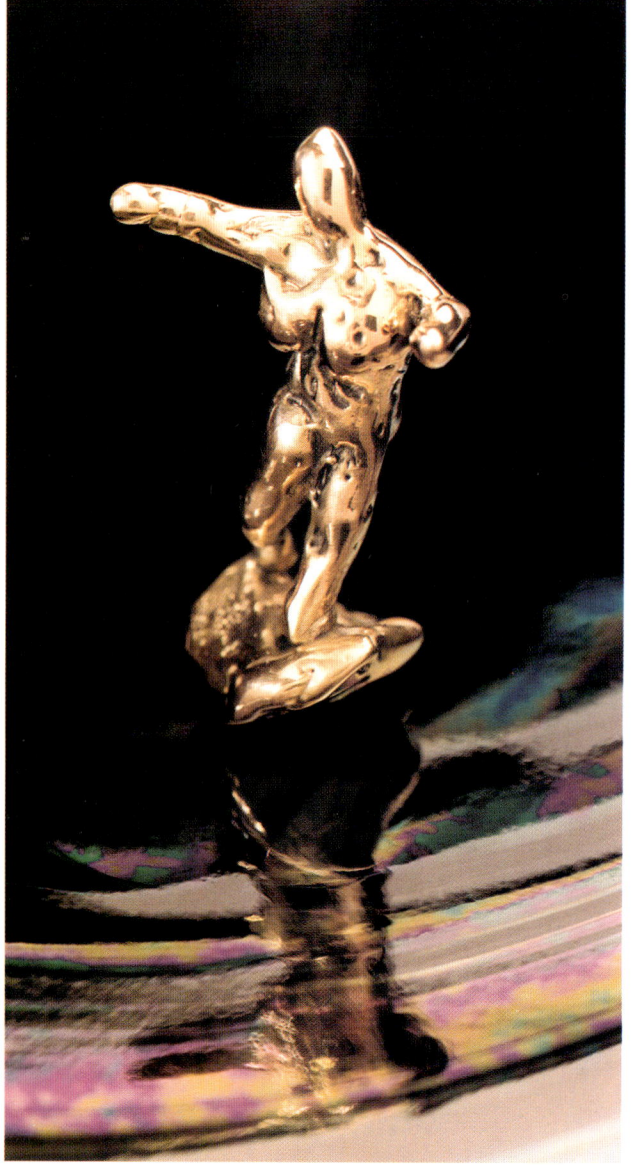

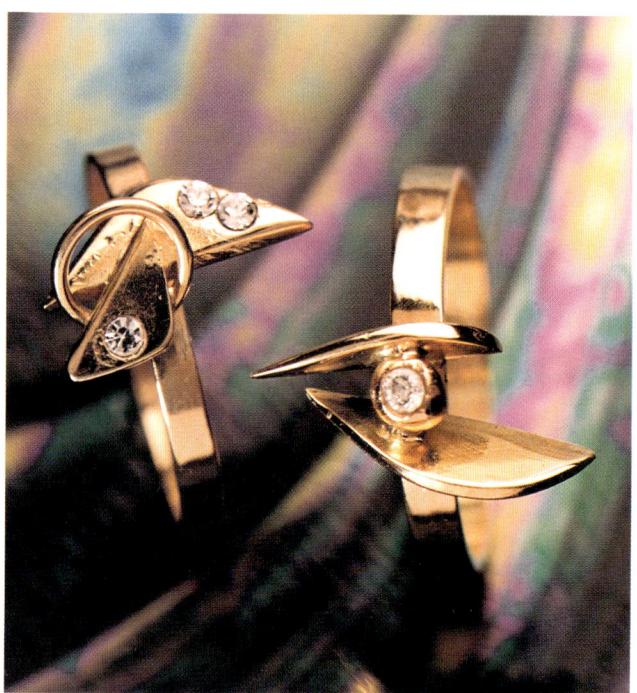

Rings in gold and zircons.

Gold sculpture. The base, left rough, reveals the raw material. A subtle contrast is obtained by various polishing techniques, which allow for different reflections depending on the light.

MARISA PALLA

Living and working on the seashore in one of the most beautiful regions in Italy, Marisa Palla creates jewels that inspire dreams.

'I think that creating jewels is comparable to any creative moment in which the artisan/artist freely transports a part of his thoughts and strength — be this mental or physical — to the material and leaves his imprint on the work that is achieved.

'The art of jewellery is not a minor art, given that the virtues that are sometimes attributed to painting and sometimes to sculpture can be found in it.

'The creation of jewels is a combination of artistic experience, professional ability and understanding of the materials. Creating a jewel is never an end in itself, but rather an open door to fantasy, to new creation, to revival of old traditions.'

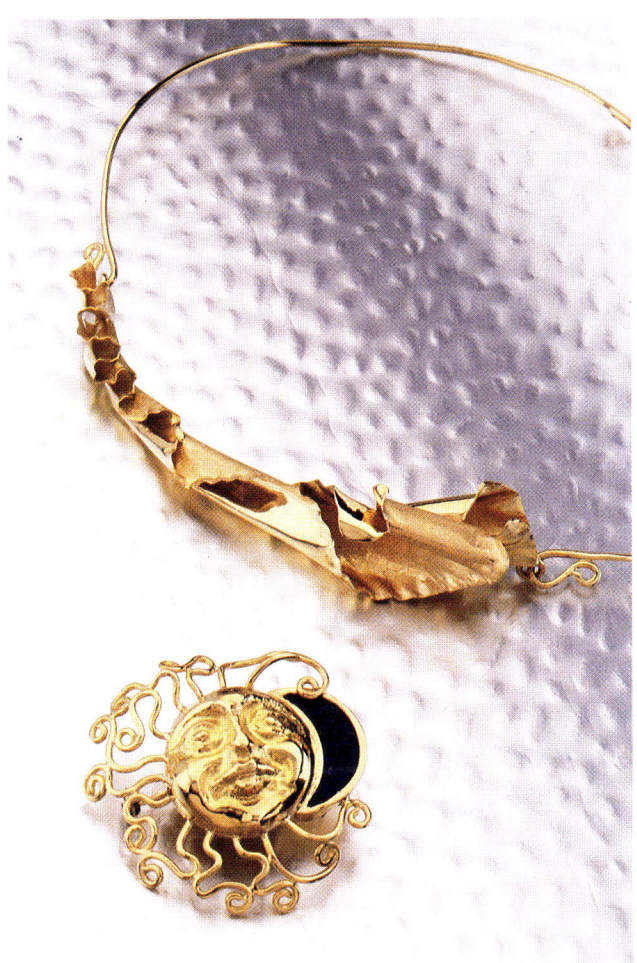

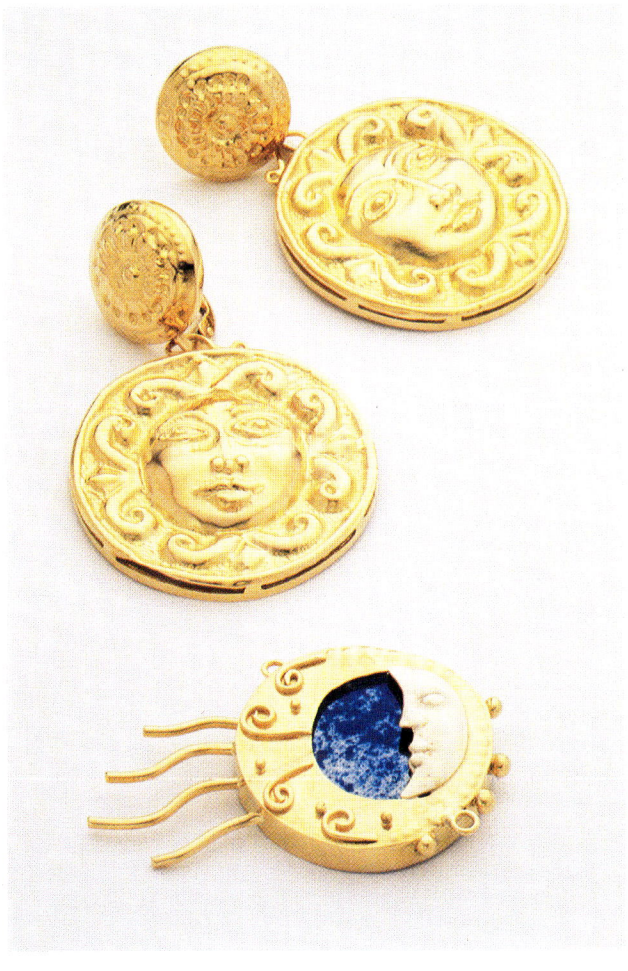

'The Sun and the Moon' and 'Alga' are two of Marisa Palla's unique pieces.

'Cosmos', brooch in yellow and white gold with a mirror. 'Sun', pair of earrings in yellow gold.

JACQUES MICHEL

Self-taught in the realm of jewellery, having been trained as a painter, Jacques Michel has also been a decorator, a haute-couture clothing designer and a theatre costume designer. But it is as a creator of jewels that he has blossomed the most. His discovery of the art of the jewel came about through his admiration for the great Masters of the past — who themselves very often came from such other fields as architecture, painting, sculpture, etc. — and for the quality of their techniques. His taste for colour is an important factor in one area he explores in the creation of a jewel. 'While rejecting neither traditions nor enchantments, I like to work on a creation in which dreams, beauty and poetry, and escape from everyday reality, are the essence of the finished work.' While he is thorough in his research in the realm of contemporary jewels, he does not abandon the styles of different eras and civilisations of the past, an aspect one senses very agreeably in certain of his pieces. 'The permanence of a material is an element that I hold in esteem; it would be very painful to me to imagine that after a few years a jewel would be terribly diminished by time. Nevertheless, the essentially precious aspect of a material is not the fundamental criterion for choosing it — not to deny its beauty, however.

'There are marvels made of copper and glass; there are horrors of gold, platinum and diamonds. Magic, tradition and nobility of materials are my references, not my prisons.'

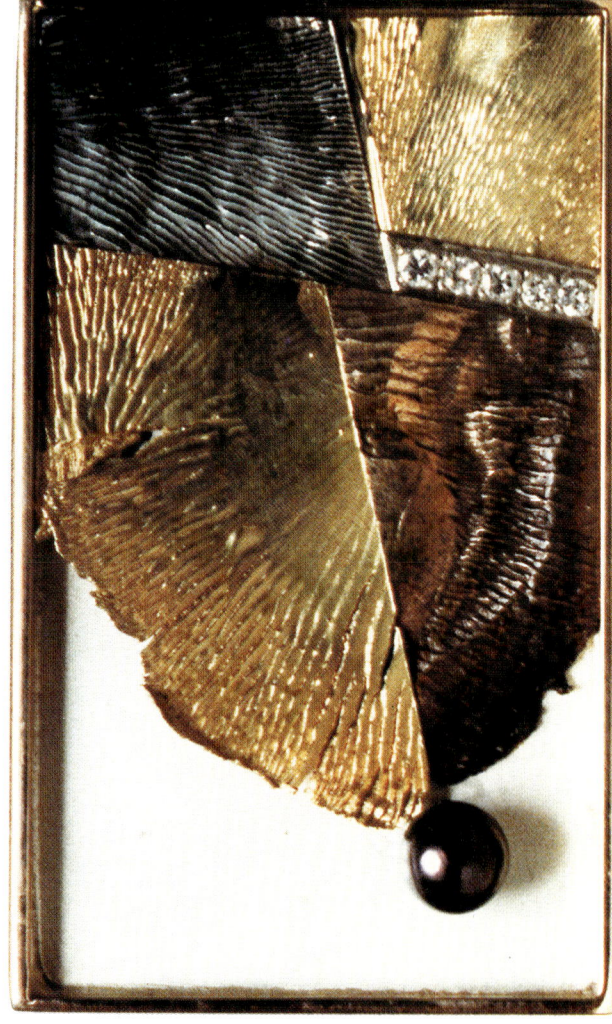

'Glaciation', brooch in gold and silver, aquamarines, pearls and black pearl.

'Cadrage' (Centring), brooch in yellow, red and white gold, silver and bronze, brilliants and black pearl.

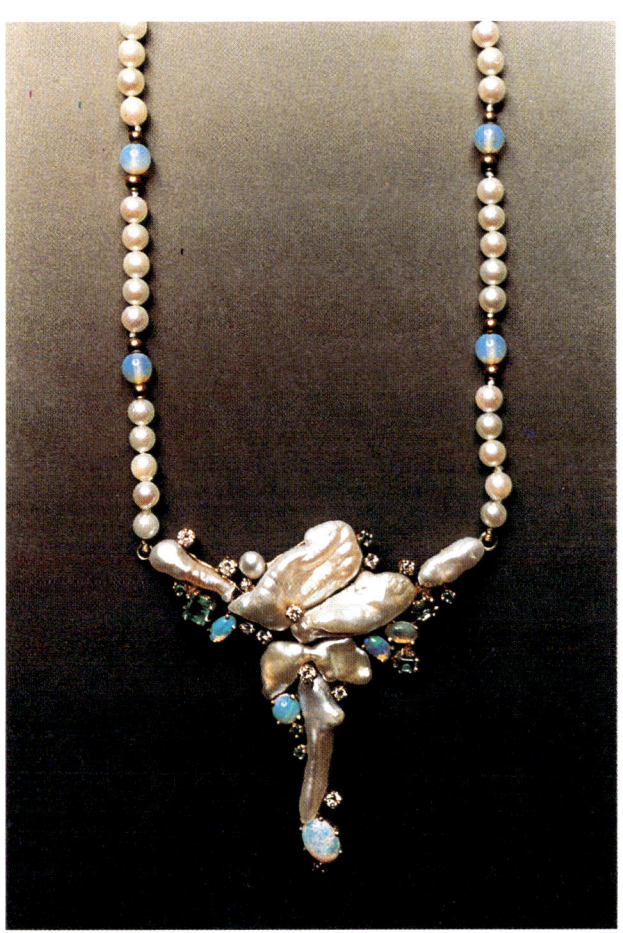

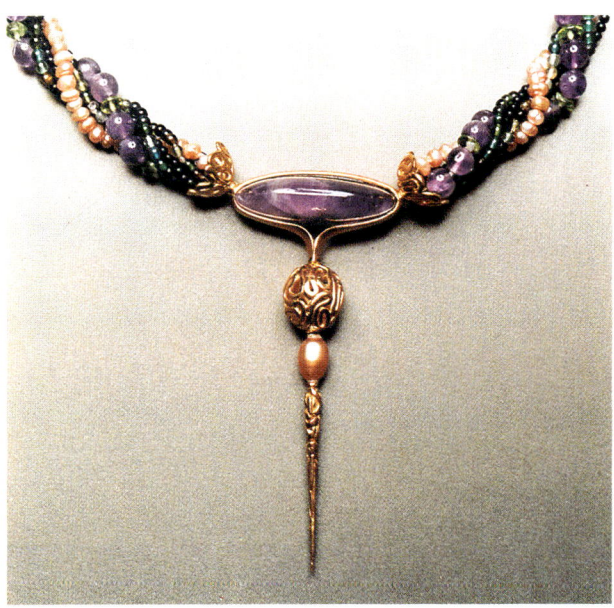

'Hans Holbein', gold necklace with amethysts, green tourmalines, onyx, peridots and pink pearls.

'Tenderness', gold necklace with pearls, baroque pearls, opals, emeralds and brilliants.

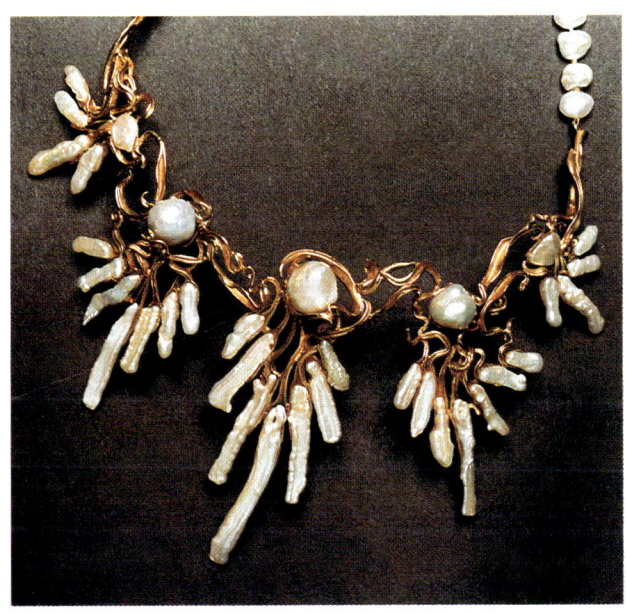

'Pearls', necklace/diadem, gold and baroque pearls.

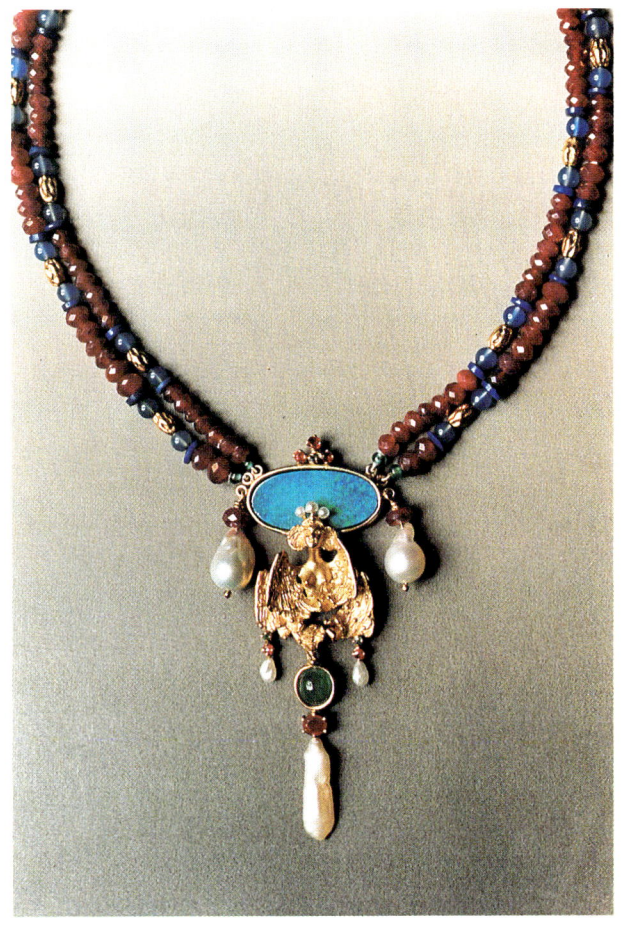

'Rainbow', gold necklace with opal, emeralds, rubies, baroque pearls, blue agates and lapis lazuli.

59

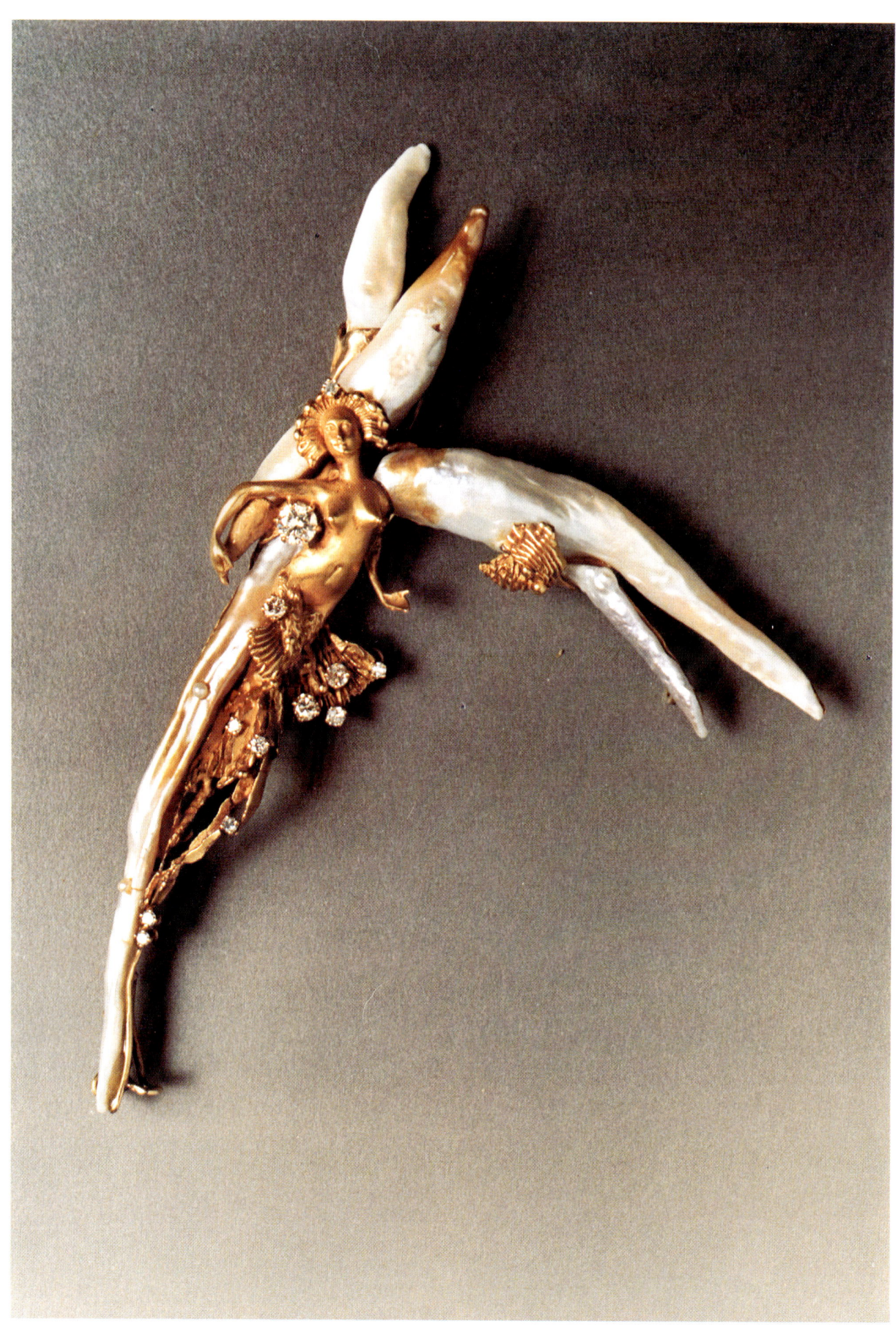

60 'The Siren's Song', brooch in gold, baroque pearls and brilliants.

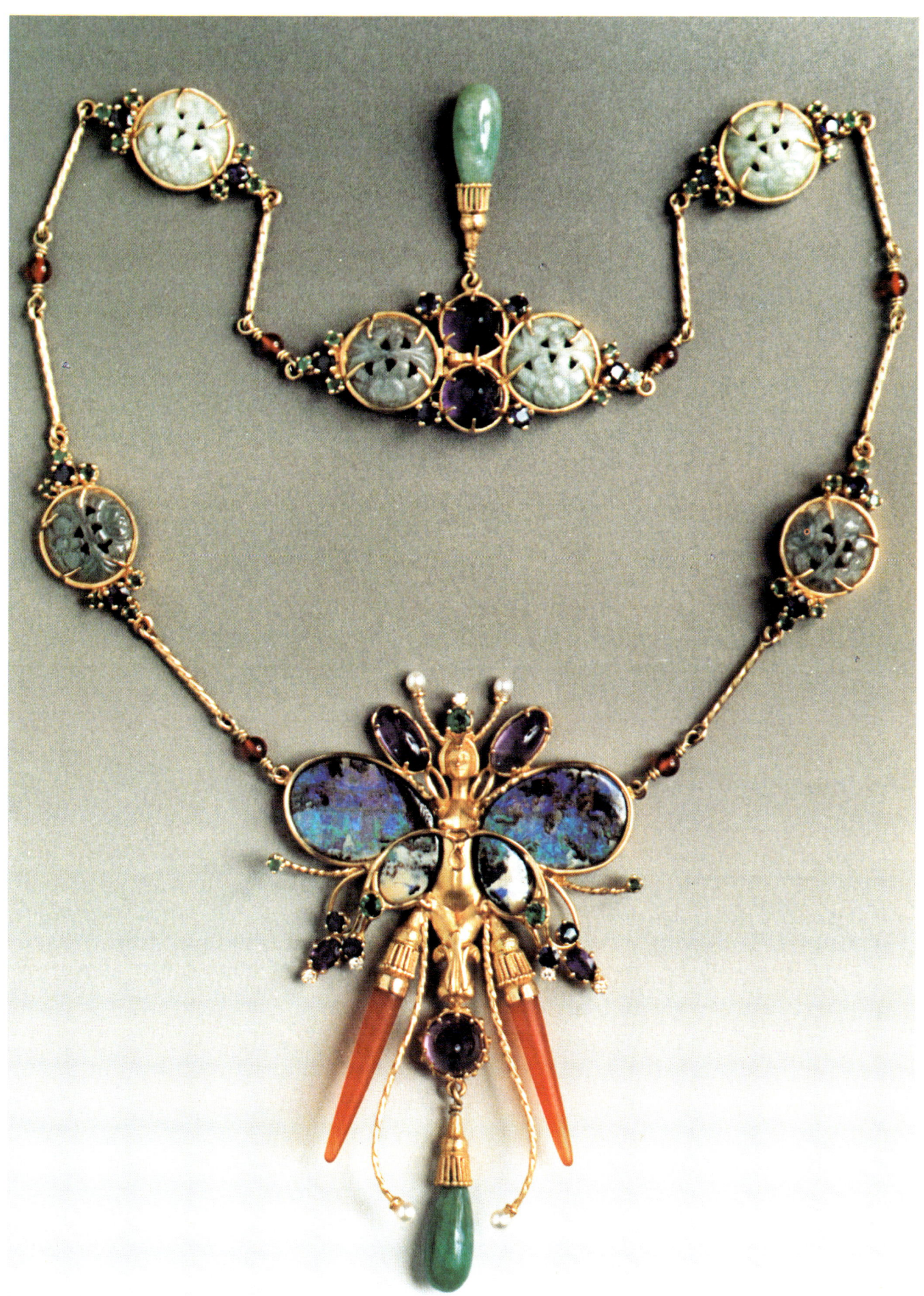

'The Unexpected Extraterrestrial', gold necklace with opals, sapphires, brilliants, pearls, emeralds, jade, carnelian and amethysts. 61

MONTSERRAT GUARDIOLA

Throughout her professional career, Montserrat Guardiola has sought to maintain a solid basis in her creative work, with the aim of preserving the continuity of traditional values within the ranks of jewellery-makers. To this end, she has committed herself to offering new ideas that provide innovation, originality and change-elements that are indispensable to opening up new possibilities in contemporary jewellery. Even the simplest of her jewels are worked meticulously, and in each new collection — however much it may differ from the preceding one — Montserrat Guardiola succeeds in imprinting her personal style which runs through her work like a conducting wire, evolving through time. Light, undulating shapes, delightful to the touch, seemingly spontaneous as if they were born from nature, are combined with other, more linear or geometric ones, in balanced proportions and volumes. Forms conceived for everyday use, in which the design concept is integrated with the very qualities of the materials. Her is own words apply here: 'It is only through design that one may proceed along a path of infinite possibilities that bear witness to the level of a society's cultural and industrial development.'

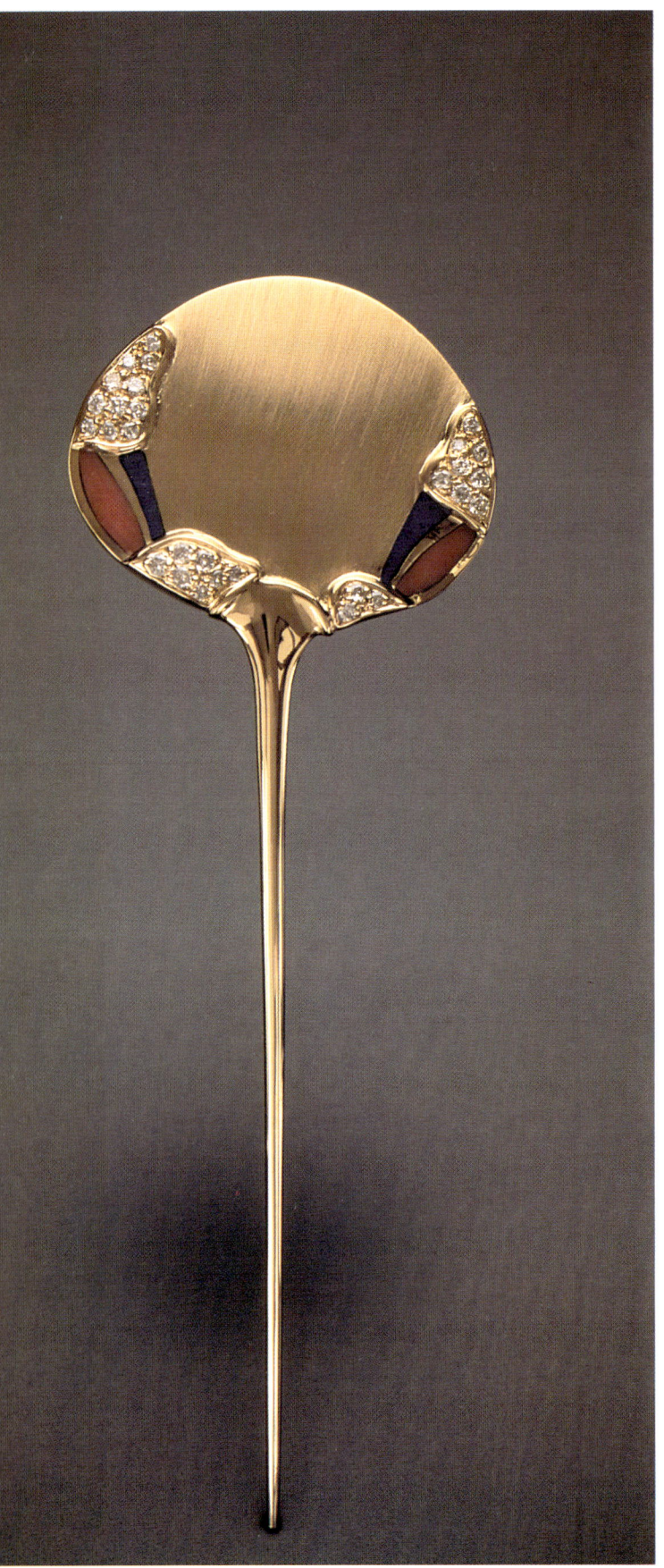

'Palma' by Montserrat Guardiola. Brooch in gold, coral, lapis lazuli and diamonds.

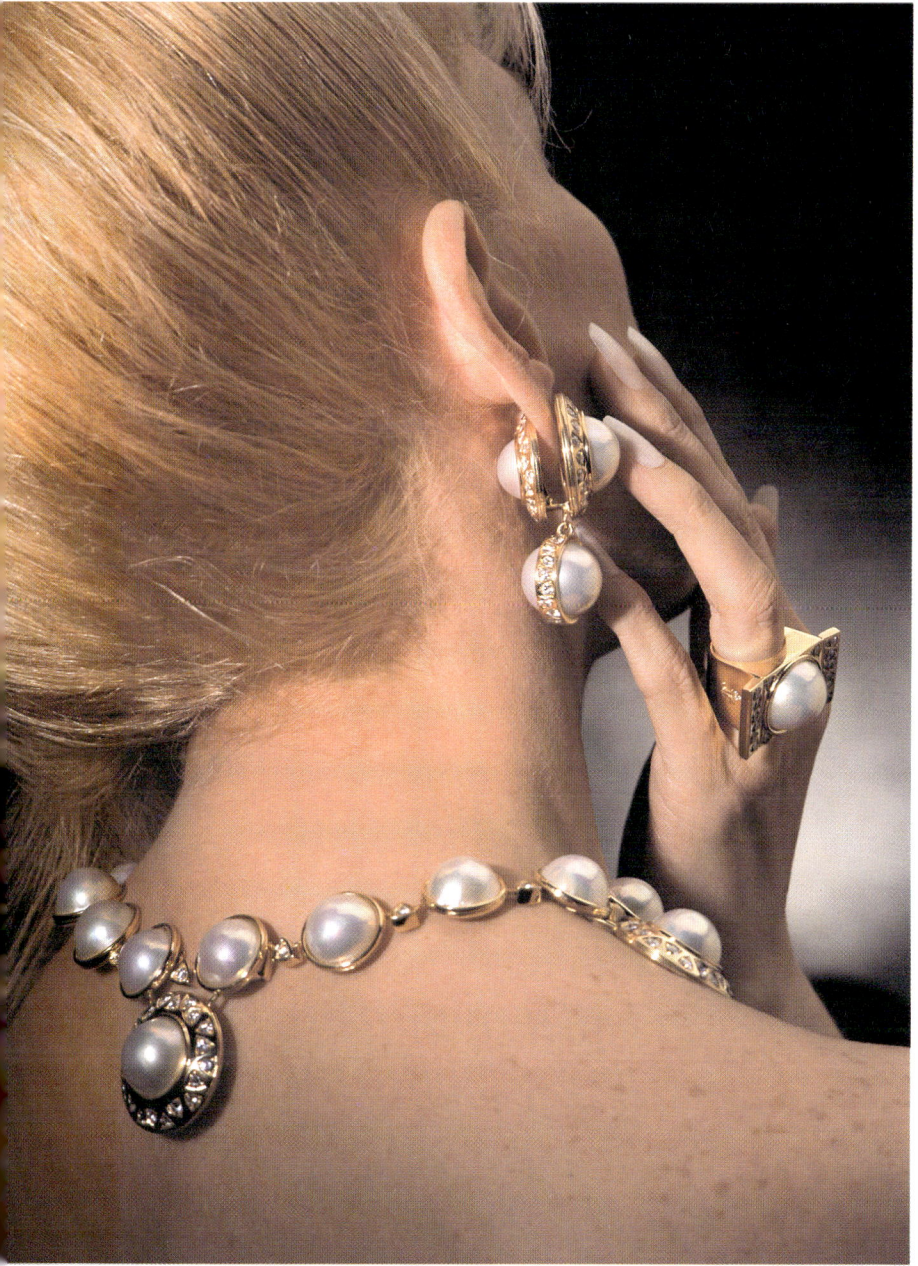

JUSSARA CARACANTE

The original jewels created by Jussara Caracante translate the fragility and elegance, the beauty and charm of a great woman. Her necklaces are the fruit of innovative design in which the very clasps are an important element, giving them charm and originality.

The ring mounted with a cultured mabé pearl, with moveable wings made of round diamonds placed on a triangular base, is a symbol of feminine strength and vitality.

As to the 'two-faced' earrings, the elimination of clips introduces a new three-dimensionality that does away with the traditional concepts of front and back, creating a uniquely harmonious effect.

SILVANO ZANCHI

A professor at the Fermo Institute of Art since 1966, Silvano Zanchi has ceaselessly collected prizes and medals. The architect Pino Gusmini describes his work thusly: 'It is clear that his art is more than a reflection of personal experience. Experience and exploration are, for Silvano Zanchi, a starting point much more complex than his destination. The style and language of his works forcefully express a series of contrasts, from whose stimulating quality no one is immune.'

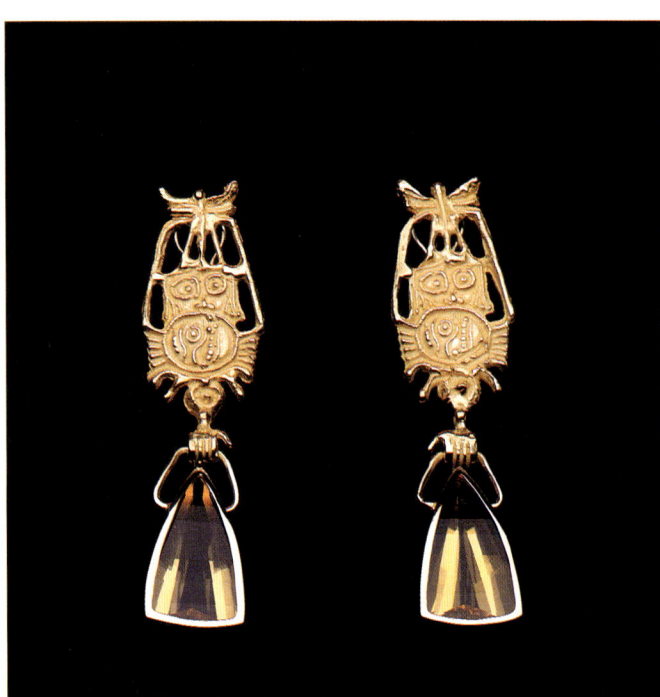

Pair of earrings in chased gold and citrine quarts.

Gold repoussé necklace with a pear-shaped citrine quartz and four rectangles of smoky quartz.

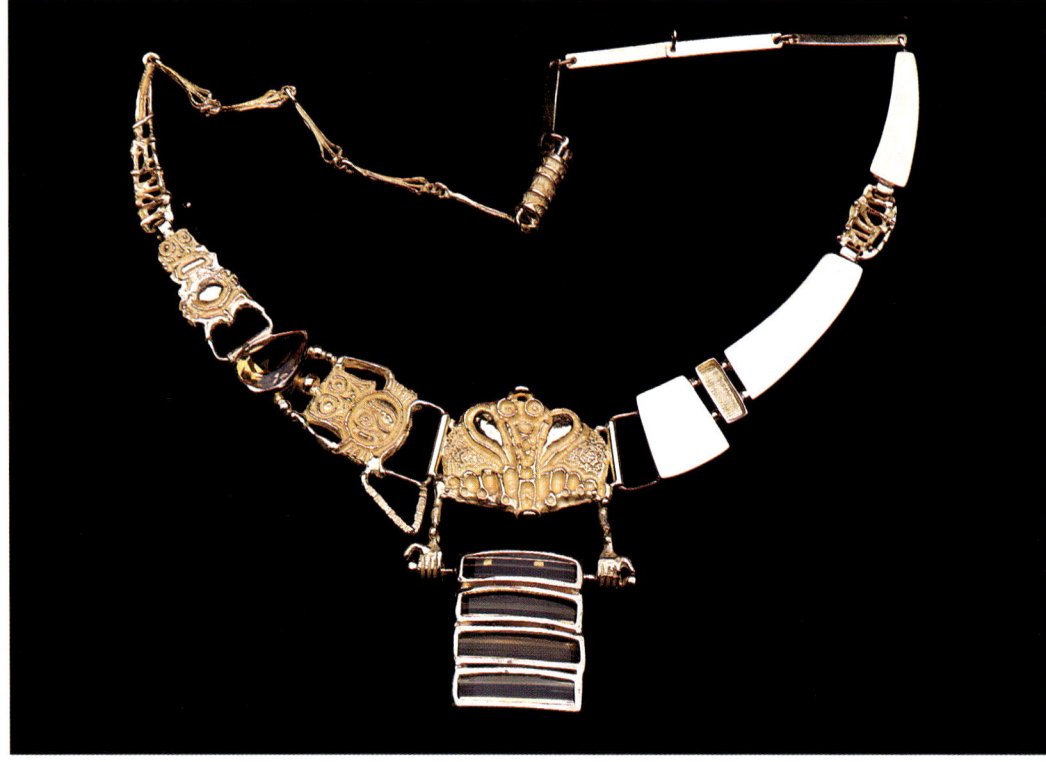

MARCELLO PIZZARI

The combination of a deep love of nature and perfect craftsmanship have allowed Marcello Pizzari to create such fabulous objects as this peacock in gold, emeralds, rubies, sapphires and diamonds, the four precious stones reunited to pay homage to nature.

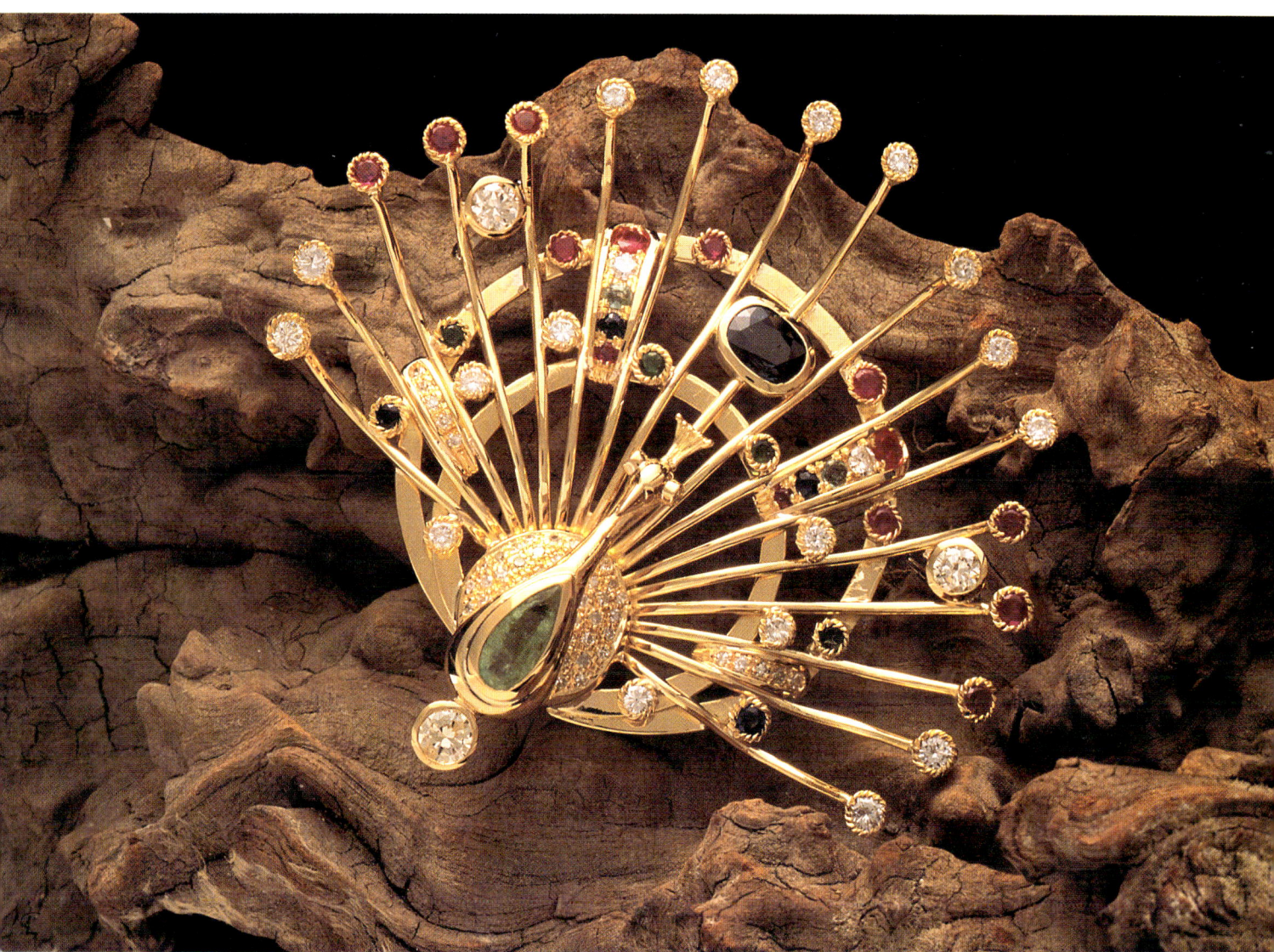

KAZUO OGAWA

He began his career as a fashion and hair advisor and only started creating jewellery in 1983. He is not limited to a single, particular style; he works with an original variety of different concepts, using a panoply of unusual materials. His collections display a vast spectrum of artistic expression, reflecting a unique mixture of culture and tradition with modernity and a sense of the present day, elegance and beauty with a faultless craftsman-like quality. Romanticism and emotions are expressed with creativity and originality. The 'Broadway Collection' was inspired by the three basic elements of theatre: dance, music and masks. For Kazuo Ogawa, Broadway symbolises the world of the extraordinary and of the imagination, a world of creativity combined with coordination, grace and emotion, as well as charisma and fire. As a designer, these elements are strongly reflected in his work; thus, for his debut in the United States, he has created this new collection showing an important facet of American culture. Japanese art is greatly influenced by nature, often delicately symbolised by subtle forms. Sensations and emotions are

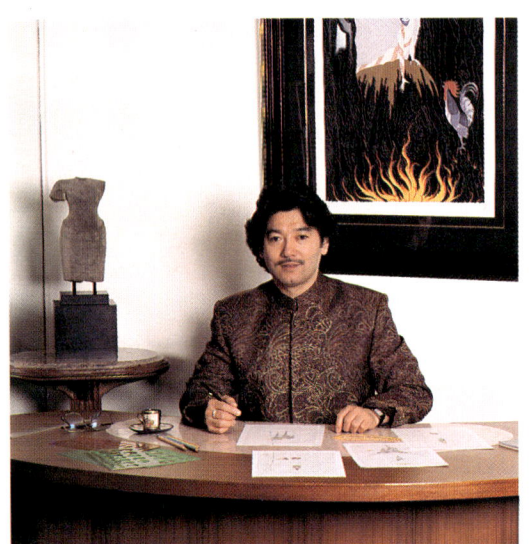

accentuated by the art of forms created by man, such as in the costumes for 'Kabuki' and 'No'. The natural shape of flowers and leaves radiate an infinite magnificence. Kazuo Ogawa has carried these exquisite expressions into two of his Japanese expressions: 'Karuta' and 'Tsuji ga Hana'. 'Karuta' describes the essence of traditional Japanese folklore, with its poetry and costumes. 'Tsuji ga Hana' is based on the artistic motifs of kimonos, whose subtle elegance is accentuated by the texture of platinum.

The 'Broadway Collection'.

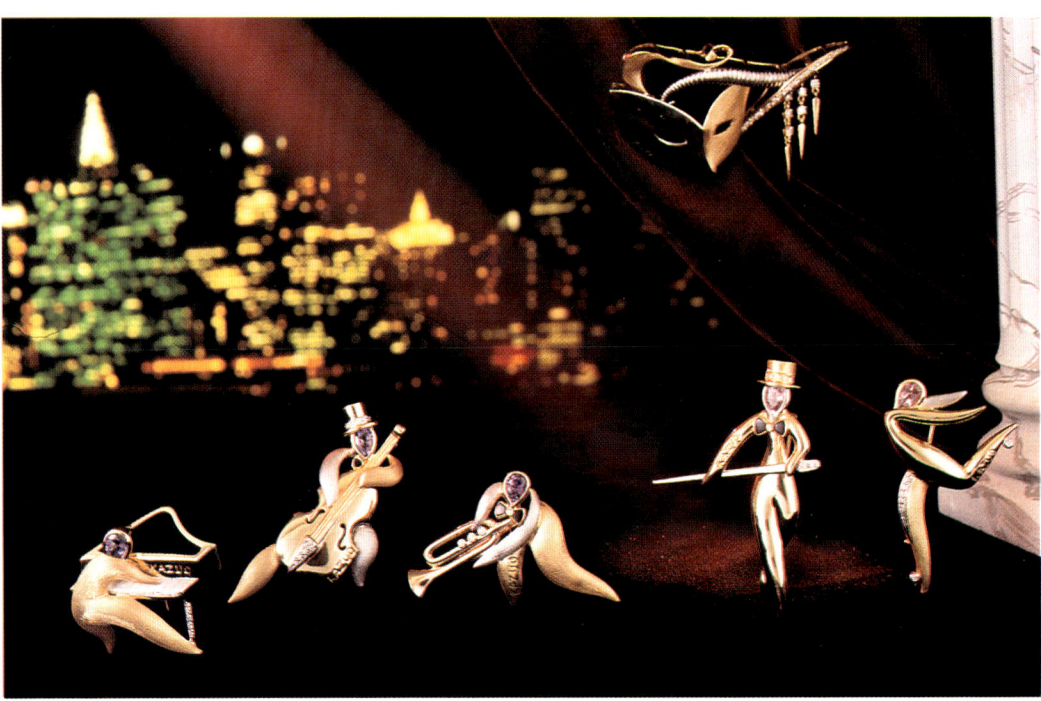

'Tsuji ga
Hana'.

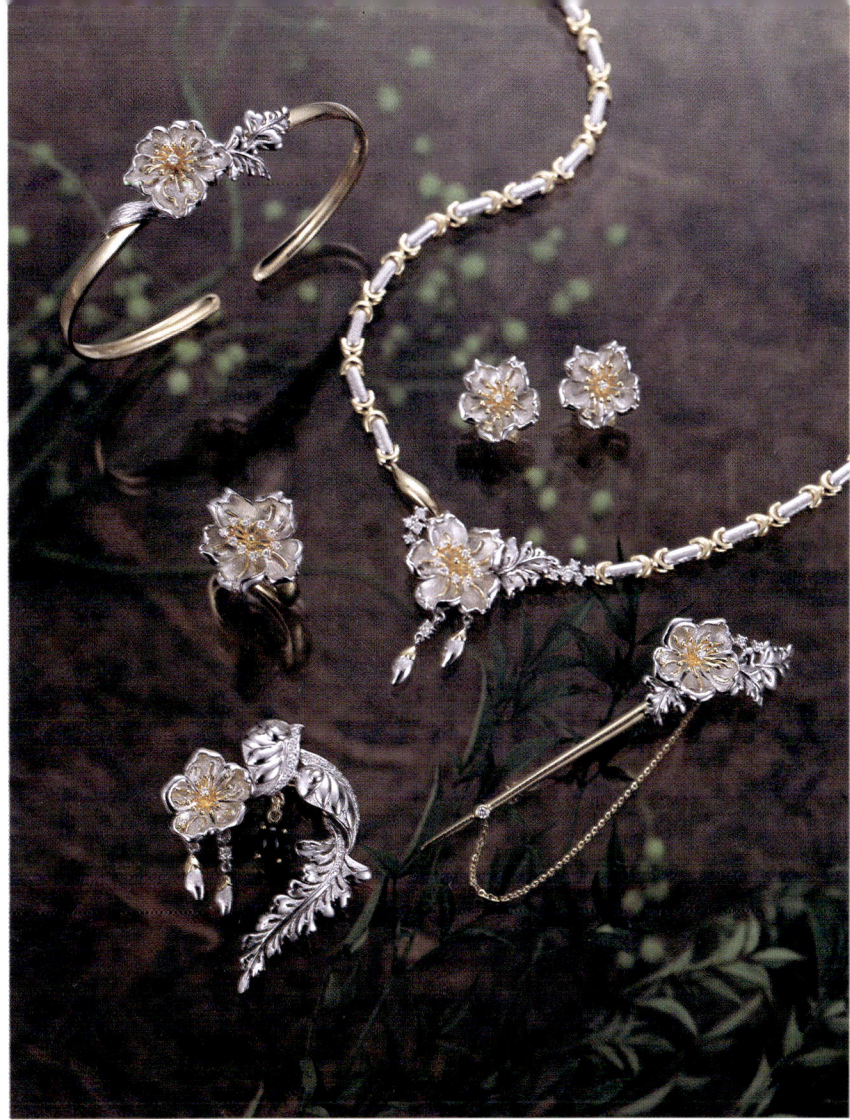

'Karuta'.

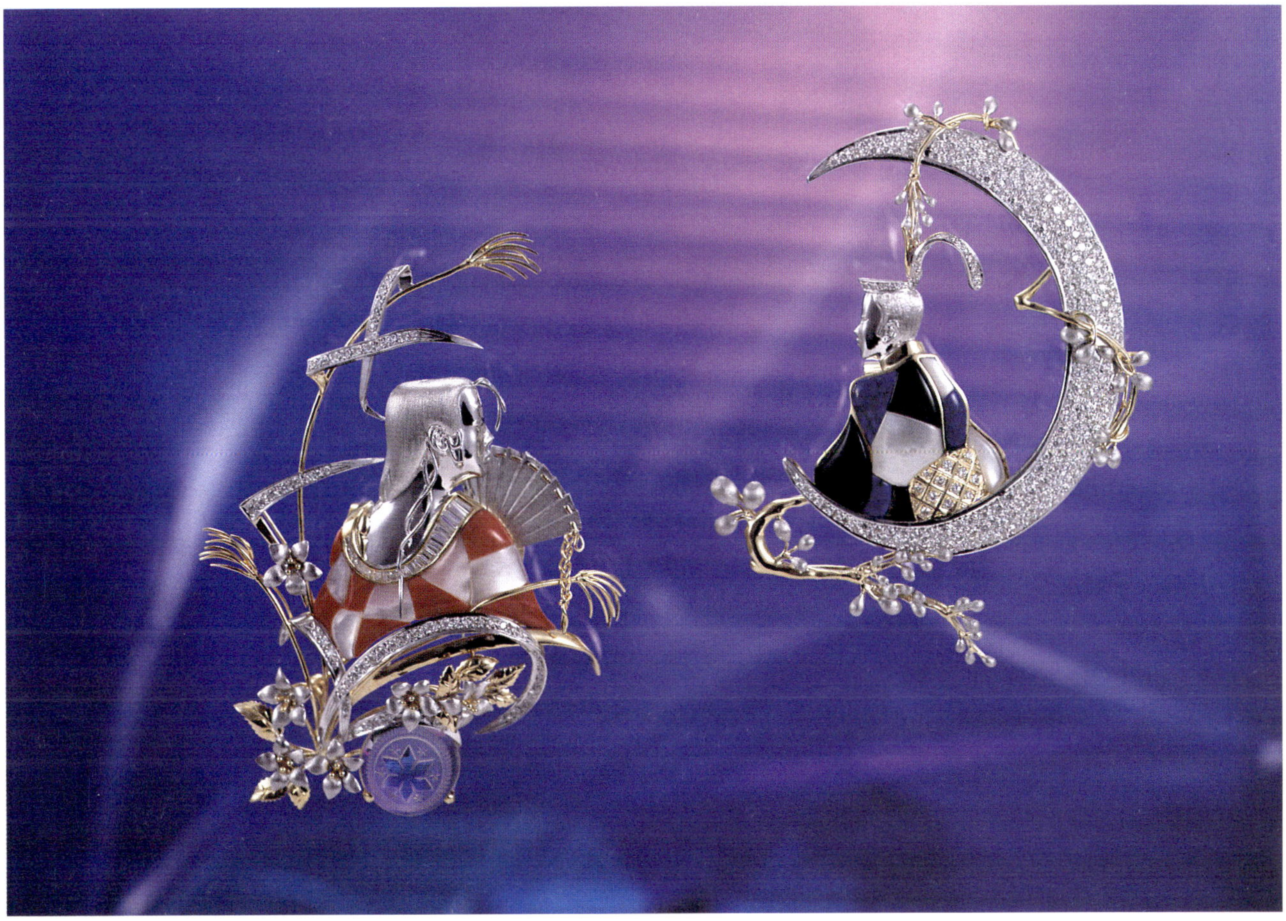

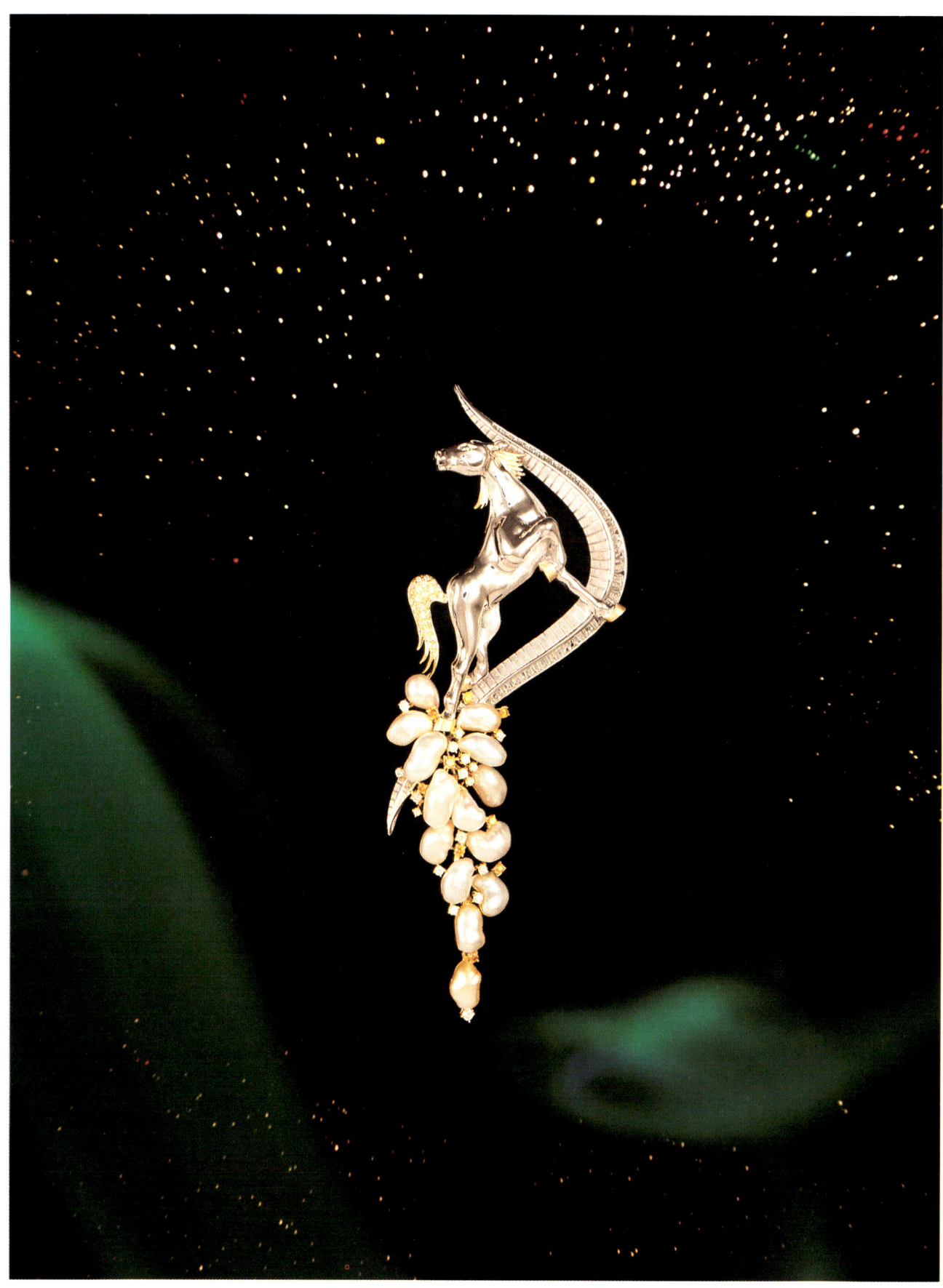

Pendant/brooch in gold, platinum, pearls and diamonds.

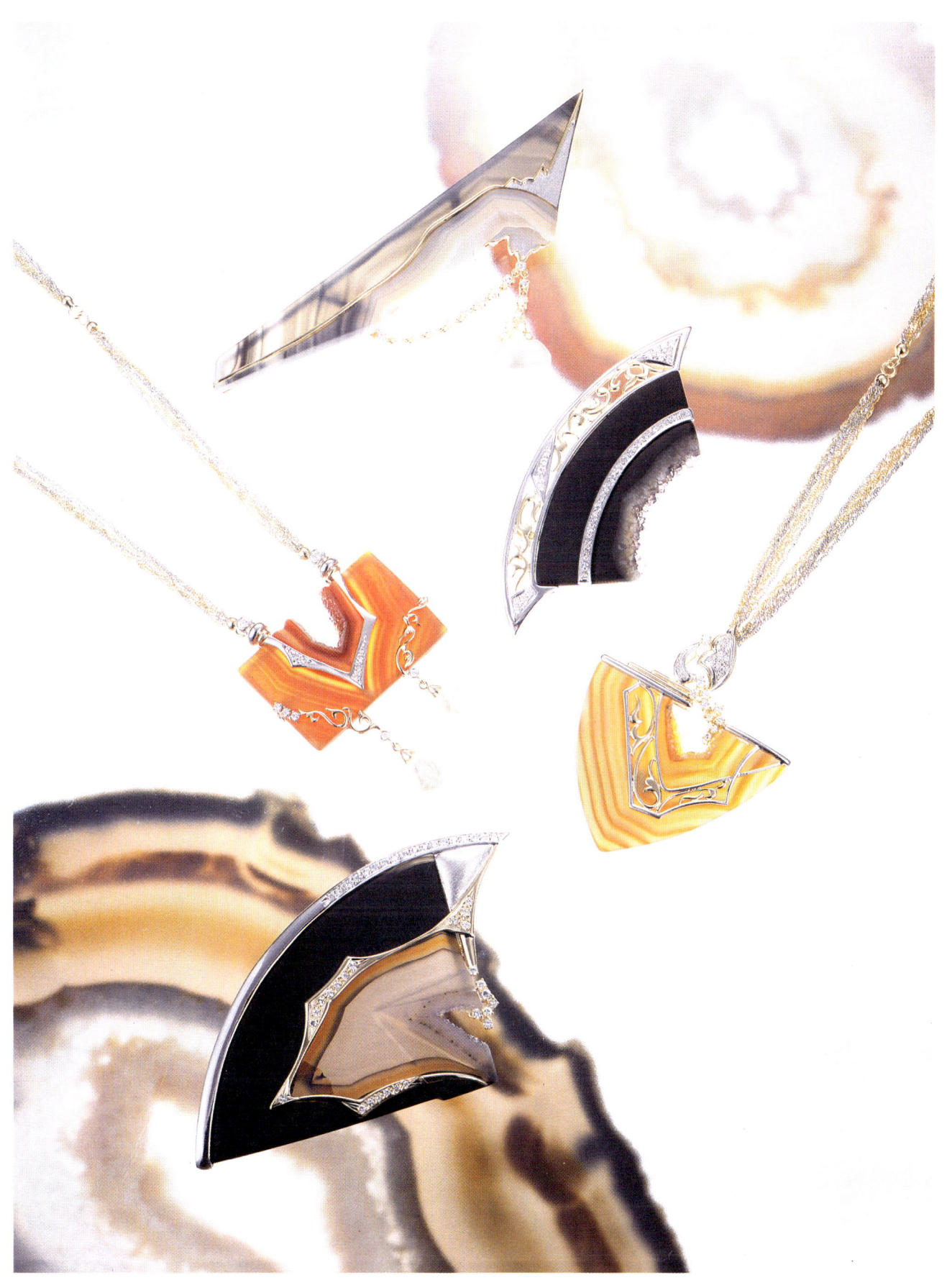

Brooches and pendants in agates, pearls, diamonds, platinum and gold.

HASBANI

These three brothers are members of a Milanese dynasty of jewellers. The Hasbani style is typically neo-classical, with some futuristic touches. Exploration and creation are the strong points of these three brothers who share a single aim: perfection of craftsmanship. Their studios are located in Valenza-Po.

Necklace in gold, pearls and diamonds. The Hasbanis have enhanced the pearls' orient with the diamonds' brilliance.

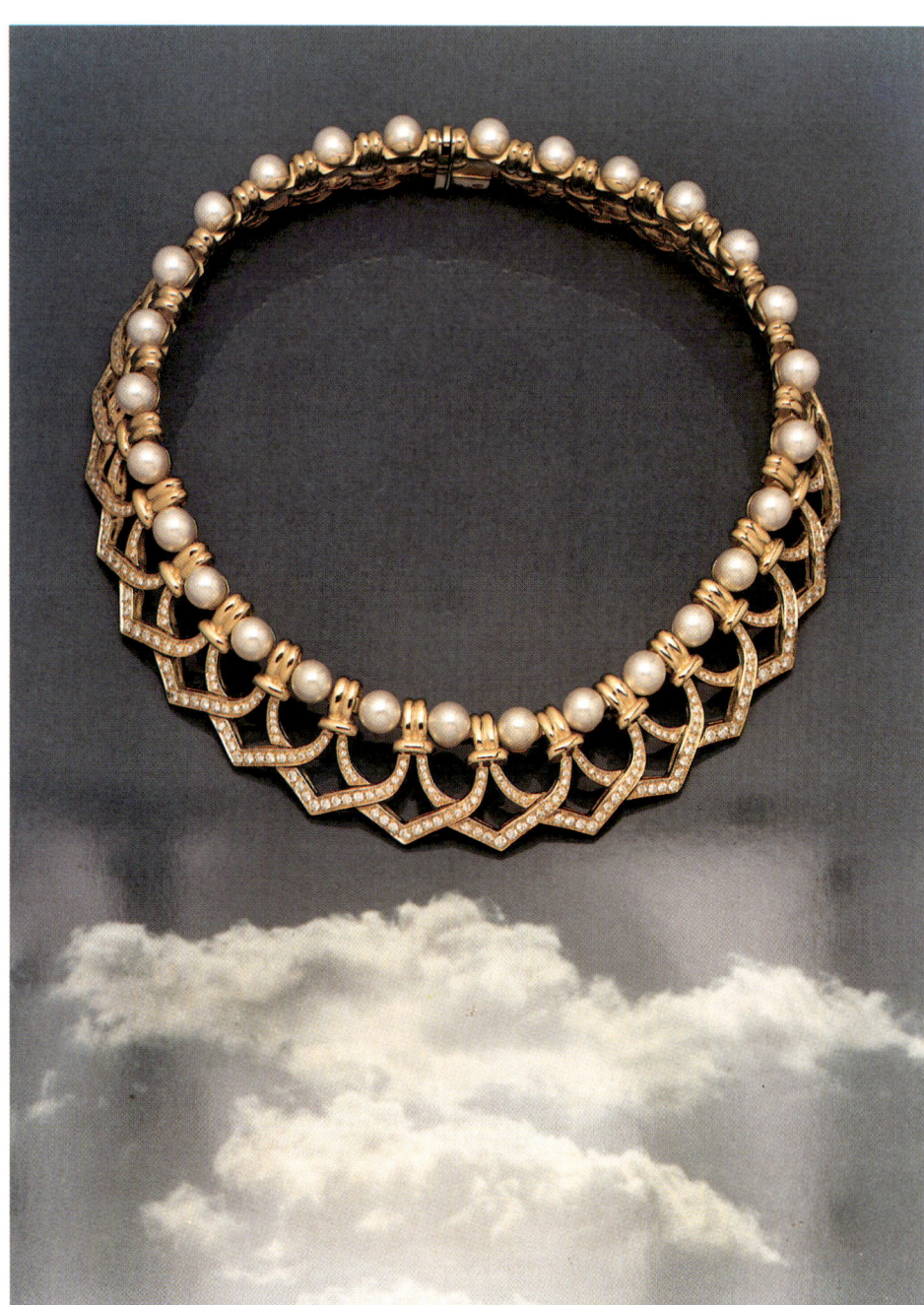

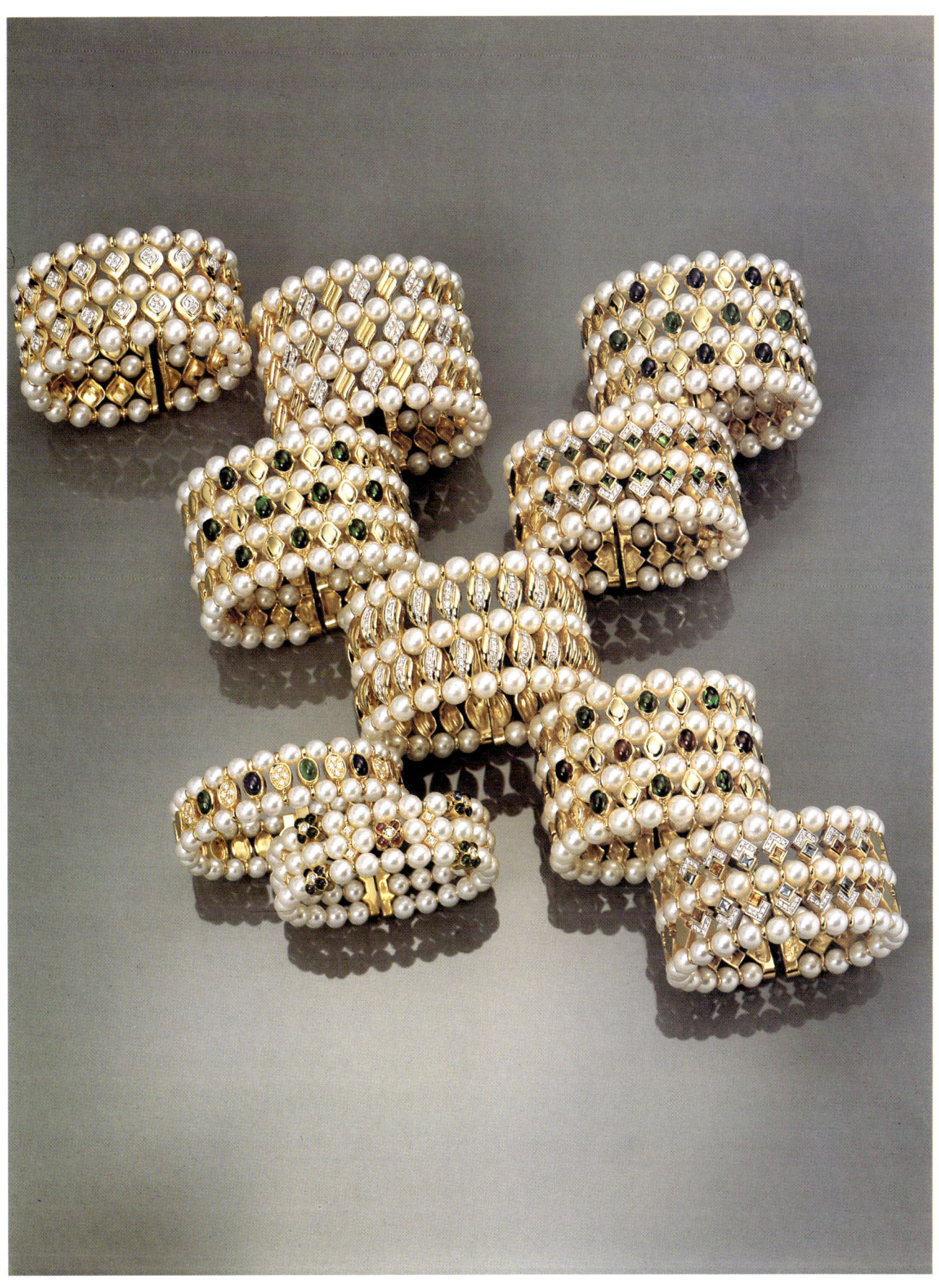

Collection of bracelets in gold, pearls, rubies, sapphires, emeralds and diamonds. The Hasbanis show the possible variations on a single theme.

DANIELA BAUMGARTNER

Originally from Switzerland, Daniela Baumgartner is a citizen of the world, which is, moreover, very clearly visible in her jewels. Her taste for round, supple forms gave her the idea of baptising one of her collections with a touch of humour: 'Diamant-terre' ('earth-diamond', a pun in French for 'diamantaire', meaning 'diamond-like').

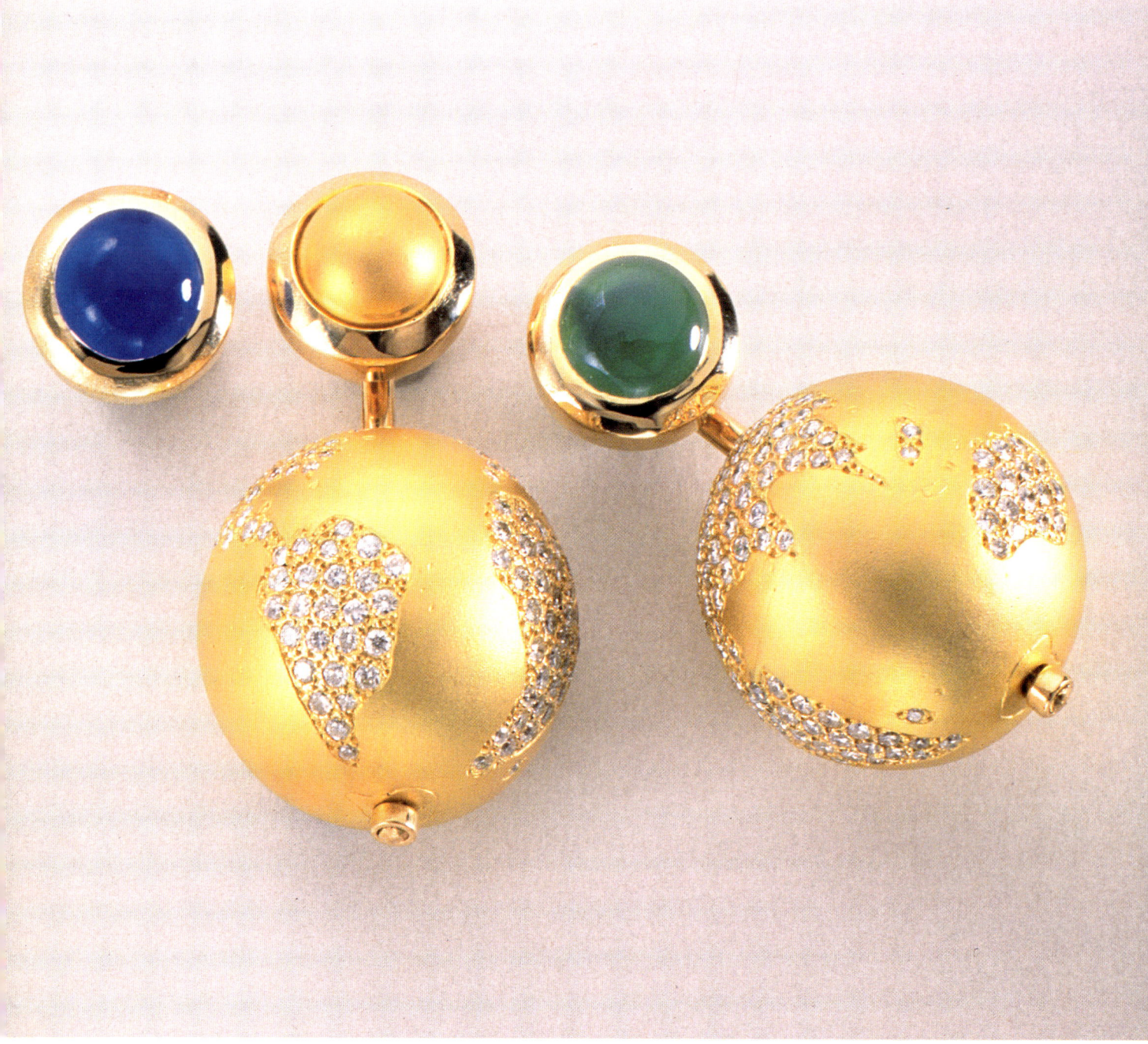

'World-Map' earrings in yellow gold and diamonds. The earring-studs are interchangeable.

RODRIGO DIEZ

He defines his works as 'jewel-sculptures', because in reality Rodrigo Diez specialises in precious sculptures made of precious stones and metals.

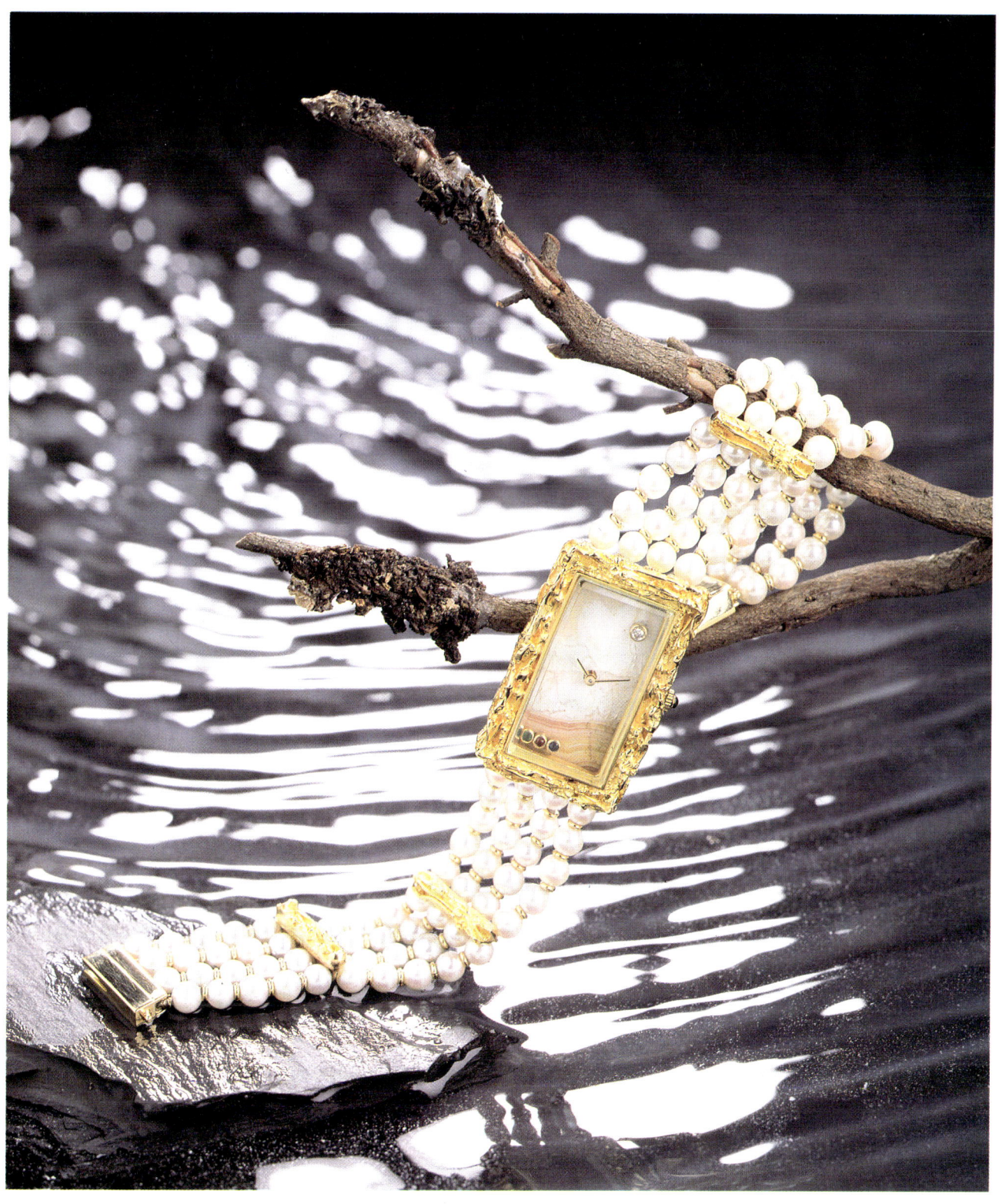

Jewel-watch in gold, diamonds, rubies, sapphires, emeralds, pearls and agates.

HANS SCHINDLER

A student of the Hanau Academy, this jewel creator has collected the most prestigious honorary titles and prizes. 'I am madly in love with colours, especially those of stones. I respect gold and platinum. My creations have a clear-cut aim: to bring greater meaning to man's everyday life through the jewels he wears; these objects must be a reflection of his personality'.

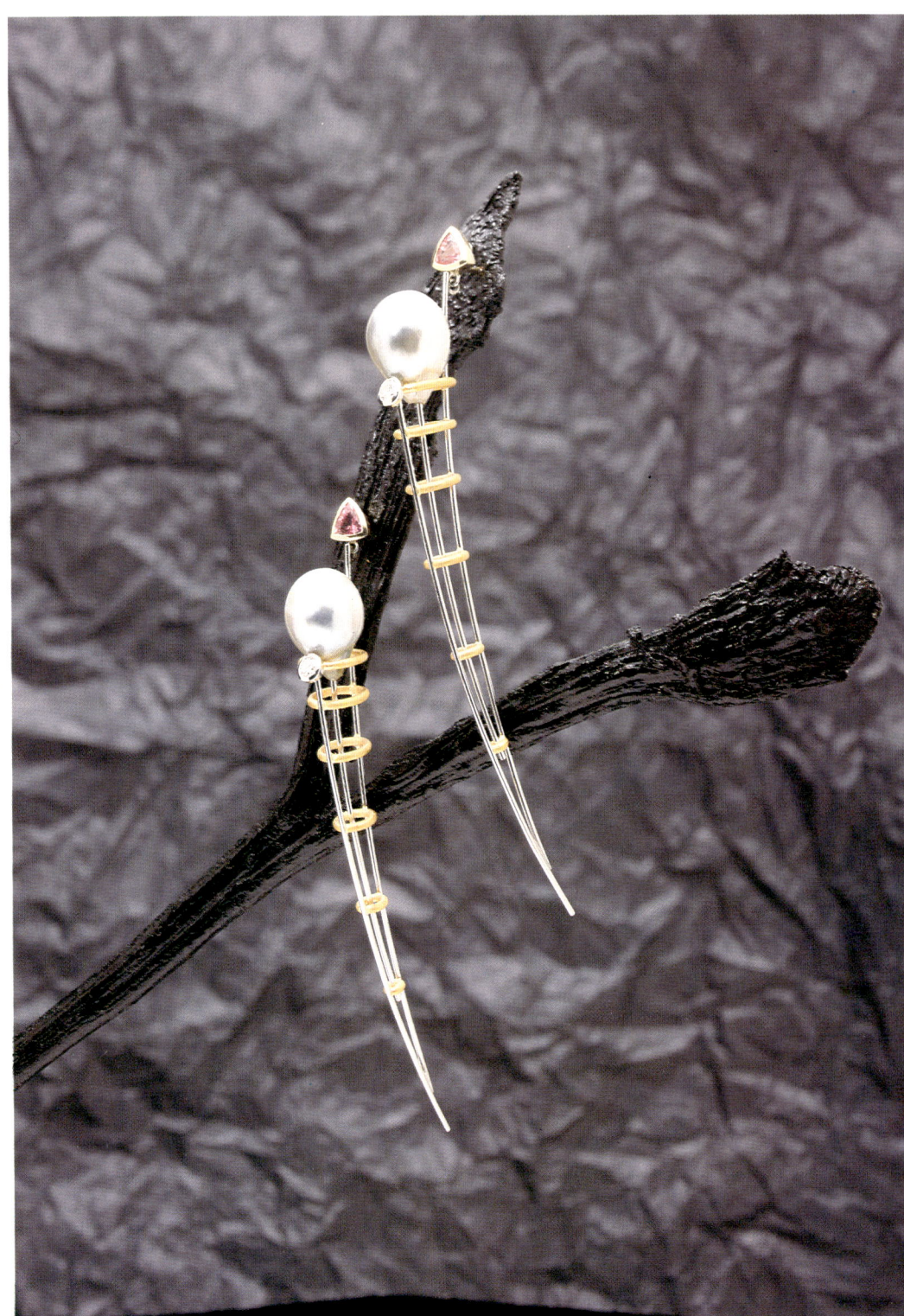

Earrings in gold and platinum with diamonds, pink sapphires and 'South Sea' pearls.

THERESE SUDRE

In her search for the authentic, she has tamed nature. Whether worn in the city or in the country, Thérèse Sudre's jewels have a relaxed air with a touch of romanticism and femininity. Northern landscapes inspired her first jewels; titanium gave her the opportunity to mix gold with greenish and bluish colours. She adds brilliance to her jewels by punctuating them here and there with diamonds.

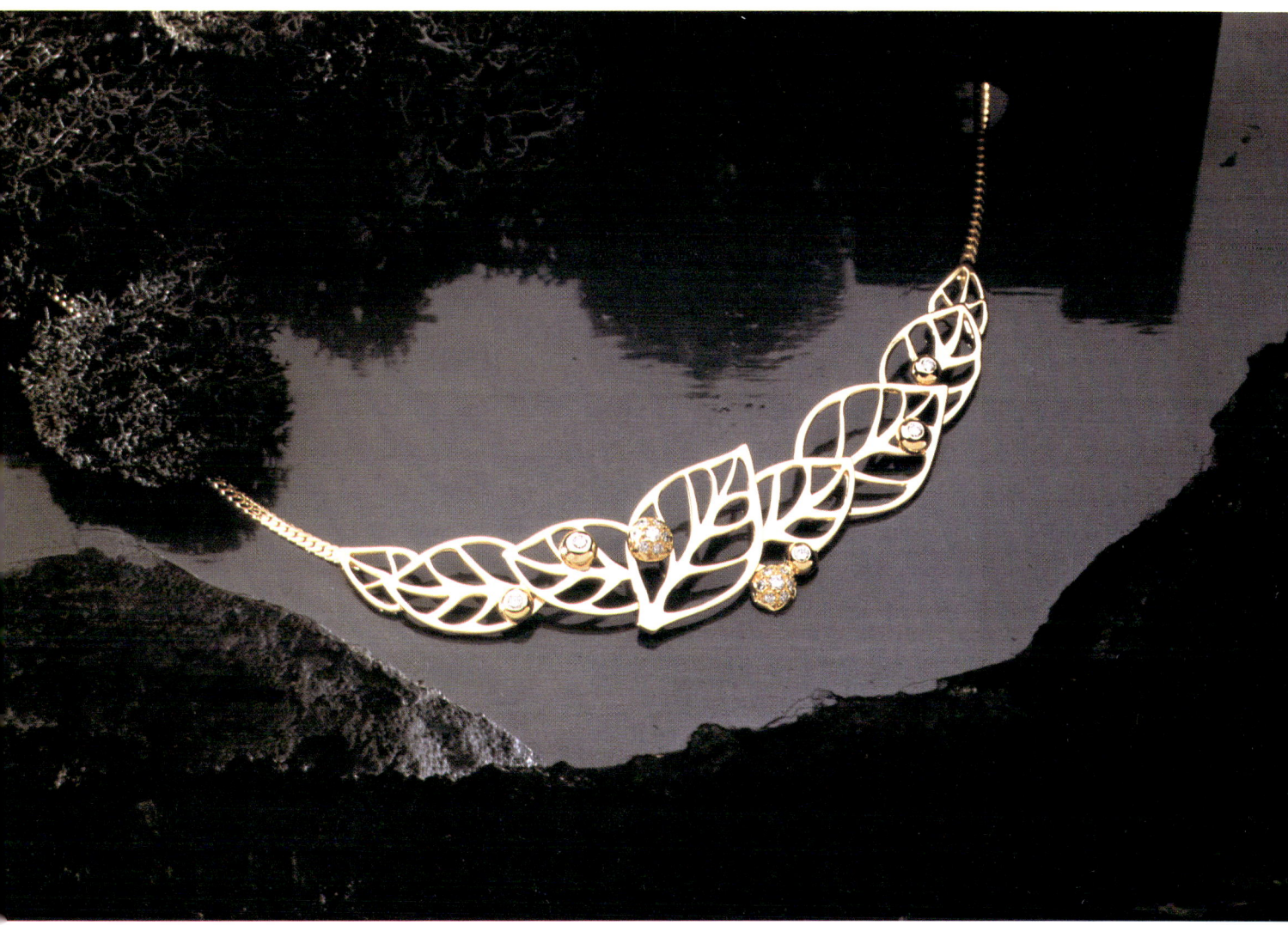

Her taste for nature and her 'country' temperament gave her the idea for a foliage necklace called 'Printemps' ('spring'), of gold and diamonds.

WOO HYUN CHOI

Closely linked to nature, especially the sun, the moon, mountains and rivers, Woo Hyun Choi's jewels instantly provoke emotion, an emotion that she likes to transmit to the persons who wear her works. Each piece has a meaning, a history. Woo Hyun Choi considers herself to be a strong link between the Far East and Italy, where she has had many shows and where she acquired her considerable experience as an artisan.

'Chiocciola' ('snail') is a brooch of gold, platinum, lapis lazuli, diamonds and enamel.

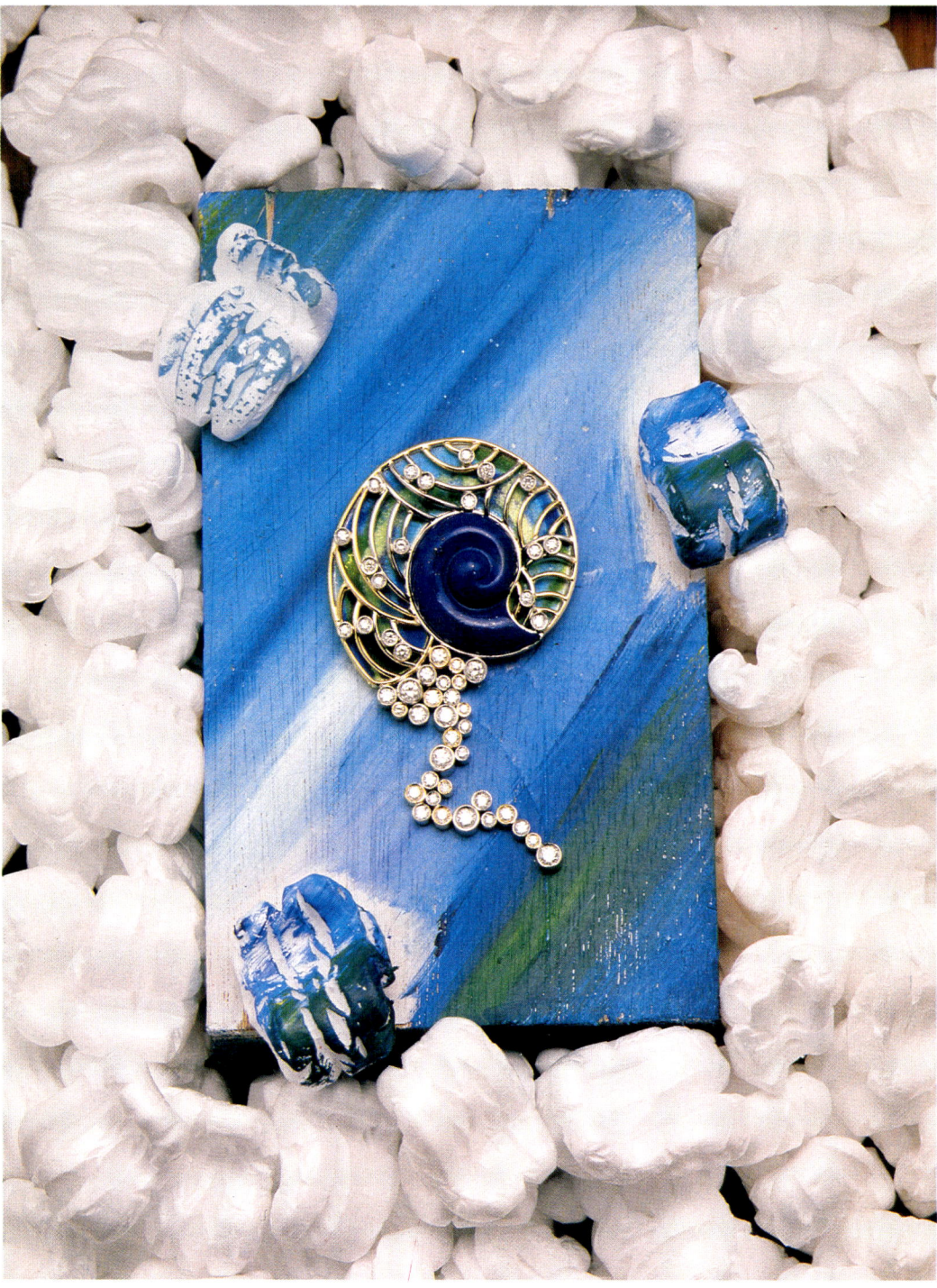

KRISTA VANDEVELDE

When someone compliments her on the beauty of her pieces, she responds, 'Creating jewels is the result of my endless passion for beauty, the reflection of my personality'.

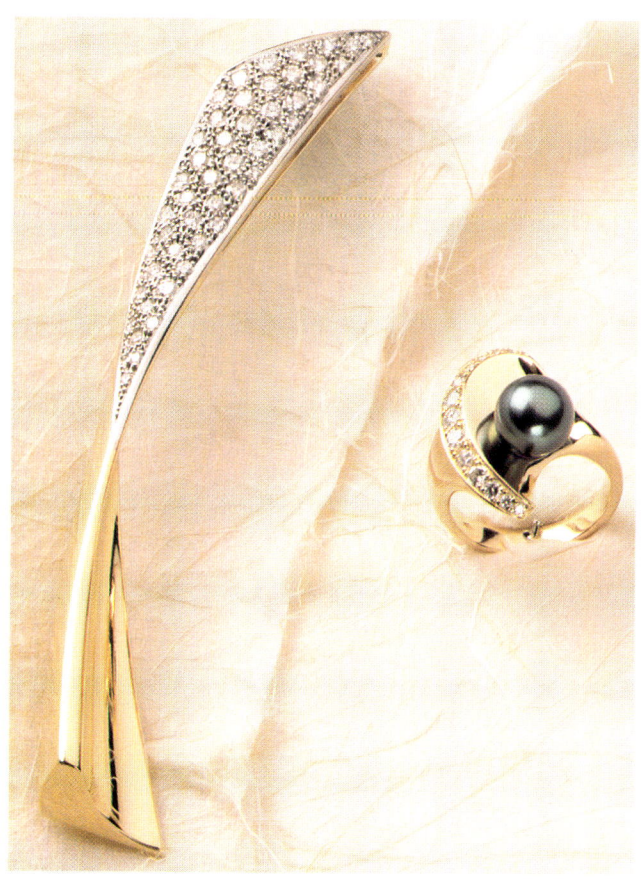

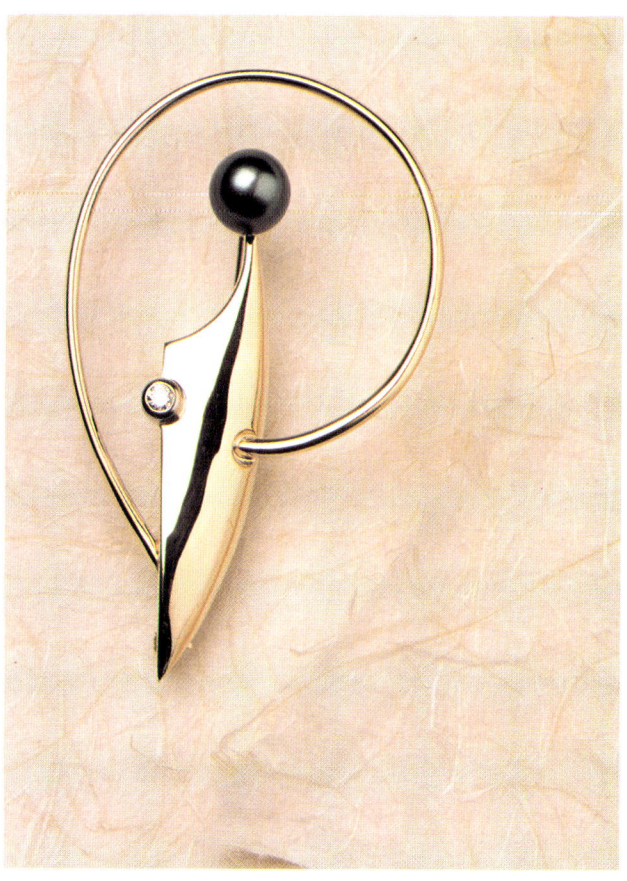

Brooch and ring in yellow and white gold with diamonds and black Tahiti pearl.

Brooch in yellow gold, diamond and black Tahiti pearl.

MICHAEL DÜRNHOLZ

'Just as a tree needs water to survive, a jewel needs a woman of character, a woman who communicates with the jewel. She is the jewel's accomplice, reflecting its qualities, but above all she is an accomplice of the jewel's creator, because she is needed to inspire its making and to show off the finished work to its advantage. When a woman is in harmony with the jewel, she makes it shine even more than the brilliance of the stones themselves.' With these few lines, Michael Dürnholz perceptively describes the relationship between the jewel-creator, the woman and precious materials. One must not forget that this creator is a student of Jean Vendome, whom he takes after.

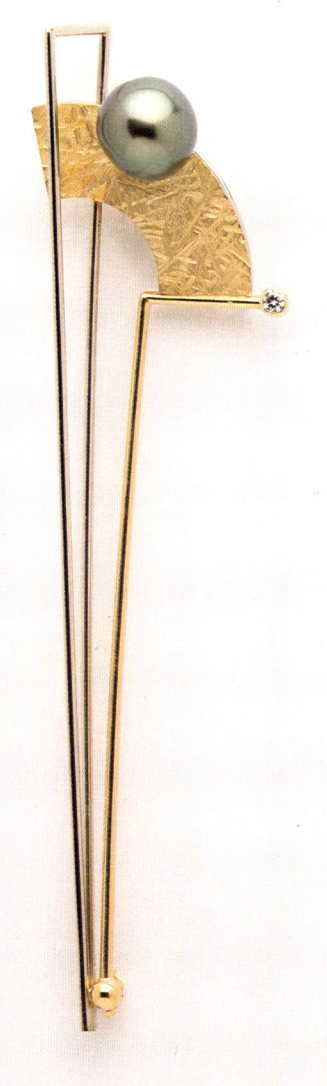

'The Sun and the Sea'. Brooch of yellow and white gold with a gray Tahitian pearl and diamond.

LENA ANTABI

She finds her inspiration in the tales of a Thousand and One Nights. When she creates, it is her heart that leads her; she is gifted with an enigmatic magnetism that allows her to communicate on the one hand with stones and on the other hand with the individuals who wear them. 'I love what I do and I do what I love' — this is Lena Antabi's guiding principle.

Pair of gold and diamond earrings.

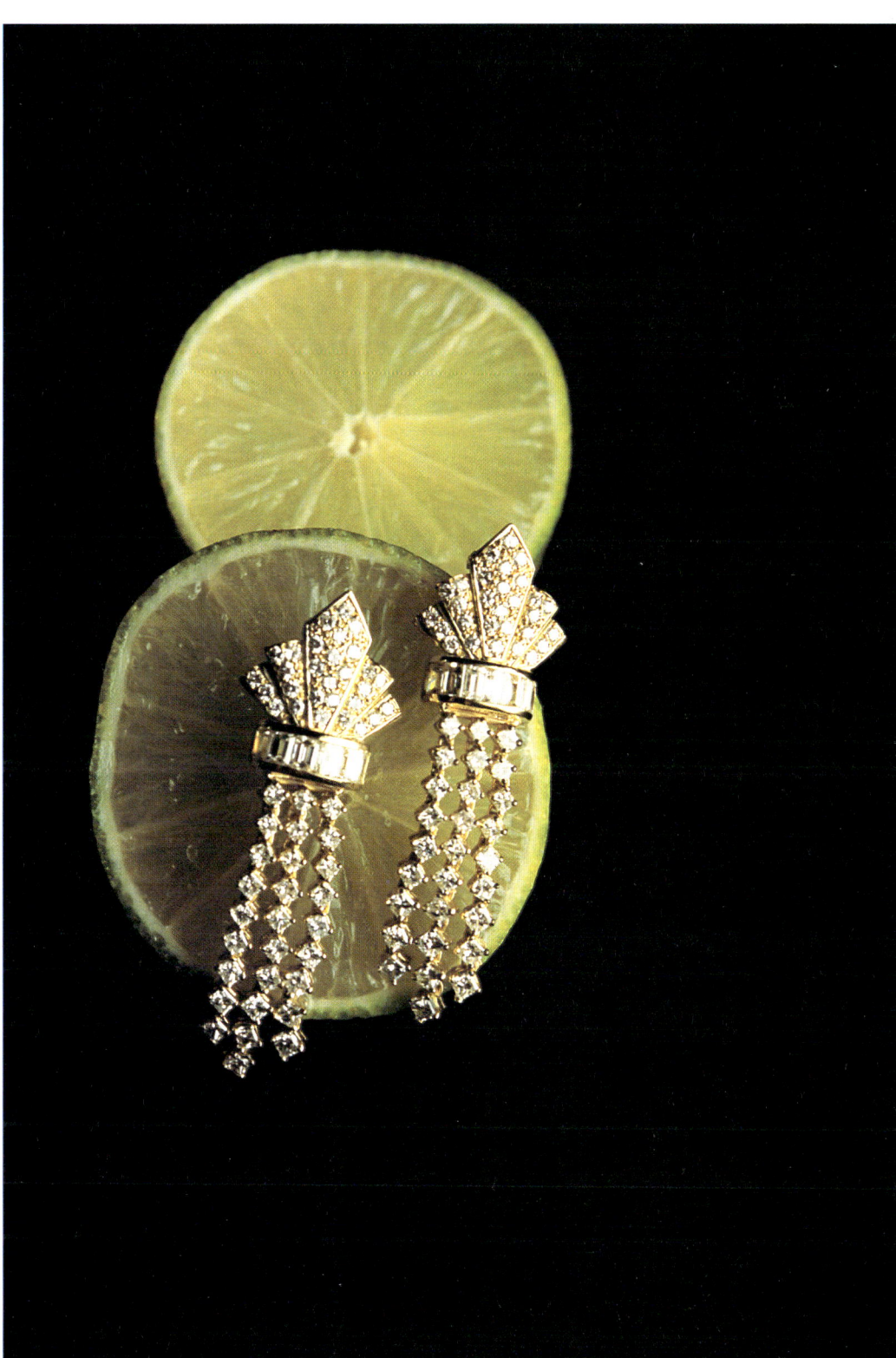

MIRIAM MAMBER

'Nature is the starting point for my work: the unique shapes and colours of minerals, the back-lit interior of a translucent agate, the organic geometry of fossils... Starting from these forms suggested by nature, I create a complement or a continuation or even a contrast. This work takes concrete form in an object called a jewel, destined for the human body, where it finds its ultimate dimension. My aim is to lead people to perceive the natural forms I use in order to inspire an emotion born of the association between those forms and my creation. In this way they can appreciate intensely how alive a jewel is.'

Necklace in silver, painted silk and Roman glass from the 4th century B.C.

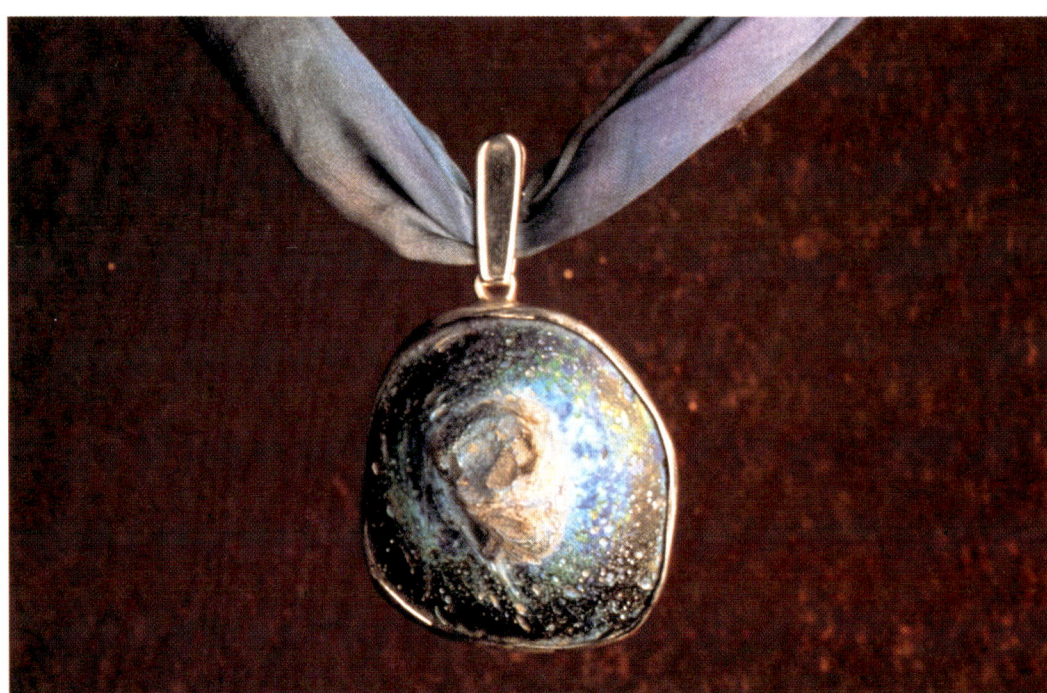

'The Fruit of the Seed', pendant in gold, sanded rock crystal and diamond.

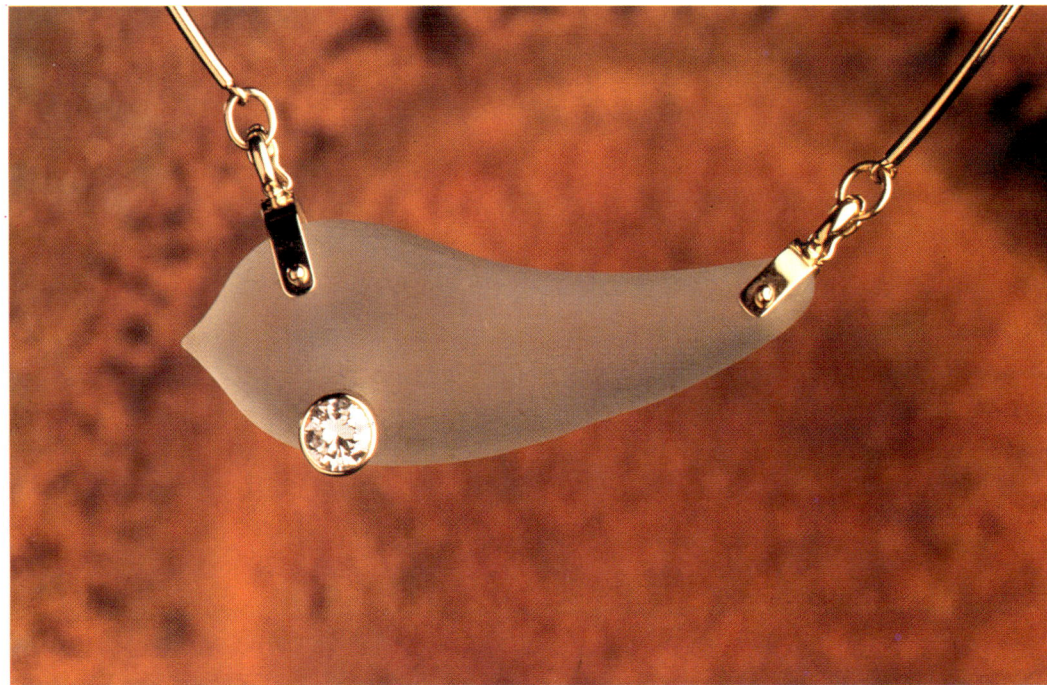

JUL DIZON

Several times the winner of the 'Diamond Awards', Jul Dizon belongs to the third generation of a jeweller-family. With great dexterity, she uses coloured diamonds and fine stones cut in the shapes of flowers and leaves. In Manila, where she is very fashionable, she is considered to be one of the country's finest creators.

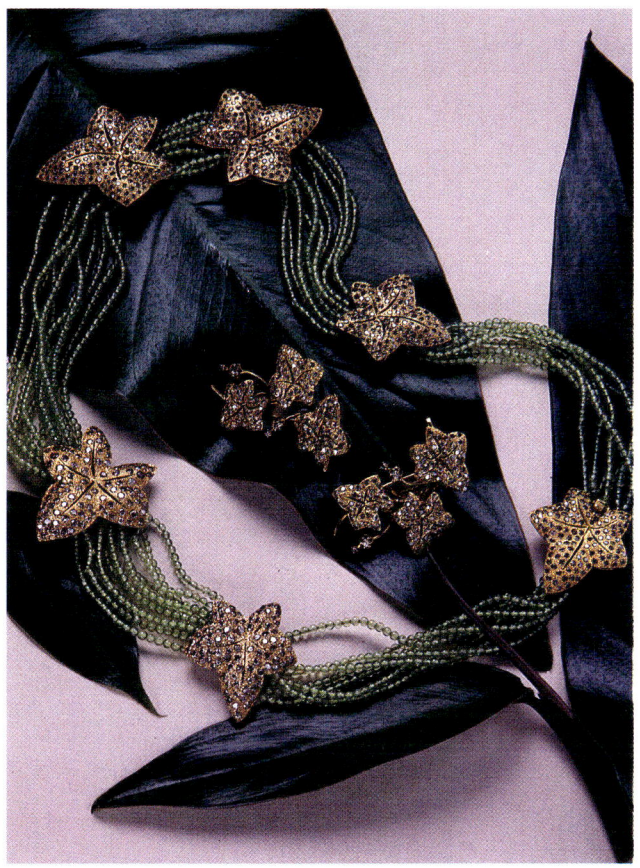

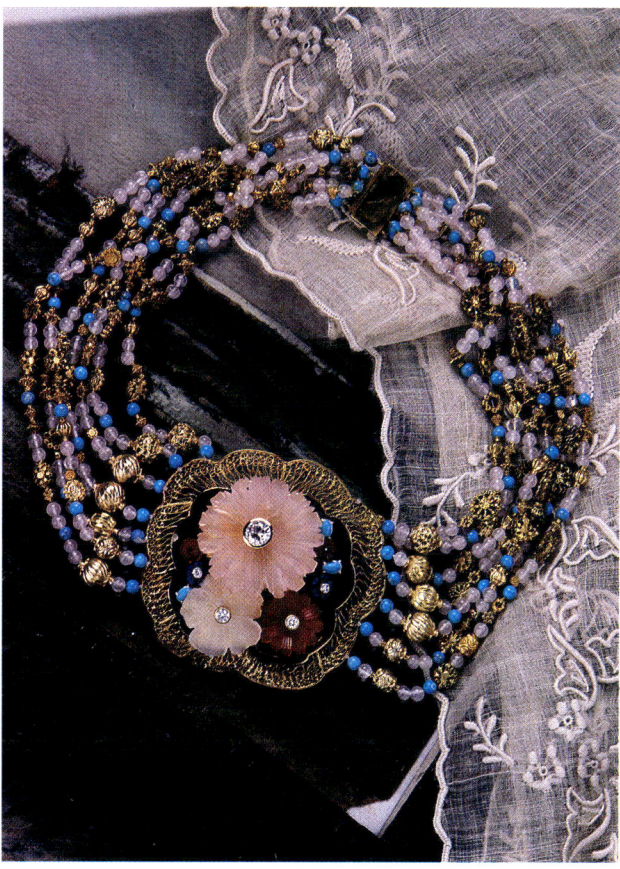

Necklace and earrings in gold, peridot and cognac-coloured diamonds.

Choker in gold, cornelian, lapis lazuli, rose and white quartz, with turquoises and diamonds.

FLORENCE CROISIER

'The bracelet was conceived as a gesture that moves at the whim of the light, letting it slide along its forms. These undulations create a movement in which the repetition of the elements sets the rhythm.' This is how Florence Croisier describes one of her creations. Such poetry.

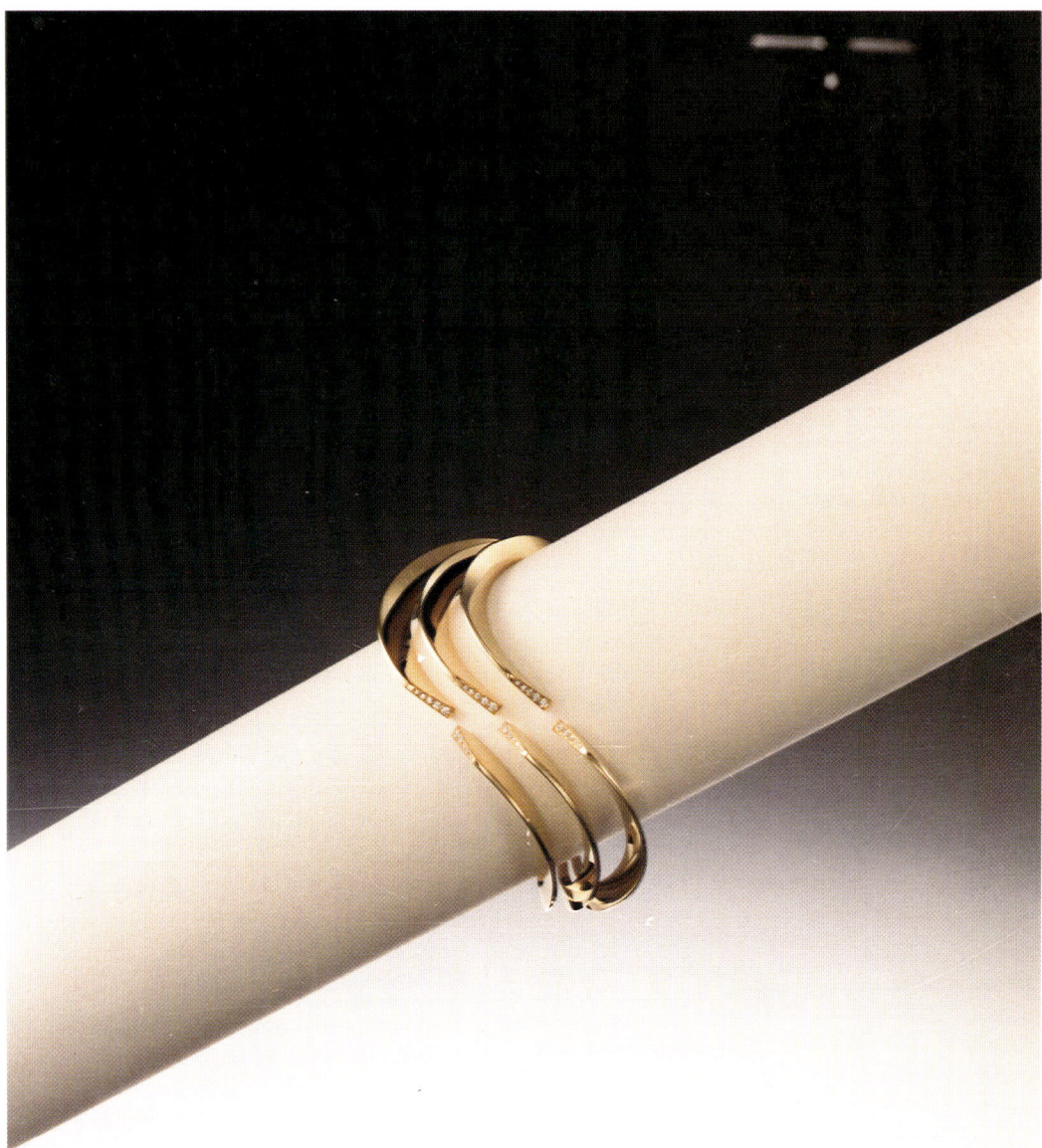

Gold and diamond bracelet.

HUBERT SCHUSTER

It was at the age of 14 that he began working as a jeweller. Highly technical, he succeeds in making pieces with very pure lines. Herbert Schuster devotes a great deal of his time to artistic and technical research.

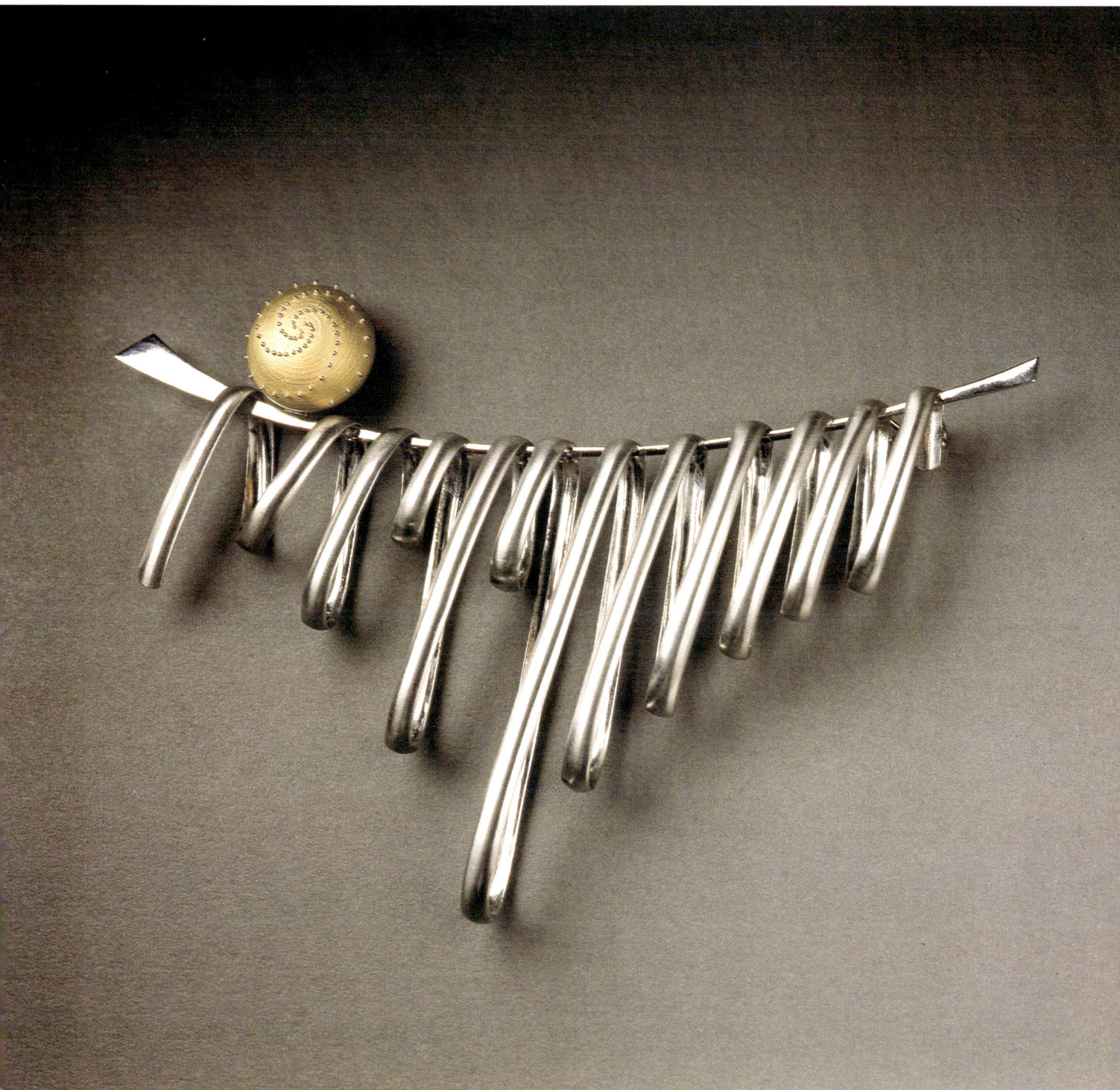

'Twilight', brooch in gold and platinum; a few lines suffice to evoke the setting of the sun.

CHRISTINE ESCHER

Christine Escher does not draw inspiration from distant voyages or vague reveries, but rather from the everyday world. Unlike those artists who like to close themselves off in an ivory tower in order to create, she prefers to move about in reality. Her most beloved material, which she knows how to make rhyme so harmoniously with diamonds, is wood — unpolished, warm, living wood. Her indefatigable eye has combed beaches and dunes to bring us a miraculous catch: ebony pebbles encrusted with diamond star-fish and sea-shells.

Pendant and bracelet in ebony, gold and diamonds.

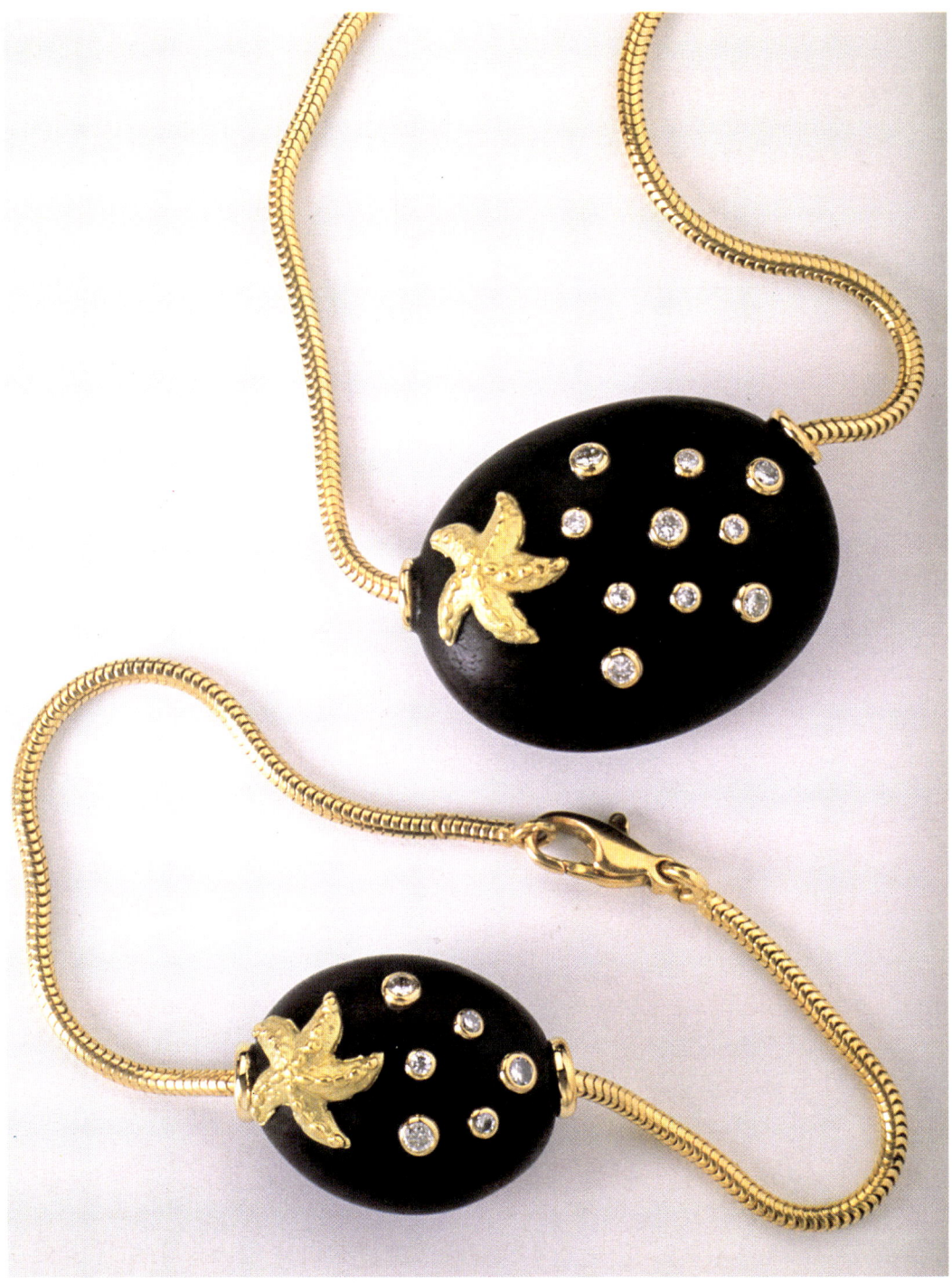

MONICA CENACCHI

After successful experience in the realm of fashion, Monica Cenacchi was drawn towards jewellery and an exploration of the creation of jewels. 'What appeals to me in conceiving a jewel is creating an element that endures through time and that may even be timeless. For me, a jewel has a magical aspect of seduction. When it is out of the ordinary, a jewel comes into contact with the human being's personality, accentuating her sensitivity, and it becomes a leading accessory through her manner of wearing it.'

'Mirage',
ring in gold,
pearls and zircons.

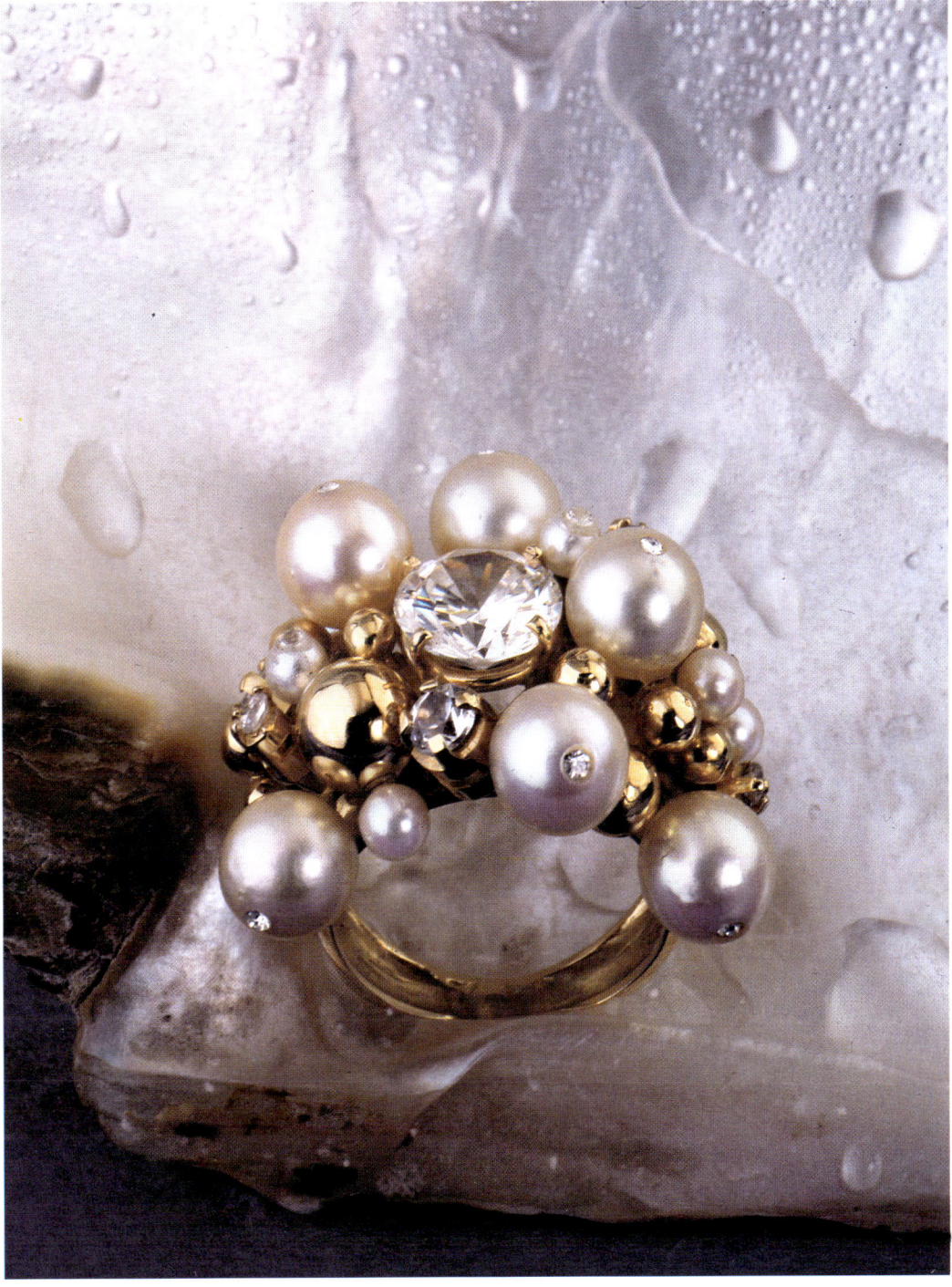

ALFONSO MAZZI

Maria Teresa Ferrari introduces him in these terms: 'His creations are born from artistic research that is accomplished thanks to his perfect knowledge of the artisan's technique.

'His creativity and sensitivity nourish a feeling for contemporary art, which results in ancient history mixed with modern times. A mixture of the figurative and the abstract, ordinary materials and precious ones, in a barely-perceptible symbolism.

'The liveliness of Alfonso Mazzi's creations bring full life to the raw materials that he plays with: humour, melancholy and aggressiveness are freed in his work.

'All his pieces are profoundly expressive and are born of an artistic intelligence; without "copying" nature, he nevertheless enhances it.'

Gold brooch with opals and diamonds.

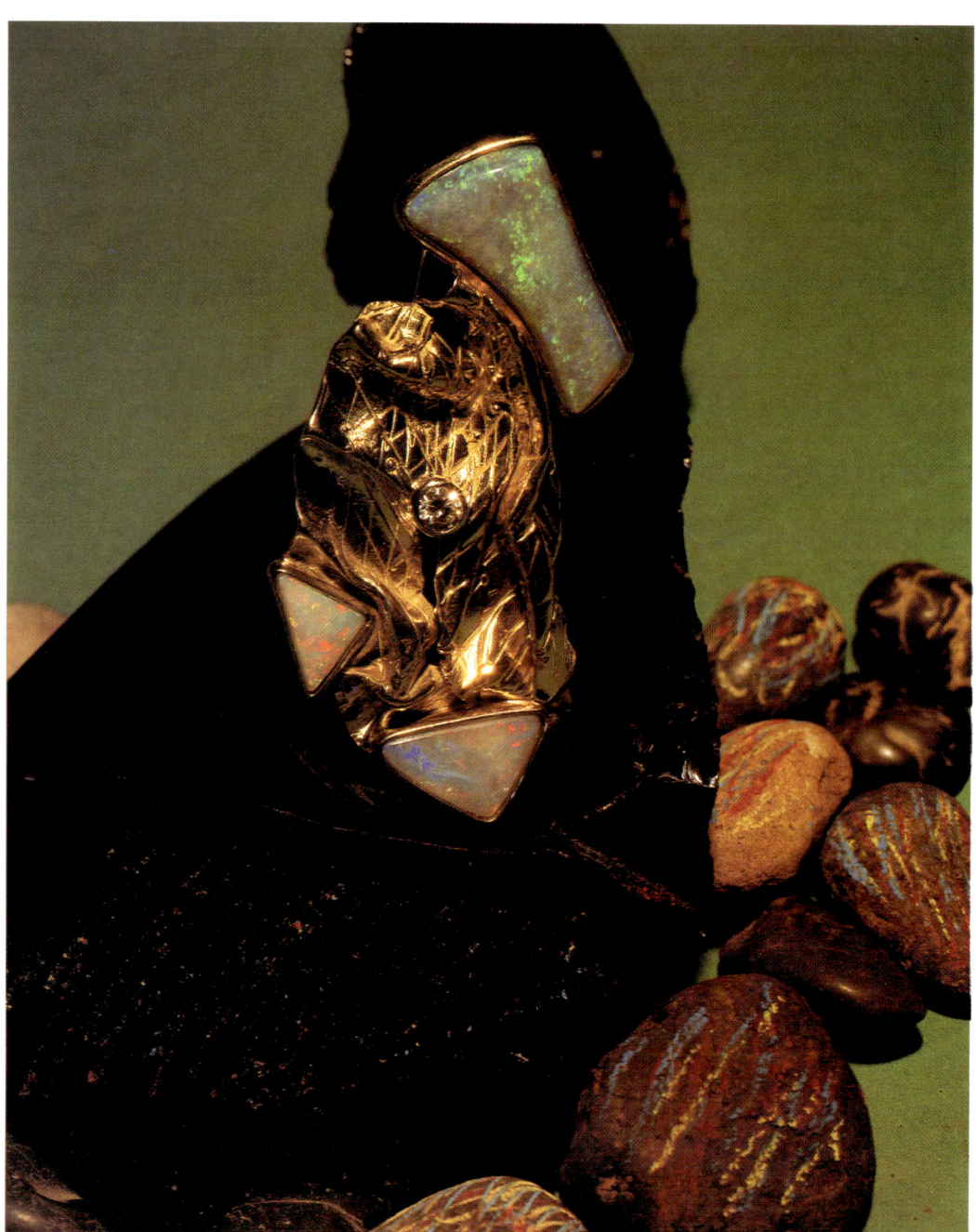

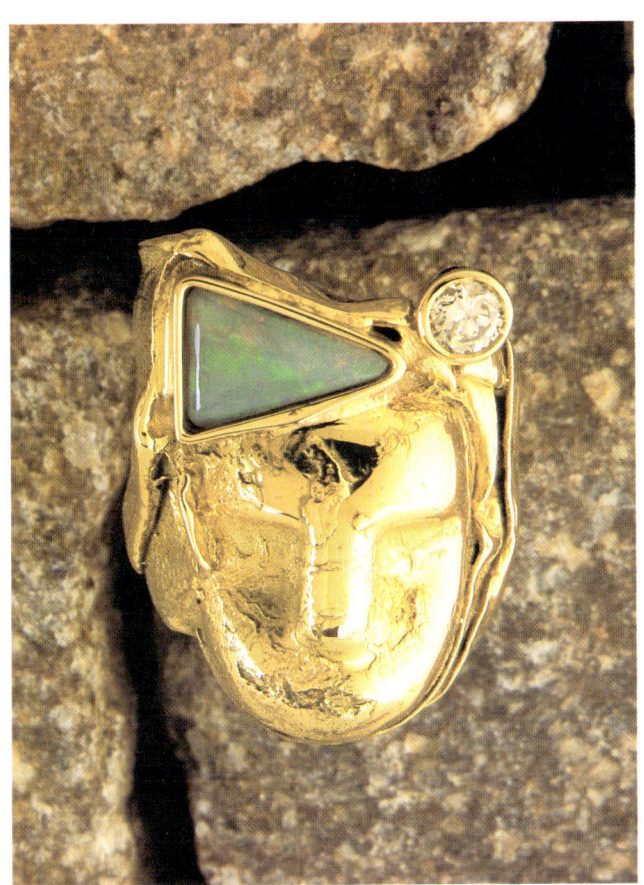

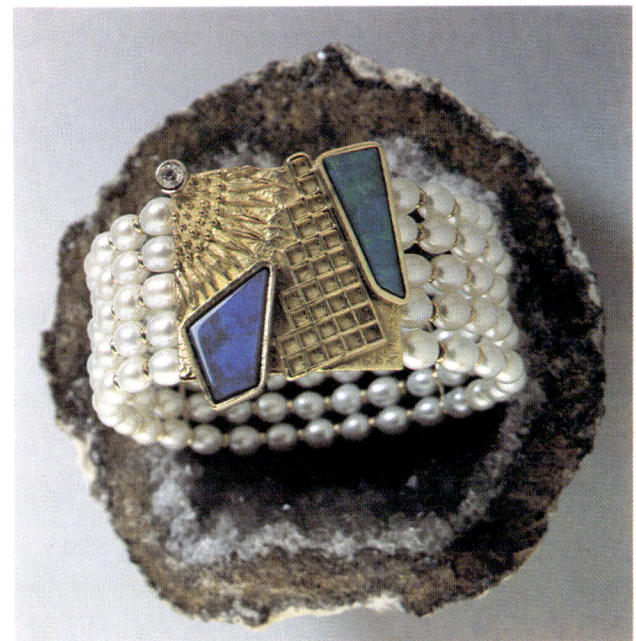

Ring in gold, opal and diamond.

Bracelet in gold, opals, diamands and pearls.

Bracelet in gold, opal and sapphire.

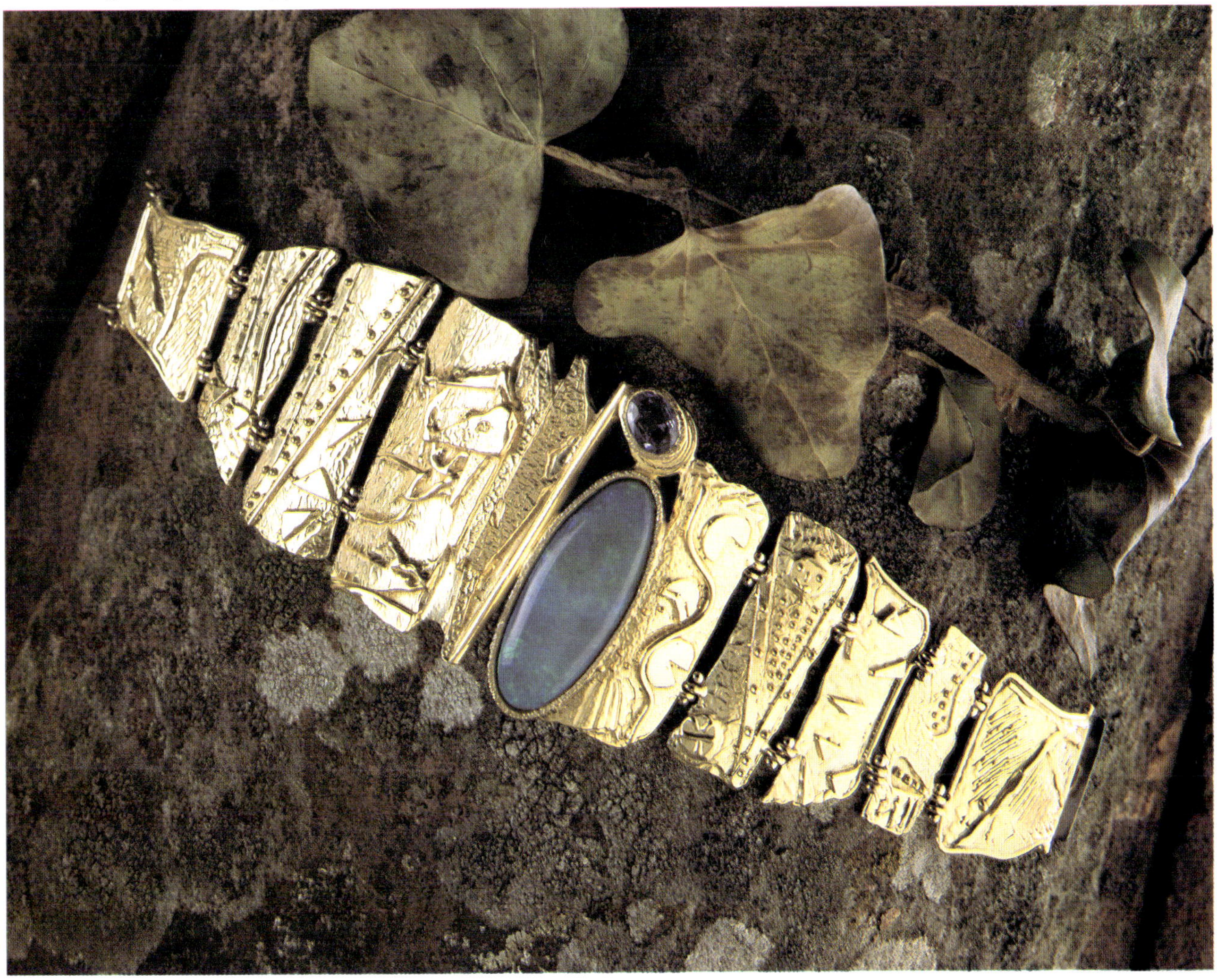

87

ANNA CELLA

Her love of nature and materials, united with an uncommonly interpretative intuition, make her jewels portable works of art. 'The form is already within the material; each object must be modelled in order to live in harmony with the human body. The hand has a very specific morphology and function, for example: a ring for the little finger must have angles and curves that are very different from those on a ring destined for the ring finger.'

Ring in satined gold and a sapphire navette practically suspended above the glossy material.

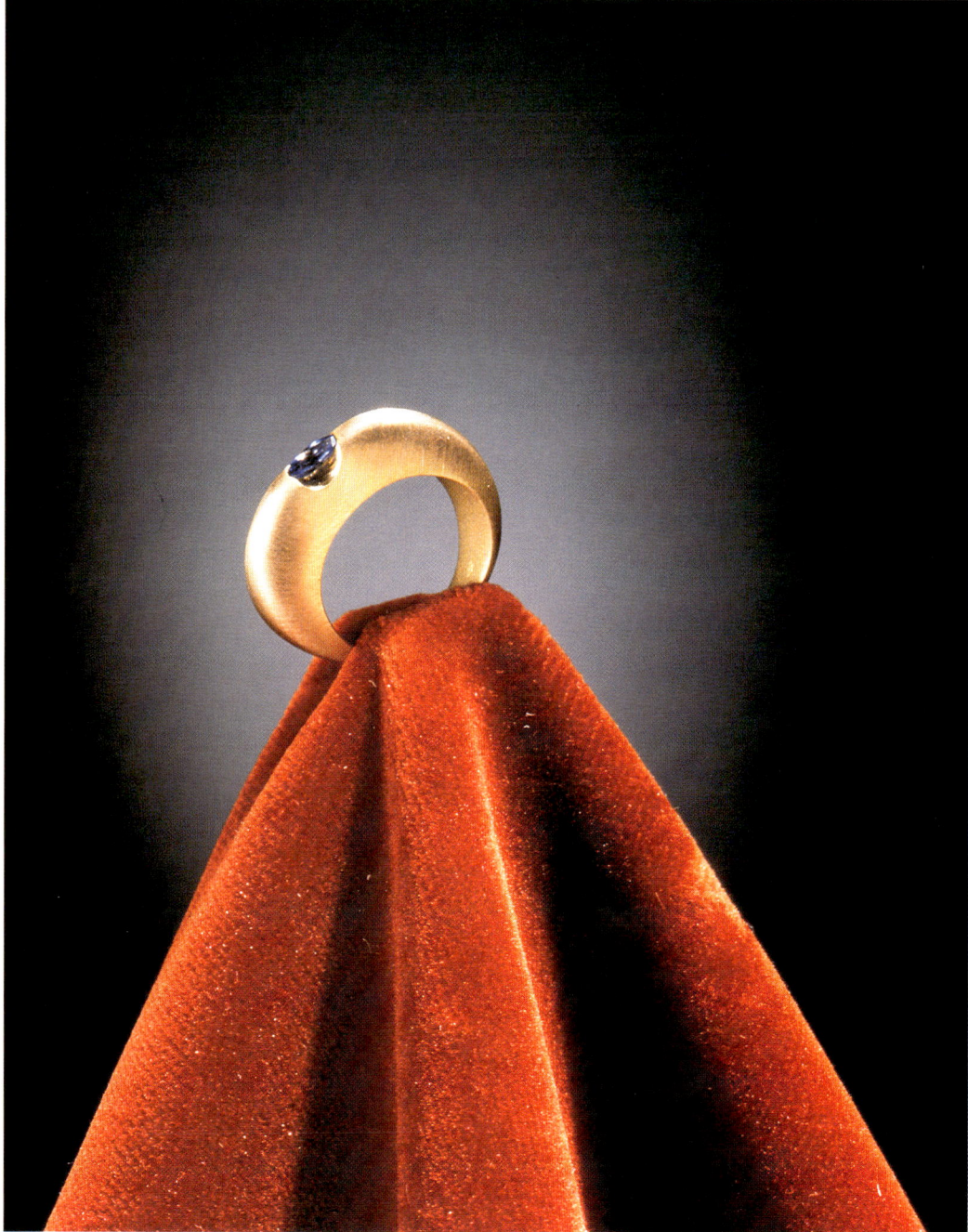

JANINE RENARD

Her sources of inspiration go back to the earliest history of the planet: insects and plants with the shapes and structures found in fossils thousands of years old. Janine Renard studies each piece from every angle. This is why a number of her rings carry a diamond on the inner side surface, the surface that is exposed only to the jewel's wearer. So that her jewels can be worn on any occasion, Janine Renard invents several variations for them. For example, certain earrings include a mobile part that may be detached or reattached as one pleases. An articulated brooch may be worn in a straight rectangular shape or bent into an angle. A pendant may become a brooch, or it may be worn with either its obverse or reverse side showing, and it can be adapted to any neckline by modifying the clasp of the chain. Finally, one must not forget that Janine Renard was the inventor of the famous 'perfume-carriers'.

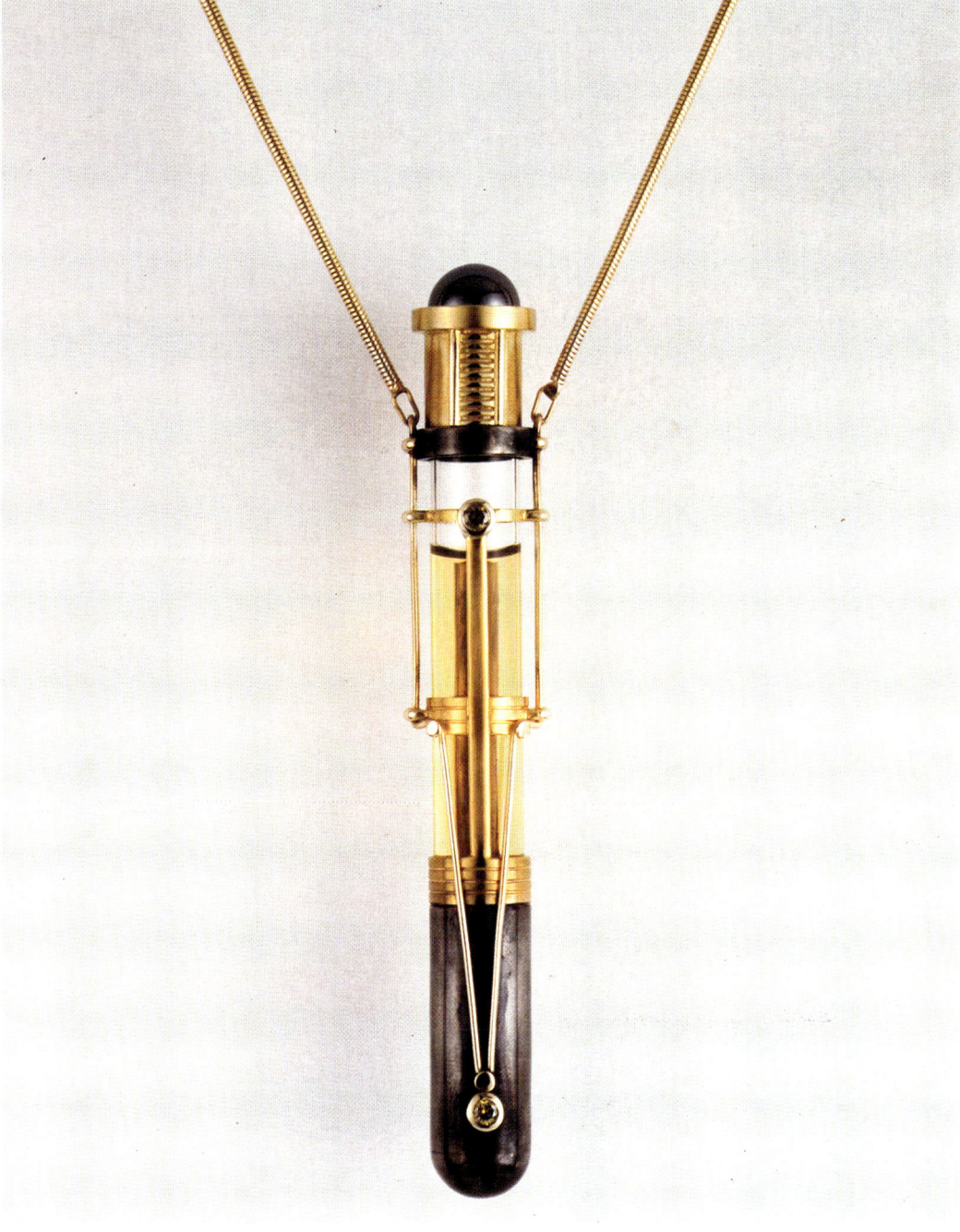

'Da Vinci II', perfume-carrying pendant in gold, oxidised silver, haematite and four olive-coloured diamonds.

SUSANNE WENZ

Originally from Düsseldorf, she chose France in which to exercise her talents as a designer, and established herself there independently. Clear eyes and a direct smile light up the frank face of a down-to-earth woman whose two feet are firmly planted in her times, and who enjoys taking great bites out of life.

An aesthete down to her fingernails, this inveterate creator is enamoured of rigour and purity. She likes spare, graphic lines. She has built a collection around the circle and round forms in which diamonds, combined with peridot and amethyst, form flower motifs.

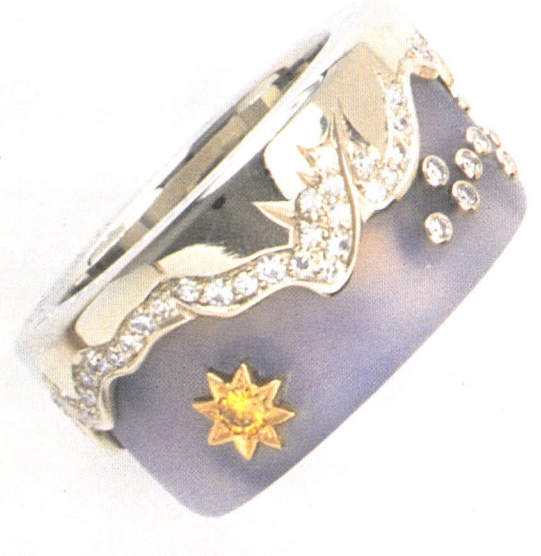
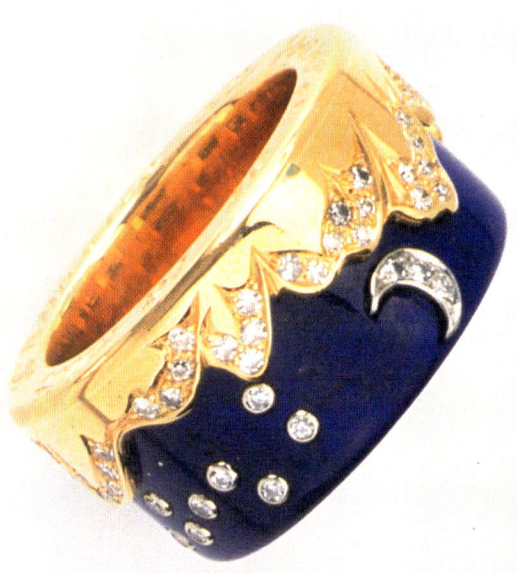

The mountains of Austria inspired this confirmed European to make 'Europe by Day and by Night': two rings with diamond-studded landscapes. Day: Gray gold ring, chalcedony and diamonds. Night: Yellow gold ring, lapis lazuli and diamonds.

CATHERINE VAVALEA

Her roots are in the richness of the Greek land, her homeland where she pursued her studies in Decorative Arts. Catherine Vavalea presently lives and works in France. Very much attached to clean, ample volumes, she creates her jewels in gold and precious stones as well as in other materials such as wood, minerals, etc., thus pursuing her aesthetic and plastic explorations rather than the object's precious effect alone.

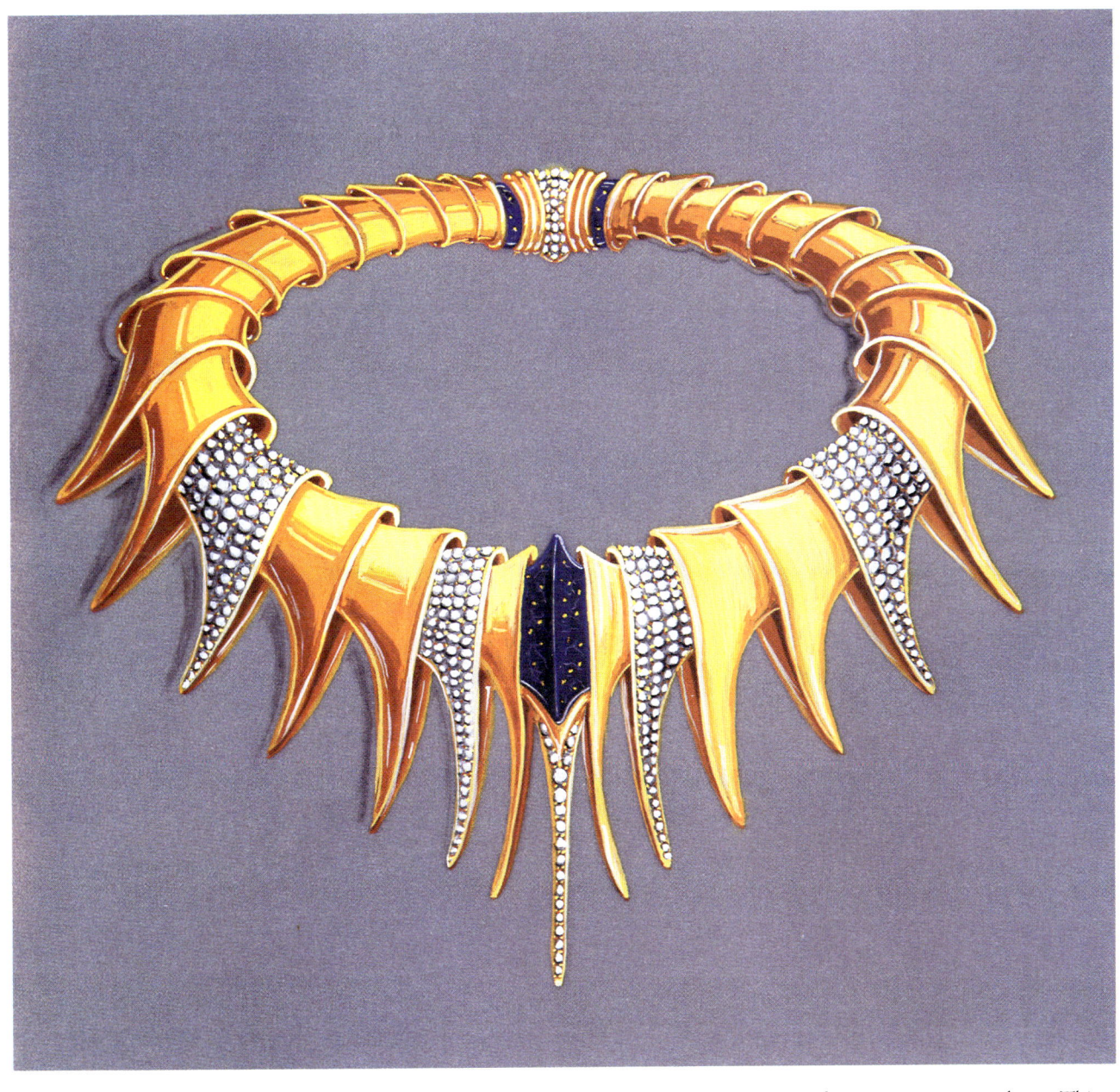

Design for 'Elxis' necklace, inspired by the extravagant morphology of certain carnivorous plants. This necklace, entirely in gold and brilliants, is set with a piece of lapis lazuli cut into double convex arches.

JEAN-MARIE AUDE

A graduate of the École Boulle and a Master Craftsman of France, Jean-Marie Aude has already completed 15 Academicians' swords and other gold and vermeil sculptures. 'The creator of jewels is constantly subject to the interpretations of fashions and markets. These constraints oblige the creator to be rigorous, to know different fabrication techniques in order to exploit them and surpass them. The "marketing" of jewels has in itself drained them of all their fine qualities and subtlety, and it is up to the creator to give meaning back to precious ornamental objects.' In jewels, Jean-Marie Aude rediscovers the qualities of sculptures, of architecture and doubtless of life.

Sketch of a sculpture joined to a necklace in gold, crystal and diamonds.

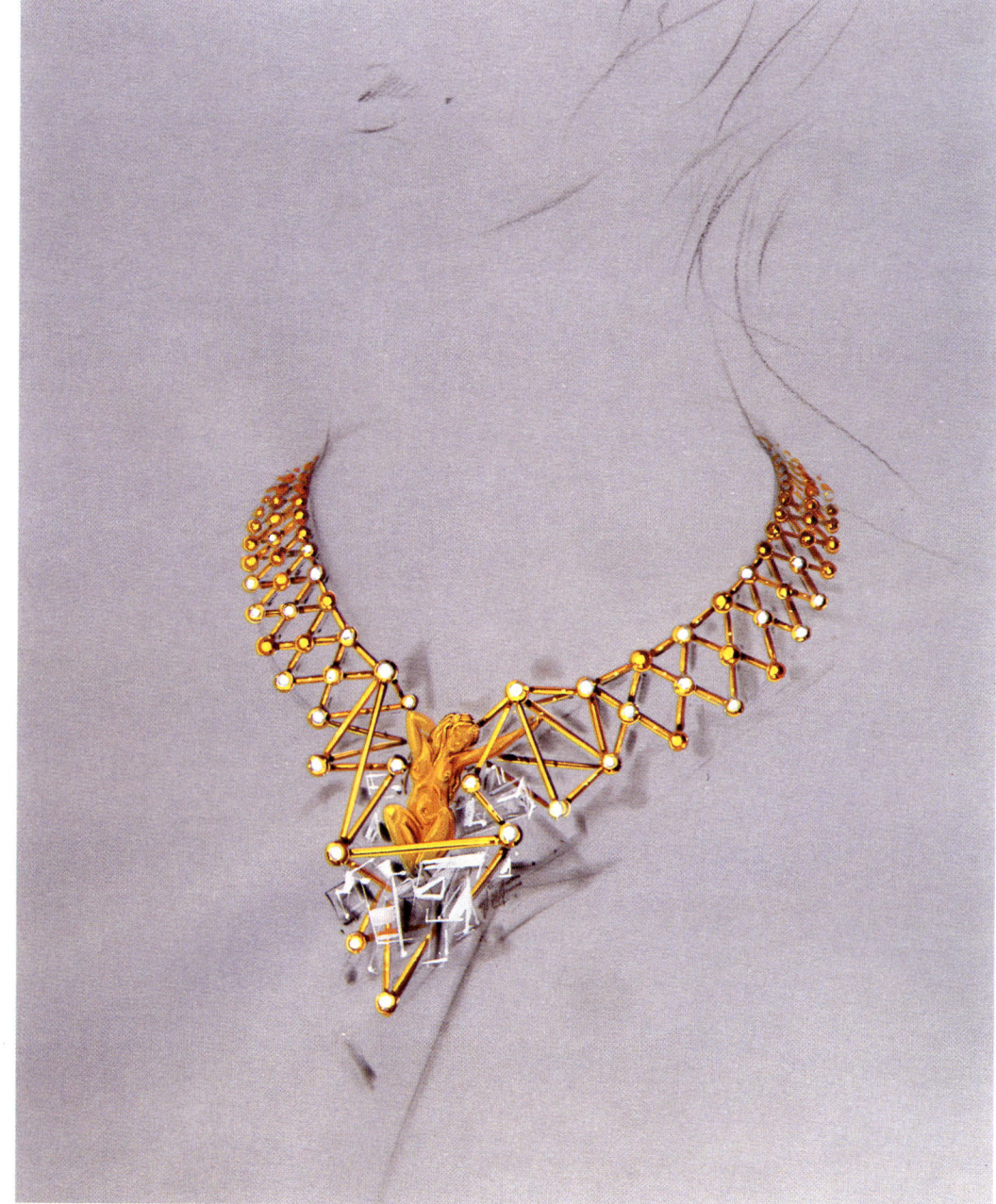

THIERRY MARTIN

His jewellery creations are audacious — he likes to mix materials and forms that may seem contradictory in order to establish a judicious equilibrium. The imperatives of technique and fabrication are gently interpreted in his pieces, augmenting their aesthetic potential. 'It is indispensable that a jewel engage a certain emotion; today a jewel should not be a synonym for wealth but a synonym for personality.'

'Pique-Fleur', sketch of a necklace in yellow gold with South Sea pearls and a real iris, interchangeable according to season and mood. The association of a real flower and a precious ensemble gives the jewel a playful air.

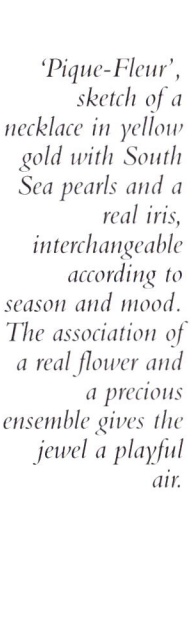

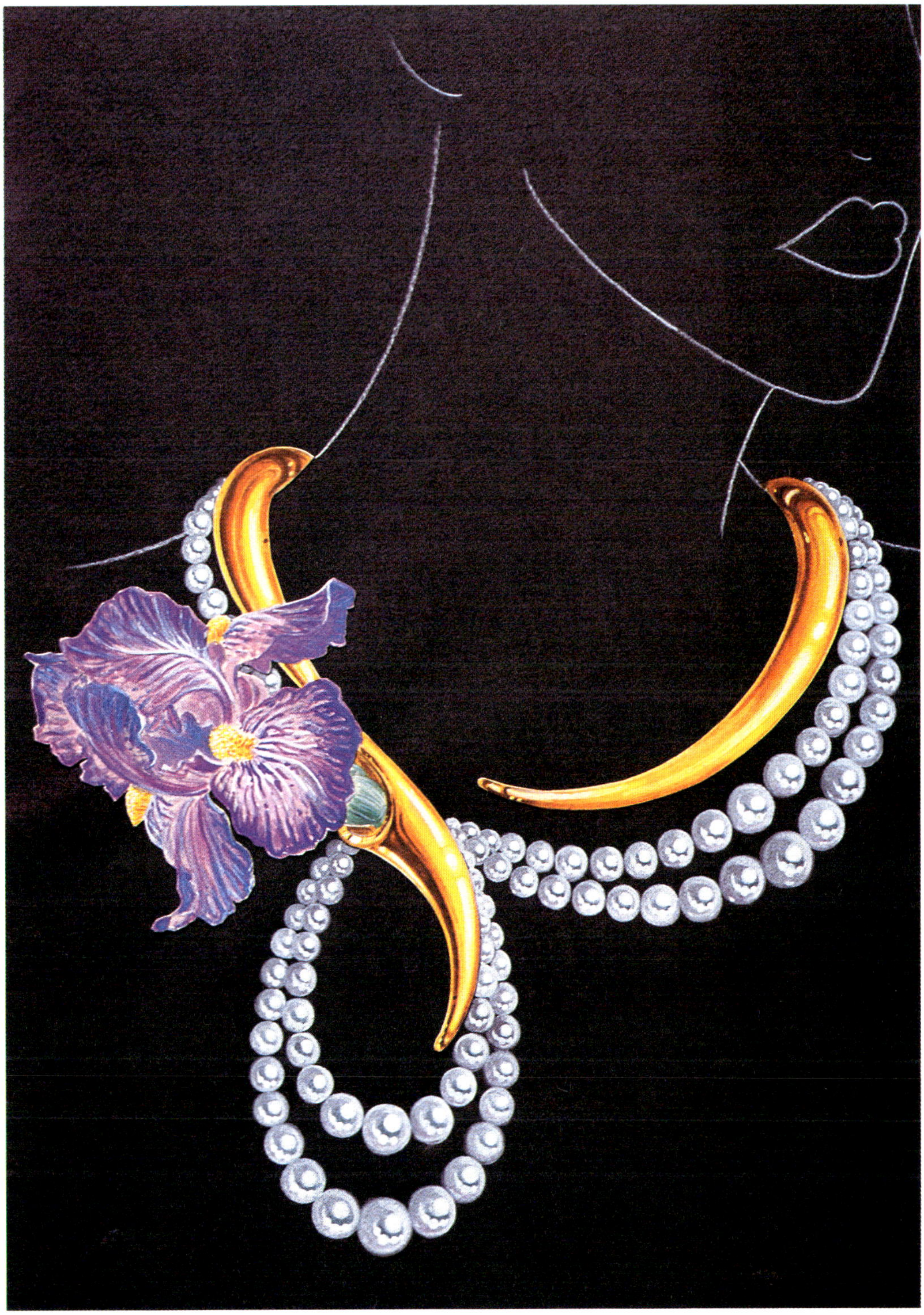

NICOLA CERRONE

He has been named as a 'Master of Jewellery Art'. He comes from Italy and arrived in Australia with his baggage full of thousands of original ideas and much goodwill. Sydney welcomed him with open arms and today he is considered to be the city's most important jeweller.

Earring in gold with diamonds ranging in colour from white to cognac to madeira.

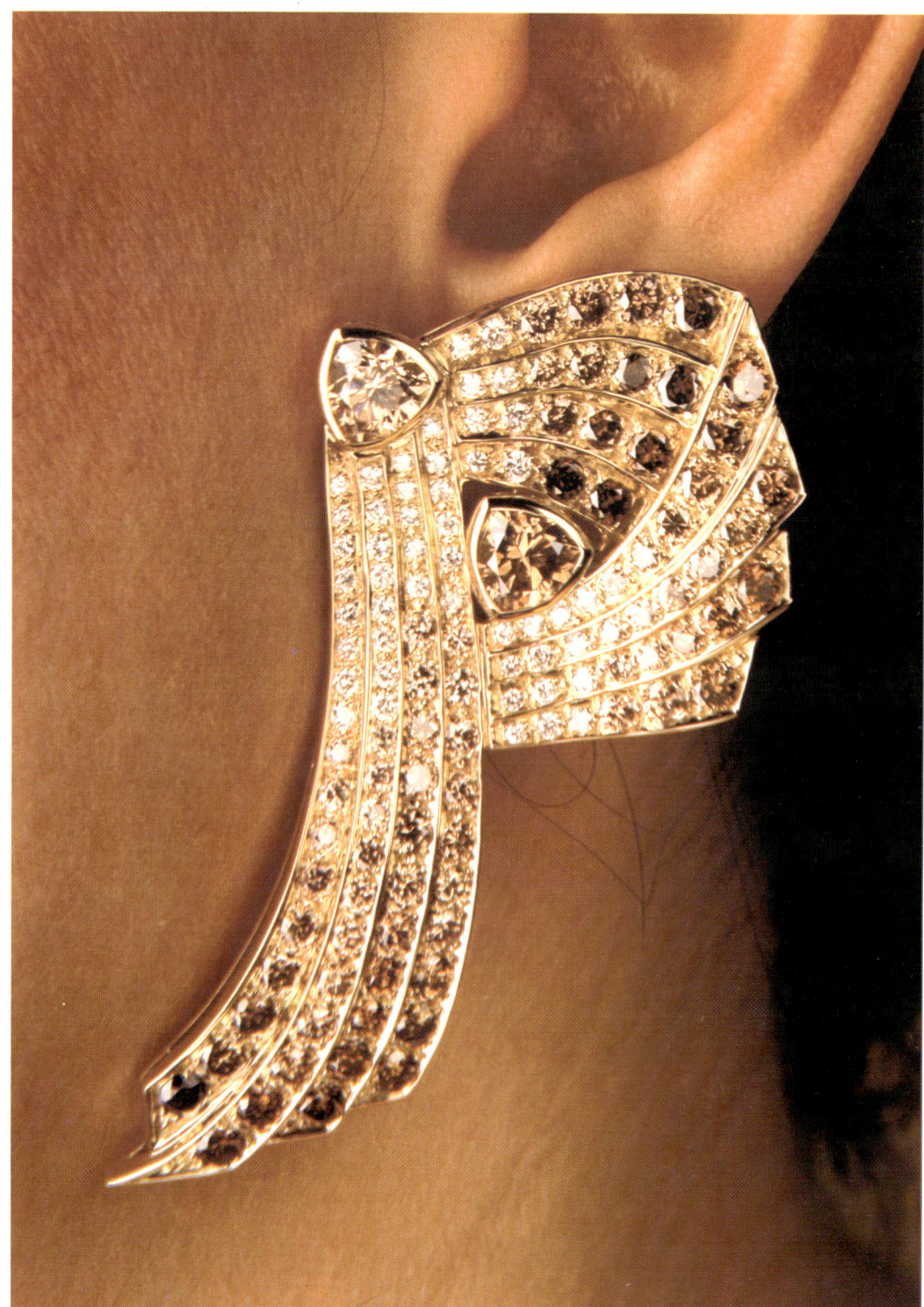

94

JACQUES PRADES

He is without doubt one of the finest creators not only in Thailand but in all of Indochina. This former student of the École du Louvre moved to Bangkok in 1971, where he maintains the traditions of Parisian jewellery, revised and updated.

Pendant in gold, blue tourmaline (indicolite), cornelians and diamonds.

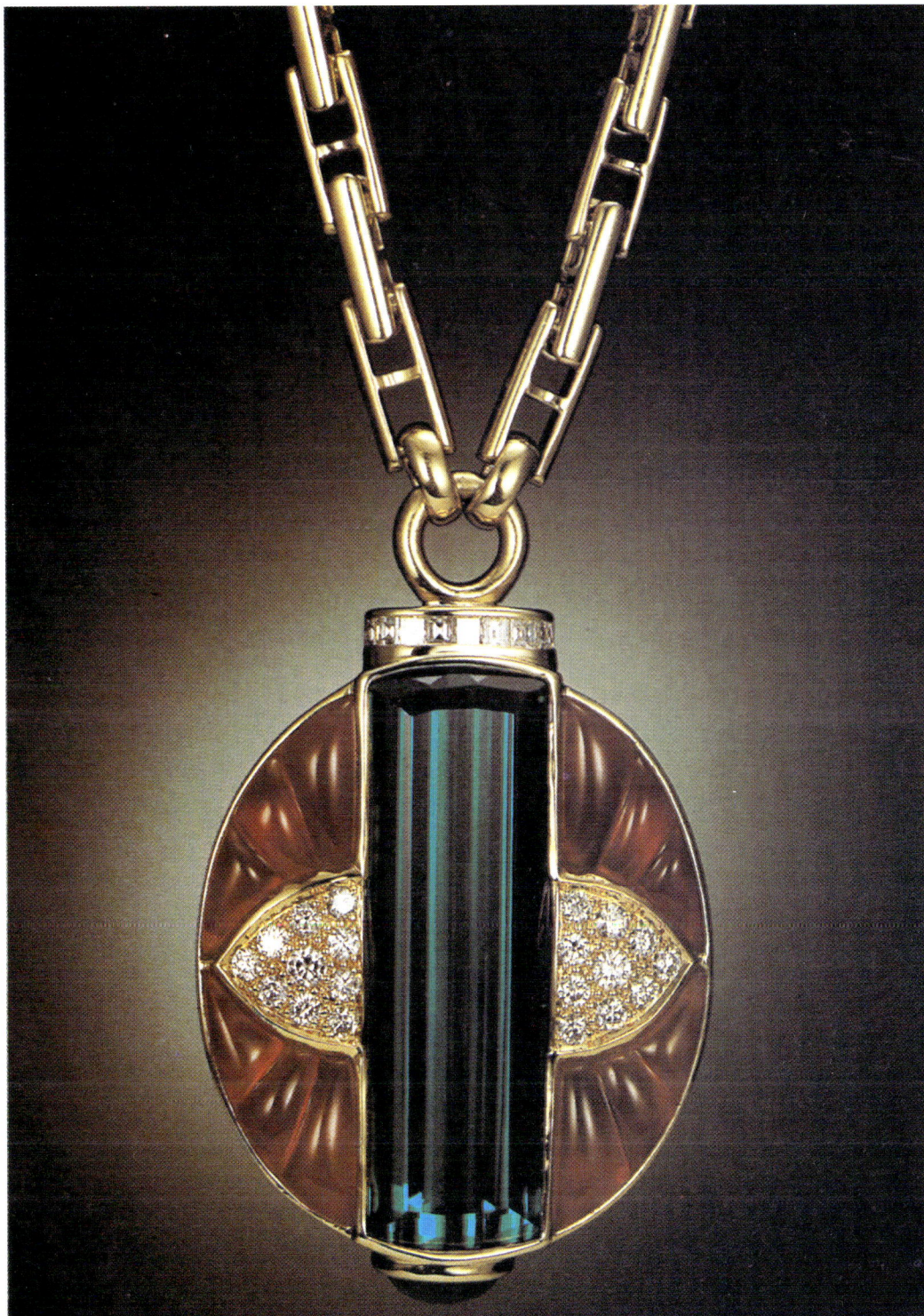

JEAN-PIERRE DUPORT

'**M**y approach to jewellery is a novel one: I do not impose any values, any constraints; I want to enjoy myself while creating, to please others when I show my work, to share ideas. My main interest is in refining the jewel; this is the alternative to evolution. I would so much like to be able to participate in mentally changing places with someone.'

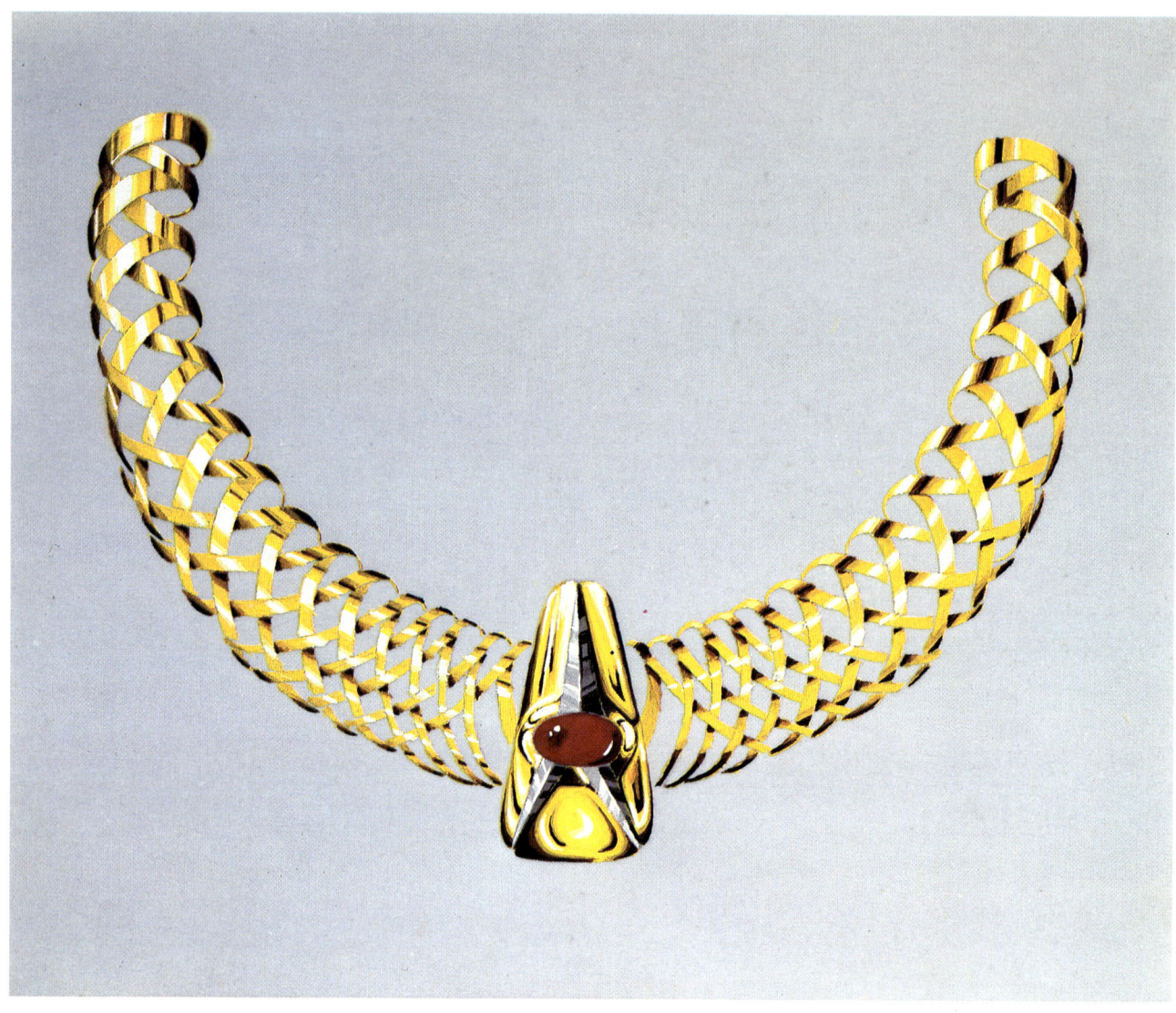

Sketch of a necklace in gold, silver and cabochon rubies. 'The spirit of the road reveals its symbols. I let myself drive to the point of intoxication.'

CLAUDE MAZLOUM

'It is of prime importance that the public have the means of distinguishing between a soulless industrial jewel and a living jewel that provokes reactions and wonder.'

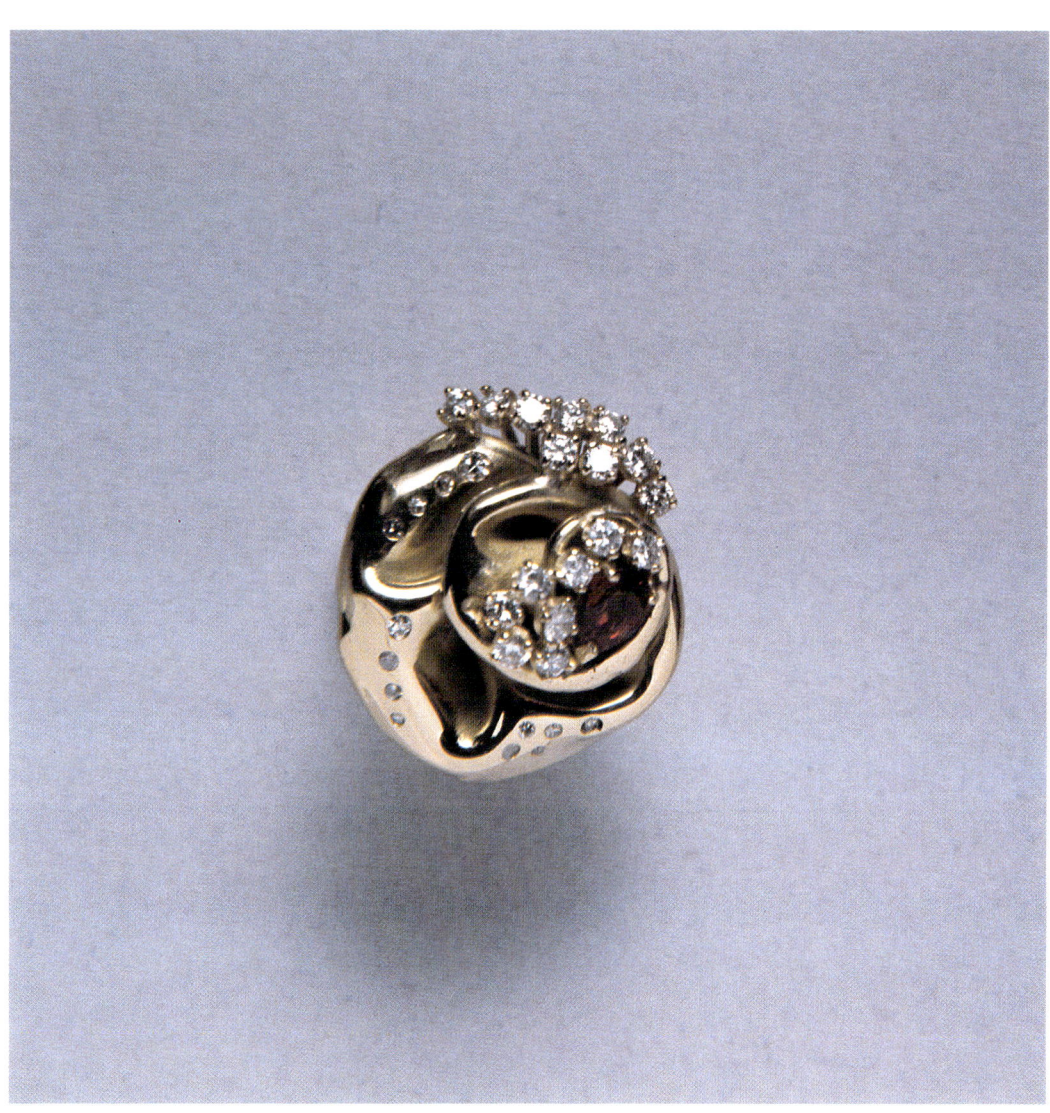

'Rosas', ring in gold, pear-shaped rubies and diamonds.

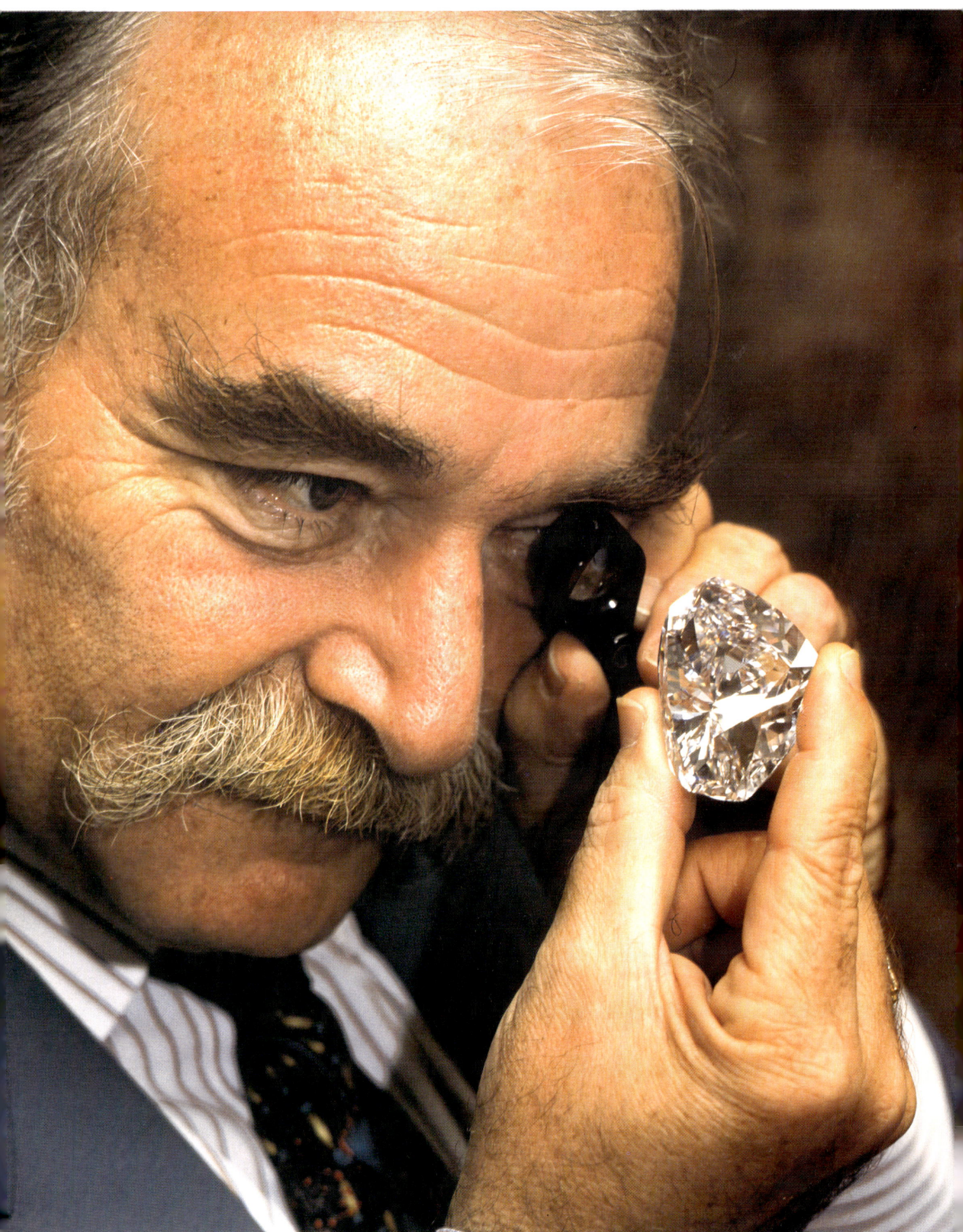

CHAPTER II

DIAMONDS: A PRIMORDIAL ELEMENT

In collaboration with Gabriel Tolkowsky

He is the inventor of 'flower cuts'; the young nephew of Marcel Tolkowsky, discoverer of the perfect cut of a diamond; a brilliant and above all sensitive man who is able to communicate with stones: Gabriel Tolkowsky decodes for us the secret alphabet that is the key to understanding diamonds. A diamond is a transparent mirror. 'When looking at objects and materials, man sees only the surface of things at first glance, yet his eye is a highly sensitive, sophisticated camera that registers the smallest details. In a diamond, the eye discovers a material whose transparency allows us to fathom its depths but which also reflects our own image.' Gabriel saw this assertion confirmed during the shooting of a film that is due to be released shortly. 'The film-maker was able to capture my face reflected in the interior of the sublime "Le Centenaire" diamond — a diamond weighing 273.85 carats, whose cutting I supervised for three years. To establish that this is a real phenomenon and not merely an optical illusion, I placed my loupe between the diamond and my eye, so that my face appeared upside-down, in the loupe, reflected by the heart of the diamond. Showing that a diamond is probably the only natural material that possesses the characteristics of a transparent mirror may help us understand man's natural attraction towards diamonds, not only because it reflects our individual personality, but also our own physical image. Of course, we cannot prove this in a very small cut stone, but our eye can. What is certain is that the image is captured in our subconscious; quite simply, a diamond confirms for us that we are quite alive!'

Diamonds are the symbol of pure water

'Part of our attraction towards diamonds is its visual similarity to water. Water is life! We are essentially composed of water, and our subconscious reminds us of this continually. In the history and language of different civilisations, the diamond's clarity has often been compared to that of pure water. In the same way, the diamond's purity is likened to water's. 'Pure as water' or 'diamond-clear water'. Light reflects — on the diamond as well as water — the fire that emanates from within and from the surface. 'The light that touches the diamond is like that of sun-rays or the

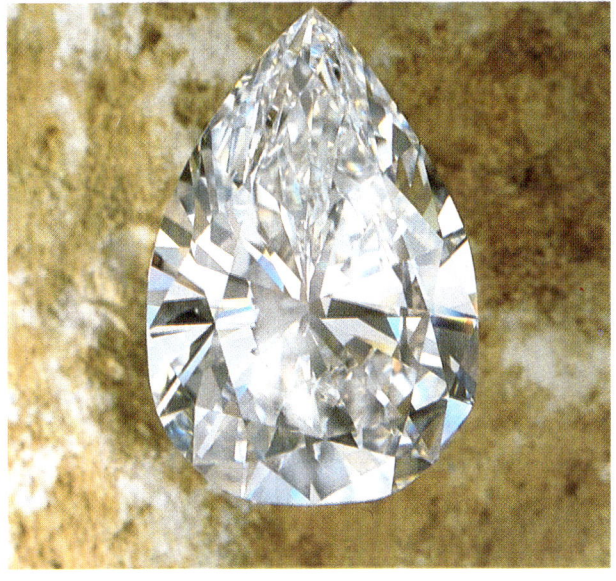

The invincible Adamas gave the term 'adamantine' to describe the typical brilliance of a diamond. In this photo there is a diamond cut in the shape of a pear or teardrop.

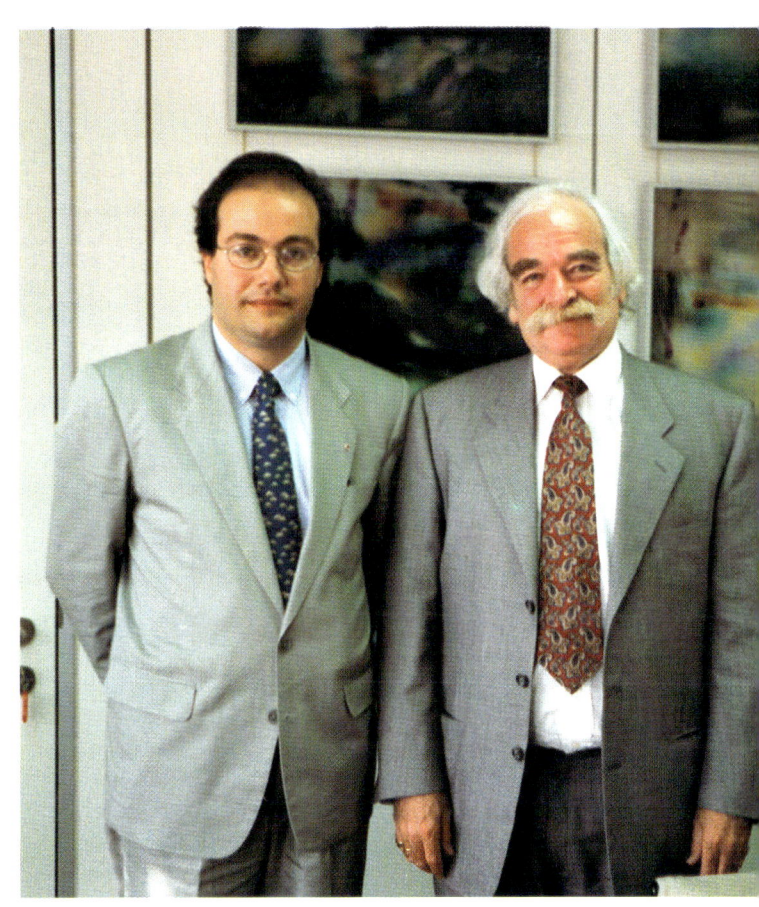

glimmer of moonlight floating on the water's surface. A human being is, and always will be, truly and intimately attracted to water; a diamond reminds him of it constantly.'

Each diamond has its individual colour

'Diamonds are probably the only crystals on earth that come in every possible and imaginable shade of colour. There are some very rare ones such as blues, reds, pinks, greens, mauves, etc.' as well as colourless ones, known as "blue white" or classified as "D" in the profession. Each human being has a colour, or rather, the nuance of a colour that attracts him personally. Identifying colours is a highly personal and individual faculty. For example, a colour described as yellow, or blue, or brown, or other is perceived differently by as many individuals as see it. It stands to reason, therefore, that each diamond, having its own nuance, will please the man or woman who is attracted by this "personal" tint. There are so many tints that, theoretically, somewhere there is a diamond for every human being. This being the case, it is nevertheless practically impossible, for throughout time, will there every be enough diamonds on earth to satisfy everyone?'

The importance of inclusions

'God created the diamond, the hardest material on earth. Despite the insurmountable difficulty, 900 or 1,000 years ago at Gilconde, man took up the challenge of transforming the appearance of a raw diamond. Was this a challenge of nature itself, or a desire to discover the sublime beauty hidden within the surface of this material? So many tools used, so many strokes of luck amassed before it suddenly revealed what was within its heart, this invincible octahedron! Today, each day, thousands of cutter-artisans make the magic gesture of cutting a little "window" on a rough diamond. Theirs is the exceptional privilege of discovering, first-hand, this extraordinary world, this transparent mirror, pure rarity, which often holds an inclusion within itself. According to scientists, a diamond was crystallised in magma thousands of millions of years ago — who knows, during the Big Bang perhaps! This material which crystallised as if by a miracle in the magma, in an environment composed of thousands of millions of other particles of all kinds, was pushed towards the earth's crust by tellurian pressures. How is it that a few rare specimens managed to stay totally pure? I will once again mention "Le Centenaire", a rough diamond of 599 carats that covered the width of my palm, absolutely free of inclusions and of an incomparable colourless tint! This is

equally miraculous for stones that are much smaller, even minuscule. Forming while surrounded by a multitude of particles yet remaining pure! This exception confirms the rule because, actually, when a diamond entirely encases an inclusion, or several inclusions, the latter are at least as old as the diamond itself. This inclusion is thus enclosed within the diamond for all eternity, coming from the very entrails of the earth, and presenting to our eyes an extraordinary package that reveals the roots of our earth's creation. Who among us does not seek to understand his roots? A diamond, with or without inclusions, makes up an important part of creation's history-book! Every diamond that contains an inclusion is unique, as are human beings. The purest diamonds are in fact more costly because they are much rarer, but this takes nothing from the unique, individualistic value of a diamond with an inclusion.'

New diamond cuts

'I am in the process of undertaking a study of the different cuts and forms of the cut diamond. There are at least 136, of which a dozen alone are round in shape. These are not only new cuts; there are many that have been in existence for quite a long time. And yet today, lapidary-artisans continue to create new ones; for instance, at Idar-Oberstein, I saw cuts that I never knew existed! We know that in the past man cut diamonds in a craftsman-like, unmathematical way, simply to facet the rough and give an agreeable shape to the stone without losing too much material. He did not try to improve refraction, only the reflection of light and transparency. By the same token, each stone was shaped differently, depending essentially on the form offered by nature. It was thus that the pear, marquise and oval cuts were born. In the course of time, diamond-cutters would apply the "Tolkowsky thesis" to these same forms. As for me, I wanted to enhance the value of coloured diamonds by perfecting the "Flower Cuts" – one of its principal attractions being the fact that it the presents the eye with homogeneity of colour. These cuts may be adapted to any natural shape of diamond, creating a perfect symmetry. The great advantage is in revealing the brilliance while respecting the initial form of the rough. Today, these cuts are highly esteemed and are requested even for white or colourless diamonds. 'Just as every colour has its follower, I have tried to make available to men and women the shape that, to their taste, is ideal, with a cut composed of new facets that reinforce the stone's fire and beauty. I shall conclude by affirming with conviction that we are merely at the infancy of creativity in the realm of cutting, and that in the years to come,

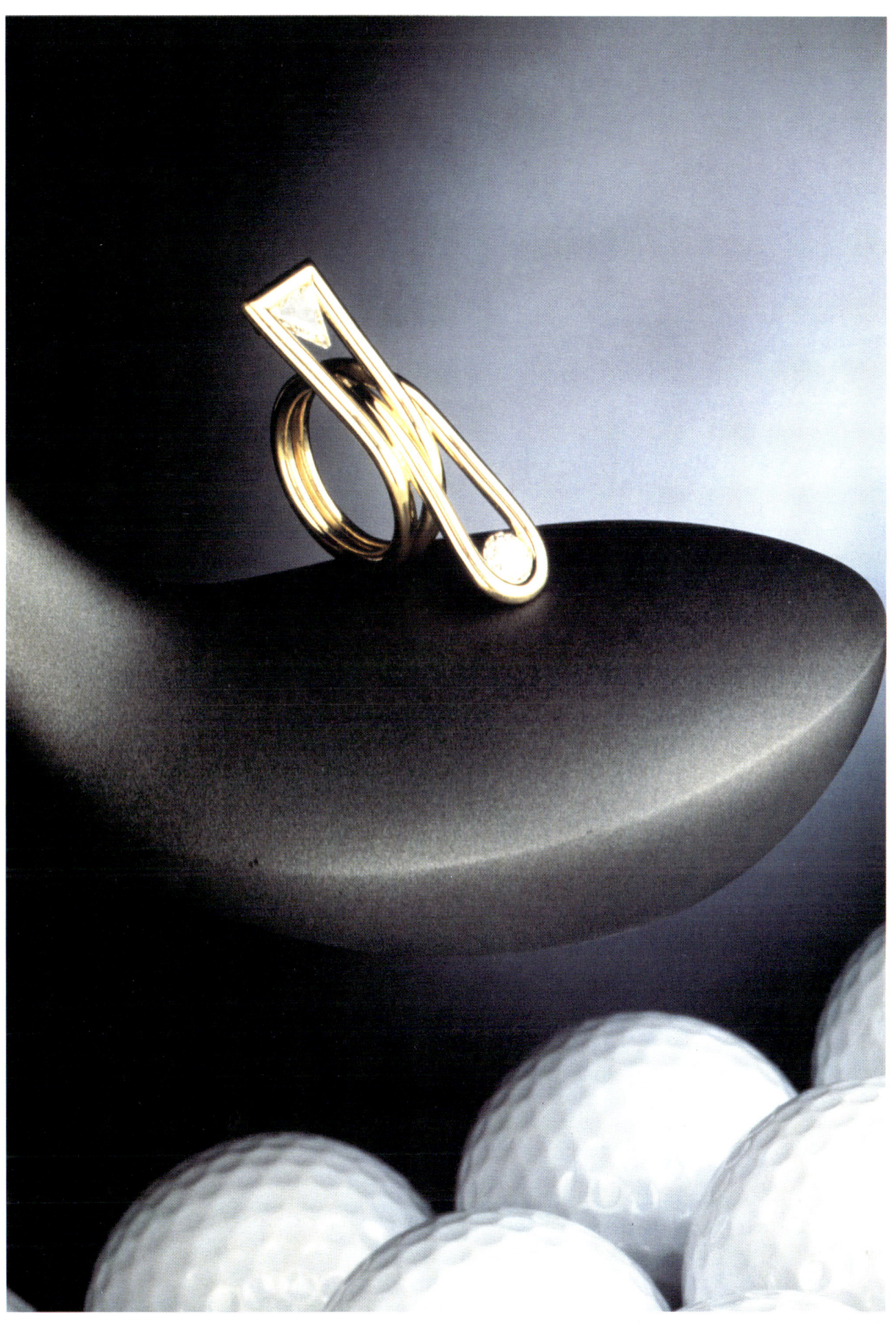

Ring in gold, brilliant and triangular diamond, created by Nancy Aillery.

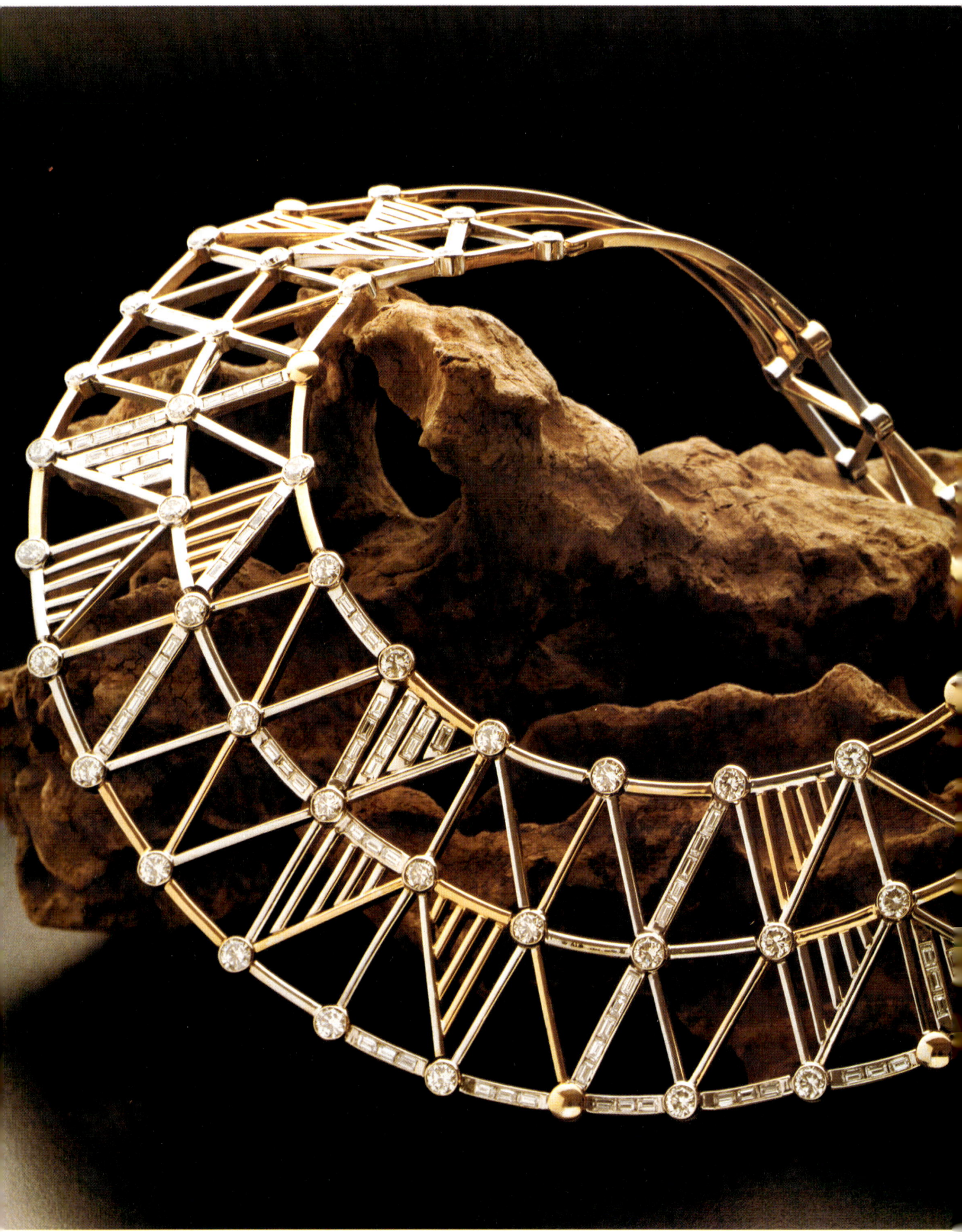

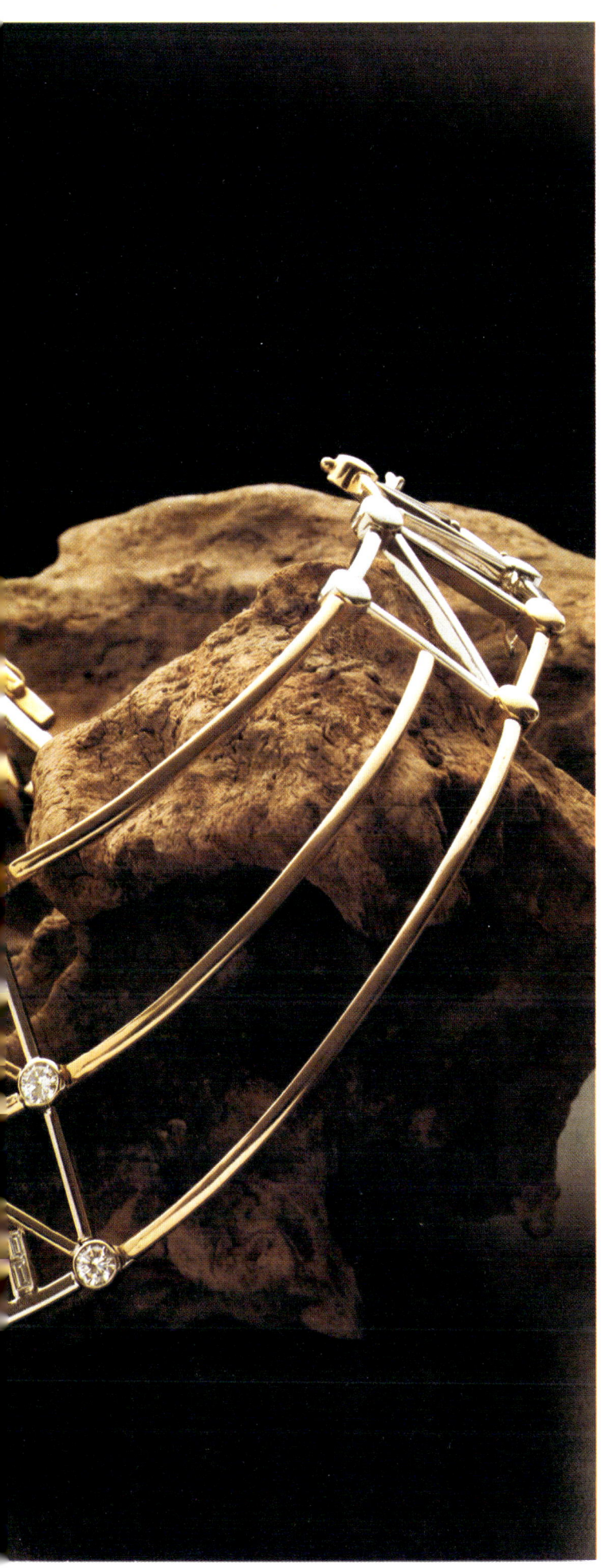

*Necklace
in gold and
diamonds by
Chelna Desai
of Bombay.*

we will certainly have more extraordinary ideas. Believe me, in today's world, it is essential to know how to "discover", and a diamond still gives us many chances for discovery. I leave the next discoveries to the younger generation. Finally, is a diamond not proof of tenderness, love, friendship? Life, beauty, mystery, history, attraction? Companion of the past and of the future, for the well-being of men!' Conversing with Gabriel Tolkowsky is certainly an enriching experience. A man who knows his craft perfectly and who, moreover, is able to convey sincerely to his interlocutors his passion for the material he loves. Here is a collection of jewels made by Belgian creators, mostly with 'Flower Cuts'.

103

'MARIGOLD' CUT

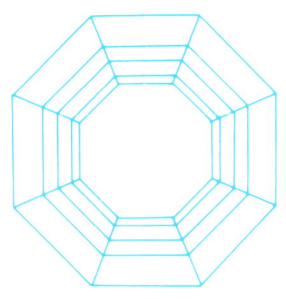

UPPER VIEW
(CROWN)

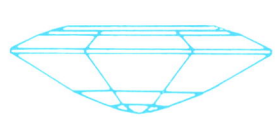

SIDE VIEW

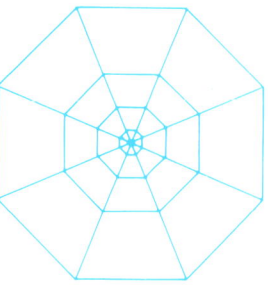

LOWER VIEW
(BREECH)

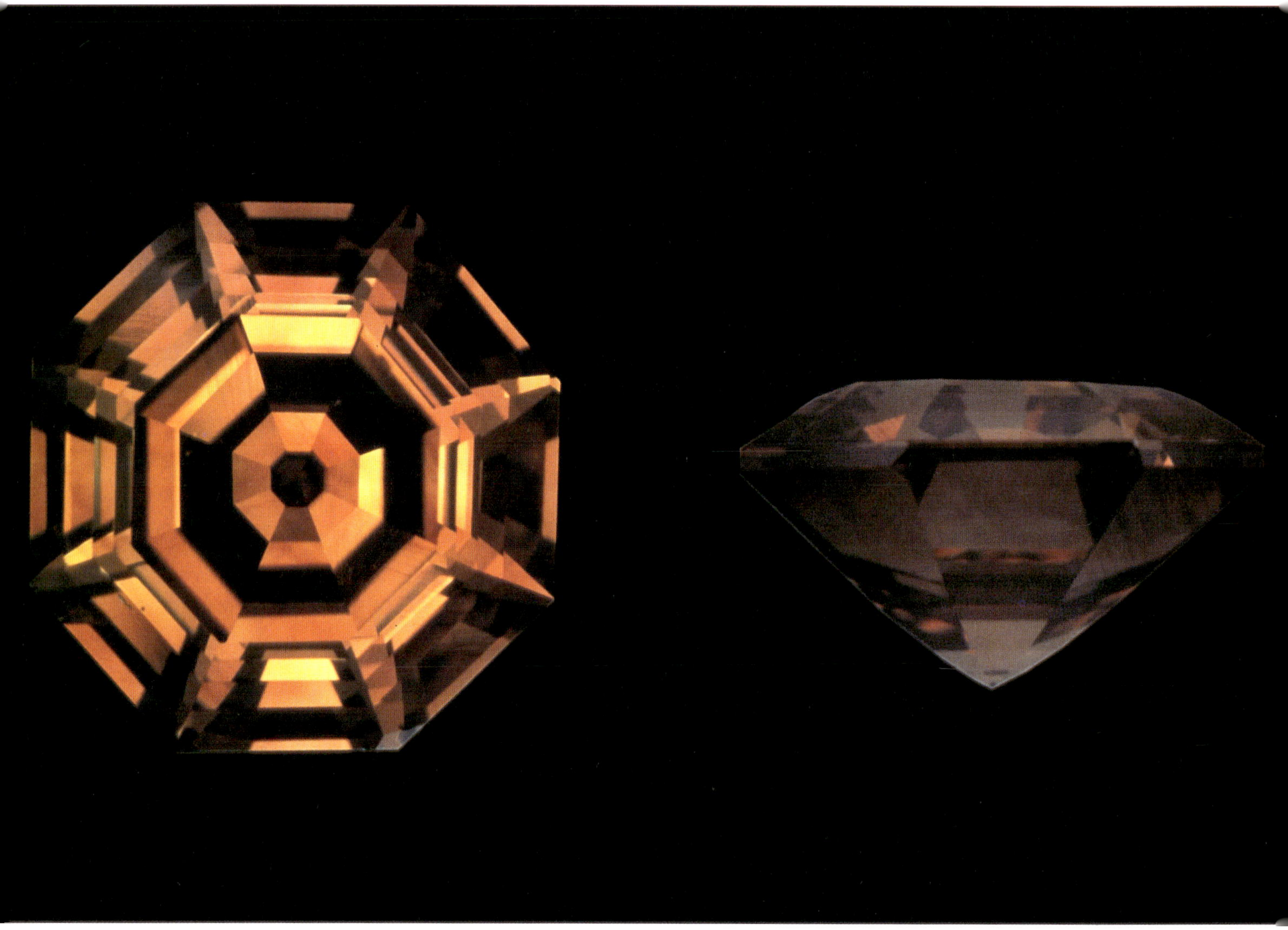

The 'Marigold' cut is composed of 73 facets.

104

'FIRE ROSE' CUT

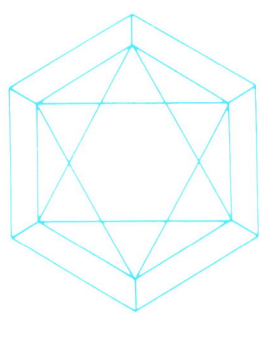

UPPER VIEW

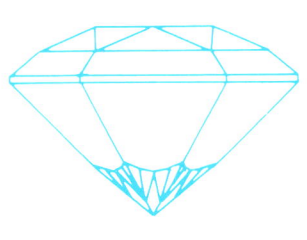

SIDE VIEW

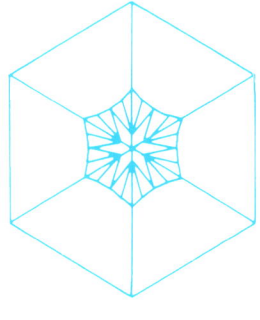

LOWER VIEW

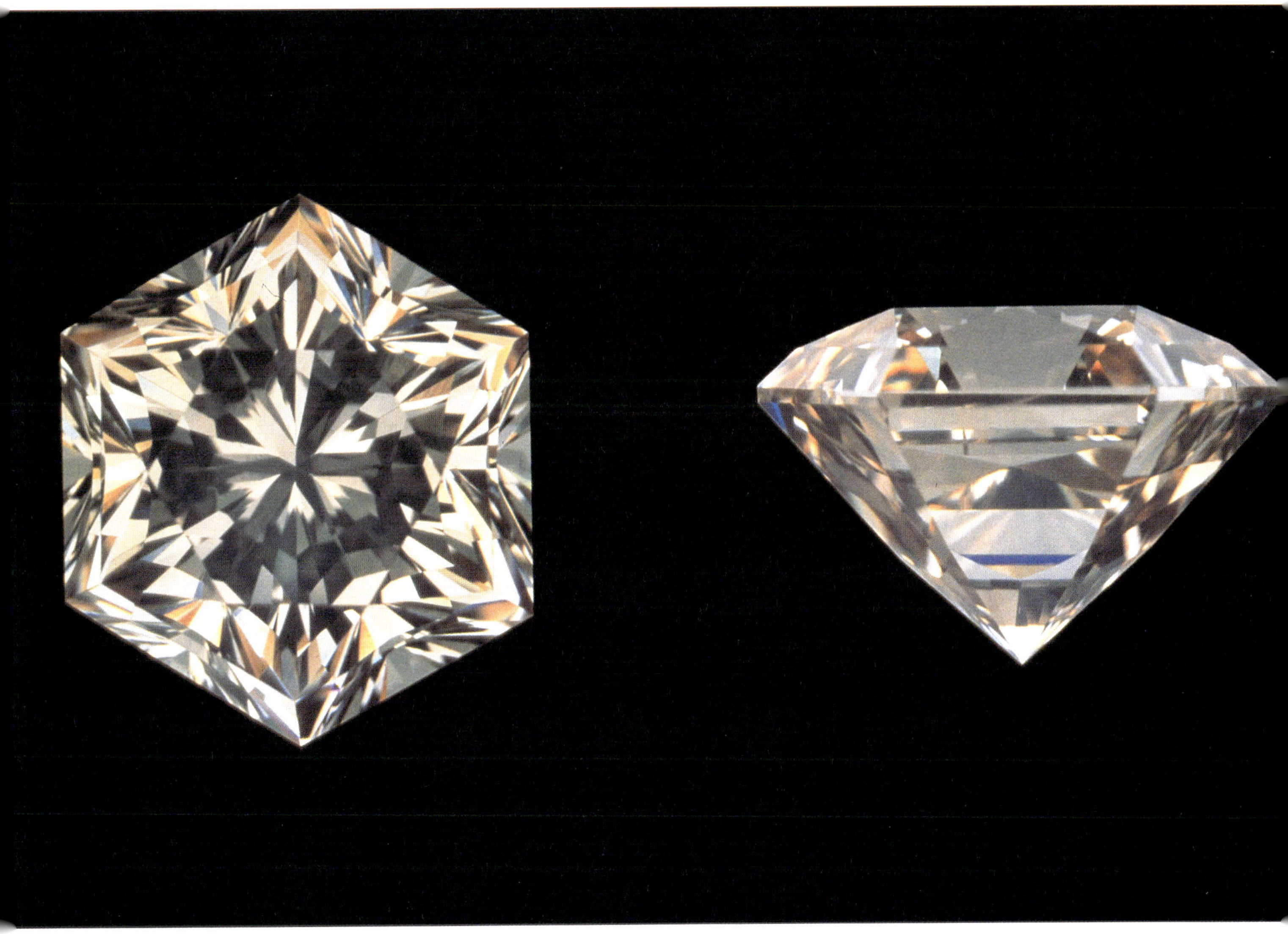

Note the multitude of little facets that garnish the bottom of the breech; these facets enhance the brilliance of the 'Fire Rose' cut.

'SUNFLOWER' CUT

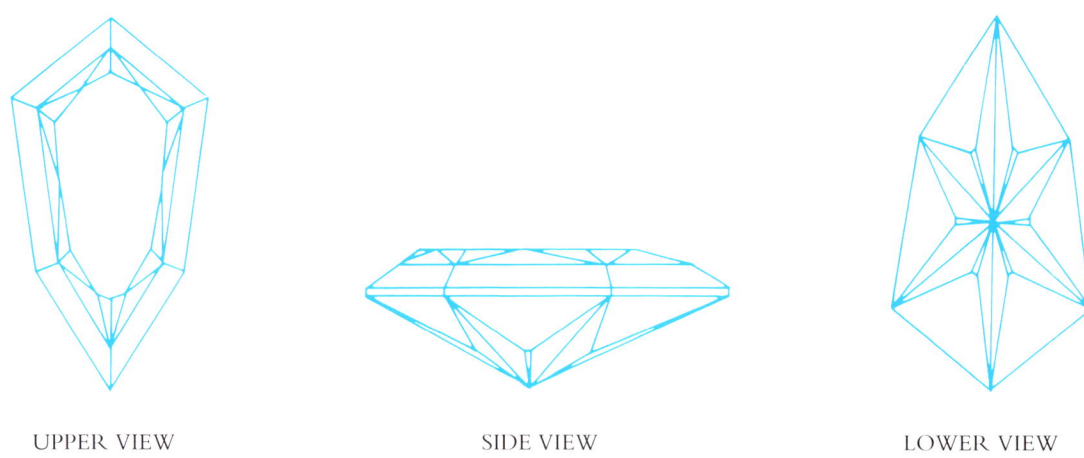

UPPER VIEW   SIDE VIEW   LOWER VIEW

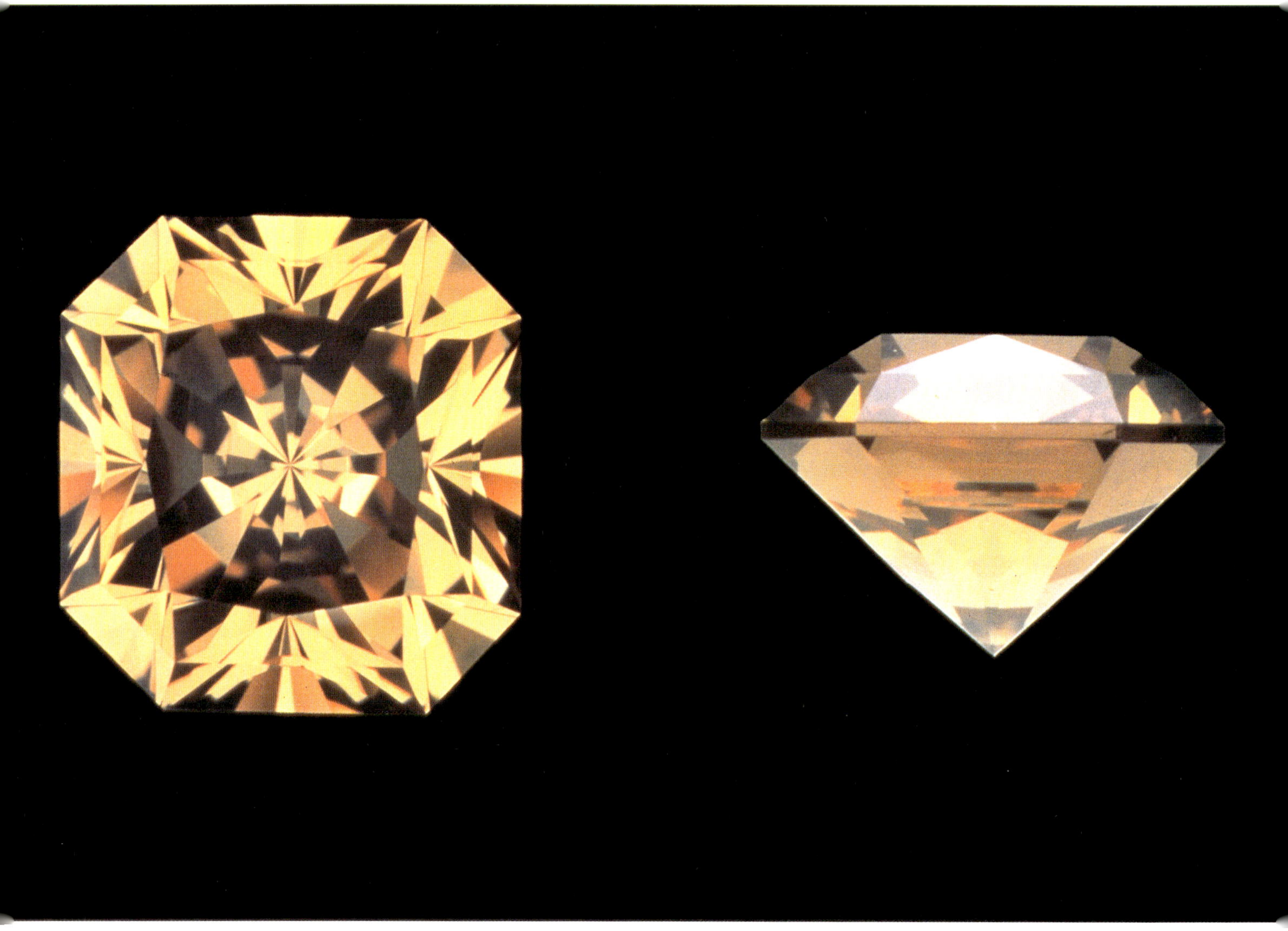

Each of the cuts in the 'Flower Cuts' series may be adapted to the original shape as well as any other shape. In this
illustration, a square 'Sunflower' cut of 43 facets.

'ZINNIA' CUT

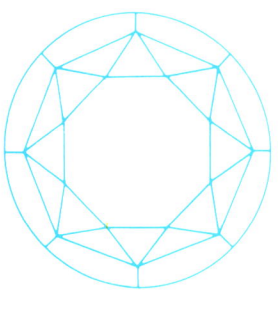

UPPER VIEW

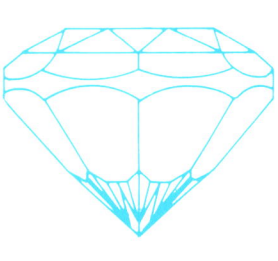

SIDE VIEW

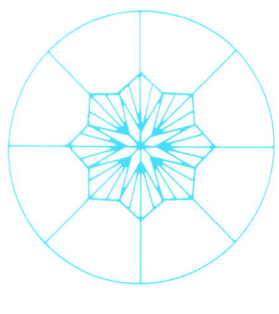

LOWER VIEW

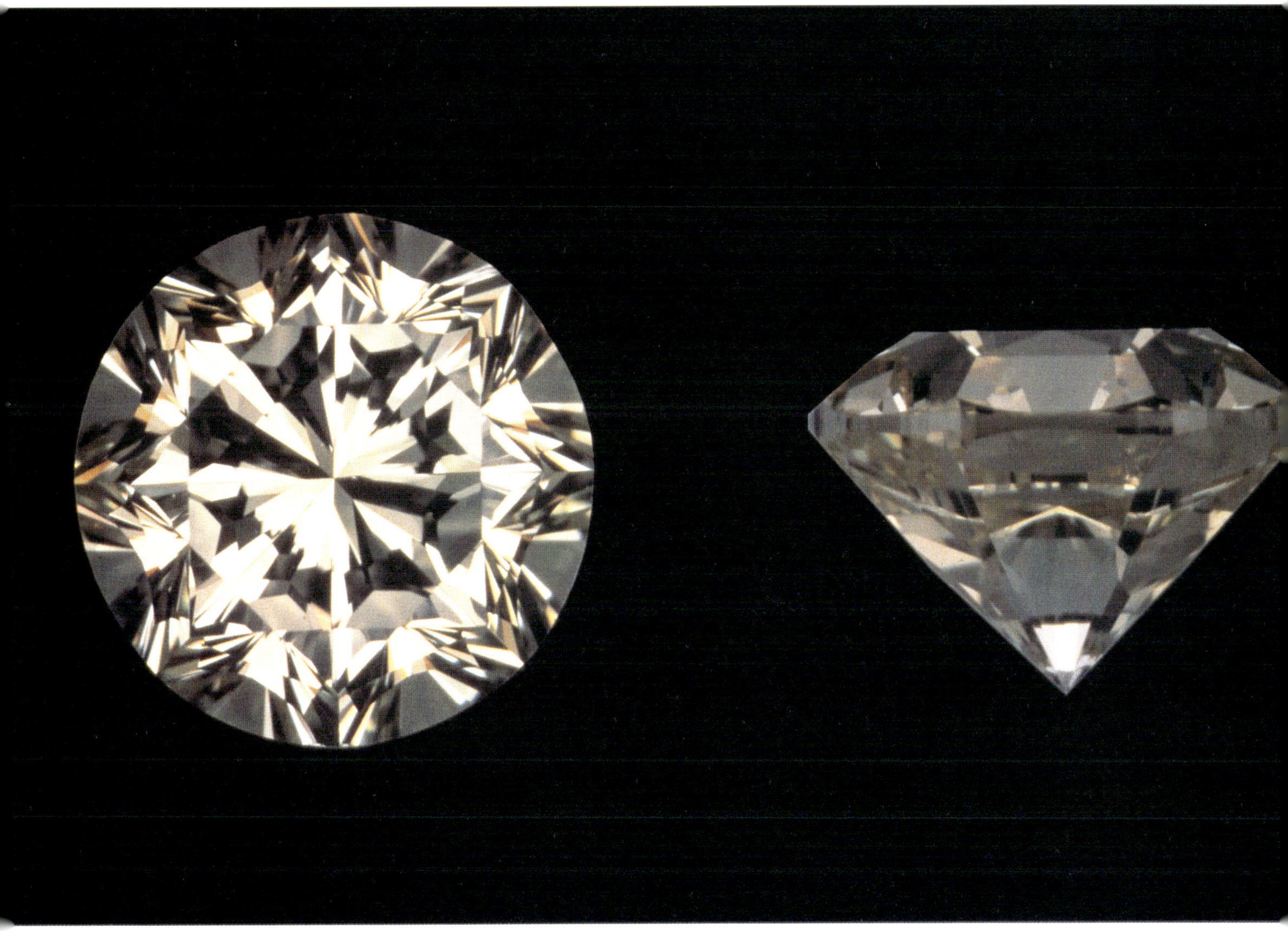

More brilliant than a brilliant, the 'Zinnia' cut has extraordinary fires.

'DAHLIA' CUT

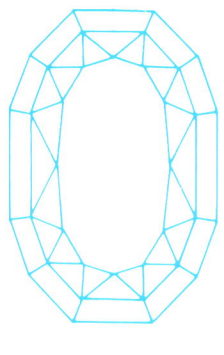

UPPER VIEW

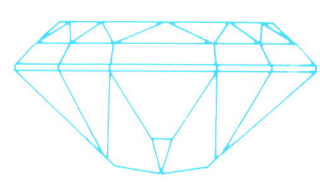

SIDE VIEW

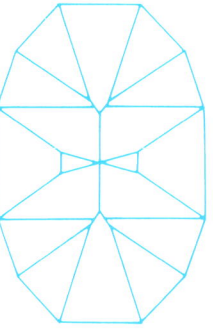

LOWER VIEW

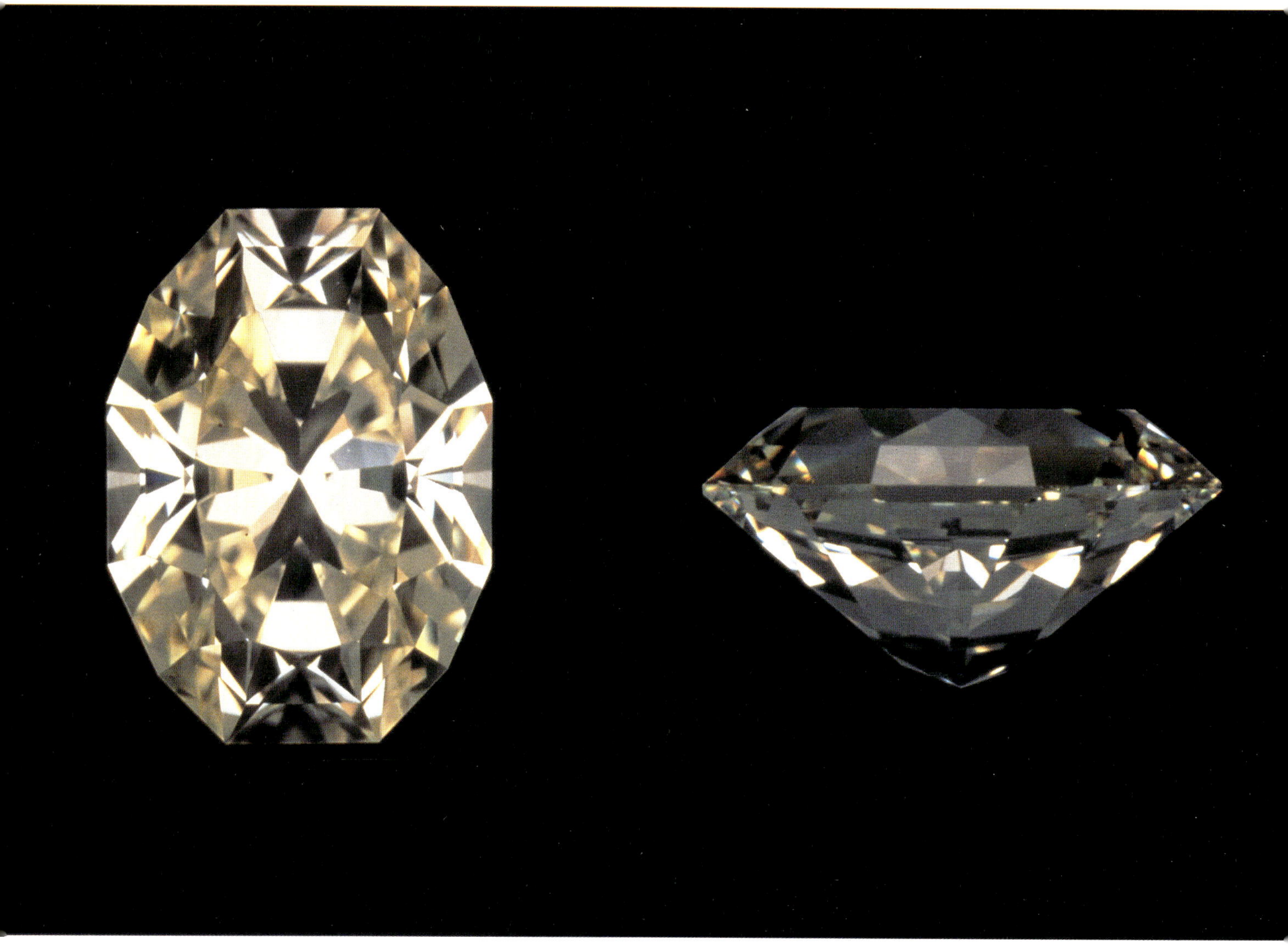

The 'Dahlia' cut is composed of 63 facets distributed on 12 sides.

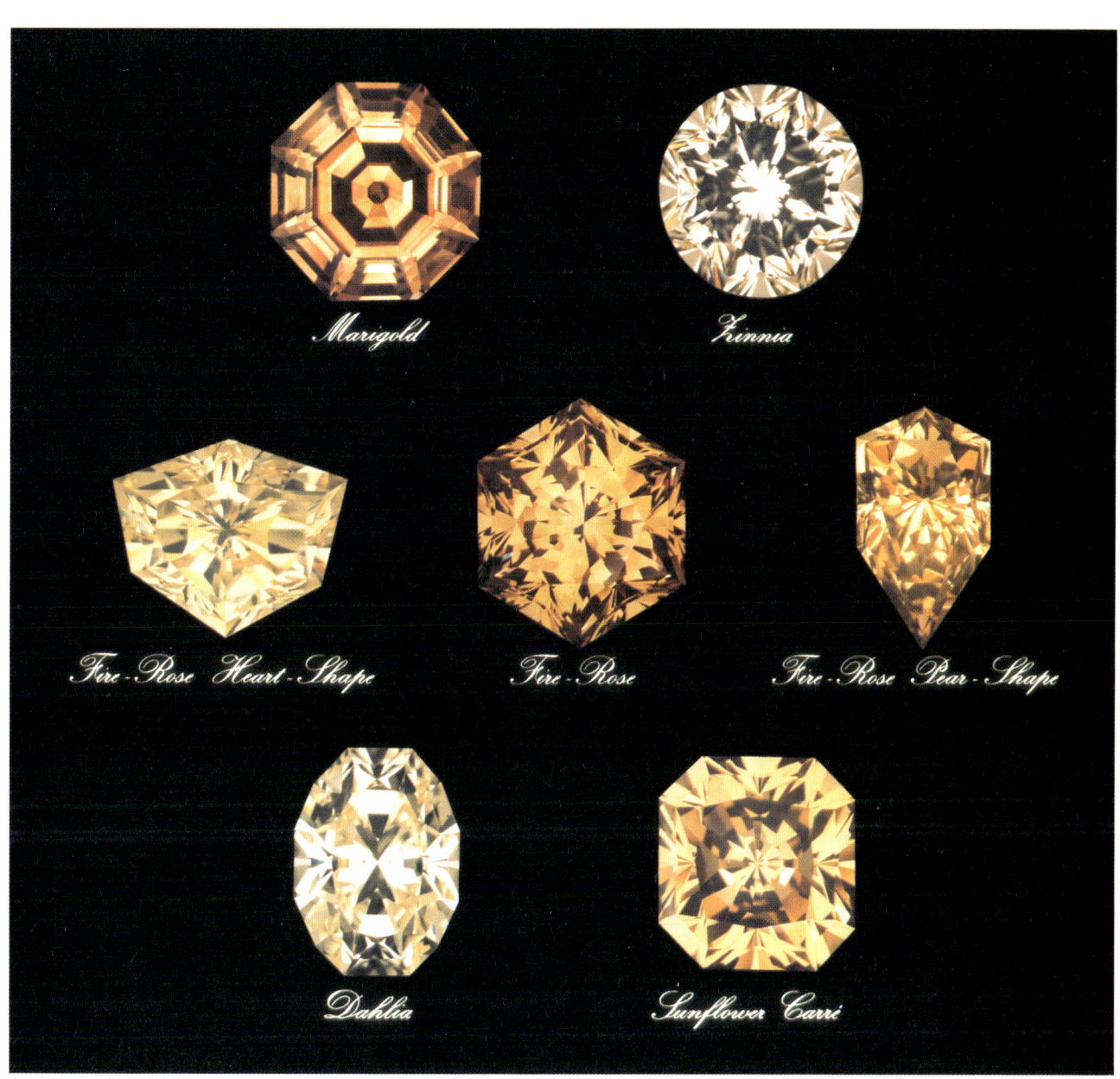

Marigold   Zinnia

Fire-Rose Heart-Shape   Fire-Rose   Fire-Rose Pear-Shape

Dahlia   Sunflower Carré

Gabriel Tolkowsky's 'Flower Cuts' may be adapted to every shape and colour of diamond.

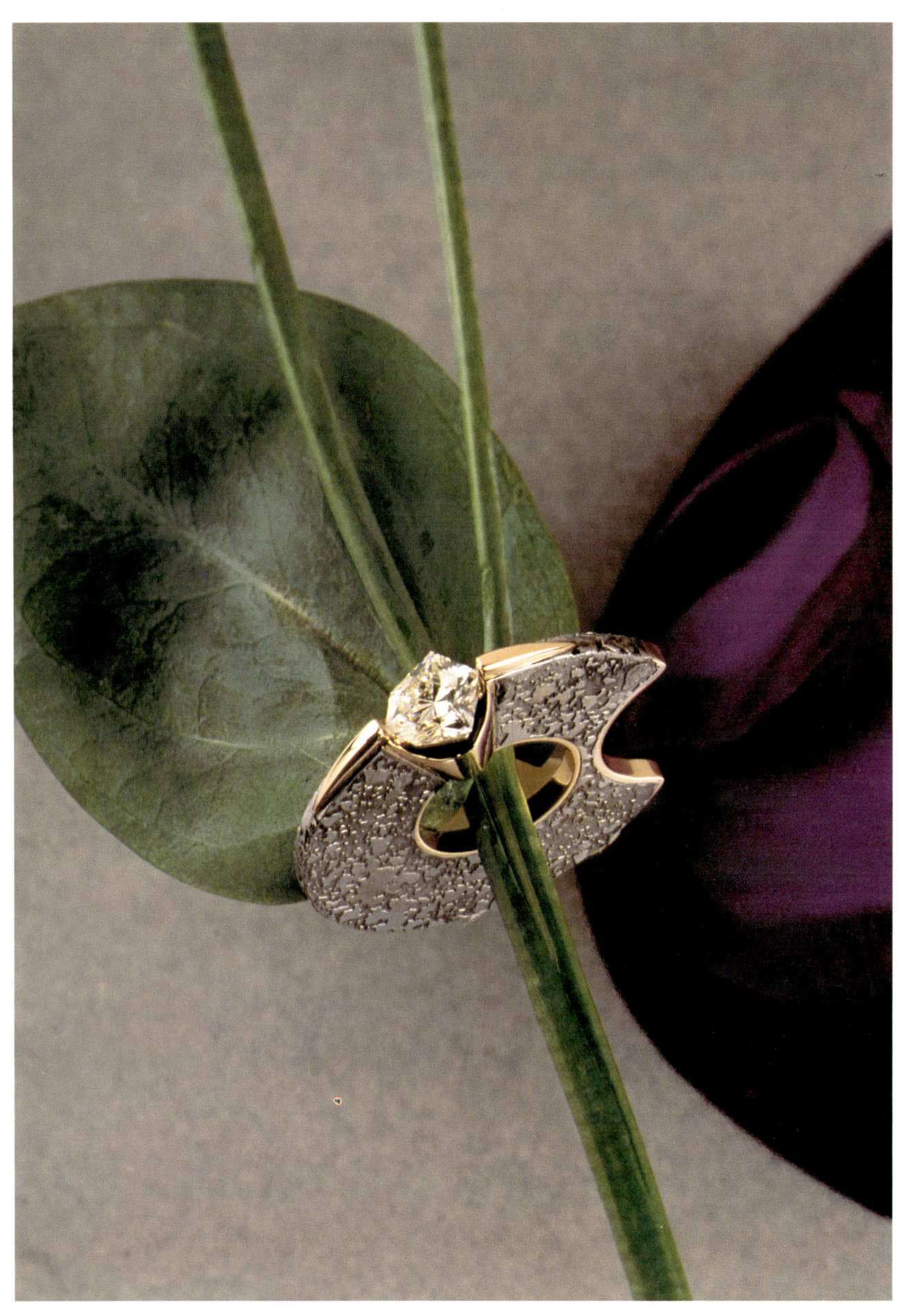

Georges Cuyvers: to be worn on the little finger! Ring in the shape of a disk in which pitted iron is mixed with yellow gold and with ebony. At the summit, a splendid 'Sunflower'-cut diamond gleams.

110

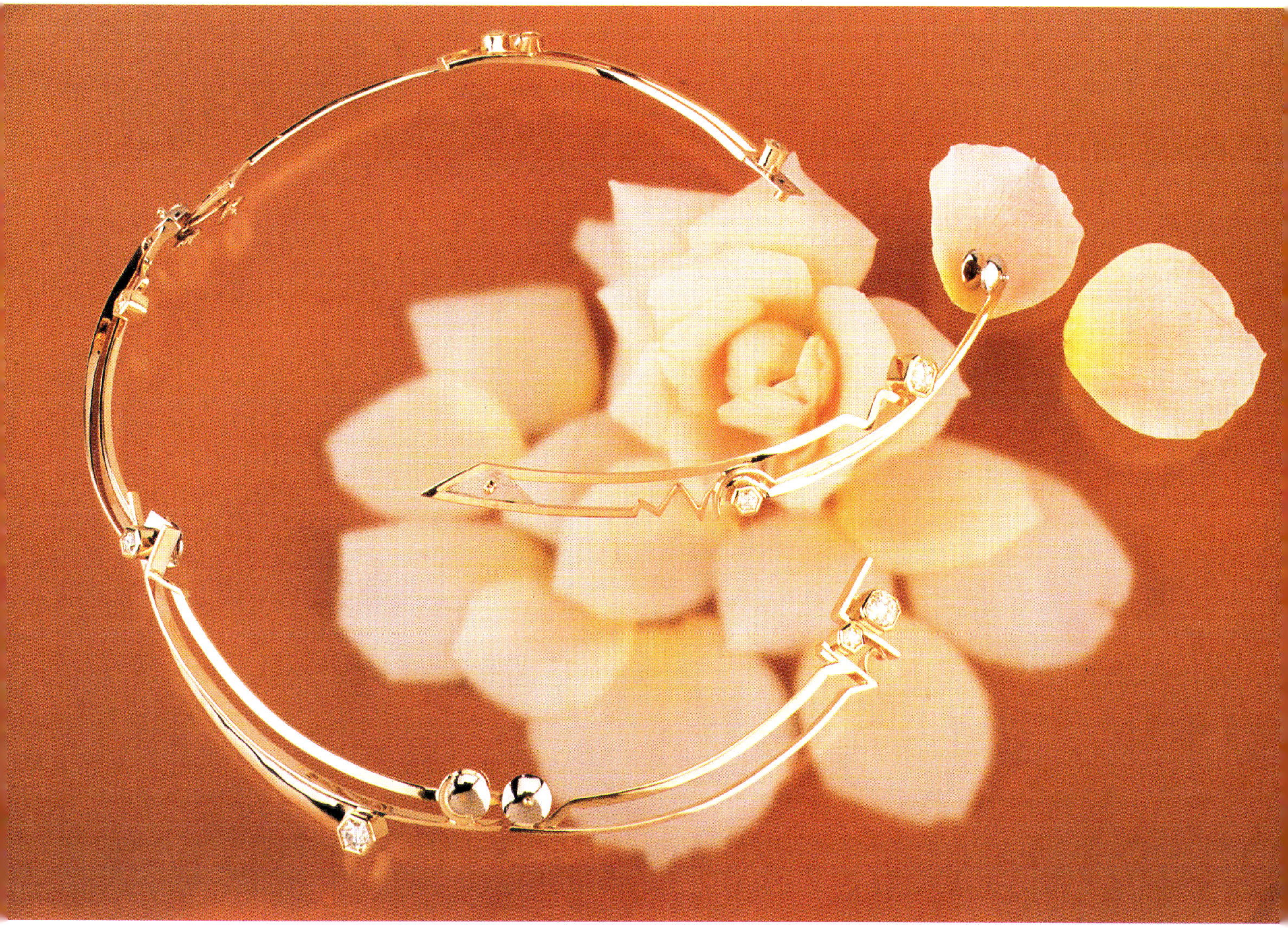

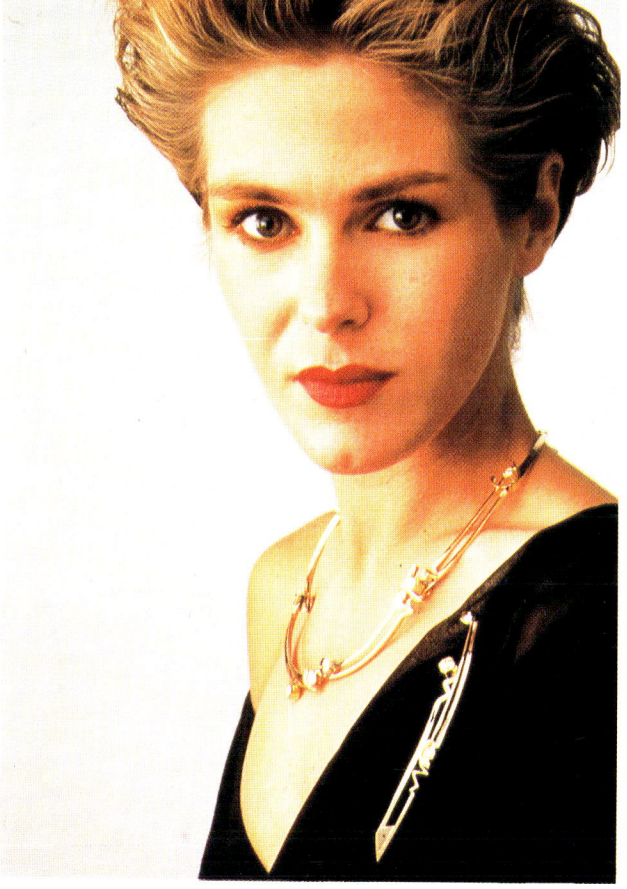

Jo Den Haerynck: five brooches whose undulating lines recall the signs of the Arabic alphabet, strung into an elegant necklace. Nine diamonds of 'Fire Rose' and 'Marigold' cuts are the sparkling links in this graceful symbol of communication.

111

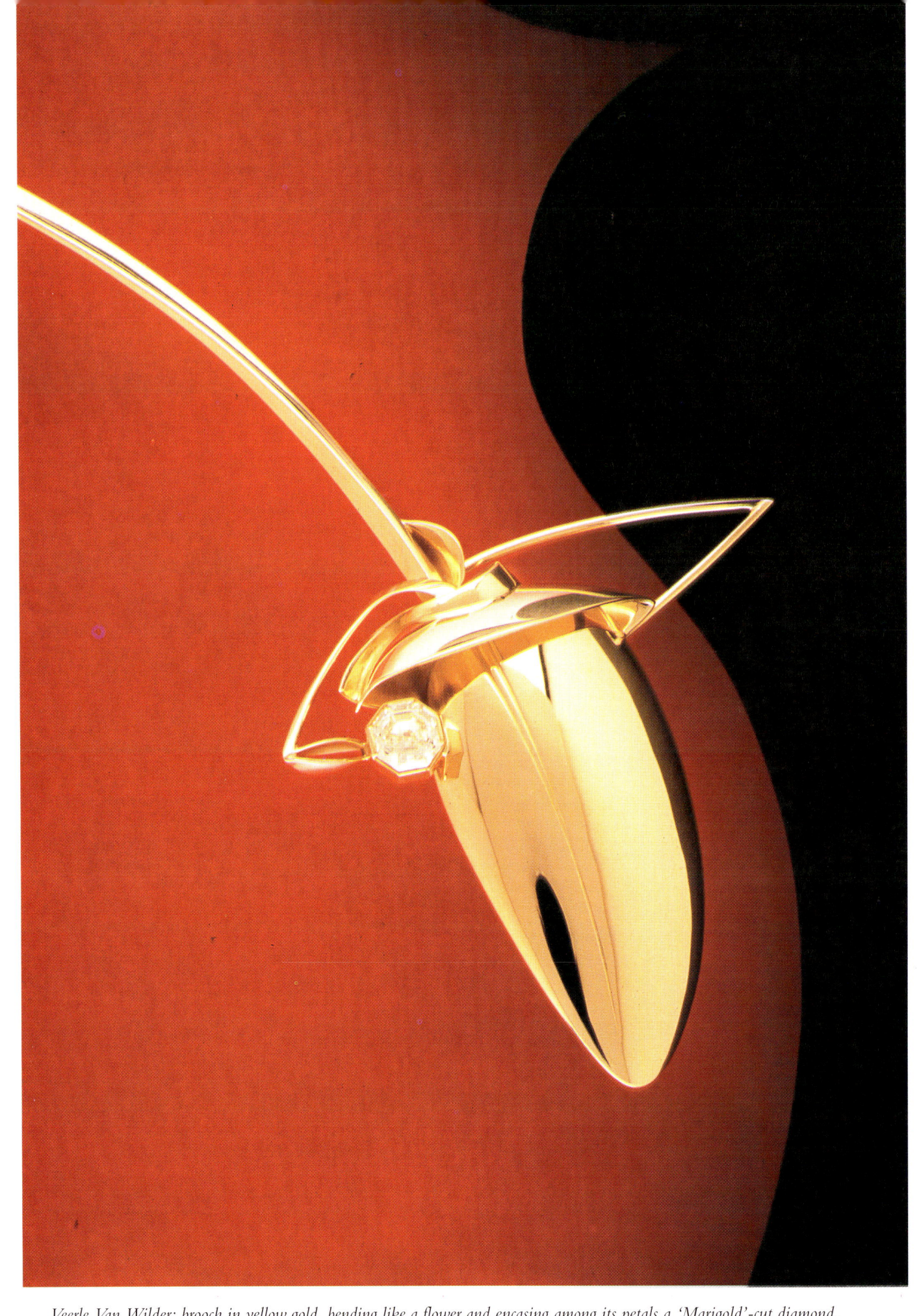

Veerle Van Wilder: brooch in yellow gold, bending like a flower and encasing among its petals a 'Marigold'-cut diamond.

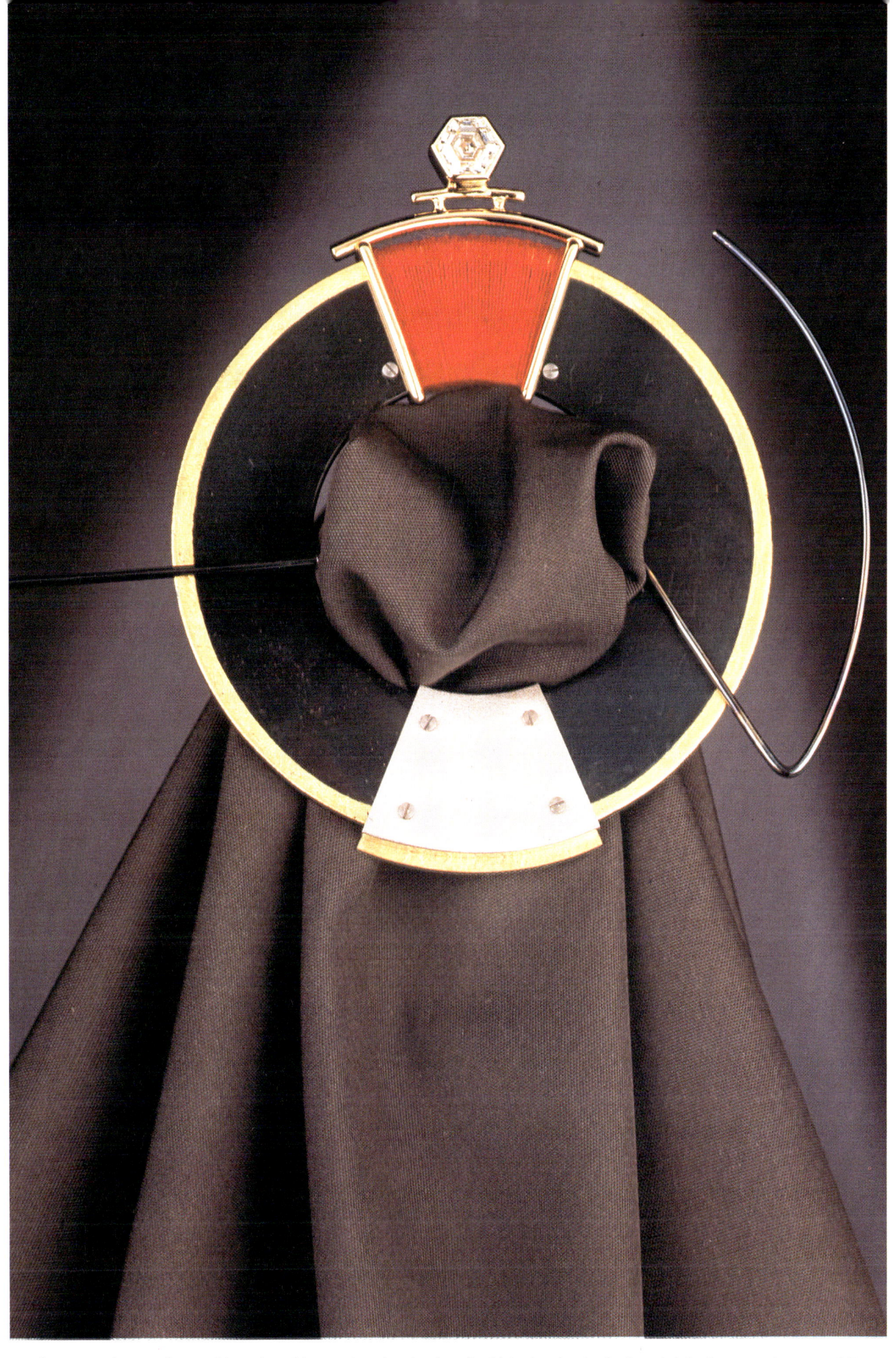

Arlette Van de Graaf: round brooch in blue steel with a border of gold leaf and red silk thread. The hexagonal 'Marigold'-cut diamond dominates the creation. When displayed on a steel stand, the diamond brooch is transformed into a contemporary work of art.

113

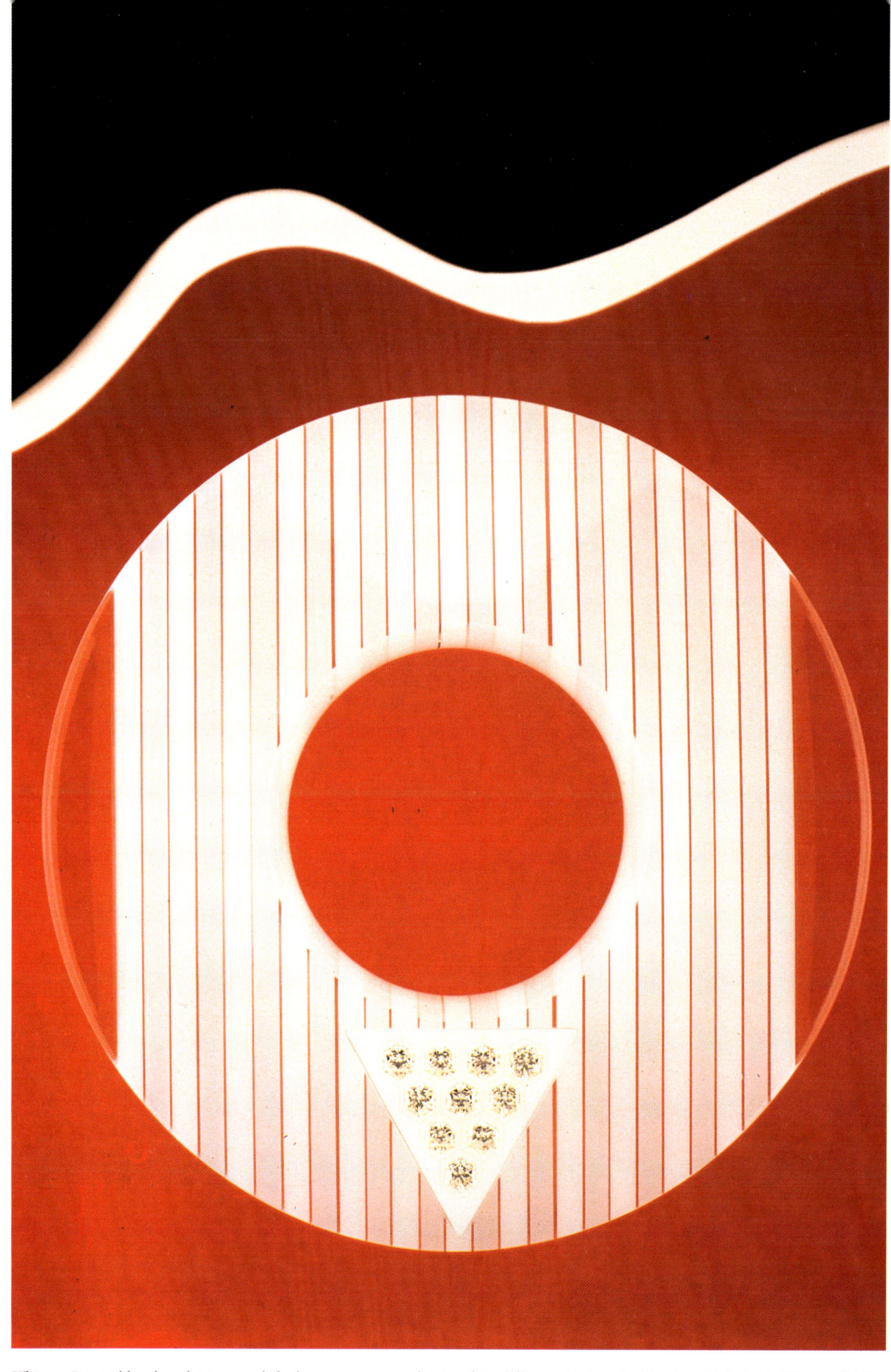

Thierry Bontridder: bracelet in unpolished, transparent acrylic tinted in different shades of white, in which the brilliance of 10 light yellow diamonds of 'Fire Rose' cut is contrasted.

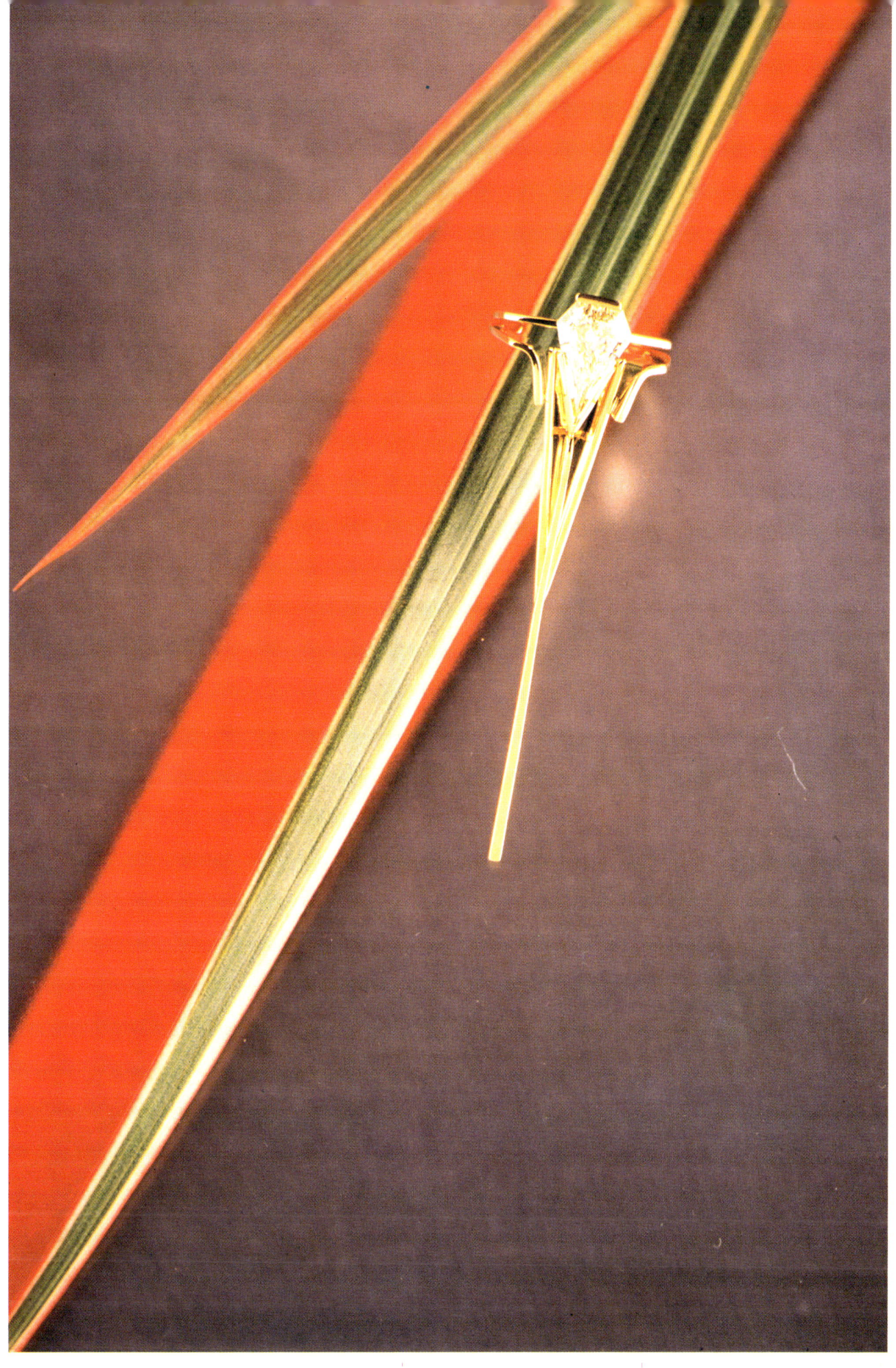

Koen Wygaerden: an elongated ring in yellow gold that recalls the elegant flight of a dragonfly, whose heart is formed by a dazzling 'Marigold'-cut diamond.

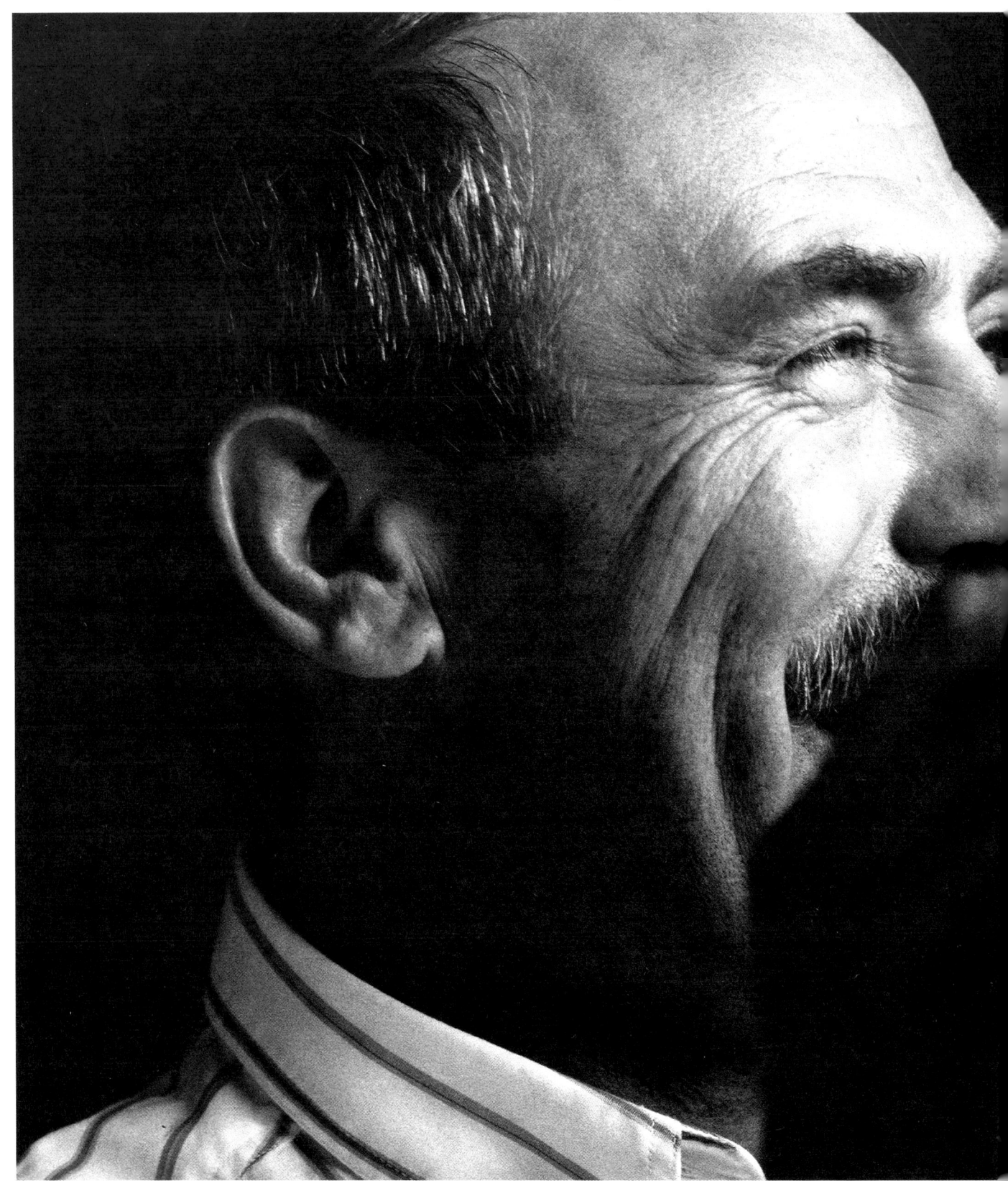

CHAPTER III

THE IMPORTANCE OF FINE STONES

In collaboration with Bernd Munsteiner

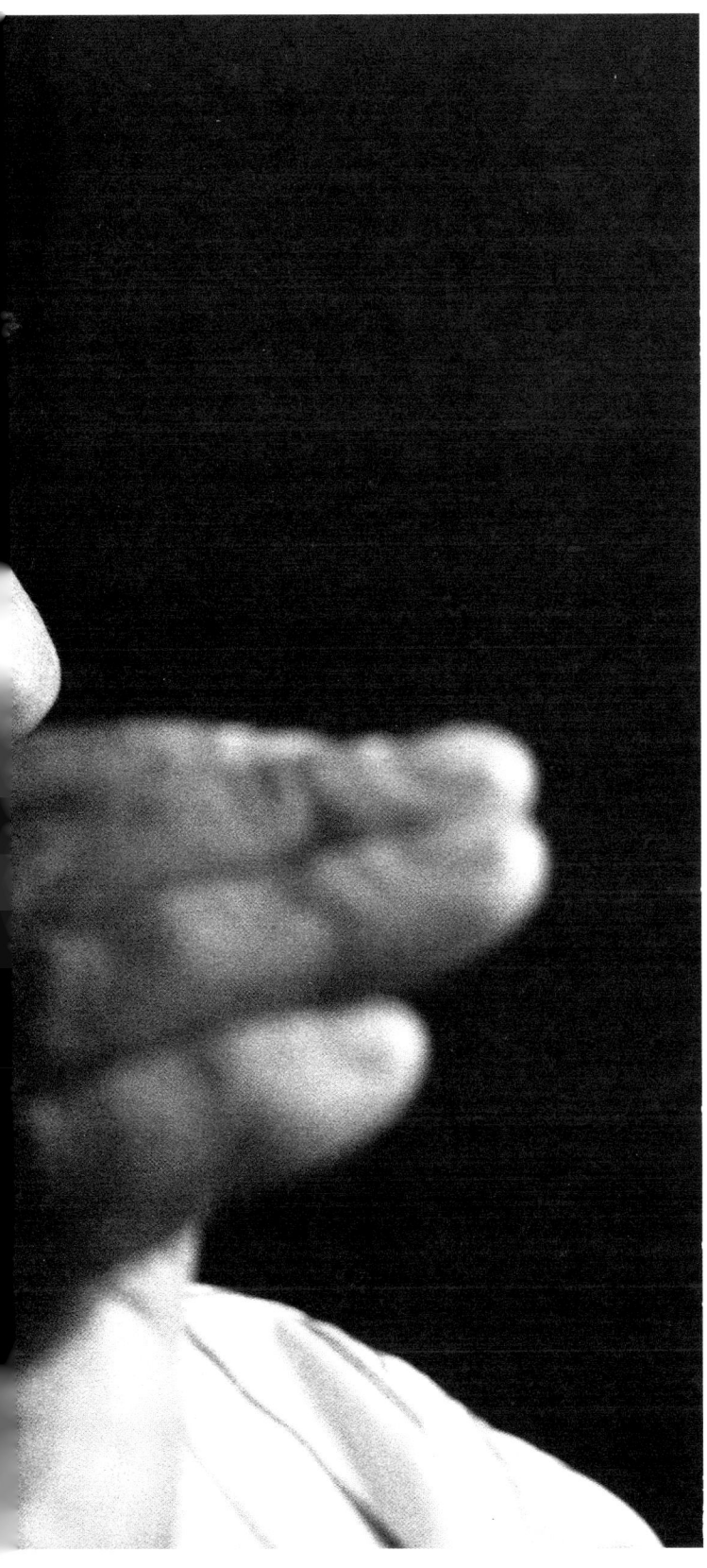

Stones offer jewel creators an infinity of possibilities, combinations and contrasts, thanks to their multitude of colours and shades.

No stone is exactly the same colour as another, even if they both come from the same crystal. As we have already seen with the diamond, theoretically every person could have his own stone that would be different from all others. These nuances are imperceptible to the human eye, of course, yet they truly do exist. Thus, when form is considered along with colour, the possibilities become literally unlimited.

Until the beginning of the 20th century, only a few hundred shapes were used in the cutting of stones. Today, thanks to modern techniques and the imagination of creators and artisans, hundreds of thousands of forms exist, and yet, according to some stone-cutters, we are only at the beginning of creation in this domain. Bernd Munsteiner, considered today to be the world's most important lapidary, has contributed greatly to the advancement of this art. Here he relates his history, his conclusions and his predilections in the field of cutting fine stones.

'Within my family, we know that my grandfather Albert was working in Idar-Oberstein by 1890. It is almost certain that he learned his trade from his father, because specialised schools did not exist at the time. My father Viktor had a lapidary studio from 1930 on. I myself began my professional activity in 1957, during the course of my studies and education at the 'Fachhochschule für Gestaltung' in Pforzheim, which continued until 1966. Finally, in 1973, I was established in my own studio in Stipshausen, near Idar-Oberstein. My two sons are also in the trade, Jurg is a jeweller and Tom has dedicated himself to stone-cutting, having opened a workshop in Pazzallo-Lugano in 1984.

'In the history of stones, it must be noted that practically nothing had changed since the Middle Ages. Even my grandfather and my father cut classical stones in response to the demands of the market.

'Right after my studies began, I decided to do something different, out of the ordinary; I wanted to change traditions while still respecting them. I wanted to give a new direction to this art; it was my deepest ambition. To this end, I was inspired by the Renaissance and what the great masters of

117

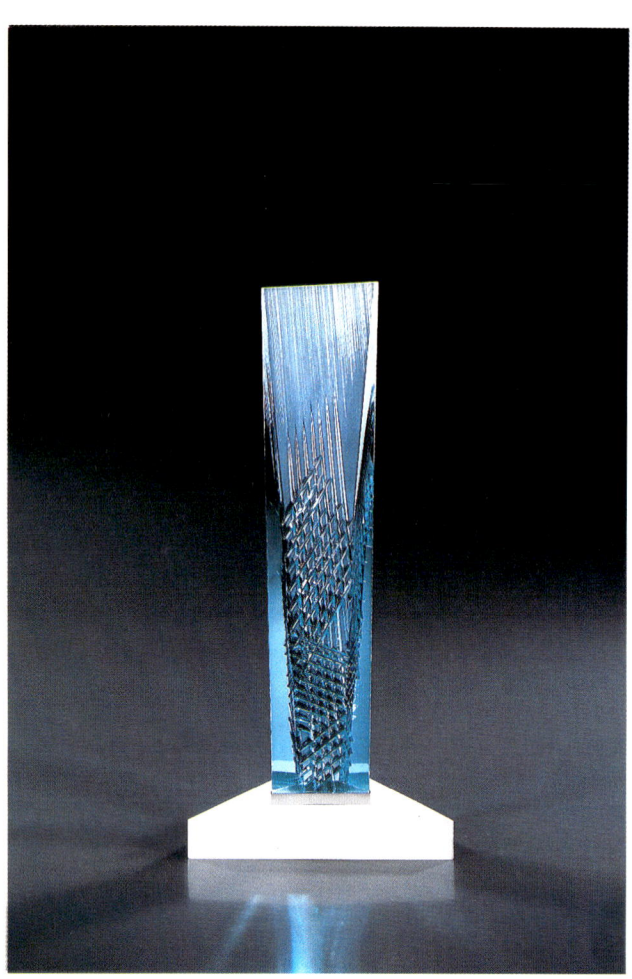

that era had done. So I was the first to cut stones in a different way, using modern techniques. From the round or oval stone, I moved to a completely asymmetrical style; I was especially concerned with total reflection and light. When I examine a raw stone, I try to imagine the places where its fires can best sparkle. Since that day in 1960, a sort of chain-reaction began in Idar-Oberstein. Today, many lapidaries all over the world are designing and working stones in contemporary and asymmetrical shapes.

'But we are only at the beginning of a renaissance of stone-cutting; today I sense that more renewal is yet to come, especially when I see my son creating extraordinary forms.

'I am profoundly convinced that the classical cuts will slowly disappear around the end of the millennium, to give way to new cuts that will certainly become the standard in the 21st century.'

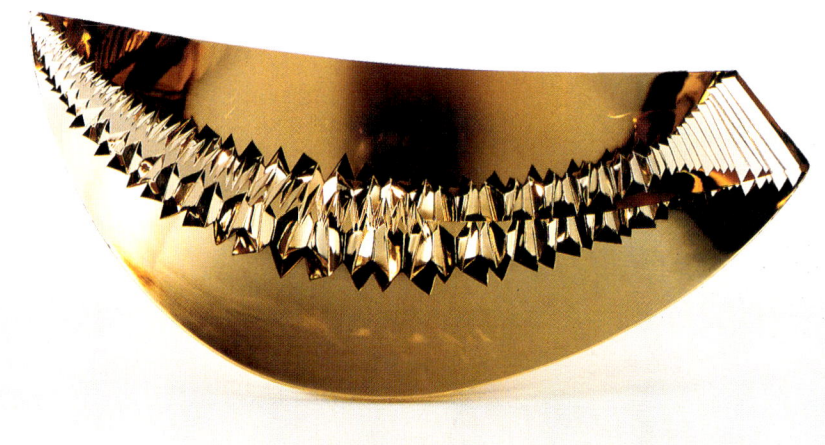

Smoky quartz cut by Bernd Munsteiner.

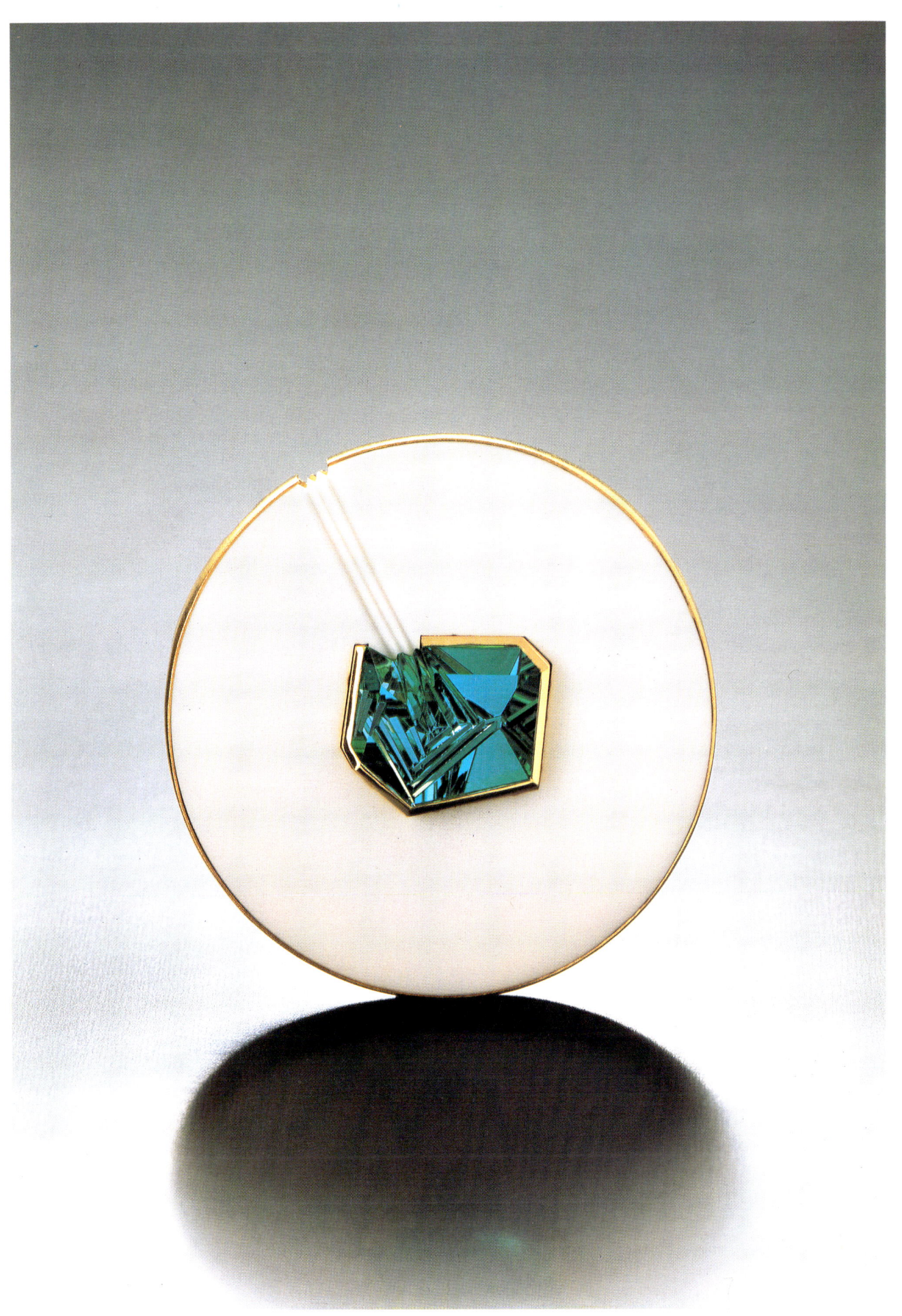

Brooch in white agate, tourmaline and gold by Bernd Munsteiner.

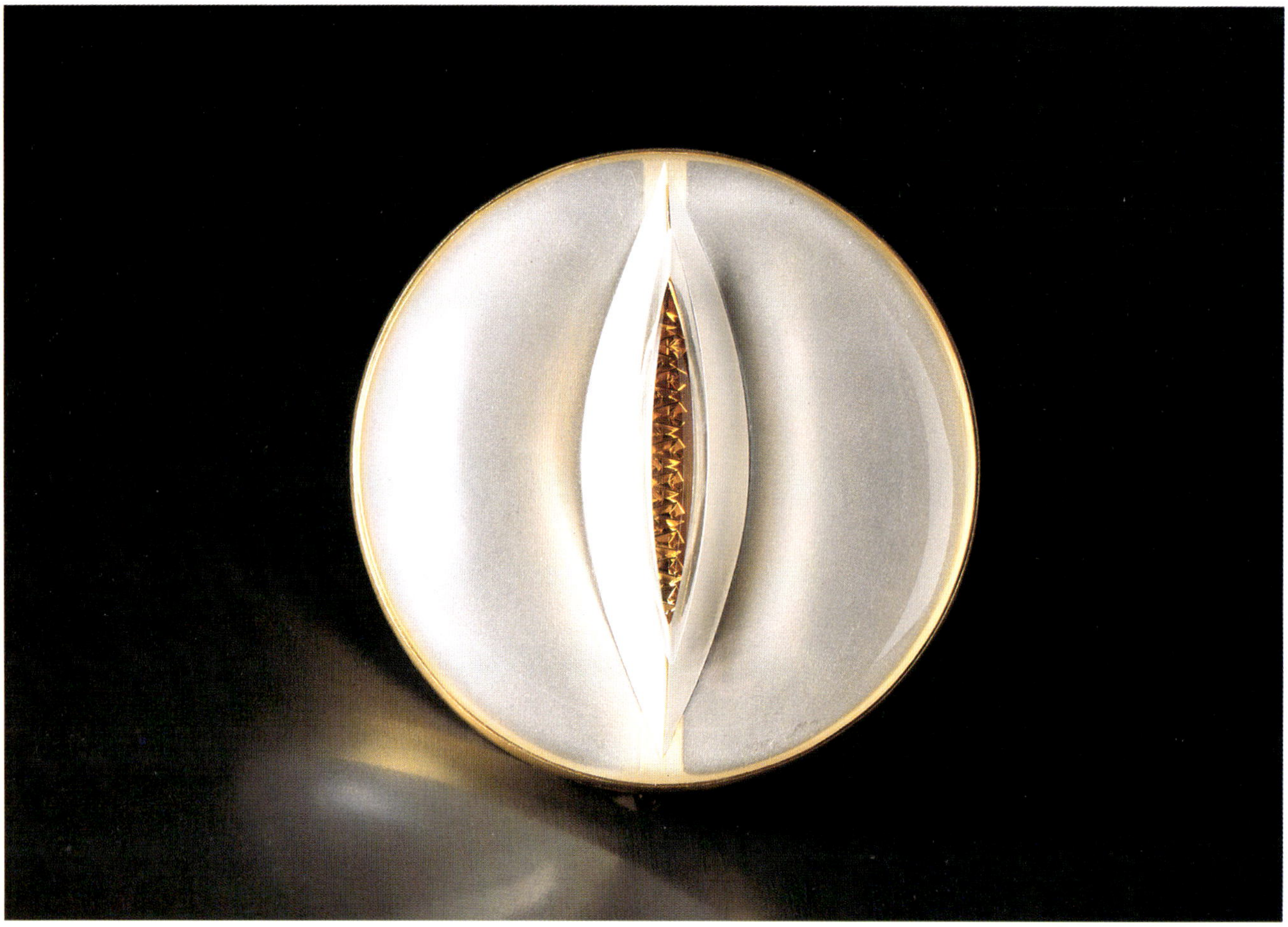

Two brooches by Bernd Munsteiner in white agate, citrine quartz, pink tourmaline and gold.

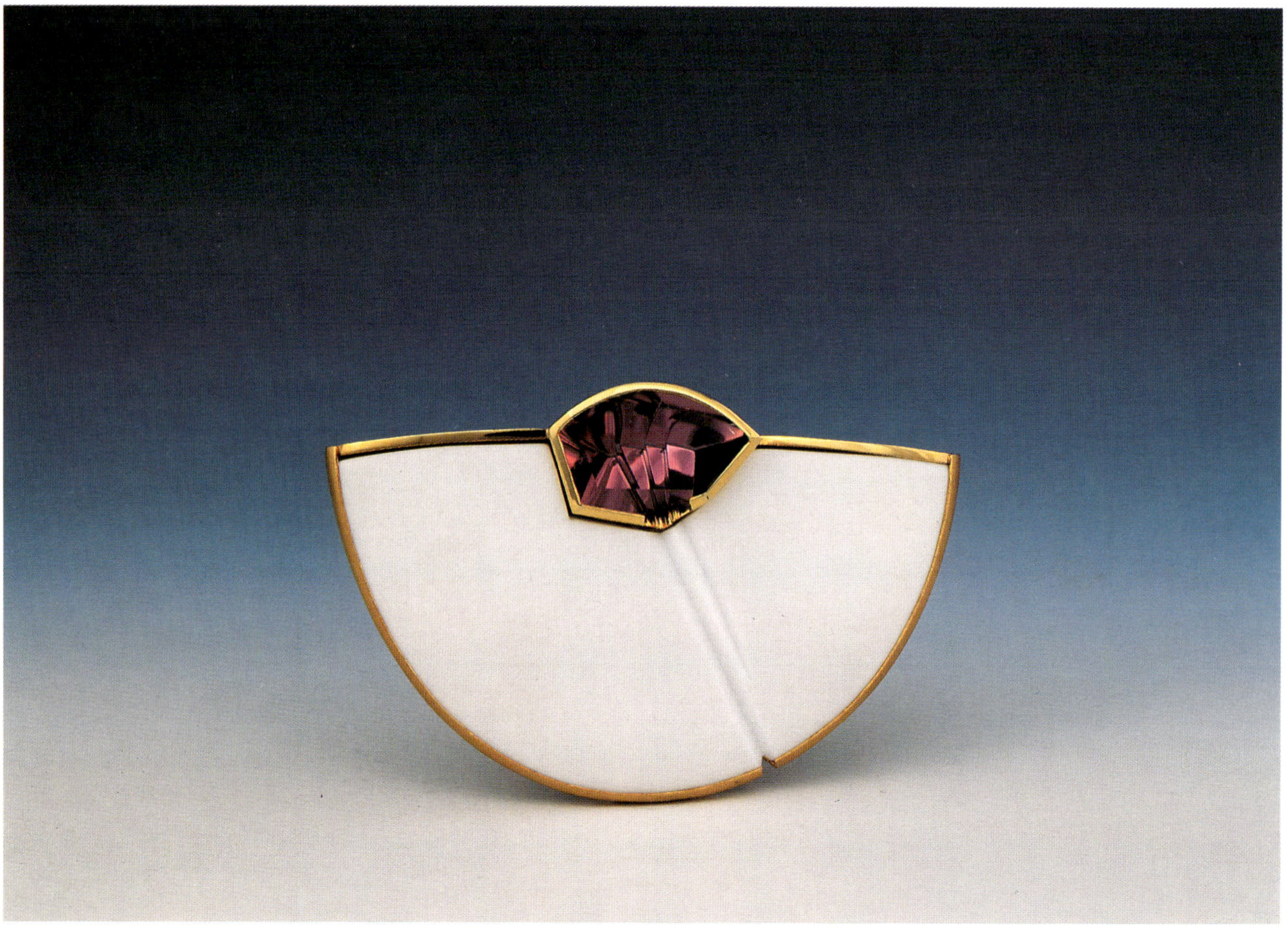

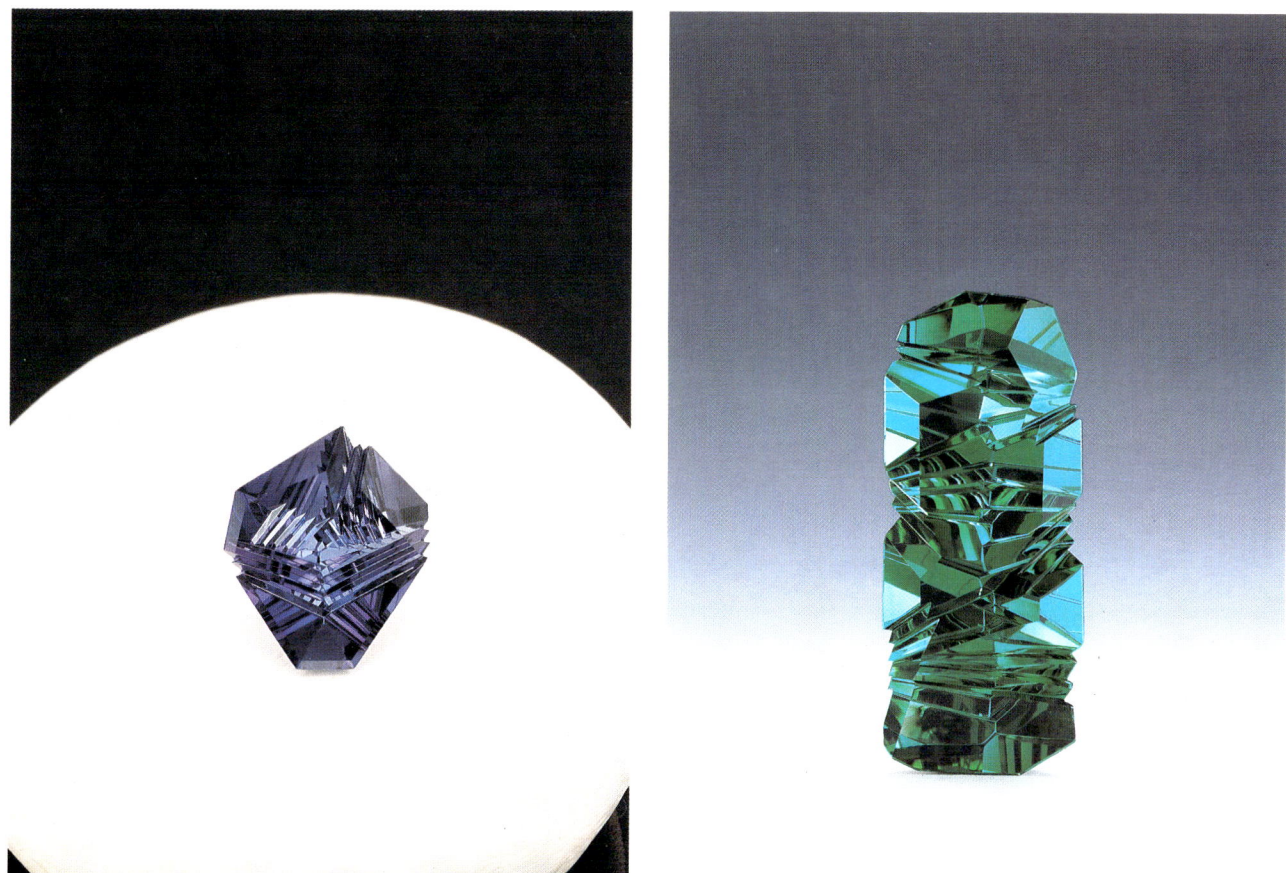

Tanzanite, tourmaline, aquamarine and blue topaz in a new style, asymmetrical and contemporary. 'We are only at the beginning of creativity in stone-cutting,' Bernd Munsteiner asserts.

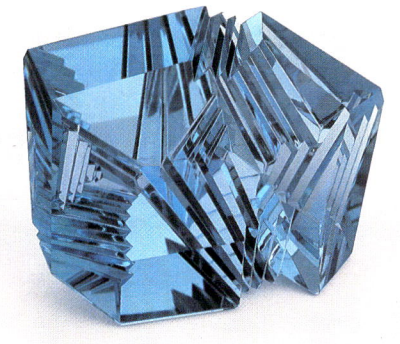

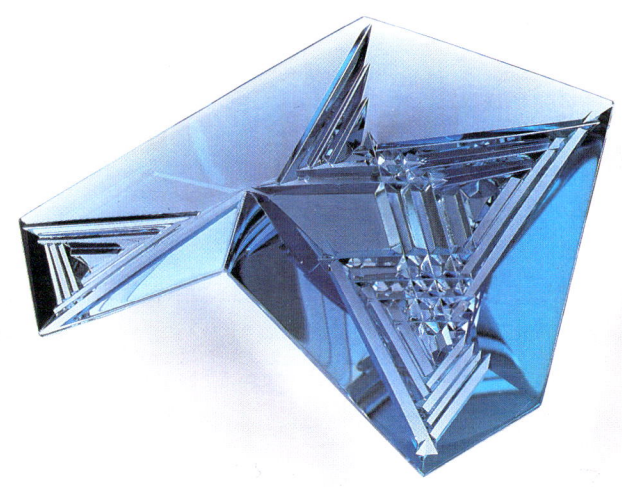

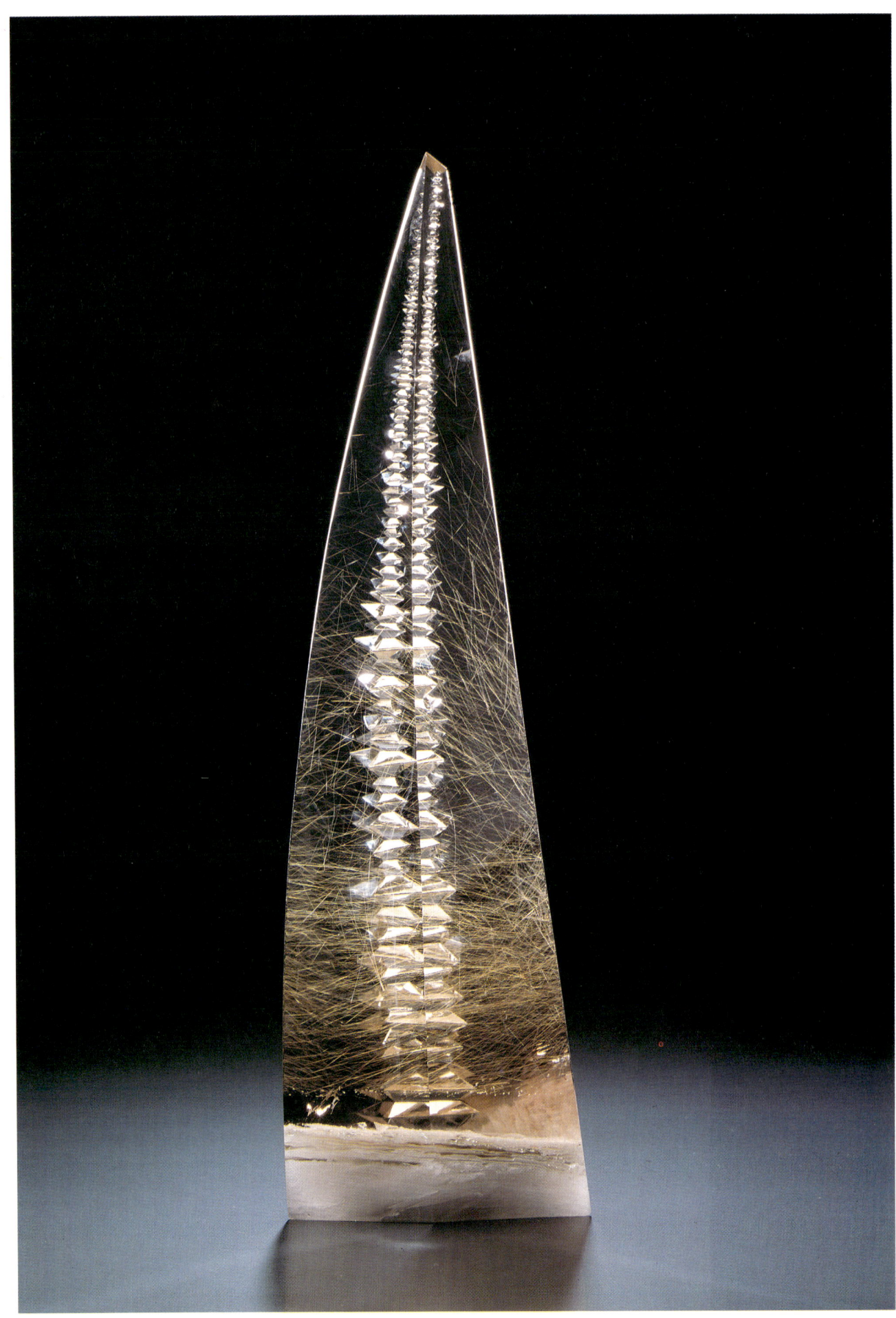

122 *'Metamorphosis', angel hair or rutile quartz cut by Bernd Munsteiner.*

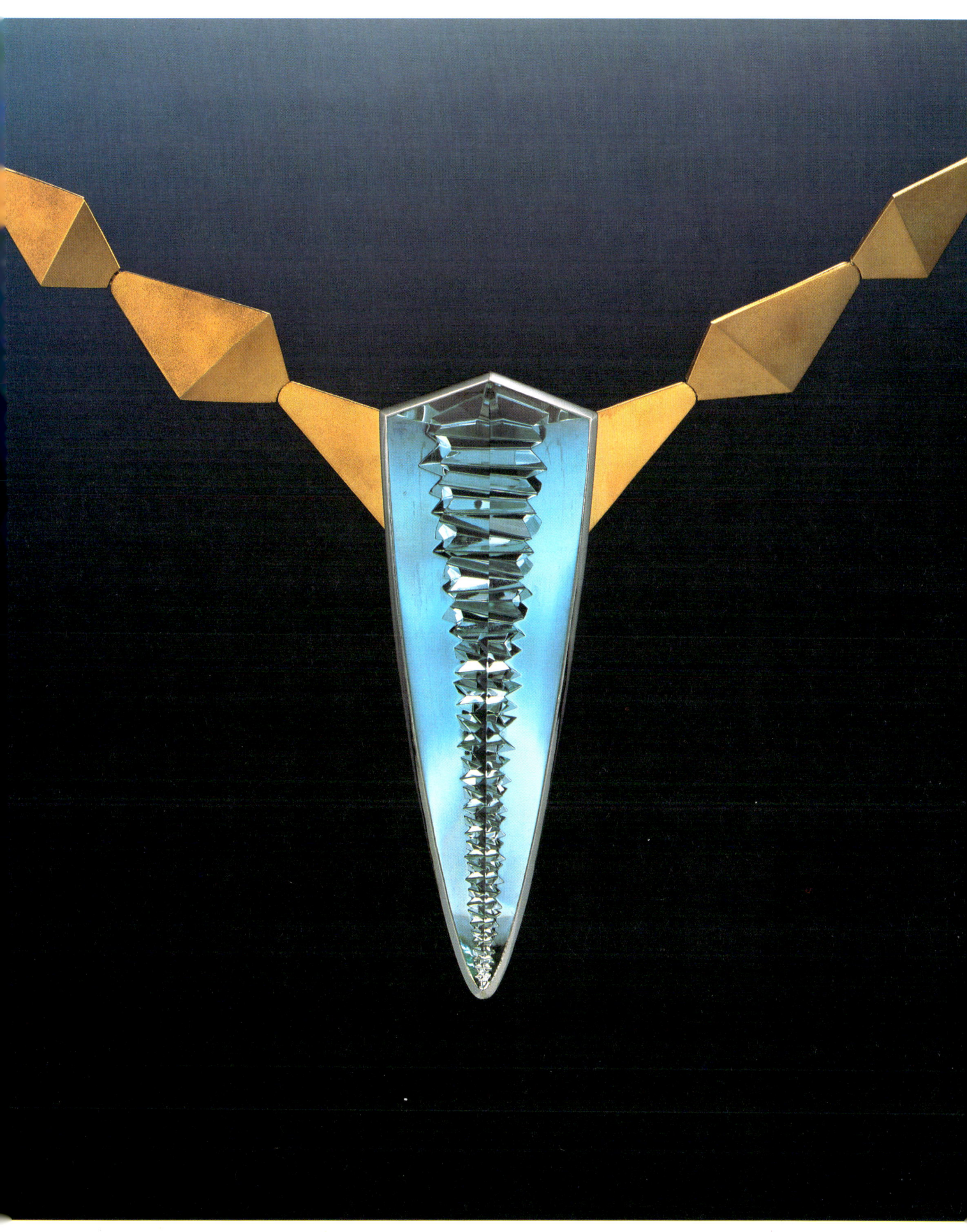

Necklace of gold and aquamarine of 134.36 carats, a work of Bernd Munsteiner.

123

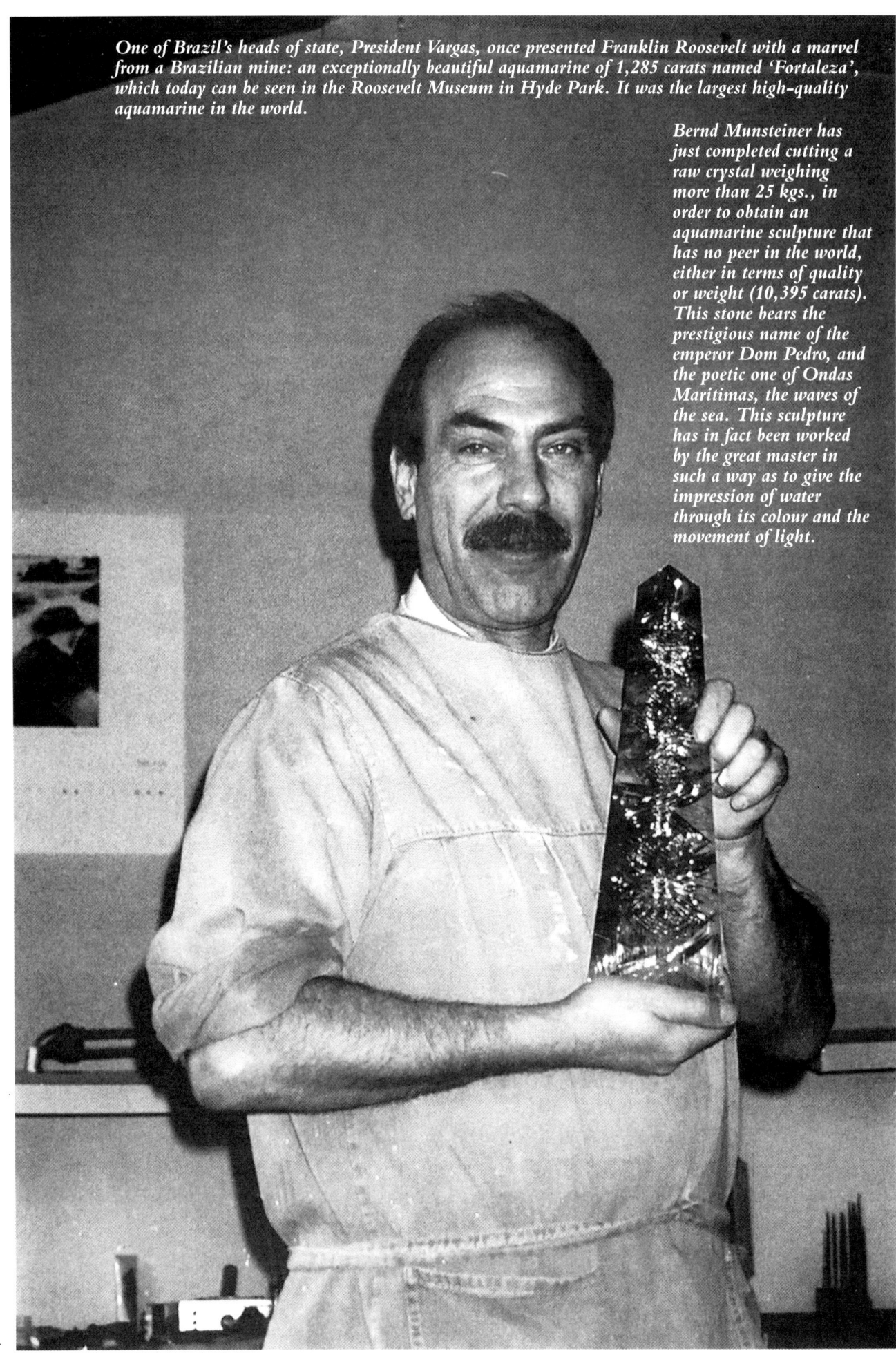

One of Brazil's heads of state, President Vargas, once presented Franklin Roosevelt with a marvel from a Brazilian mine: an exceptionally beautiful aquamarine of 1,285 carats named 'Fortaleza', which today can be seen in the Roosevelt Museum in Hyde Park. It was the largest high-quality aquamarine in the world.

Bernd Munsteiner has just completed cutting a raw crystal weighing more than 25 kgs., in order to obtain an aquamarine sculpture that has no peer in the world, either in terms of quality or weight (10,395 carats). This stone bears the prestigious name of the emperor Dom Pedro, and the poetic one of Ondas Maritimas, the waves of the sea. This sculpture has in fact been worked by the great master in such a way as to give the impression of water through its colour and the movement of light.

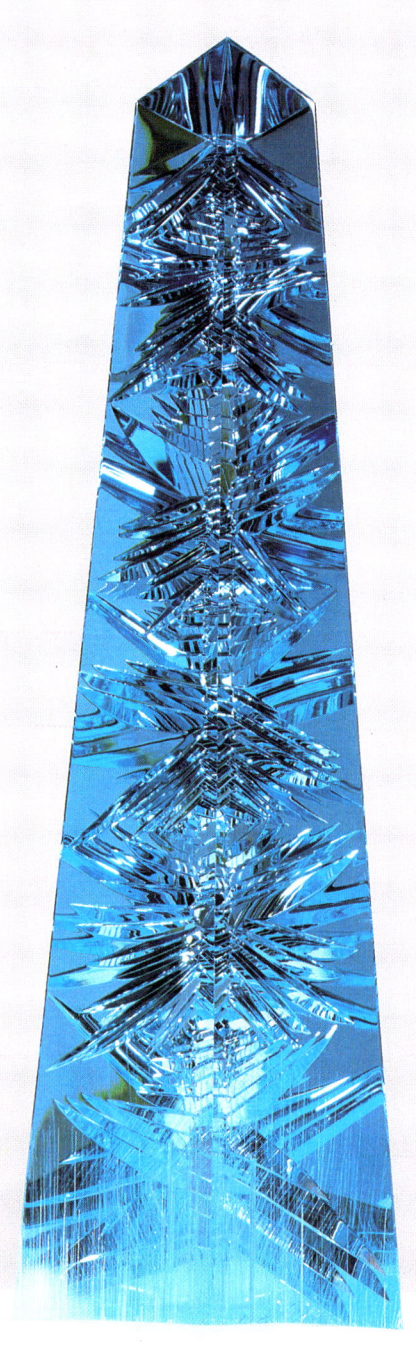

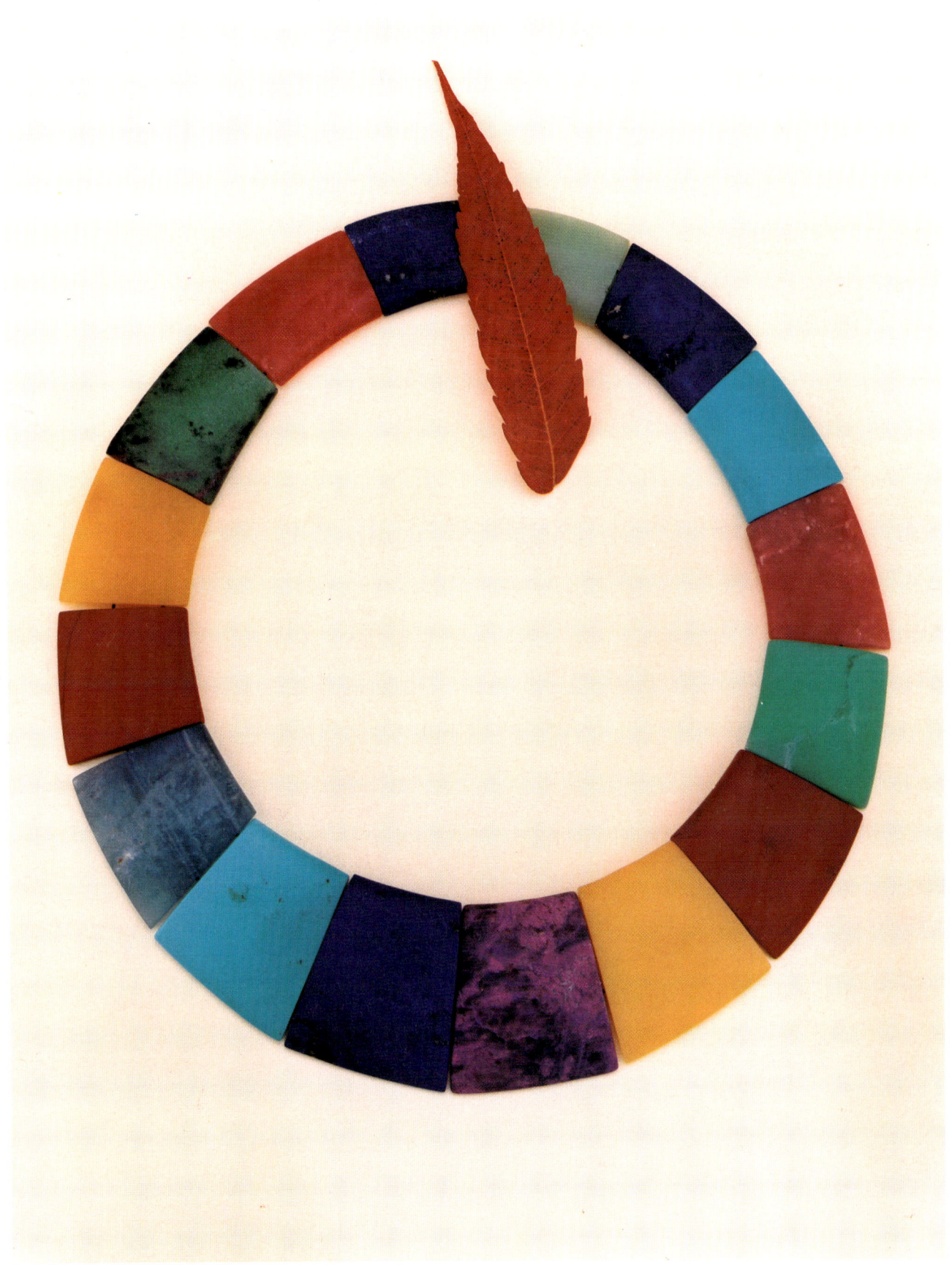

Necklace in aquamarine, yellow agate, jasper, coral, jade, zoisite, rhodocrosite, lapis lazuli, crysoprase and turquoise. This ingenious melange of stones and colours is the work of Habib Asadullah of Idar-Oberstein, who shows us that a jewel may be created without metal, with stones alone.

126

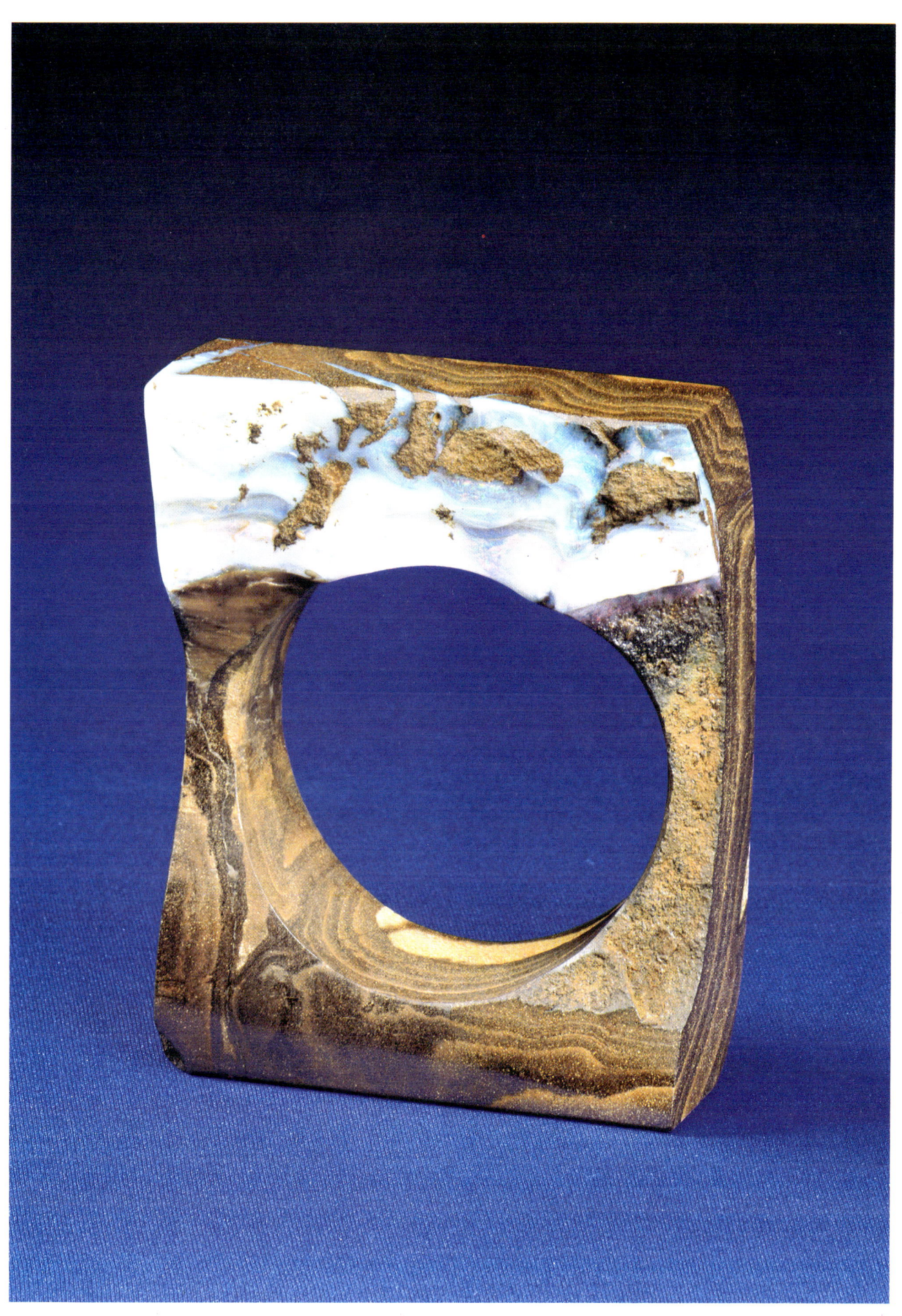

Bracelet sculpted from a block of opal by the Philipp Becker group; these objects have been designated by the trade press as 'the new stone age'.

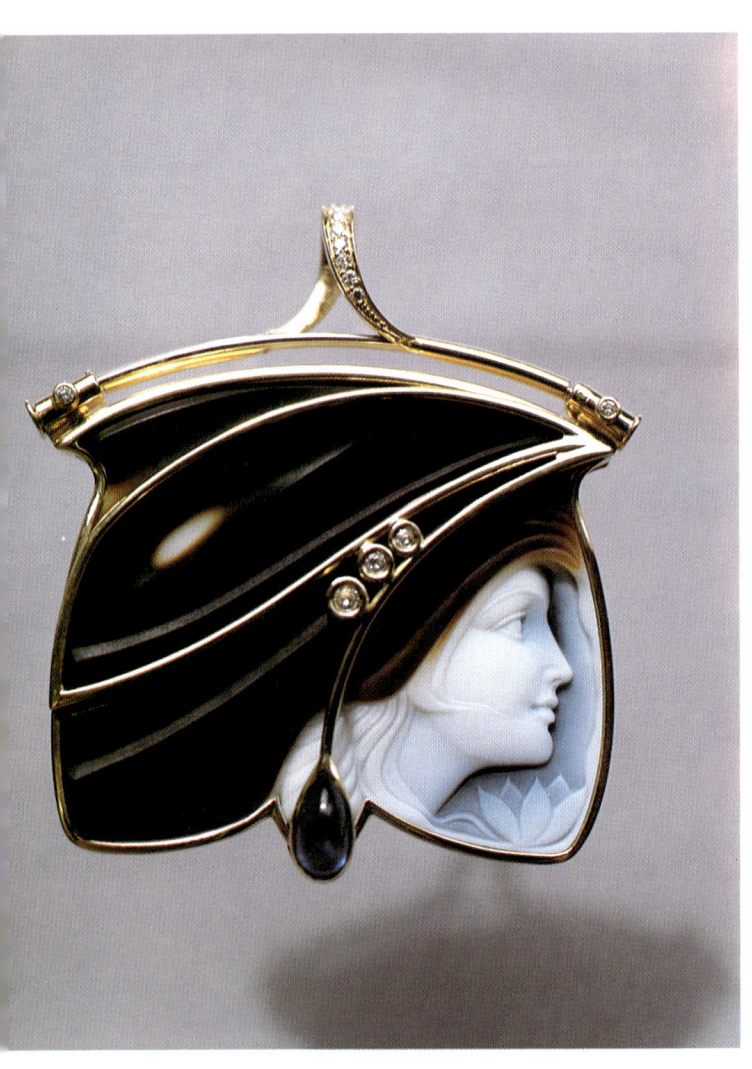
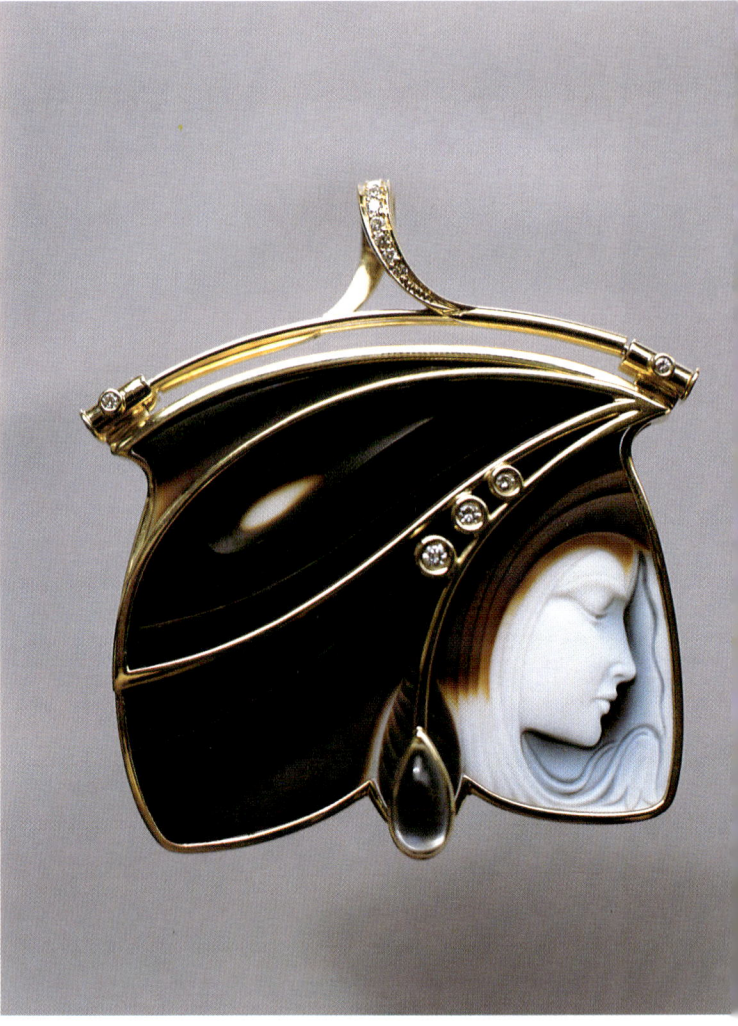

Erwin Paul: 'Comedy and Tragedy' is the title of this double-sided jewel made of gold, diamonds, moonstone and an exceptional cameo of striped agate.

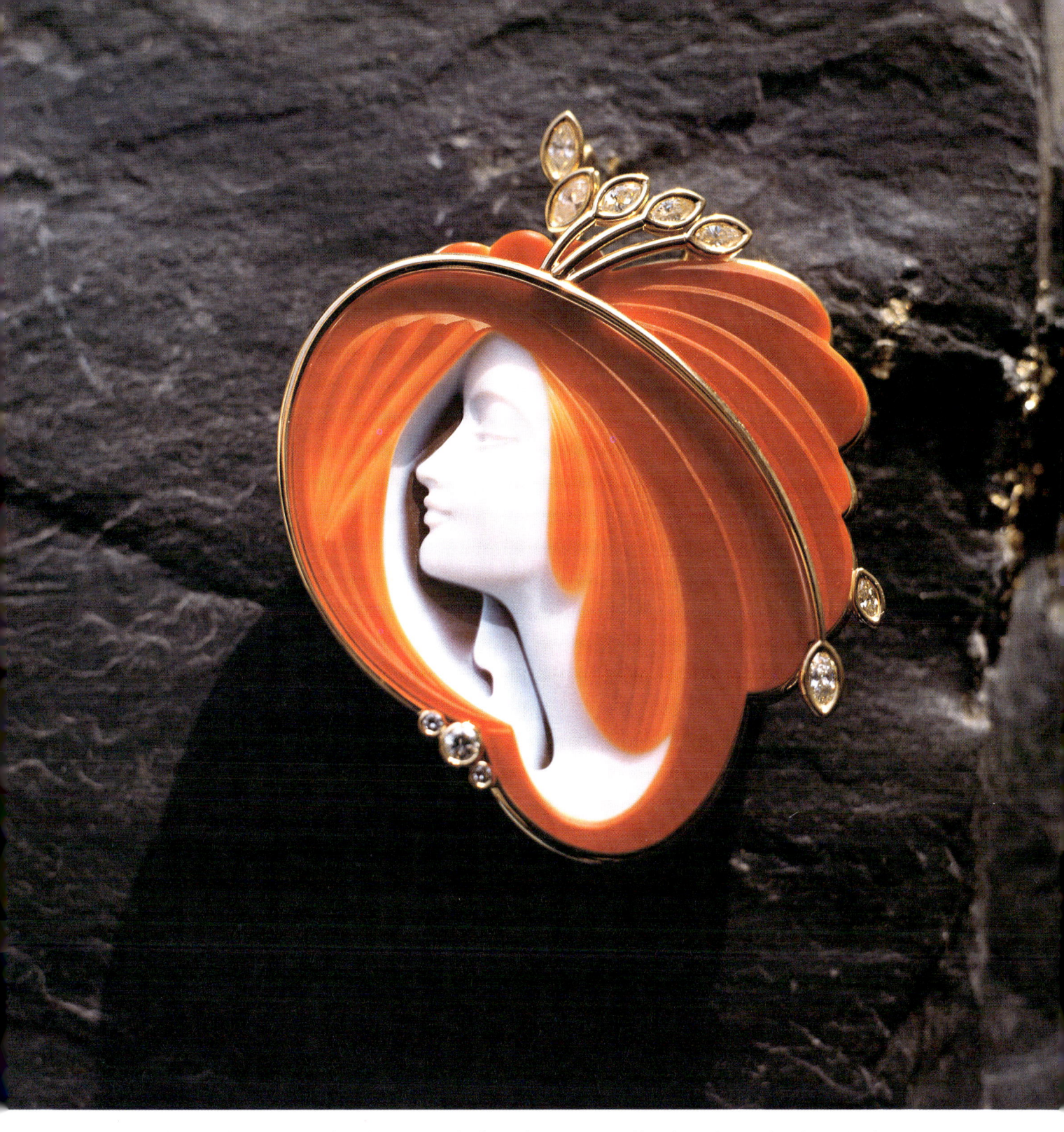

Erwin Pauly: 'Psyche', represented by the artist in the form of a cameo on gold with 10 diamonds. The myth of Psyche is neatly symbolised by all the proofs that the artist must execute before achieving the final work.

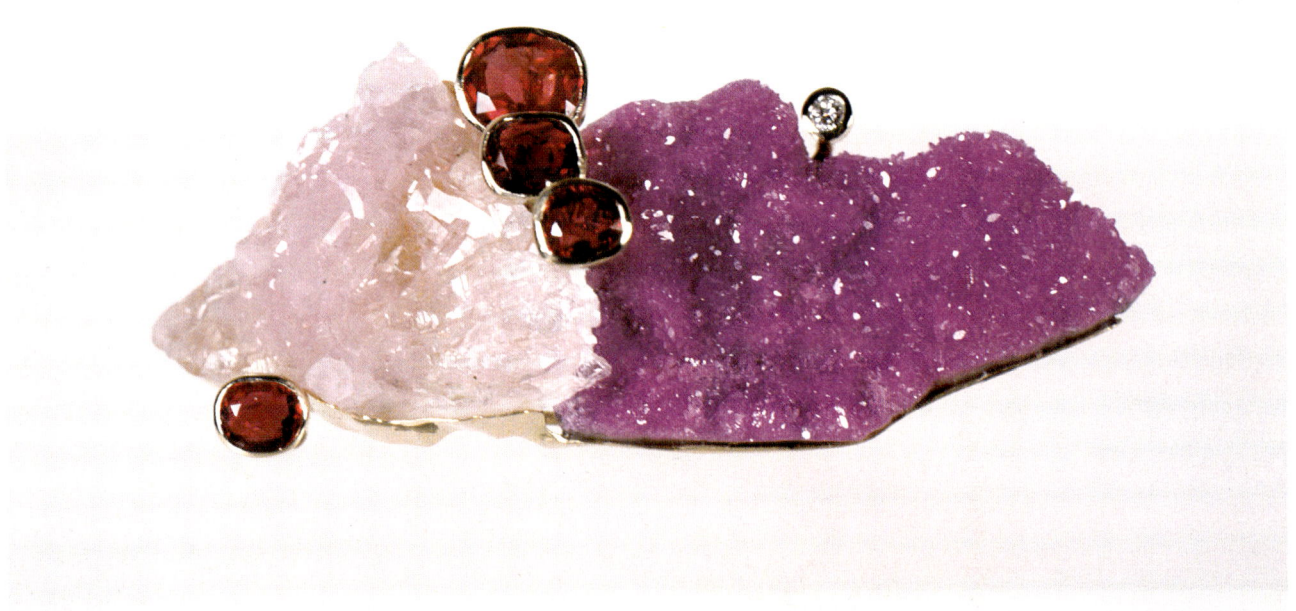

Beautiful minerals and coloured stones have always been one of Jean Vendome's principal sources of inspiration. Brooch and necklace created from raw and cut stones.

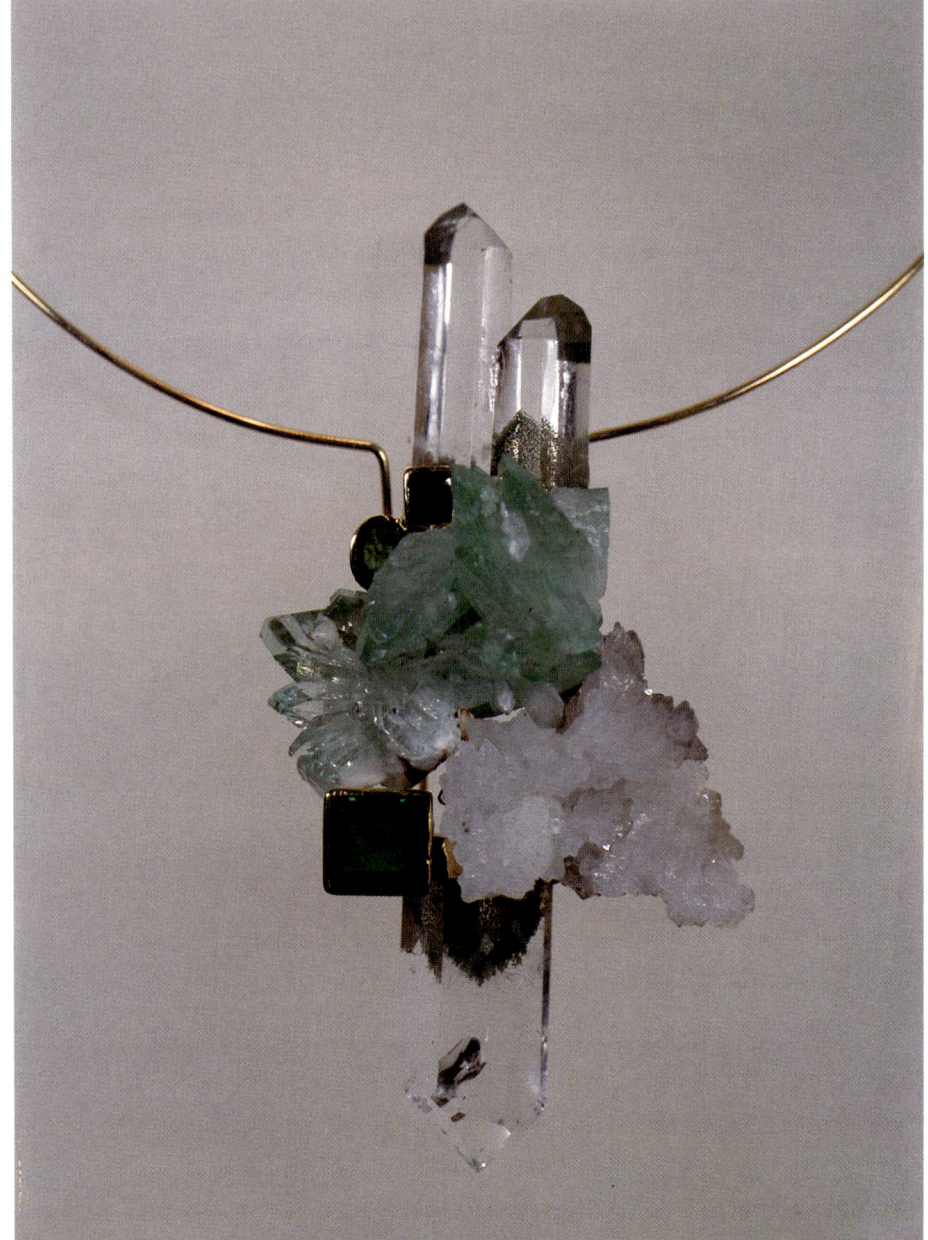

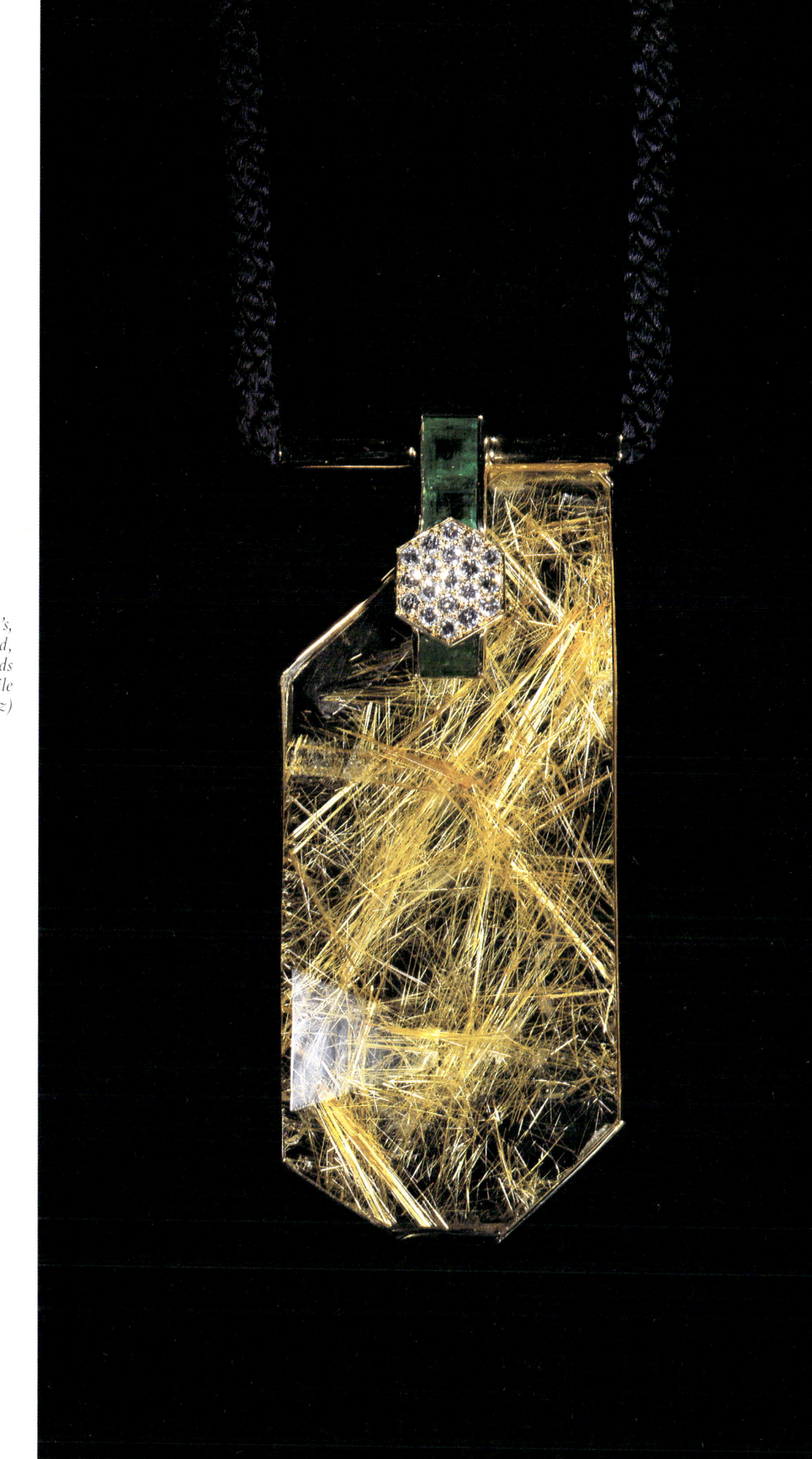

Jean Vendome's, pendant in gold, emeralds, diamonds and angel hair (rutile quartz)

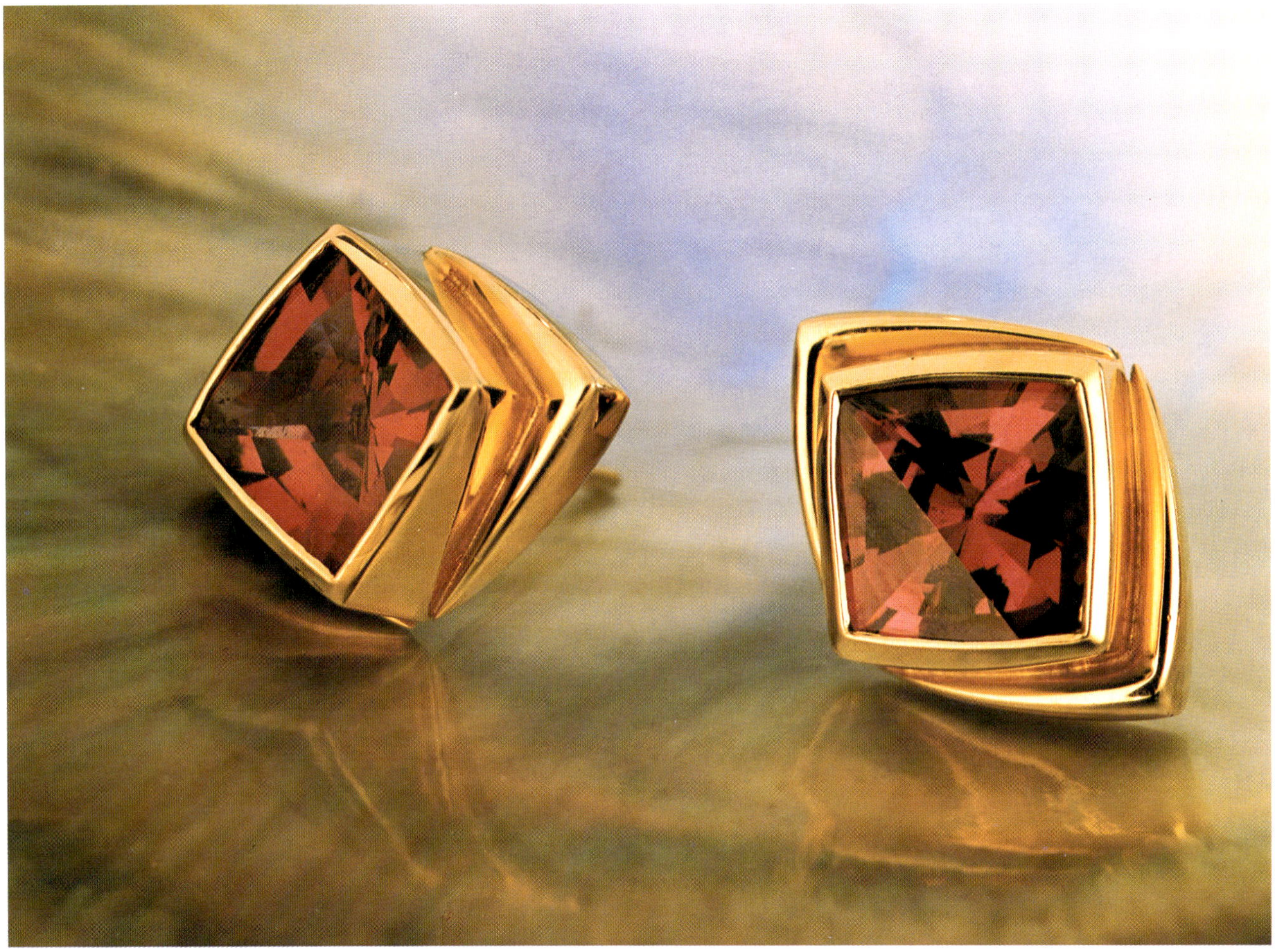

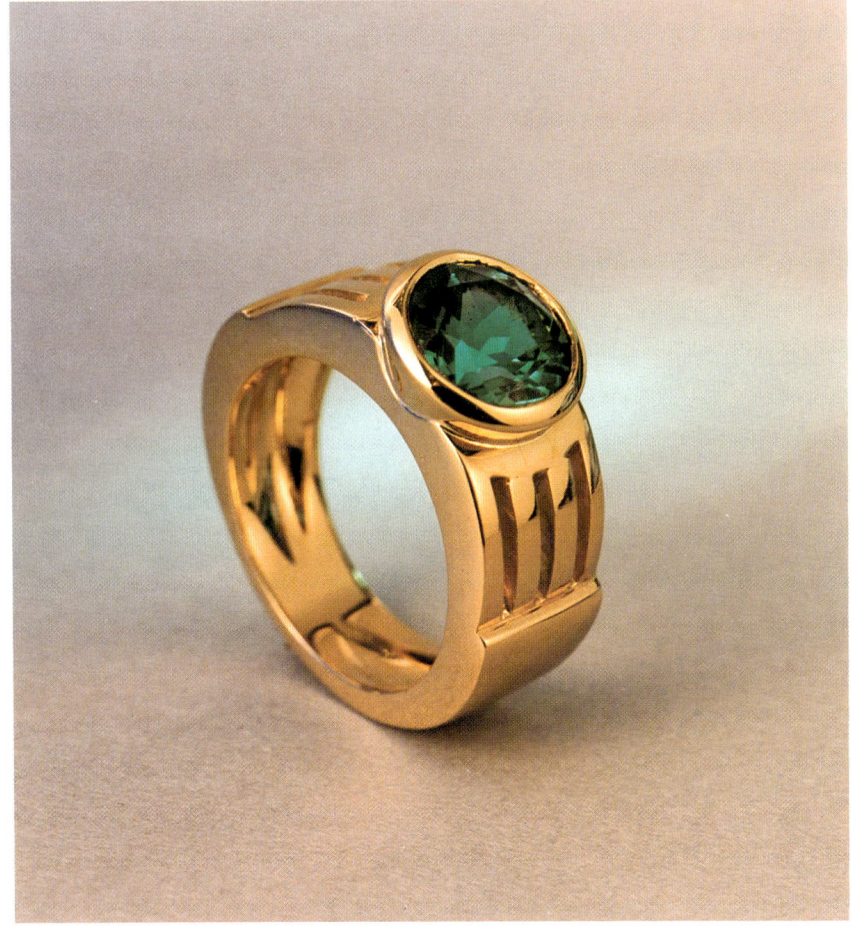

Earrings by Pascale Van Havre. Two pink tourmalines were cut in a special way to give them maximum brilliance, then set in gold.

Pascale Van Havre: ring in gold and brilliant-cut green tourmaline.

132

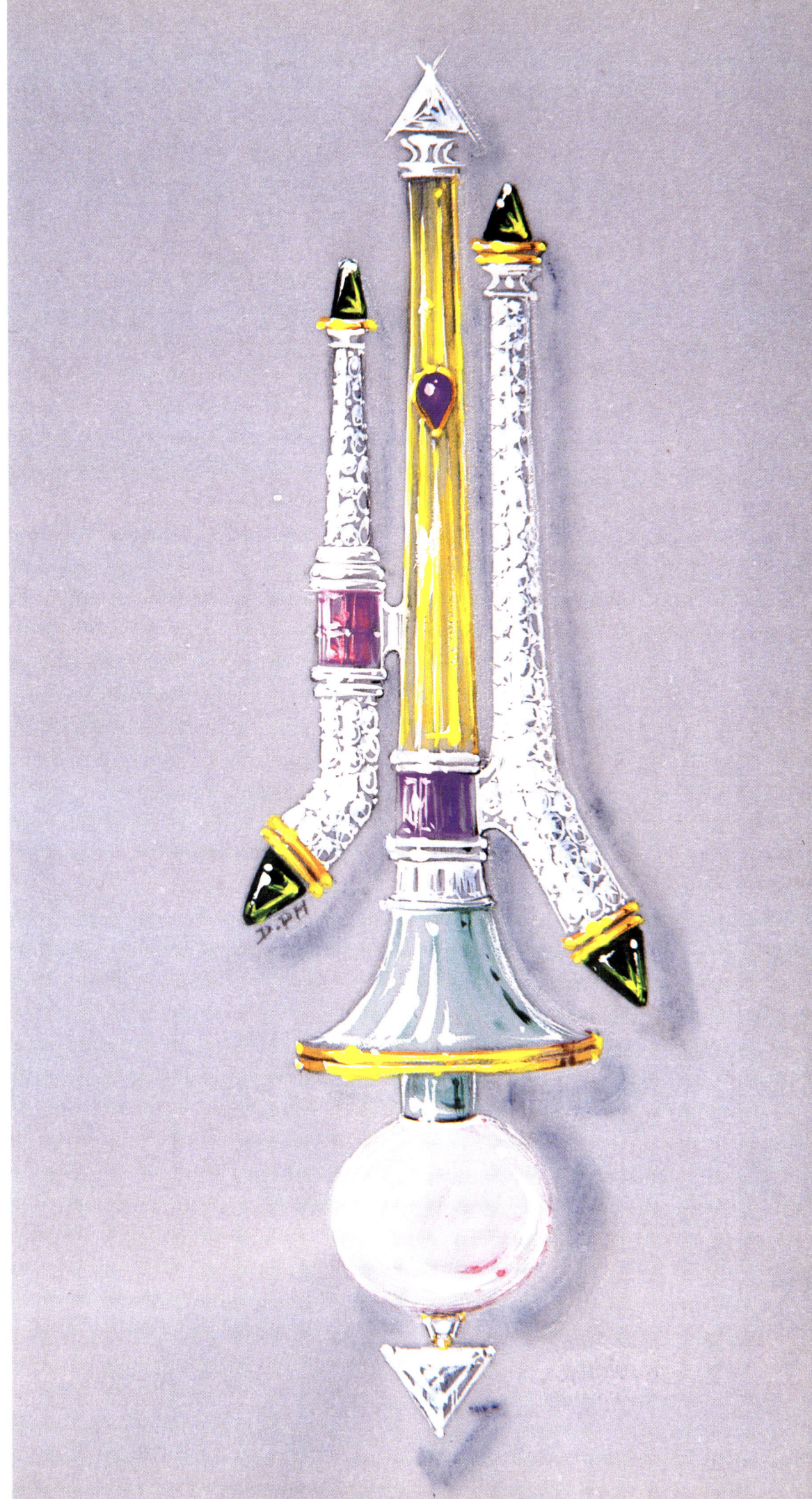

Design for a brooch in gold, diamonds, rubies, aquamarine, amethysts, tourmalines and rock crystal by Philippe Deloison. A subtle mixture of stones that enhance one another.

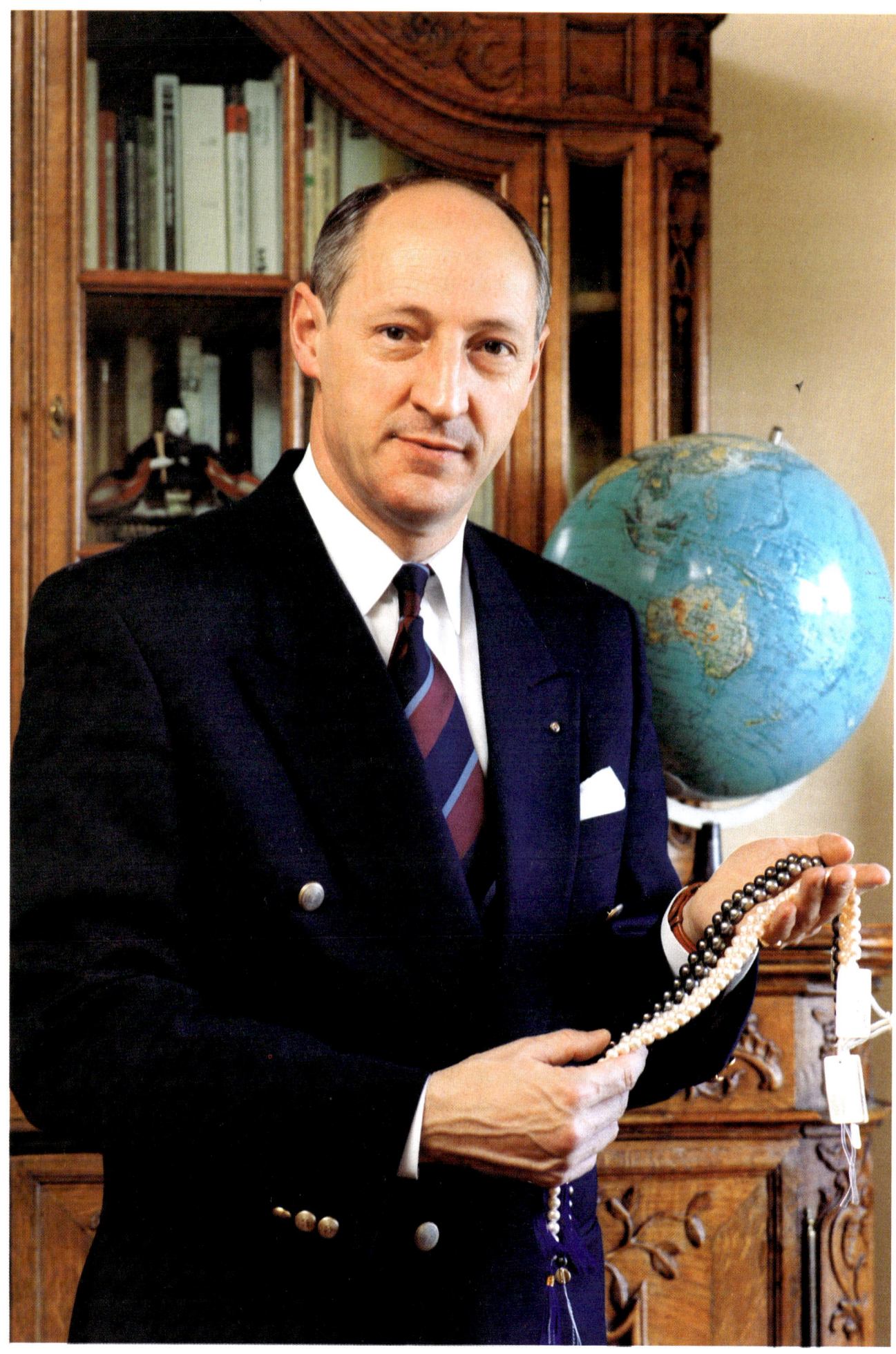

CHAPTER IV

GOLD AND PEARLS

In collaboration with Vincent de Jaegher

The pearl holds a privileged place in the domain of jewellery, and notably in the creation of jewels. This natural rarity offers an infinity of forms and colours that stimulate the artist's imagination.

To present diamonds and fine stones, I had the kind collaboration of one of the world's greatest cutters, but for the pearl there is one major difference: man can only assist it, it is an animal that creates, shapes and perfects it. In order to talk about pearls, it was necessary to enlist a great expert, an enthusiast, a lover of these marvels of nature: Vincent de Jaegher, globe-trotter and perfect connoisseur of this material, gives us the primary elements for understanding the only gem that comes from the animal kingdom.

From legend to reality

How can it be that one oyster in ten thousand offers a pearl? For a very long time, this enigma was believed to have a divine and legendary origin; myths and surrealistic explanations fused and became more poetic still.

It was said that on nights with a full moon, oysters were drawn to the light at the sea's surface, opened themselves up and were impregnated by the rays of moonlight, causing a pearl to be born. Other legends declare that wherever a rainbow touches the earth, a fairy comes to deposit a magic pearl there. Scientific reality is another thing entirely, yet the aura of mystery and magic that surrounds pearls nevertheless endures.

A pearl is born of an injury to an oyster, either natural or man-induced.

Fine pearls and cultured pearls

Fine pearls are never subject to human intervention during their formation, whereas cultured pearls are conceived through a graft. The grafting technique was invented by the Japanese at the beginning of the 20th century,

and it is still they who practice this perilous surgery today, as it requires as much experience as it does skill.

Pearl-breeders graft three-year-old oysters, place them back in the sea for three years more, and during this period the oyster tries to isolate the foreign body that has been placed in it by

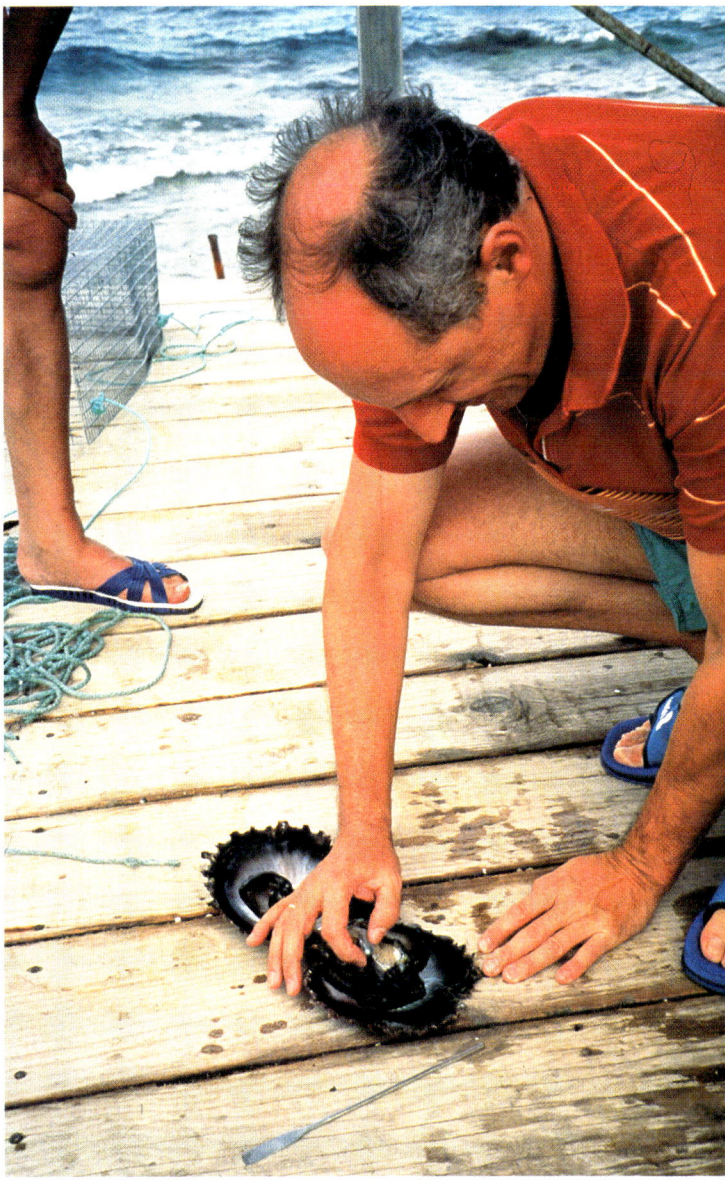

Vincent de Jaegher at work in his office and at his pearl farm.

135

covering it with mother of pearl. A true surgical operation, pearl grafting is a delicate procedure that succeeds in only 20% of cases. Finally, some three years after the intervention, the oyster gives birth to a superb cultured pearl; unique, because each oyster reacts differently. Each pearl thus has its own personality.

Jewel creators are especially interested in one type of pearl: this is the incomparable Tahitian pearl. What is it that sets these pearls apart from all the others?

Its size. The Polynesian cultured pearl is clearly larger than the white Japanese pearl, as it may grow as large as 14mm in diameter, compared to the 9mm maximum of the Japanese article. The average size is between 9 and 12mm. It should be noted that the larger the diameter, the rarer the pearl.

Its shape. Throughout the ages, the round, symmetrical and perfect pearl was sought after for its rarity, and was considered the *summum* of beauty. Nevertheless, other forms have their own purity and charm. The creator's talent gives birth to marvellous jewels that start with a pear-shaped or baroque pearl. The more or less elongated pear-shaped pearl is especially appreciated in a pendant or earring.

Its colour. Whether it be an iridescent deep black, silvery gray, bronze-green or blue green, eggplant, tan or coppery, these can all be designated as a natural, coloured, cultured Tahitian pearl.

Although the basic colour is generally black or dark gray, some specimens are found to have a light gray or moon-white tint. All of them are as beautiful as the black pearls; however, even though they do not lack in appeal, they are slightly less prized than the black ones.

Why are these pearls black? Mainly because the kind of oyster in question naturally produces a black mother of pearl. This oyster, *Pincta Margaritifera,* lives only in the warm waters of Polynesia, which favours the oyster's metabolism, its strong growth and copious mother-of-pearl production. Moreover, the abundance of plankton and the high level of mineral salts provide the greenish or bluish highlights that make the pearl unique.

Its brilliance. Light is reflected on the surface of the pearl, which gives it its brilliance. This

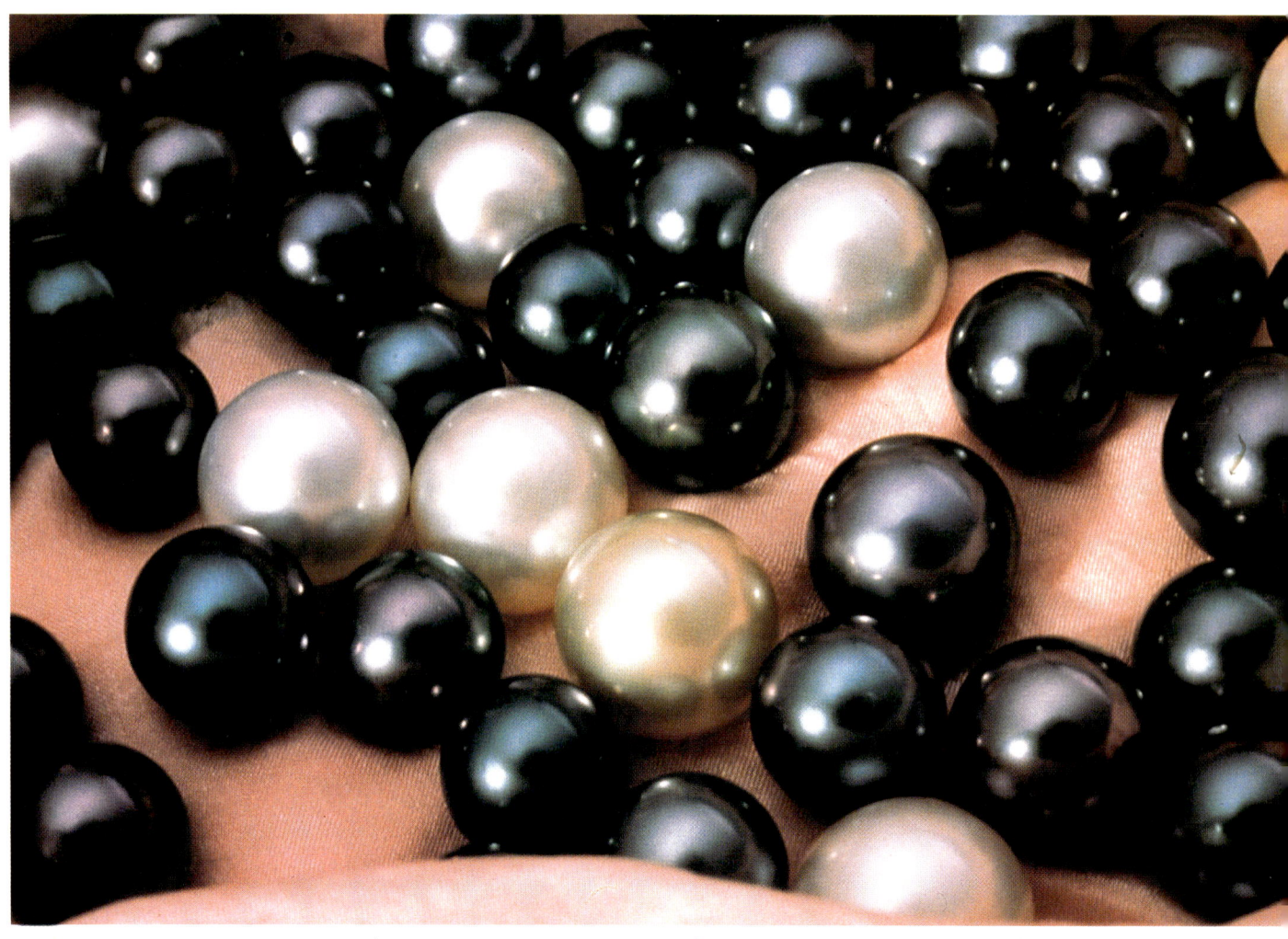

136 *Black and polychrome Tahitian pearls.*

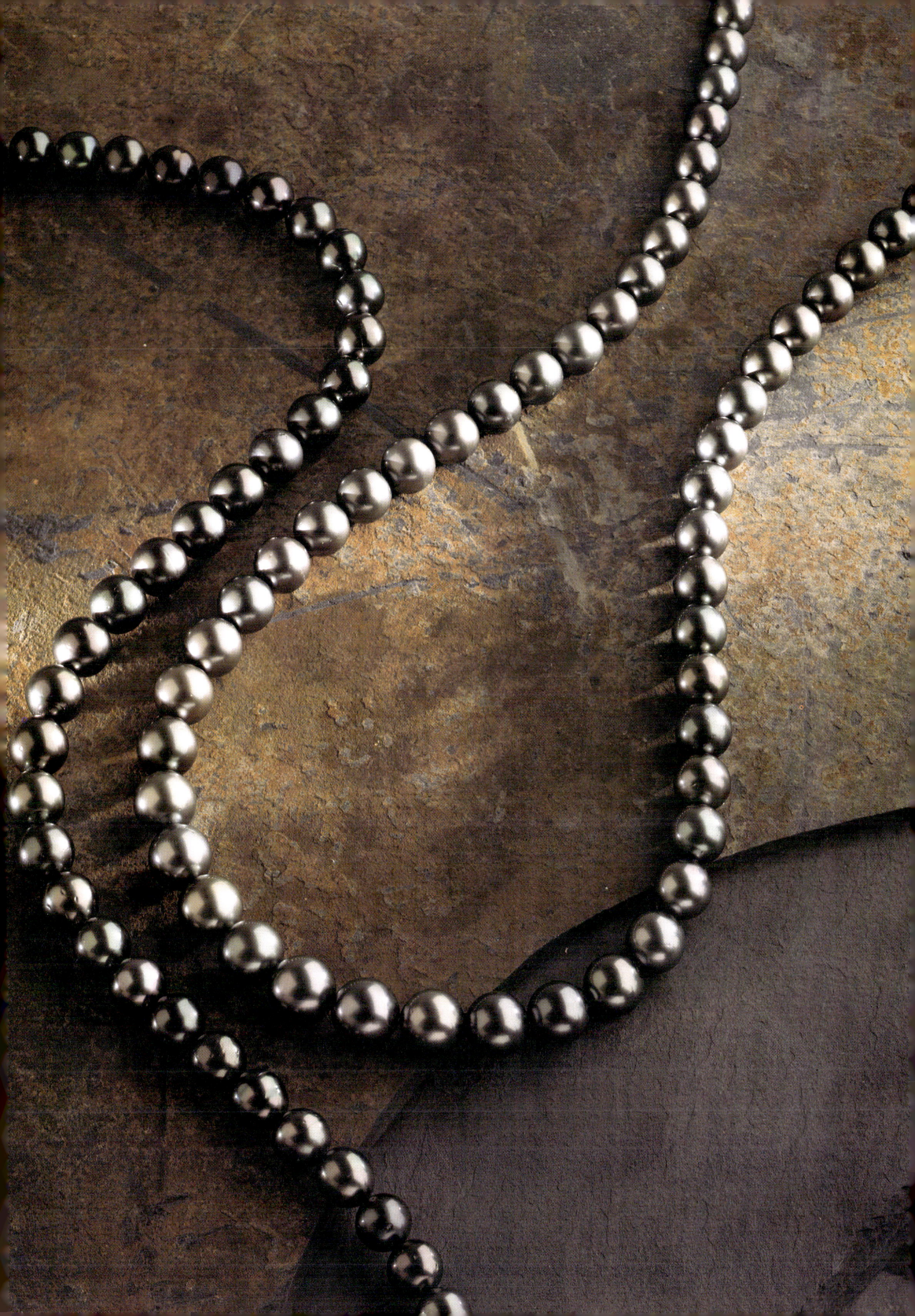

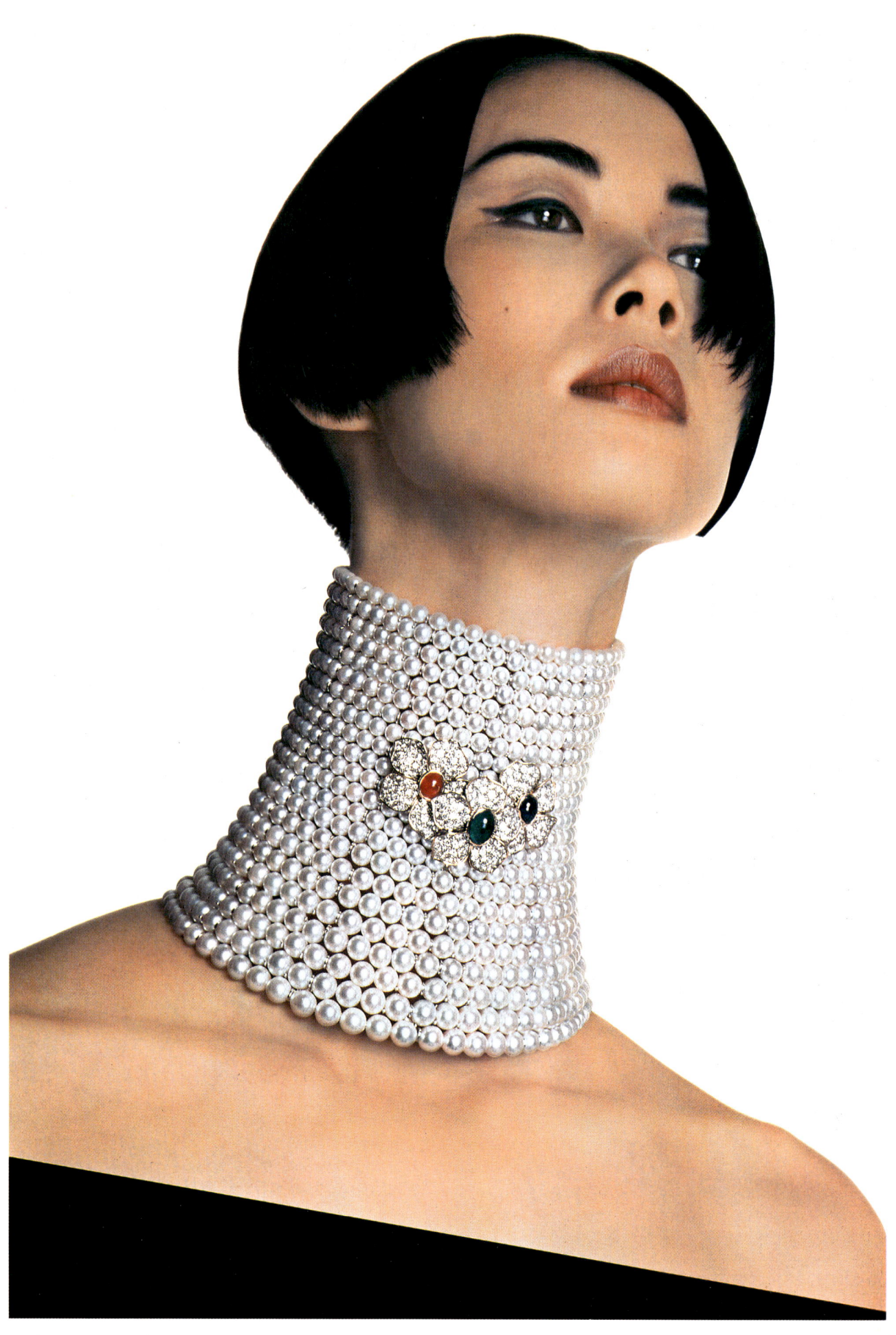

138 'Mikana': very sophisticated rigid necklace, composed of 22 superposed necklaces adorned with gold and precious stones.

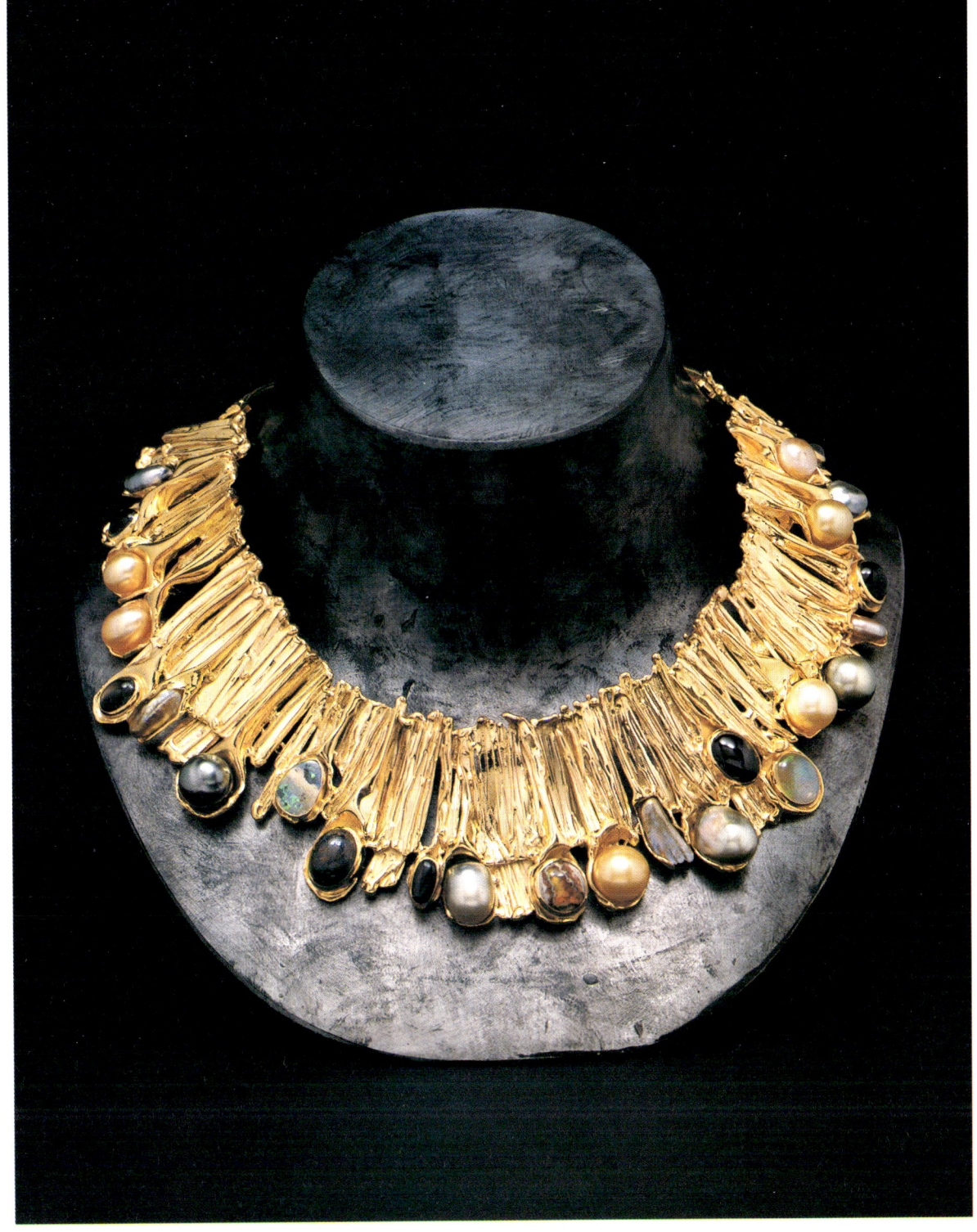

Simonne Muylaert Hofman: necklace of gold, stones and pearls in all colours and shapes.

brilliance, called lustre or orient, depends on the thickness and uniformity of the coatings of mother of pearl. The black pearl reflects everything that surrounds it, like a mirror. The more abundant the thickness of the mother-of-pearl coating, the more brilliance the pearl has. The thickness of the mother-of-pearl coating may vary from one pearl to another. Generally, a cultured Tahitian pearl has a mother-of-pearl coating of about 3mm around the central core; this coating may reach up to 4mm in a highly developed pearl.

Its purity. Sometimes the surface of a pearl shows certain irregularities or pits. A pit is a small, shallow depression, normally about the size of a pin-head. A pearl without a single pit is considered to be flawless. A single flaw is not fatal, because the pearl must be pierced in order to be mounted in a jewel or strung on a necklace. However, numerous pits on several places on the pearl will greatly lower the pearl's value, unless they are barely visible.

To sum up, what matters is the overall appearance of the pearl, taken as a combination of its qualities: diameter, shape, colour, brilliance and purity.

139

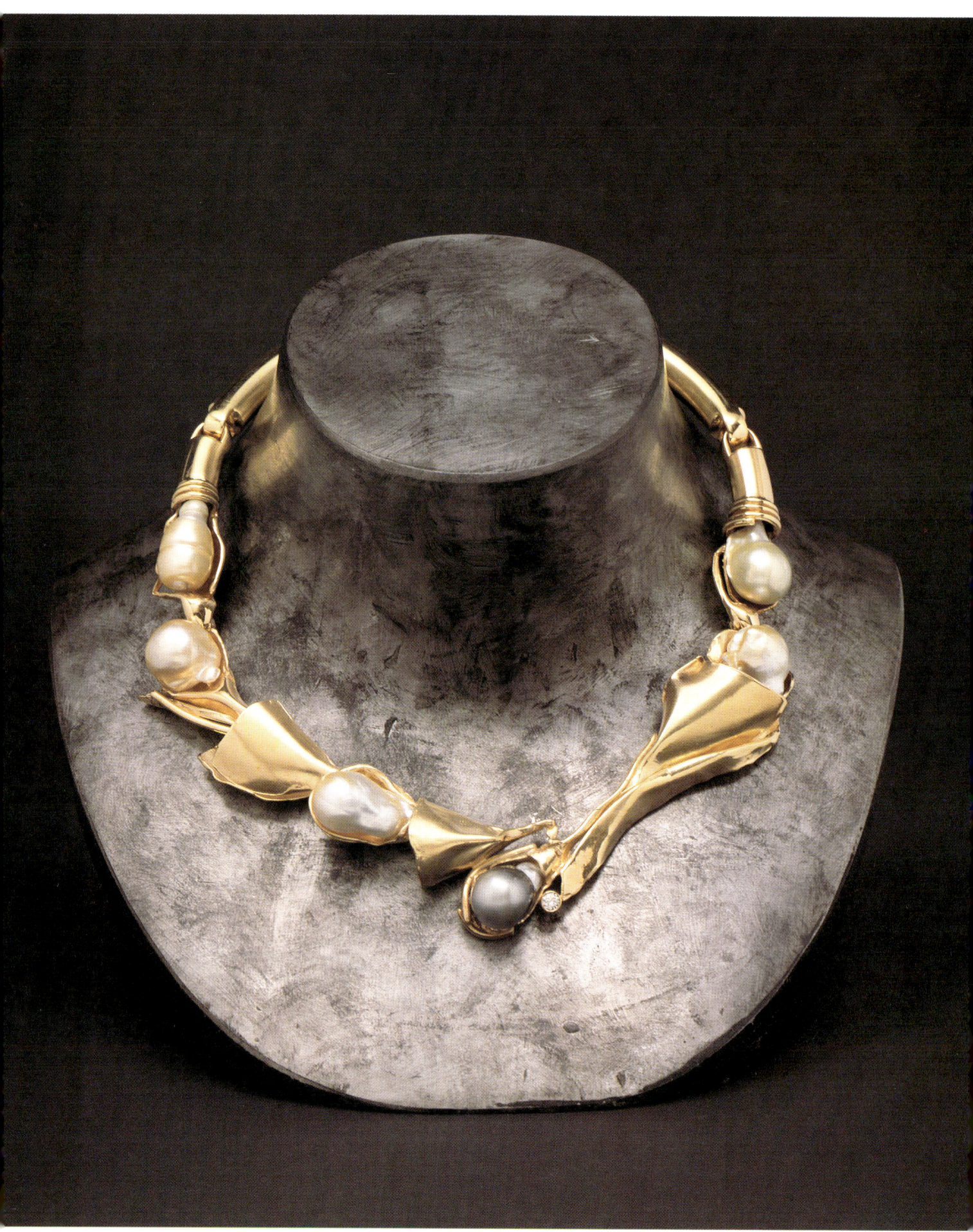

140 *Simonne Muylaert-Hofmann, necklace in gold, diamond and polychrome Tahitian pearls.*

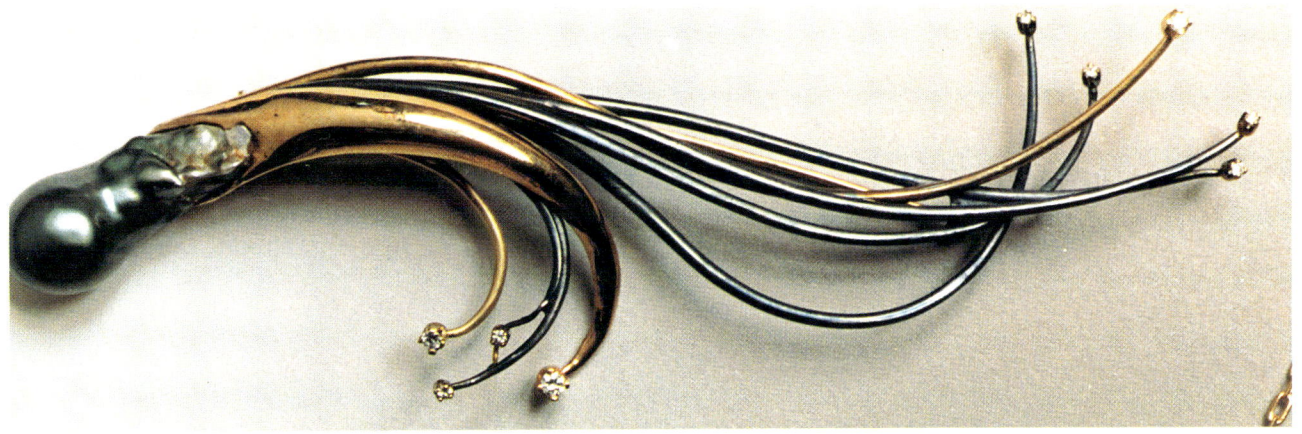

'Sea Comet', brooch in gold and silver, baroque black Tahitian pearl and diamonds..

Alfonso Mazzi:
necklace of
diamonds and
Argent pearl.

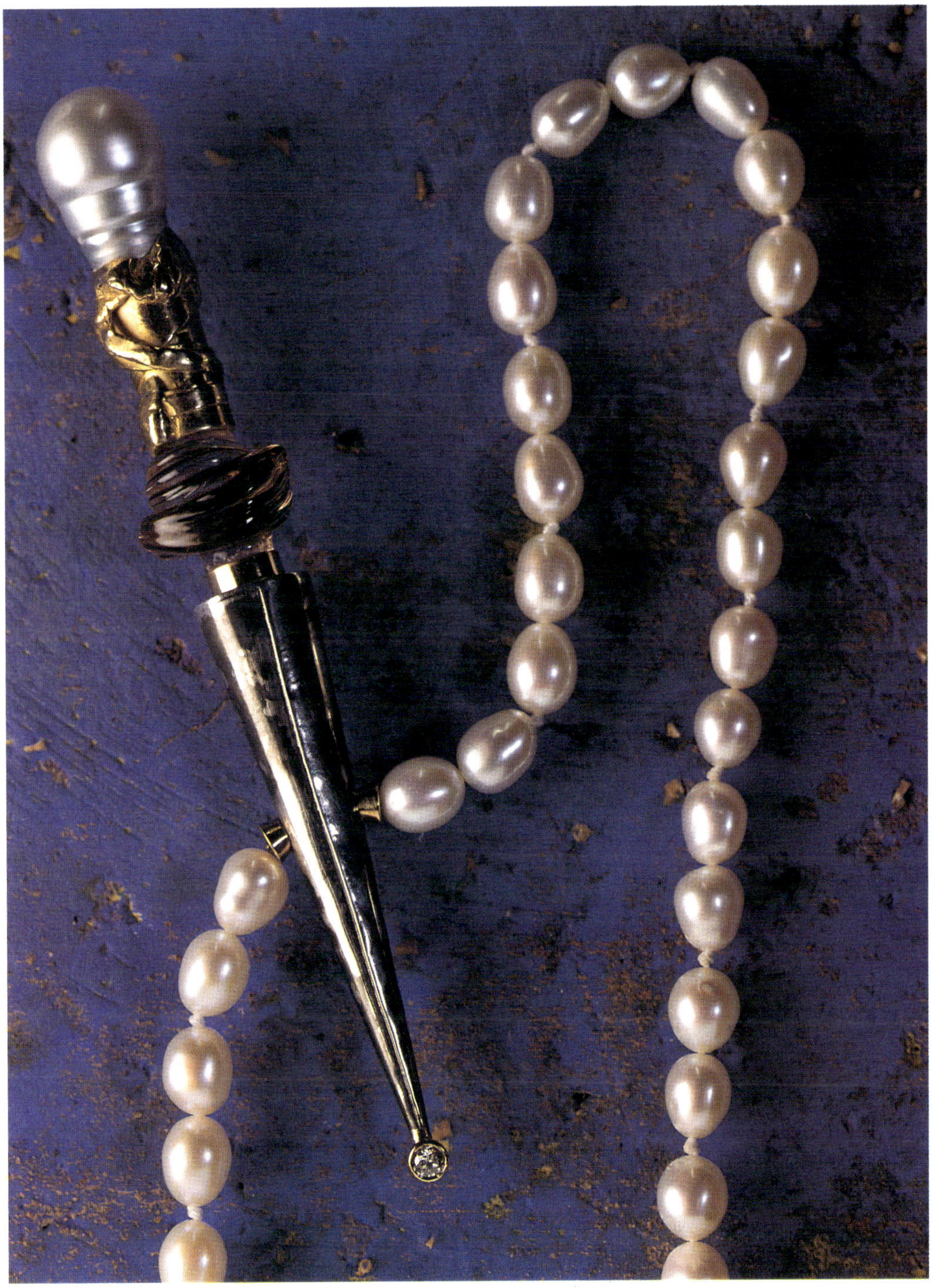

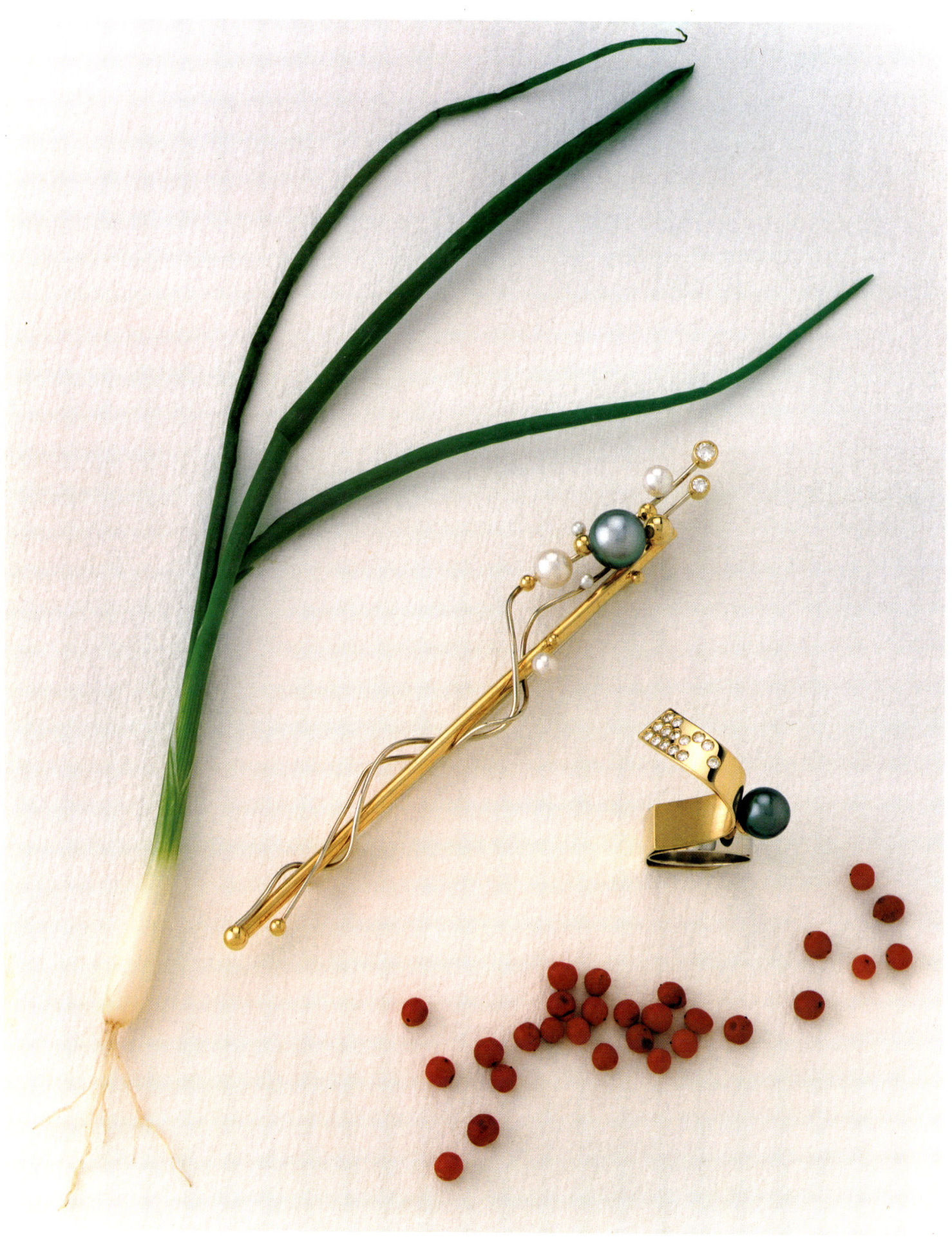

142 *Michaël Dürnholz, brooch and ring in yellow gold, white gold, Tahitian pearls, Japanese pearls and diamonds.*

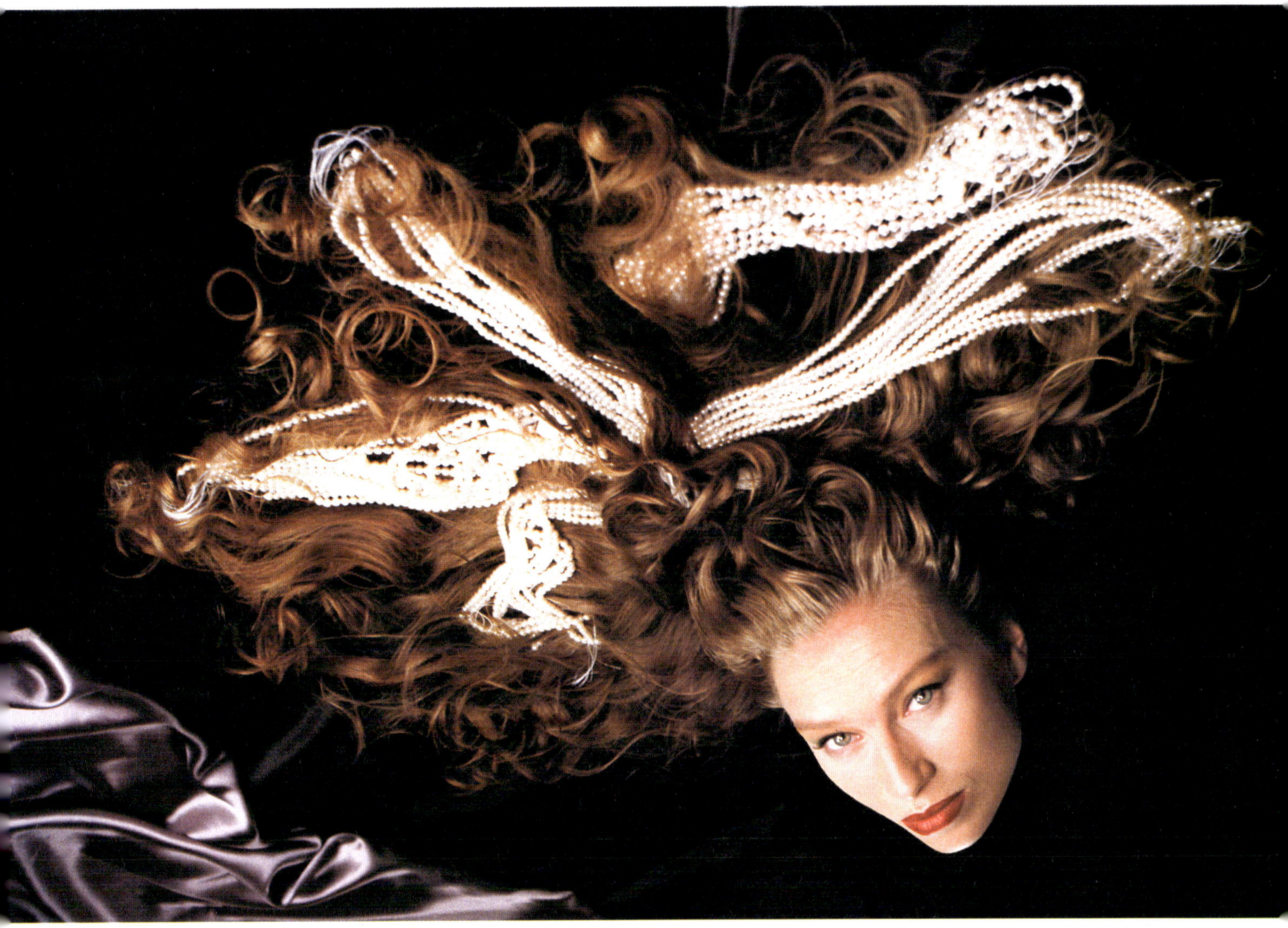

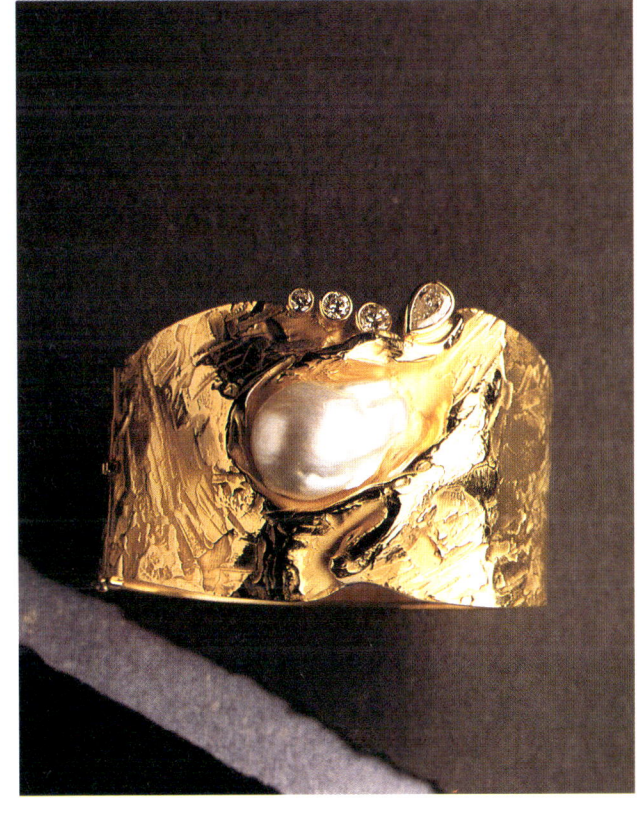

Pearls have often
inspired Jean-Pierre
de Saedeleer in the
creation of his
collections.

Jean-Pierre de
Saedeleer, ring in
gold, diamonds
and baroque pearls.

143

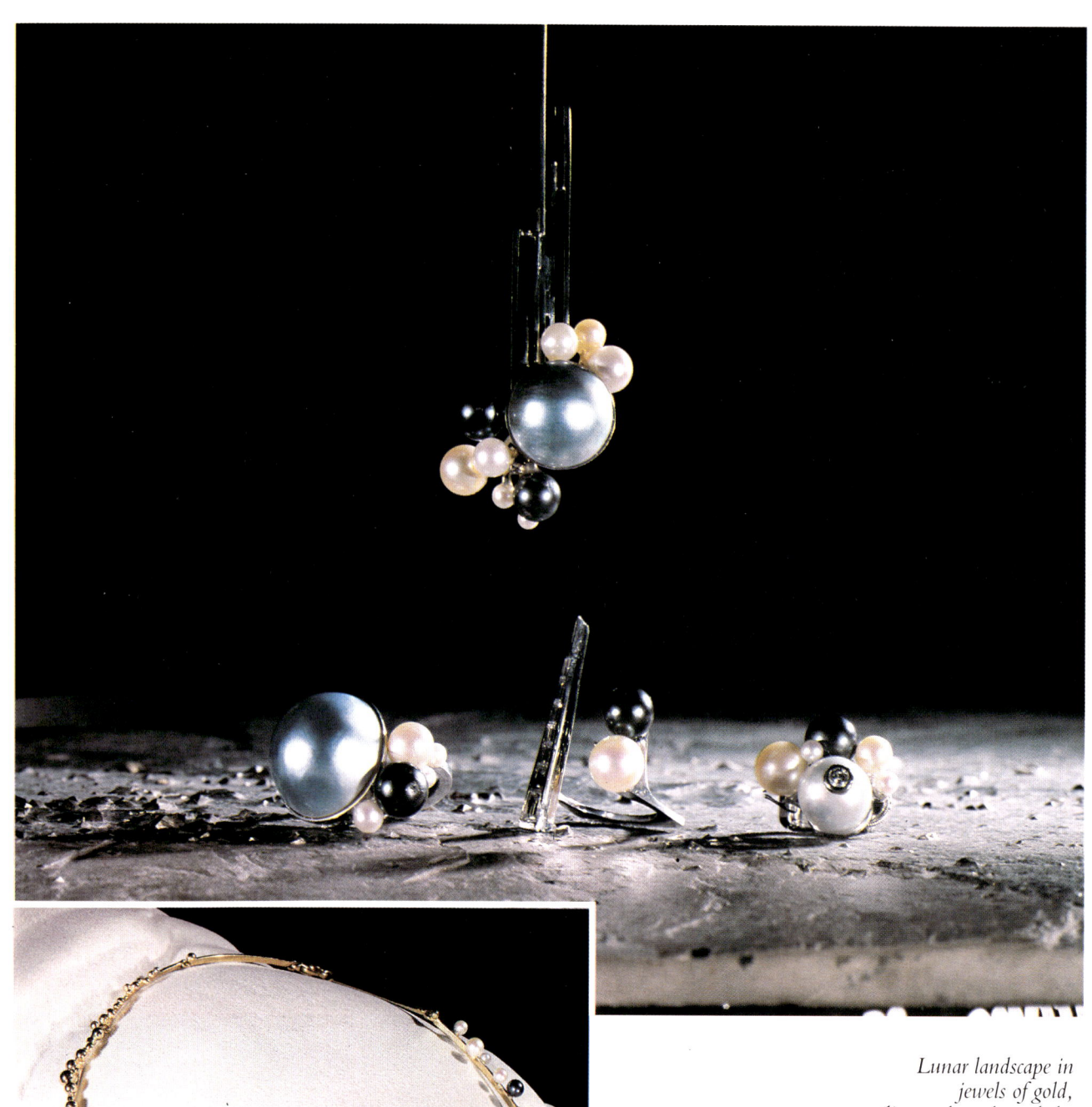

*Lunar landscape in
jewels of gold,
diamonds and pearls by
Jean Vendome.*

*Jean Vendome,
necklace in gold, opal,
diamonds and pearls
of all colours.*

144

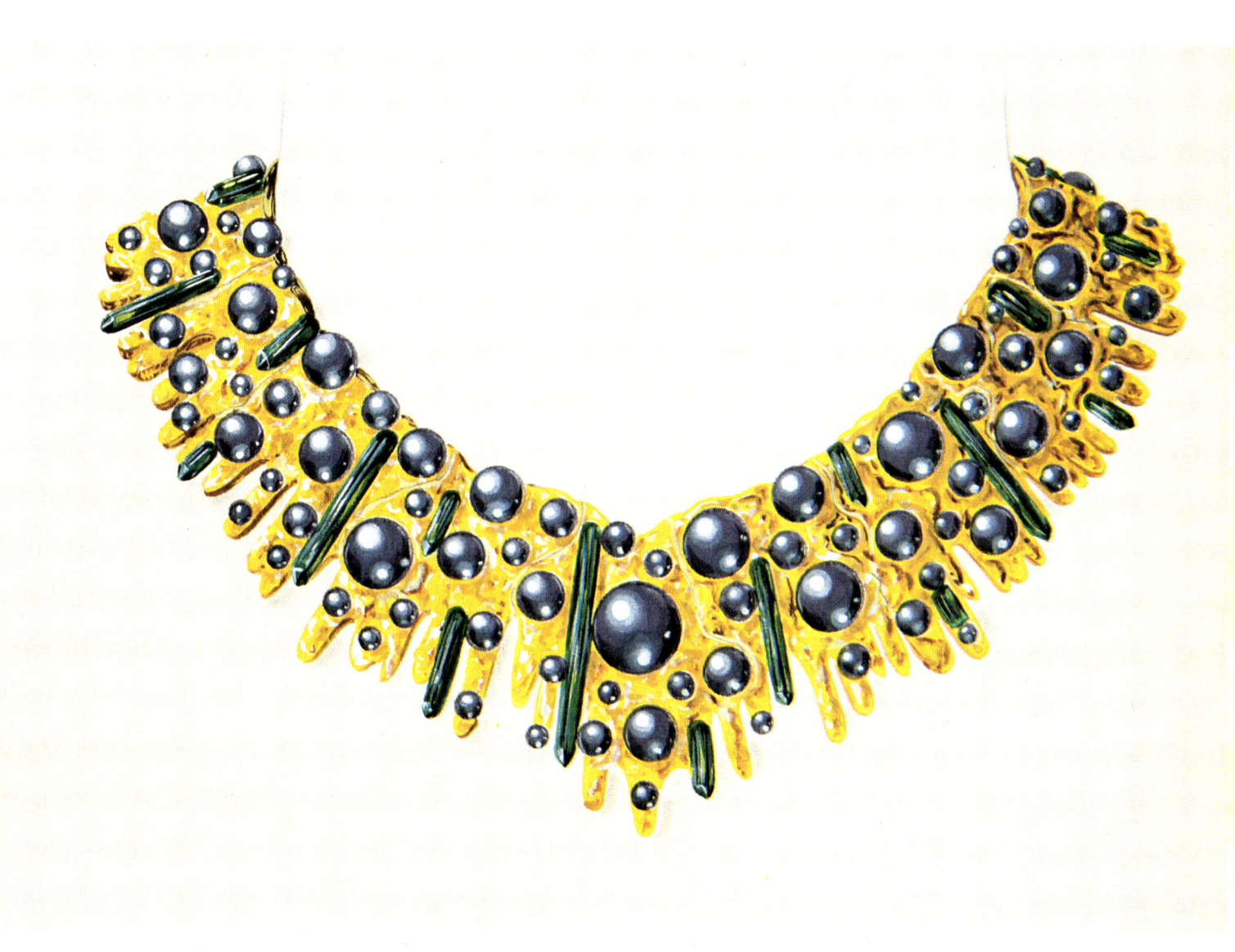

'Ocean', *necklace by Thierry Martin designed to be made in gold, raw crystals of green tourmalines and gray Tahitian pearls.*

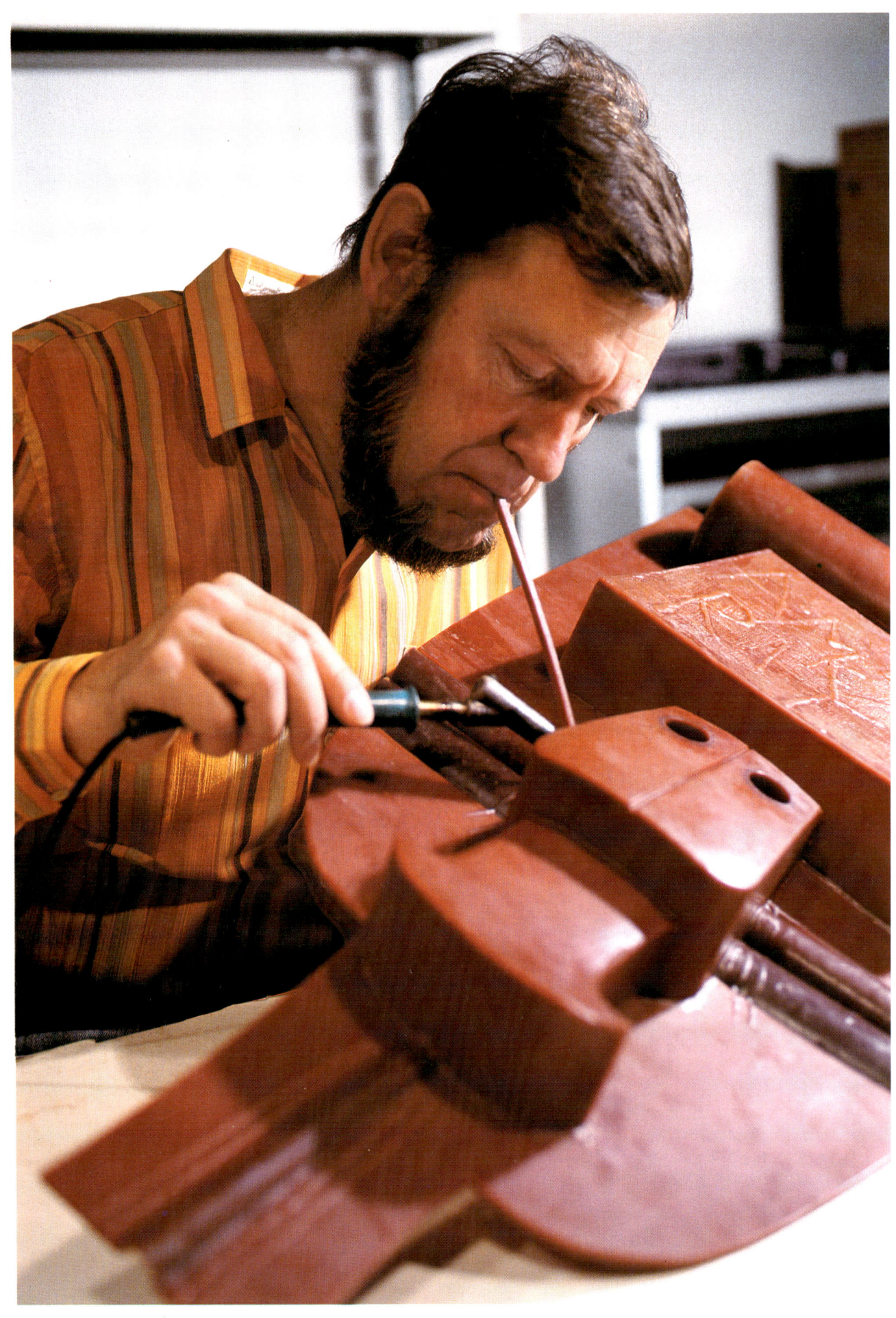

146   *Hubert Minnebo at work in his studio.*

CHAPTER V

SCULPTOR'S JEWELS

In collaboration with Hubert Minnebo

There is no doubt that an art-jewel and a sculpture are such similar entities that sooner or later virtually all sculptors find themselves drawn to creating jewels.

On the other hand, jewellers are often tempted to create precious sculptures, even if the results have not always been very satisfactory. Jewel-sculptures or sculpture-jewels? It is not only a question of size! Ultimately, what differentiates the two categories is the means of presentation: the former need a chain, a ring or a pin; the latter are placed on a column, a pedestal or a plinth.

Hubert Minnebo, a world-renowned Belgian sculptor, creates gigantic sculptures of bronze and copper, and small works in gold and diamonds that he calls wearable sculptures. In a book written on this artist and his work by Fernand Bonneure, one chapter is specially devoted to jewels. I discovered that the author, a friend of the artist's, was able to describe perfectly the vision that a sculptor works with in order to arrive at creating jewels. I present it here in its entirety.

The Jewels of Hubert Minnebo, by Fernand Bonneure, Éditions Lannoo.

'"Reducing a statue to a small format makes it wearable as a jewel, while retaining its monumental nature: this to me seems an important undertaking." It is with these words that Hubert Minnebo himself introduces his jewellery.

'Throughout history, man has always wanted to accentuate his appearance, his social standing, by his clothing, his hairstyle, his personal objects, his language. Jewels are part of this type of signal. They enhance the brilliance of his body, distinguishing it from others.

'Originally — and even today in certain parts of the world — it was the man who was the most bejewelled, in order to underscore his worth and prestige. Among animals, the male is often not only larger, but also more elaborately adorned with manes, feathers and colours. Today it is more often the woman who wears jewels, but it is the man who selects them and pays for them. This affirms his self-worth as much as if he wore them himself.

'For centuries, highly skilled artisans have made jewels; one can still admire their works in our museums. But during the course of recent decades, the artist-creator, and especially the sculptor, has become active in this realm. Hubert Minnebo began designing rather late, having already earned great renown as a sculptor. In 1975, he broke into the design and creation of jewels. Of this he himself says: "Speaking from the solitary corner of my consciousness, I let the creative impulses surge forth, I put them on paper, I redo them, I close my eyes, I imagine my creation already completed, knowing full well that the physical form that I want will only be achieved through a struggle with the raw material of the wax blocks. During the process of creation, in the transformation of wax-to-void-to-gold, one

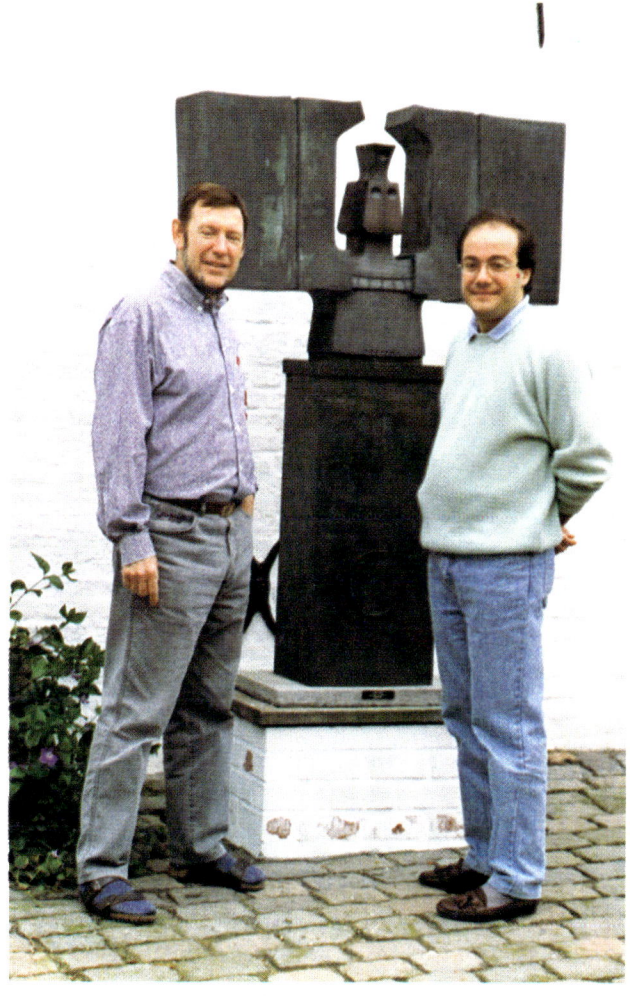

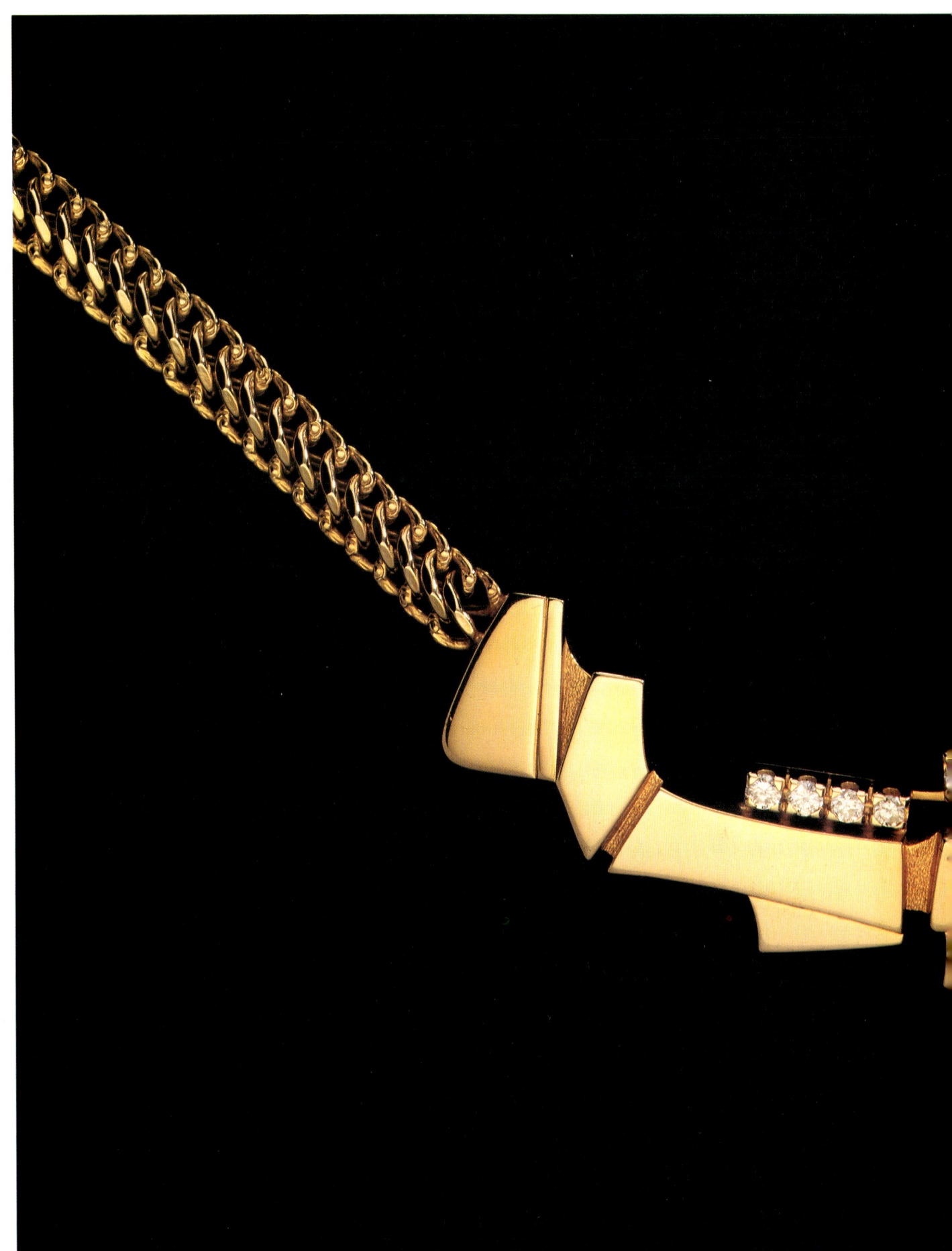

148 *Gold and diamond necklace, a unique piece.*

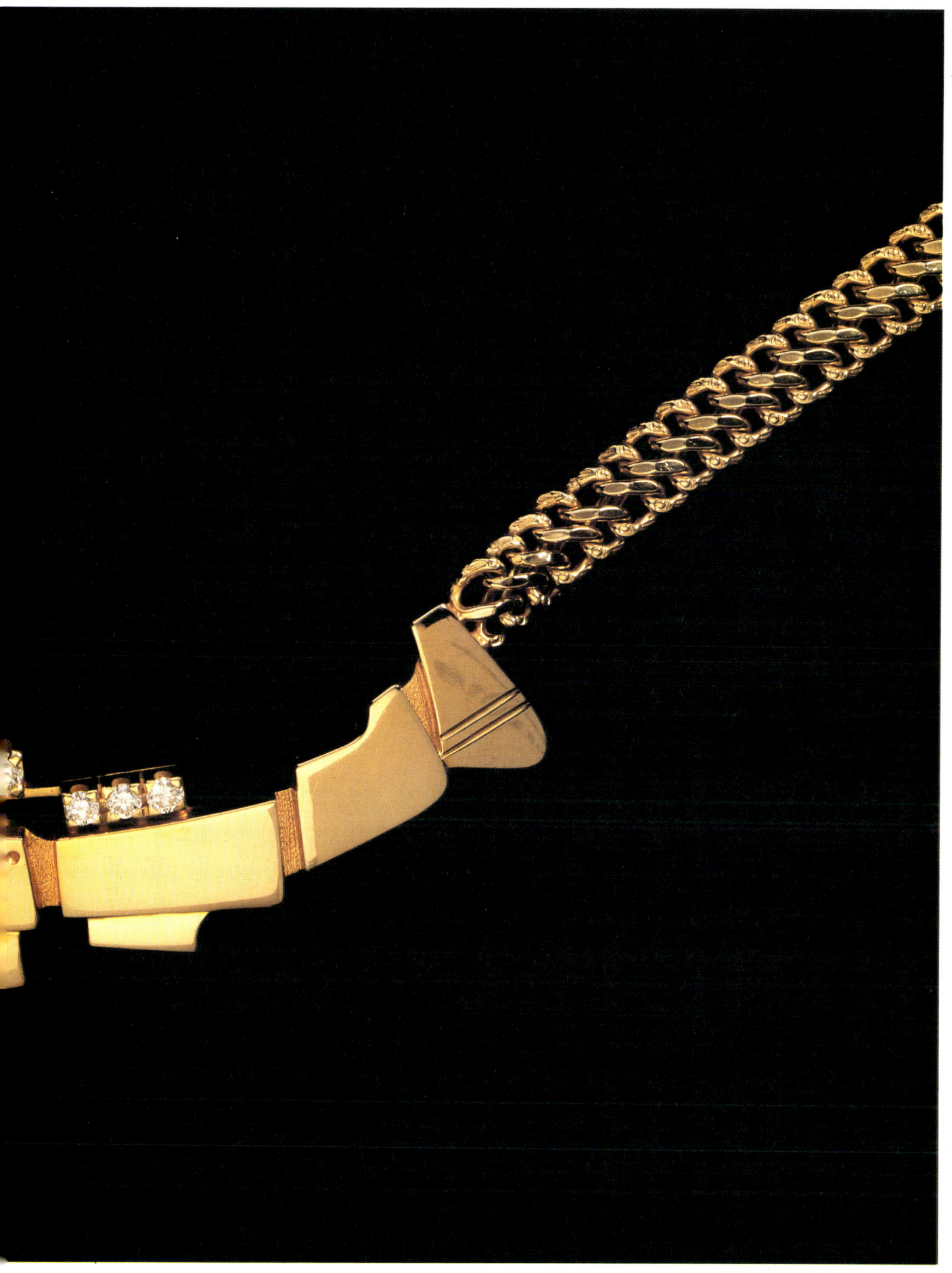

must drain off the wax gently, so as to bring a brilliant, almost sacred beauty to the fragile, tender piece, with a cautious and agile prudence, in order to achieve the vessel, the dreamt-of summit, and make its dignity endure like a luminous summer day,... this reflexion of images." Although he has created bronze jewels, such as belt-buckles, the artist has from the beginning shown a predilection for gold and the use of the lost-wax technique.

Gold is one of the oldest known precious metals. It is a very soft material, easy to laminate and stretch. Gold has become a virtual synonym for power, property, divinity. Artists could make the soul glow with it. They did so for centuries before our own era, at a time when nations and civilisations were founded and taxed on their possession of gold, and perished if they had none. Countries were named for their gold, such as Nubia, or at least they were imagined, such as Eldorado. Everything that King Midas touched turned to gold; this became his curse. Jason set out in search of the Golden Fleece; he was *crushed under the prow* of the Argo. Croesus, the last king of Lydia, learned Solon's lesson: gold does not bring happiness; when he tried to corrupt the Delphi oracle with his gold, he was overthrown.

'Now, gold is brilliance and reflection that has an almost supernatural power. Clerics kept their relics in it. Kings' tombs are lined with it. Alchemists of all times have tried, in Aristotle's words, "to change one into the other", the inferior into the superior, copper into gold. Paracelsius still prowls among us. Gold continues to attract man because it embraces power, science, discovery and creativity, even in an era in which prosperity is based on commerce, production, work.

'It is said that barely half of the production of gold falls in artists' hands. The largest share remains in the coffer-fortresses of banks, or used in industry, technology and scientific research. But artists make the most precious objects from it. Just remember the golden casket of King Meskalamduk of the Sumerian Ur, the death-mask of the Egyptian King Tutankhamen, that of Agamemnon, the golden Buddha in the British Museum, the reliquary of the Magi in Cologne, the treasure of the Golden Fleece in Vienna, to name only a few of the dozens of major jewels in the history of art.

'In contemporary art as well, jewellery is distinguishing itself more and more. This is due to the fondness for gold, because, as Aldous Huxley pointed out, "The goldsmith's products are priceless and form the core of all mystery."'

The subtlest irony hides herself in a delicate and spiritual way just under the skin; smilingly, little by little, she lets herself be discovered.

'In his romantic comedy *Two Gentlemen from Verona*, William Shakespeare writes: "Dumb jewels, in their silent kind, more than quick words, do move a woman's mind...".

Herbert Minnebo has become very particular in this field of jewellery creation. He works the gold. He uses this precious material to transplant the monumentality of his sculptures into the miniature art of his jewels. And, like his bronzes, his jewels are the creations of his own hands. One can recognise the characteristic shapes, the very expression of his eyes, even when he adds precious stones as noble accents.

Minnebo's jewels are conceived, first and foremost, to adorn a woman. In all of history, in every culture, the precious jewel has a proper place and a distinct approach. It represents prestige, initiation, accord, election and consecration. It is an adornment, a characteristic, a symbol and a talisman. A jewel has always been a sign of taste, and very often a unique work of art, sometimes even created for a special occasion. In this way, a jewel reflects the wearer as well as the creator. One pays homage to the other.

Minnebo has a special relationship with jewels. "No other work of art," he says, "can dream of a lovelier or more worthy bearer than a jewel's: a beautiful bosom." With jewels he pays homage to woman, thus joining a long line of poets, painters and sculptors, from minstrels of the Middle Ages to Gainsbourg. The king of Israel and Judea sang of the beauty of woman, and no plastic art can be imagined without her: as myth, as model and alibi. The sculptor knows her body and thus understands where his embellishments will give the most brilliance without ruining the lines or shapes of the whole. These are not recent discoveries. As early as Egyptian and pre-Colombian cultures, and among so-called primitive peoples, the earlobe, neck, waist, navel, fingers, wrists and feet have been the privileged bearers of jewels. And they still are for the contemporary artist. These are the zones that refer to a woman's functions and to the vital junctions of her psyche. It is not only with gold that Minnebo has this intimate relationship. Especially in this aspect of his art, he wants to know where his work will end up. A jewel is a personal act, a privilege and a mirror. It is important to know who will wear it. Thus the jewel will depend on the character of bearing and personality of the wearer. At times, a certain bravura is required on her part. Minnebo sometimes creates jewels of sizes and shapes that demand some courage.

'A third relationship is the one that exists between gold and skin, since there will be a great affinity between the work and the body. The contact of precious metal with the neck,

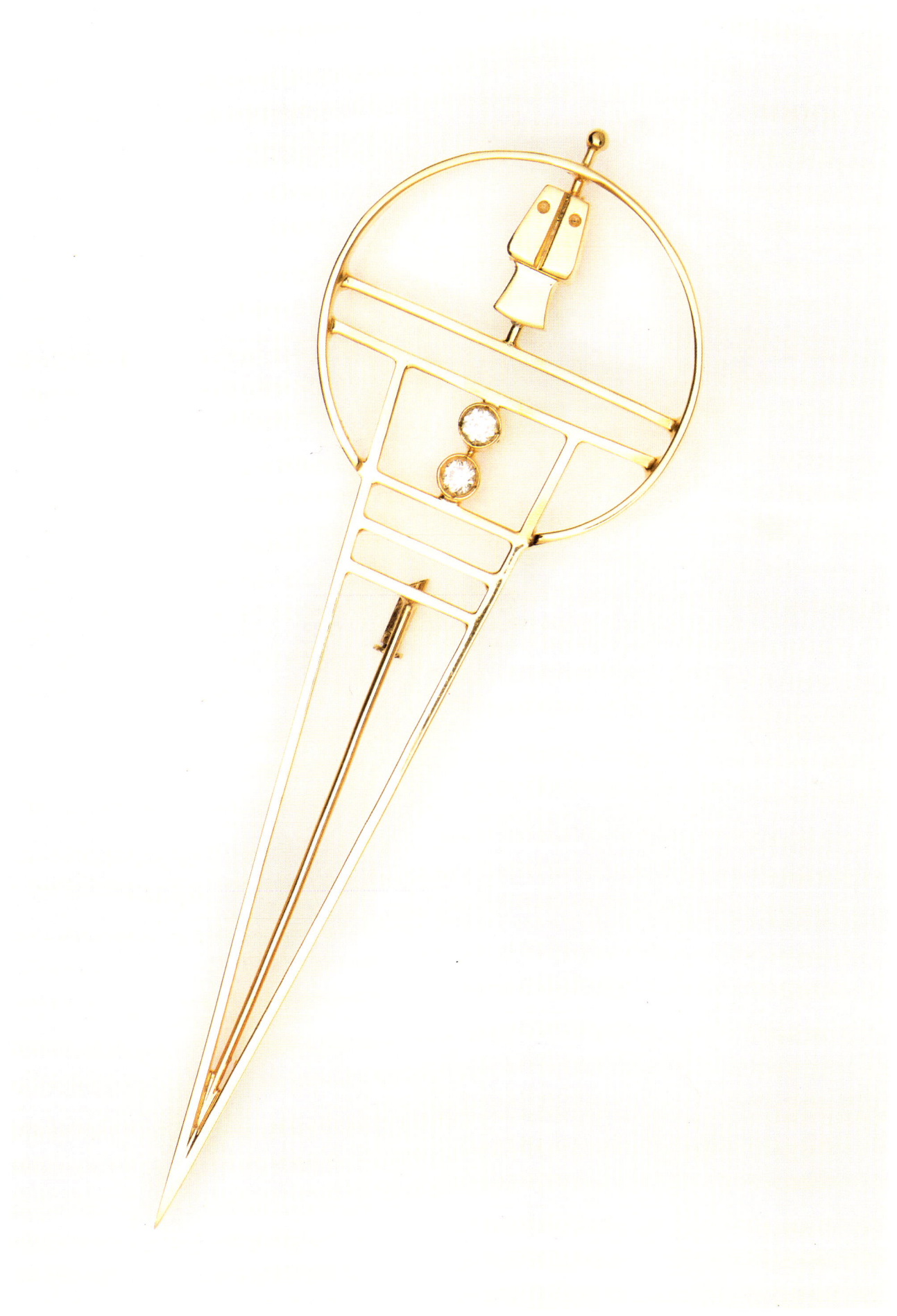

Gold and diamond brooch, a unique piece.

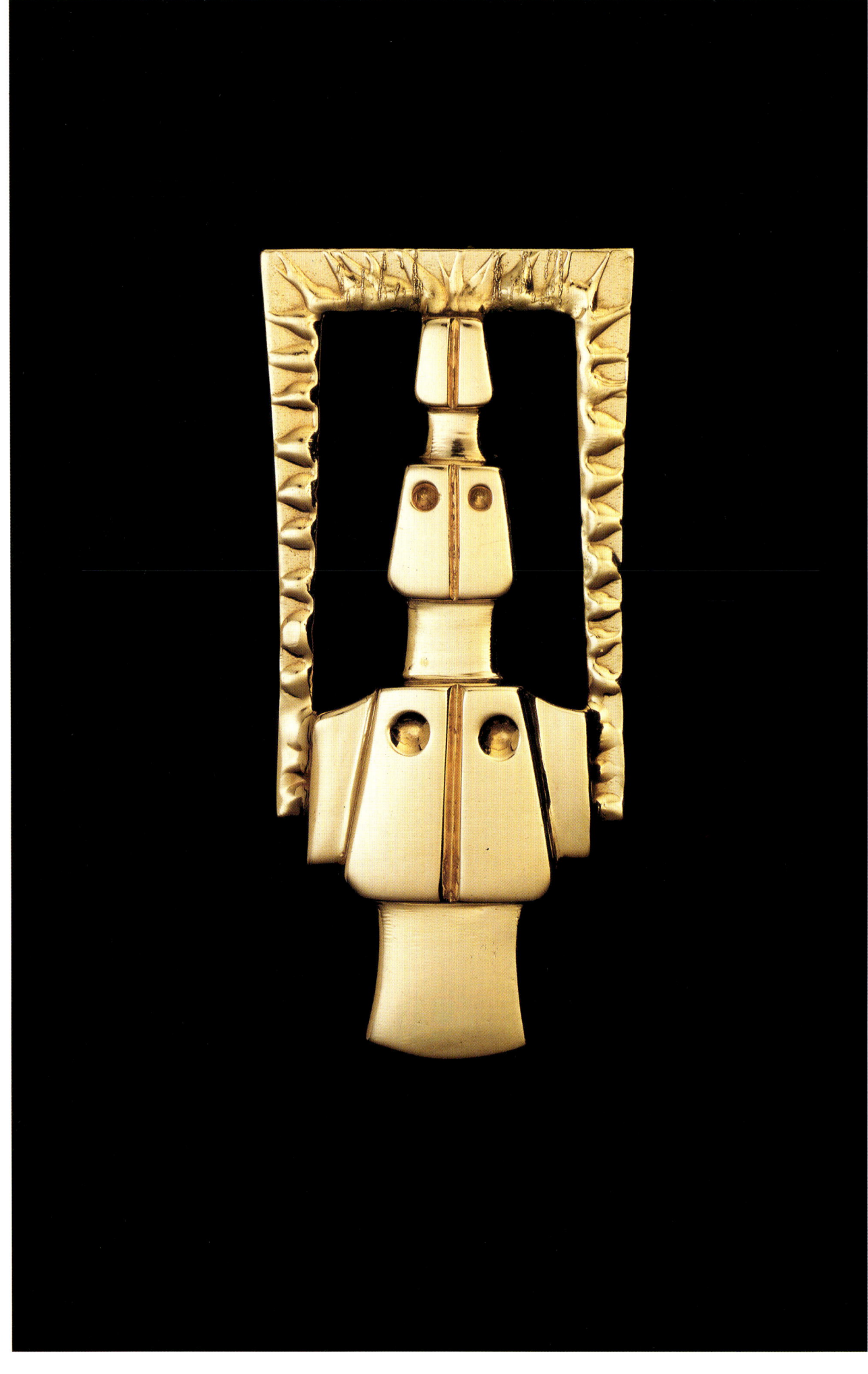

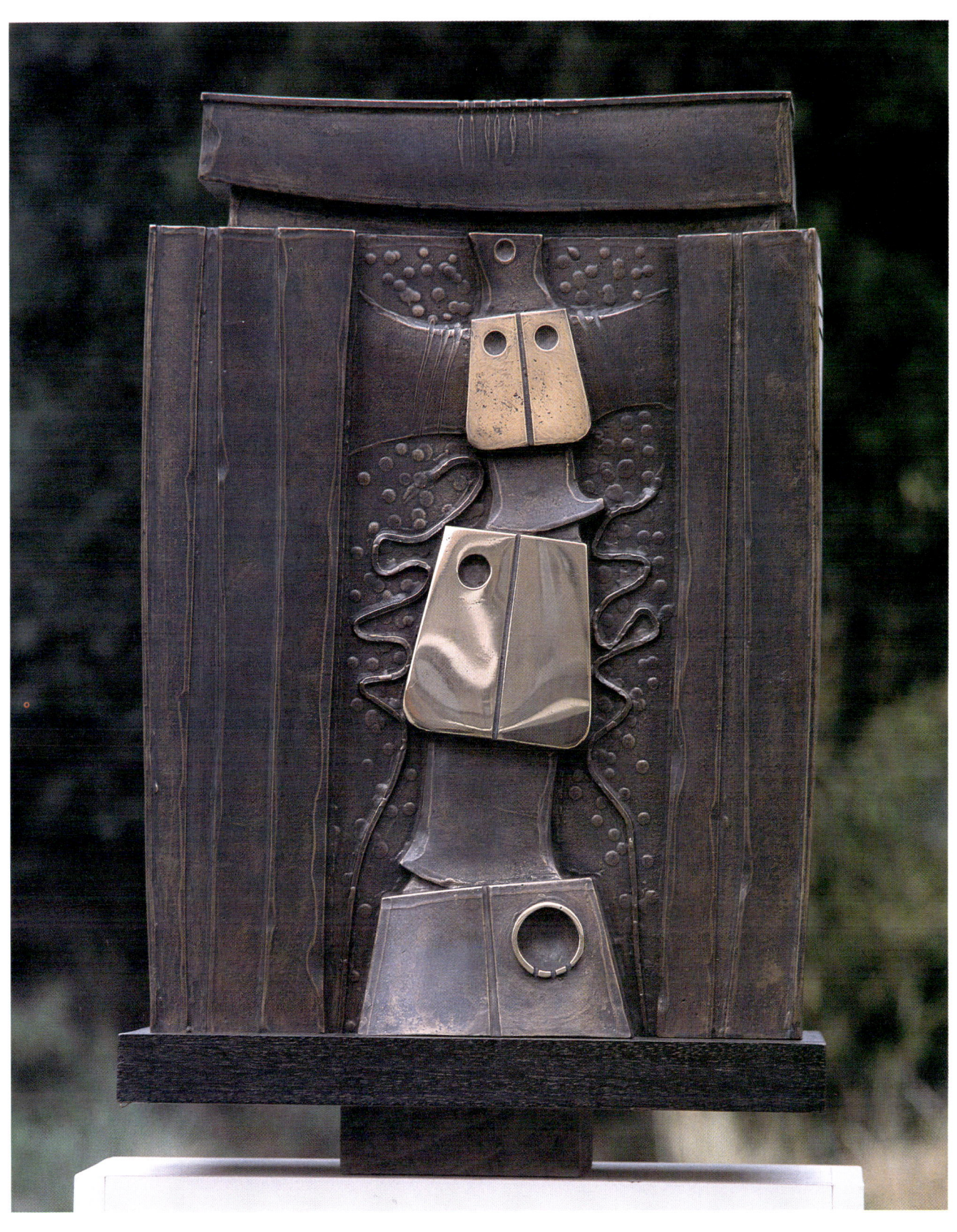

Tho works by Hubert Minnebo: gold pendant and bronze sculpture. 'Working several tonnes of bronze or several grammes of gold requires the same effort.'

153

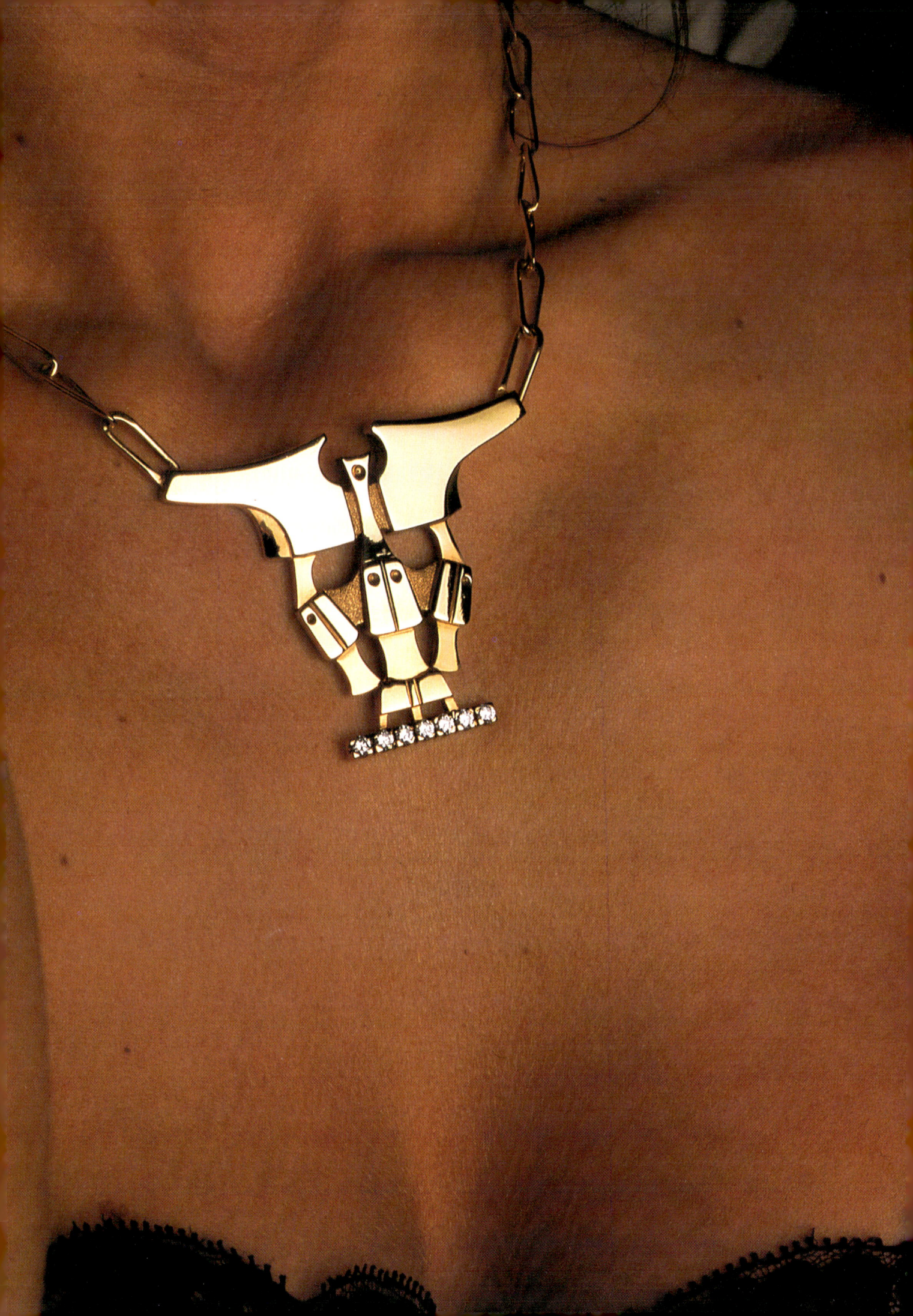

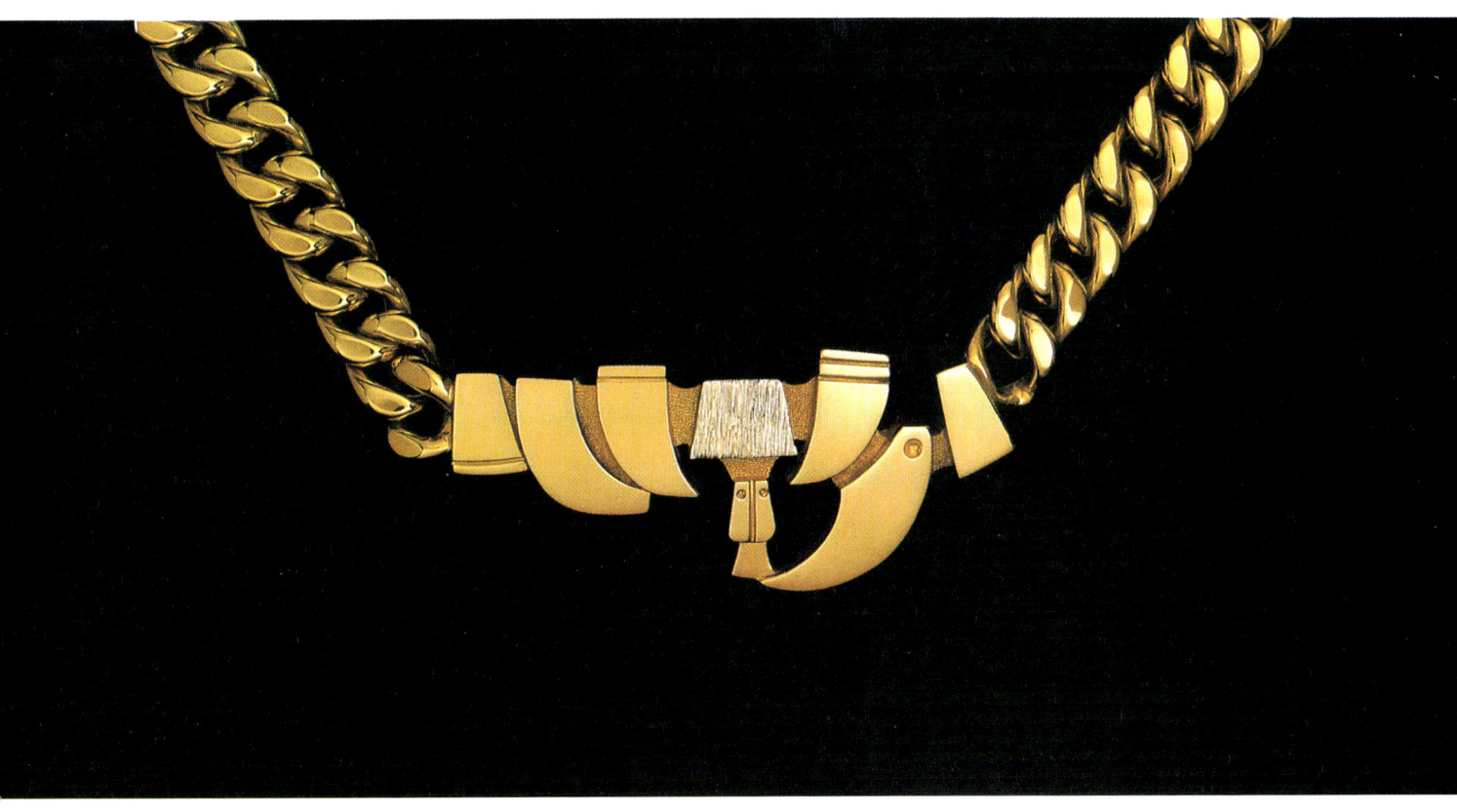

Gold necklace by Hubert Minnebo.

breast, wrist or finger grandly overcomes the objects frivolity. It is more profound than a simple decoration, and in turn it becomes a symbol. This object, which sets a woman apart and which will always be seductive, plays a universal role; it is an homage to the body and soul of the beloved. As Minnebo gives much importance to these relationships, he creates his works with a great deal of love and passion. If his jewels are functional objects, they are also works of art of very great value.

'If the creation of a bronze demands a great deal of strength and time, Minnebo uses as much effort and precision for his jewels. To begin with, the artist makes an exact sketch of the object. Next, the wax model is produced, which in this case is a very precise work in miniature. The rendering technique, which requires as much care, is performed sequentially. As he casts several pieces at once, the mould comes to resemble a tree, with the future jewels as its branches. In fact, they are not cast, but rather the gold is injected into the moulds by centrifugal force. "To make my jewels, I can imagine no material but gold," the artist says. "Gold is the most fantastic material there is. It is a magical experience." Here Minnebo joins the view of jewellers who, in so many cultures, have experienced the inexhaustible mystery of this metal so rich in effects, matte and shiny, and

that carries within itself the seeds of true works of art.

'In his jewels, the artist»s characteristic expression gives rise to new and very singular representations: the face with large, wide-open eyes; the eccentric, sometimes daring placement of forms and planes; the serious, noble and calm appearance. Even though Minnebo creates completely functional objects, he nevertheless finds the means of giving free rein to his inspiration, especially in the unusual poses of his figurines. Neither function nor presentation seems to impede him: on the contrary.

Even in oldest times, the ring – in the form of an amulet, seal, key or other – represented the dignity of its wearer, a woman's chosen lover or, more generally, a job or trade. Minnebo continues this tradition according to his own very personal vision. Creating a ring, for the very limited space of a finger-joint, is a great technical challenge. In this minuscule format, the artist succeeds, for example, in creating a face, surmounted by a circle that unwraps into symbolic rings.

'In the space of a belt-buckle, he manages to superimpose a face on a plane that is almost a square, almost a cloud, in which his characteristic three magic points appear. Bracelets allow him even greater freedom. He knows how to enhance the jewel, to make it

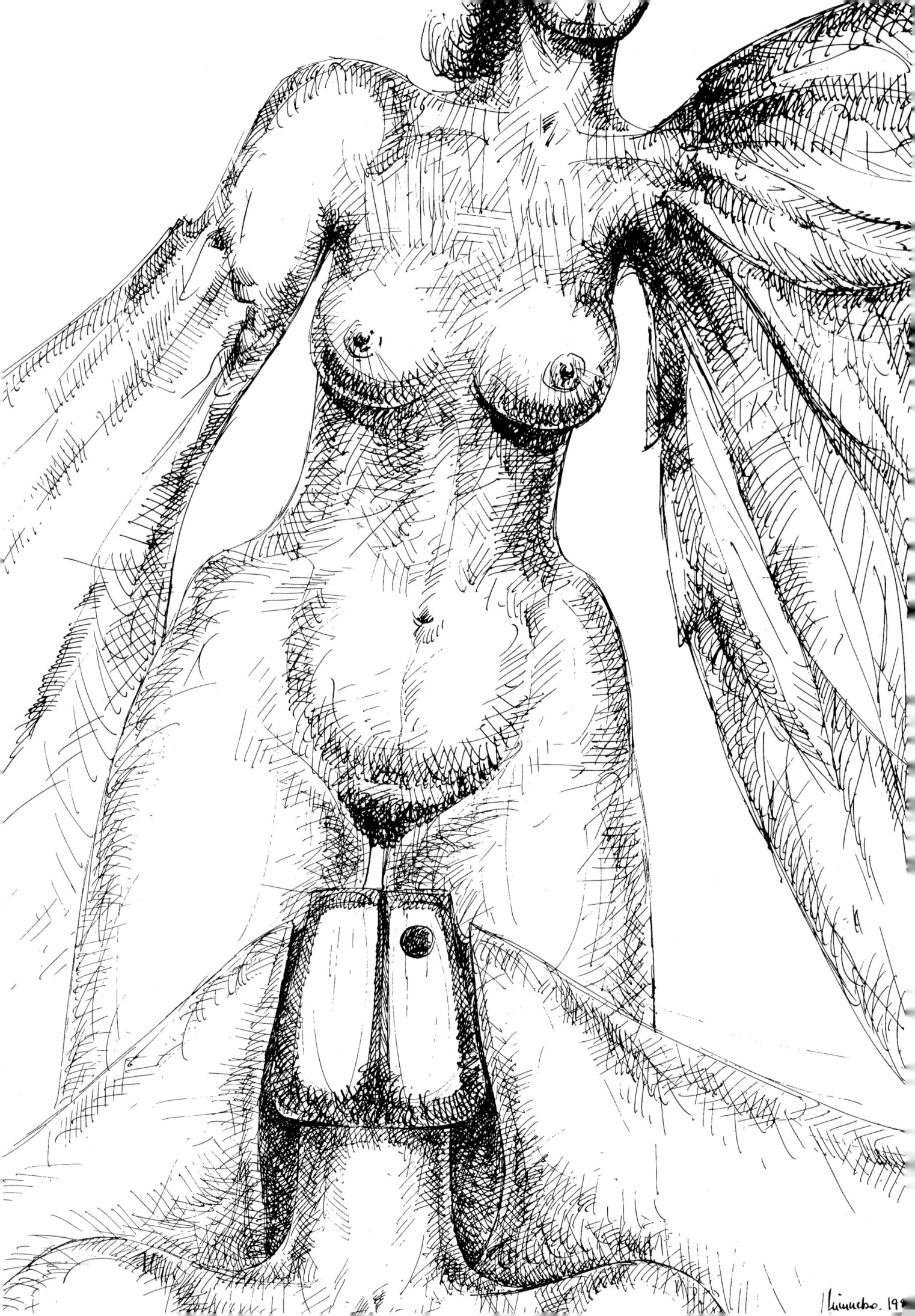

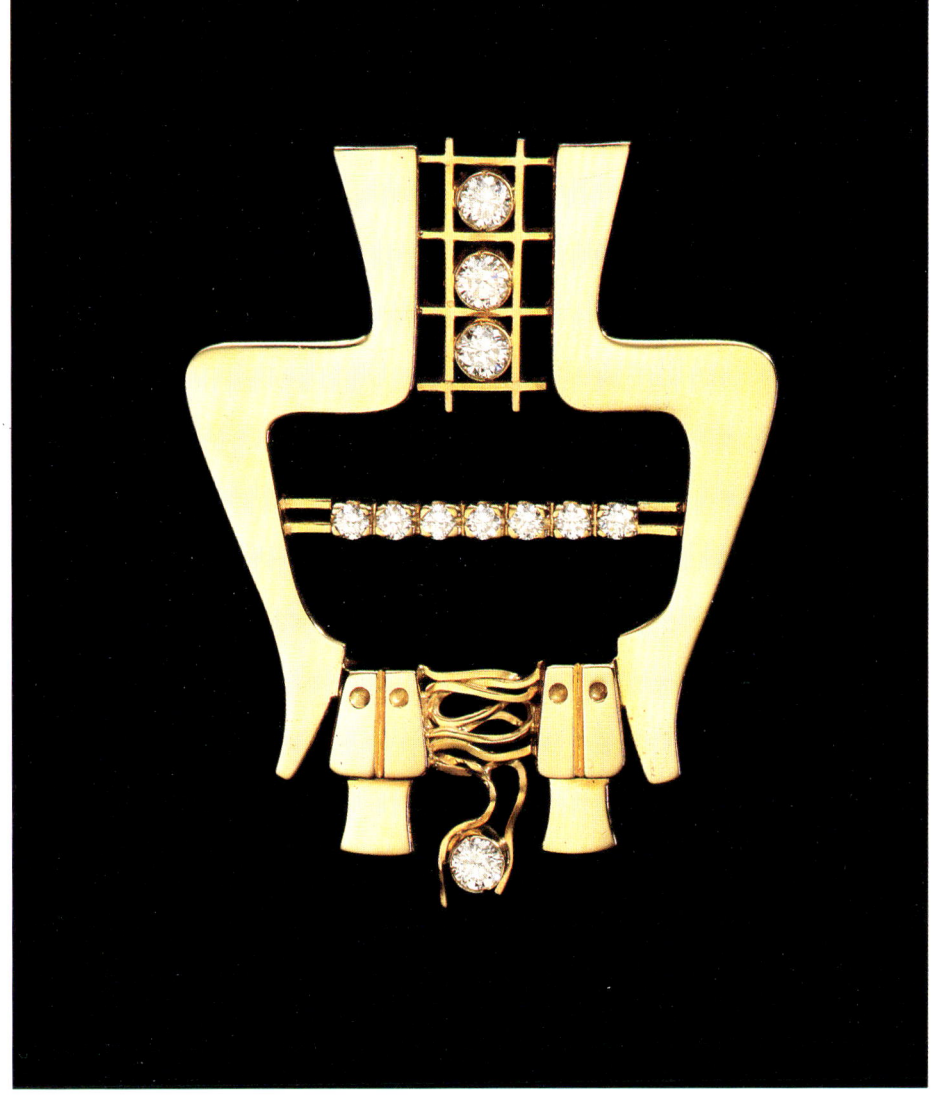

Gold and diamond pendant, a unique piece.

thick or light by its lines, by its subtle decorations, especially small planes on which little two-faced angel-heads capture the attention.

'Brooches, derived from antique fibulas, are extremely light and graceful. They are based on a play of triangles and circles. With just a few lines and a few support points, the artist arrives at perfect compositions, little jewels of balance.

'Since he began creating jewels, Hubert Minnebo has made pendants. They constitute the major part of his jewels and they are the ones that most resemble the forms of sculptures. The same characteristics are found in them, but with a charm enhanced by their small size and brilliant material. There is the famous Minnebo face and the three magic points, but above all a seductive and harmonious play of planes. They suggest a bird's head or sundial, a bust of a woman with a curl in her eye, or a double image emerging from a bumpy plane. Here are the outstretched crowns, a perfect circle or two wrought

squares. Elsewhere it is the detailed figure of a woman that strikes us, draped just as a sculpture would be, or three superimposed heads enclosed in a frame. Precious stones give even more brilliance to the whole. Sometimes certain symmetrical or asymmetrical planes are left rough, thus accentuating the shiny parts. All these elements form the key to the different levels of meaning, which are always present in these tiny sculptures. For certain pendants, the artist has chosen a chain; it becomes part of the whole. This enables him to produce a more voluminous and elegant arrangement. In this case, he especially likes to use little rounded triangles and precious stones, placed in the centre, distributed unevenly, or integrated in the chain.

'All of Minnebo's jewels radiate the same characteristic style. These great works of art of small size contain strength and refinement, sensuality and spirituality, confrontations and combinations that are very unusual but still very real. To this quality is added the important dimension of flawless craftsmanship.'

157

PAOLO
SPALLA

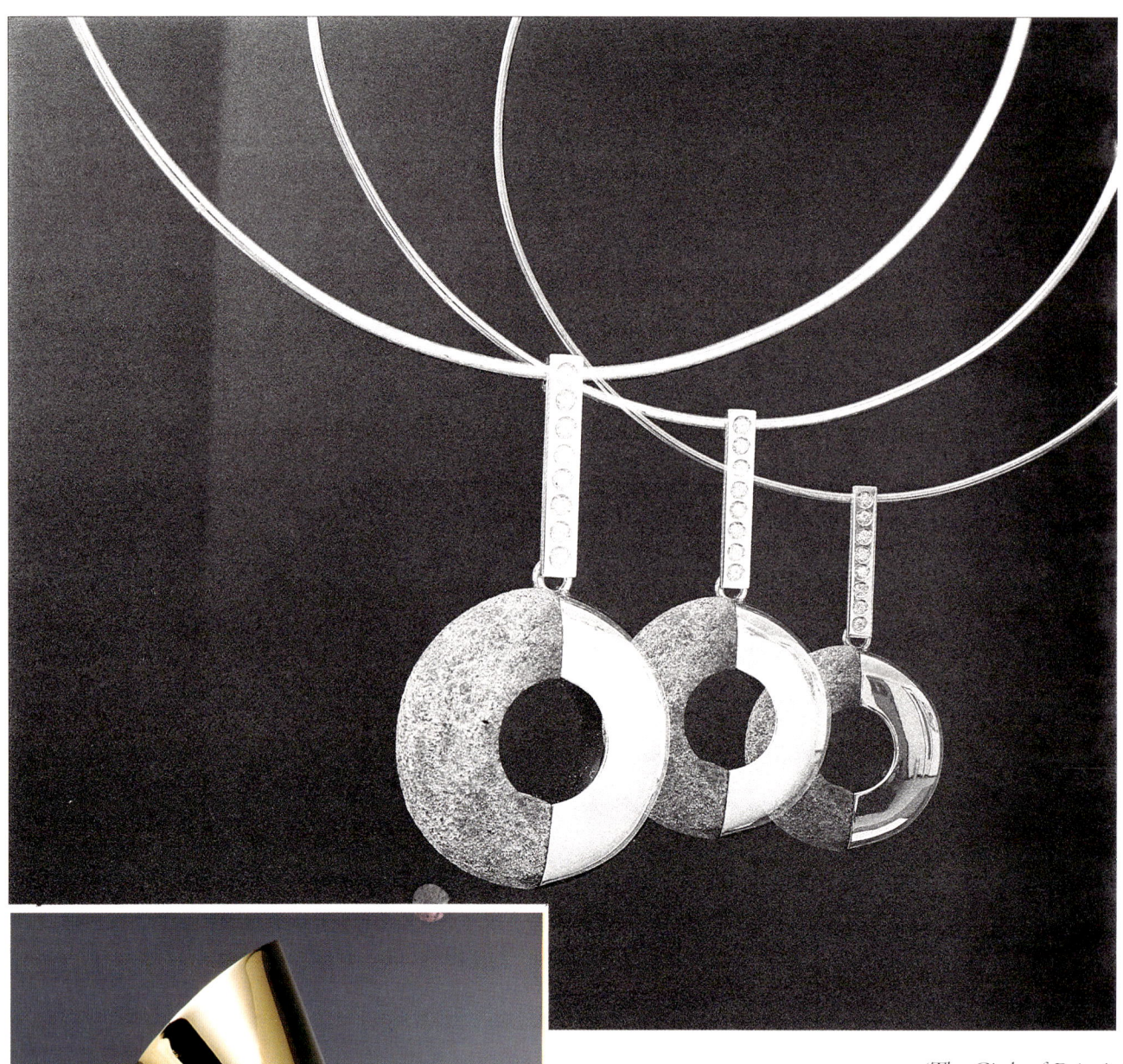

*'The Circle of Being',
necklace in gold,
diamonds and pebble
from the Po River by
Paolo Spalla.*

*Ring and bracelet by
Paolo Spalla.*

158

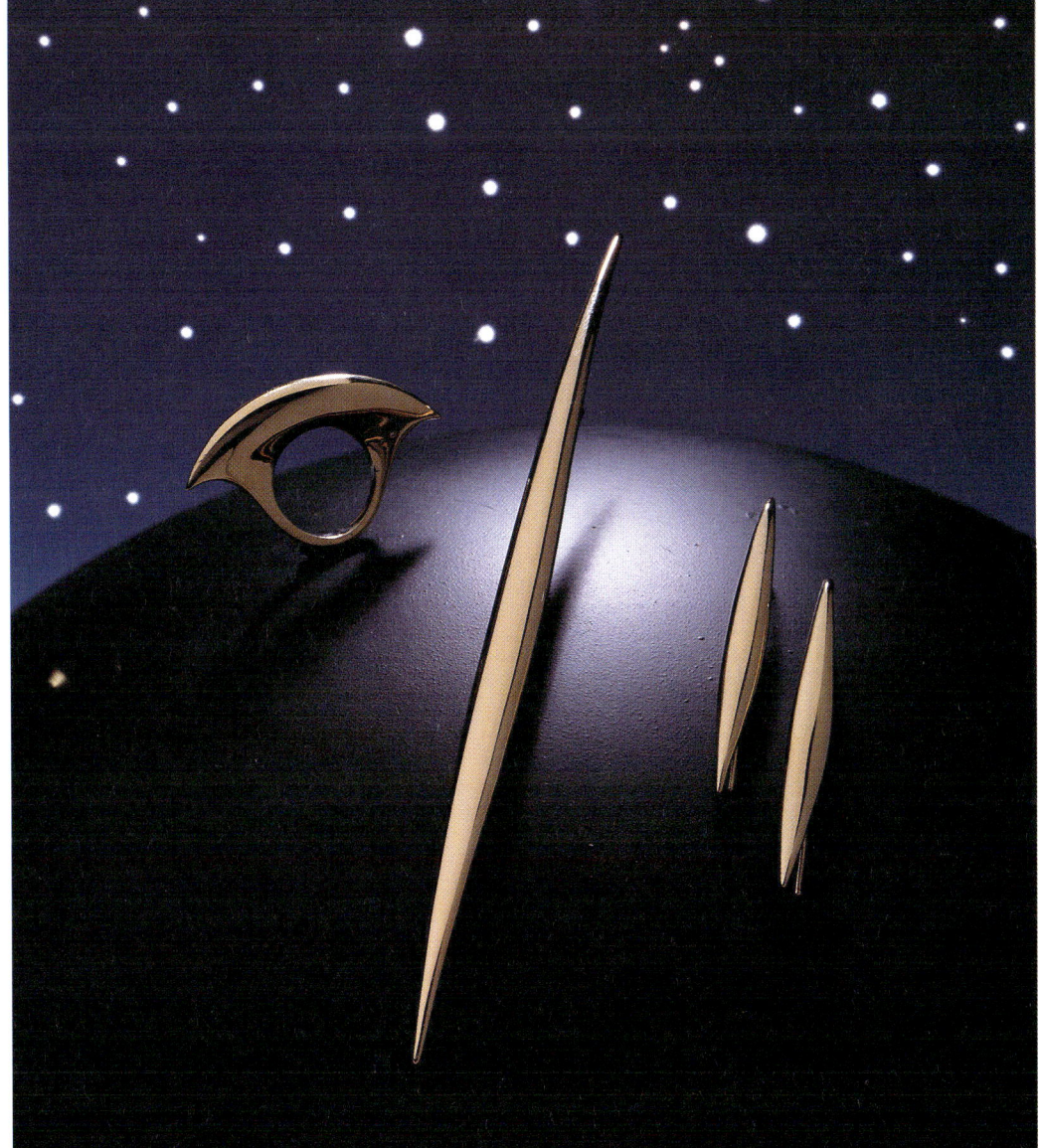

'Whistling', ring, brooch and earrings in laminated gold by Paolo Spalla.

Certain great sculptors have been so captivated by the art of jewellery that they have made it their principal activity. Paolo Spalla, whose works are seen throughout the world, creates jewels and precious sculptures. In an article appearing in the journal *l'Orafo italiano,* Ivo Sedezzari describes, very poetically, Paolo Spalla's work and philosophy:

'The seed...perceived. If you take a pebble from the river and sculpt it, you will change its form: you will have used this stone as a raw material. But if, from this pebble, you manage to capture its meaning and you accept the action of the water, its shaping, its polishing as they are, then you understand this pebble for what it really is, which its form represents in its continual mutation.

'If you take a tree-trunk from the river and you sculpt a figure from it, you will have changed its form: you will have used this trunk merely as a common material. But if you know how to seize the essence from this trunk and you succeed in penetrating it, you will revive the slow flow of water that worked to the bottom of its soul; then you will understand this trunk and what it really is, you will enter into its innermost structure and become saturated with the most profound aspects of its character and you will feel the time pass.

'If you take the seed of a fruit, if you know how to perceive the life that this grain encloses, you will repeat the gesture by breathing its essence... I mean to say that in the air there was the whistling of a seed sailing by, attracted by an infinity of centripetal forces; this grain burst open, luminous and pointed like an arrow in a bow... the bow of the infinite. I mean that this seed was captured by Paolo Spalla as it drifted through space. I mean that this seed, touched by the hand of man, blossomed while giving life.'

PHILIPP
BECKER

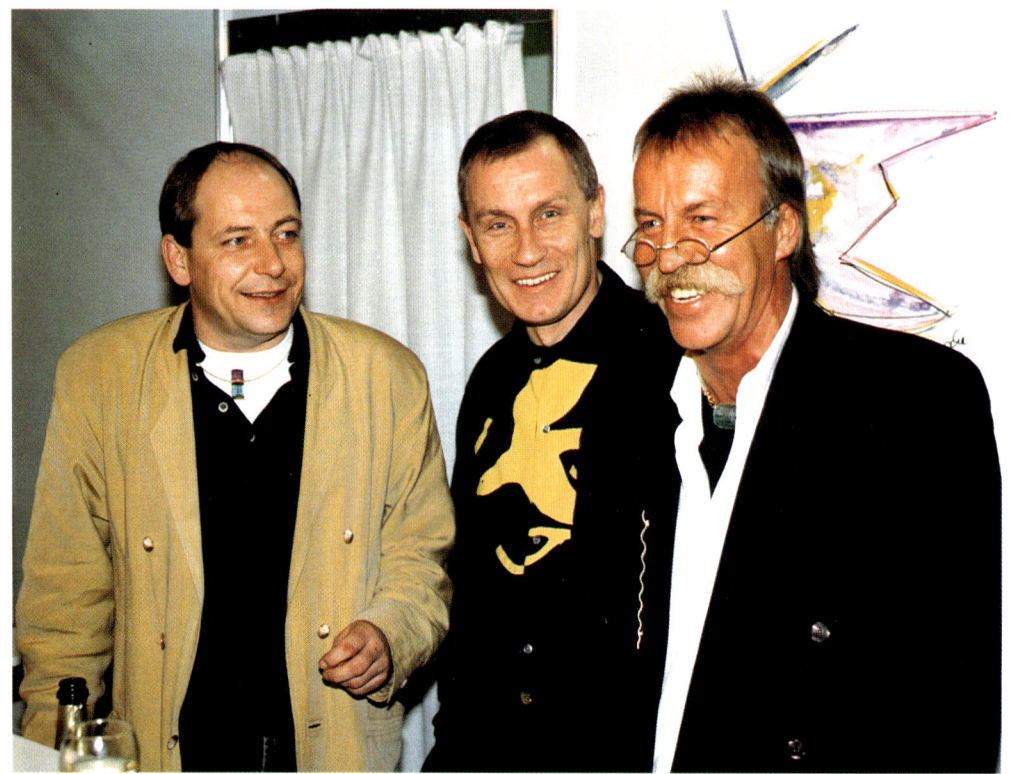

The sculptures of Phillip Becker & Co. are objects created by a group of lapidaries in Idar-Oberstein: Friedrich Wilshaus, Karl-Heinz Neumann and Veit Helmut Goris. They collaborate in cutting stones for contemporary jewellery and also in creating 'precious sculptures'.

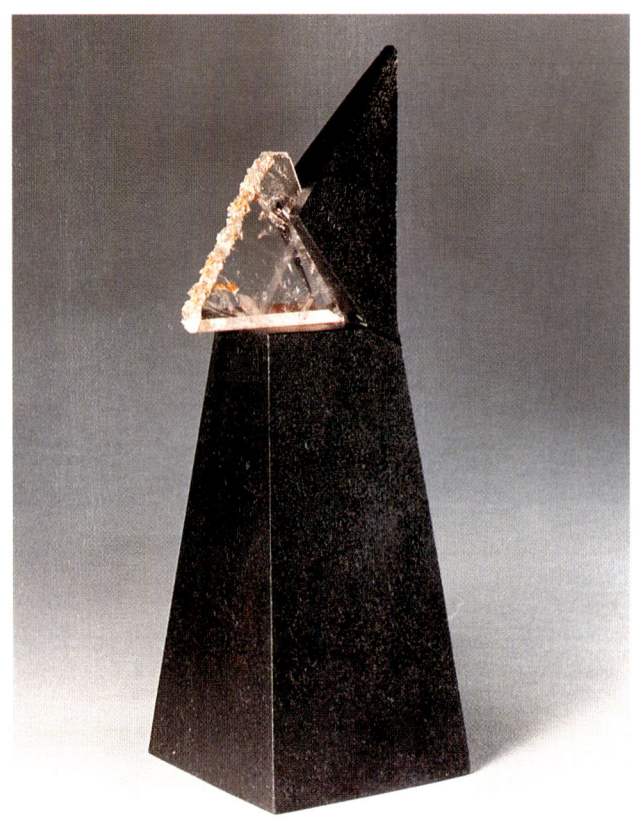

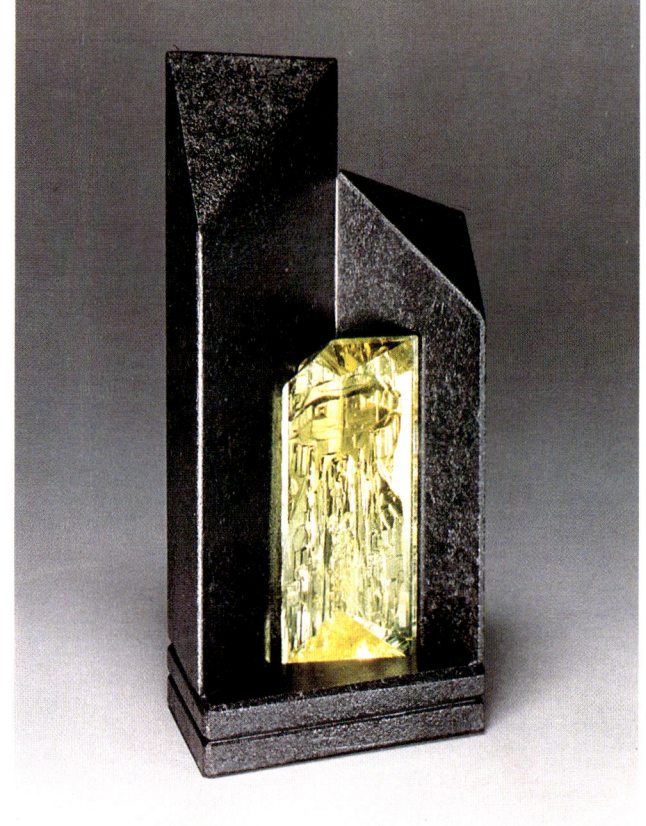

160 *Black granite and morganite. A unique piece.*   *Black granite and yellow beryl. A unique piece.*

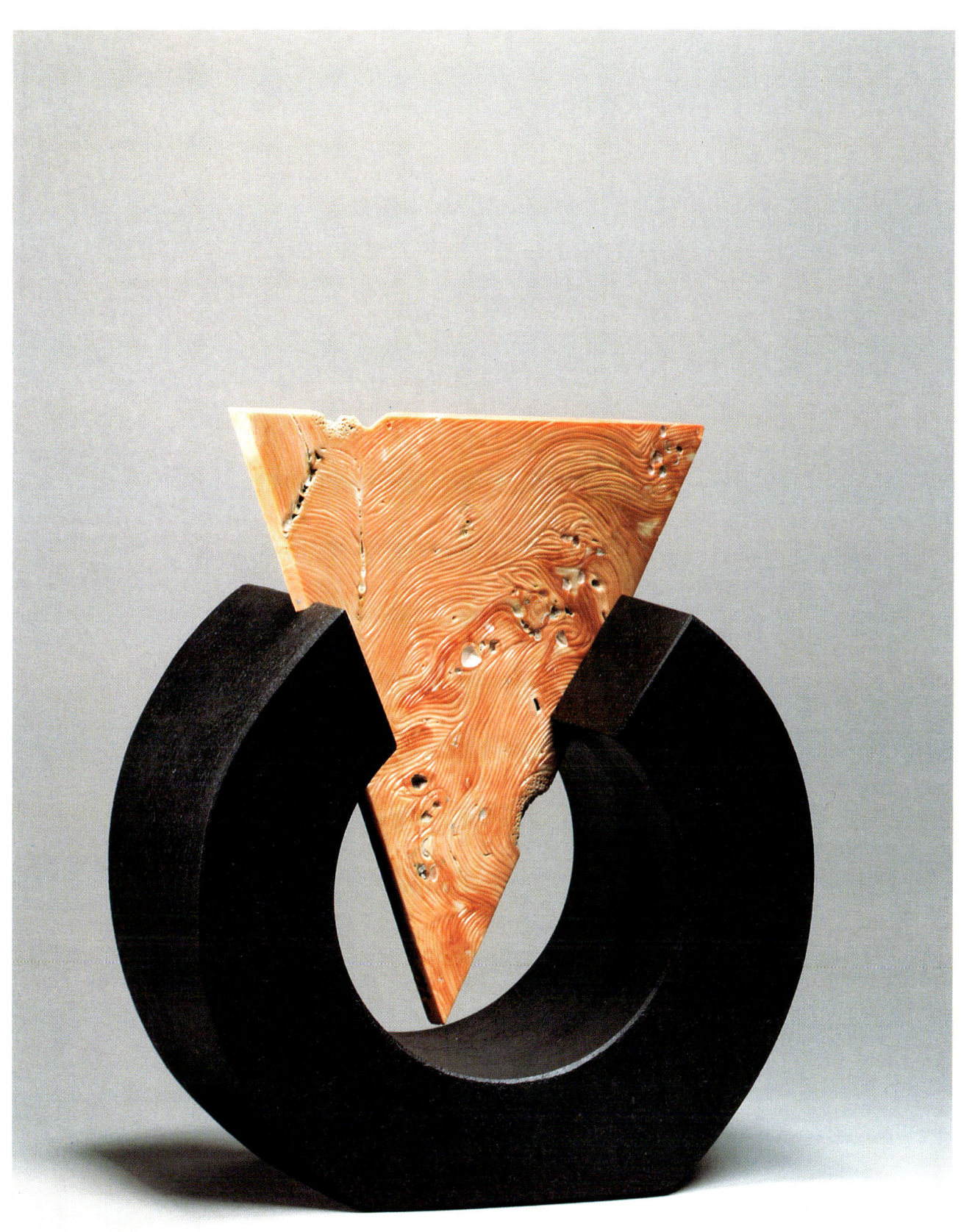

Sculpture by the Phillip Becker group: black granite and coral. A unique piece.

JORGE LUPIN

Stones inspire him, sculpture is his passion. In combining these two elements, Jorge Lupin succeeds in creating works in hard stone of a peerless finesse, such as this 'Equestrian Fantasy' in rainbow fluorite, amber fluorite, diamonds and gold.

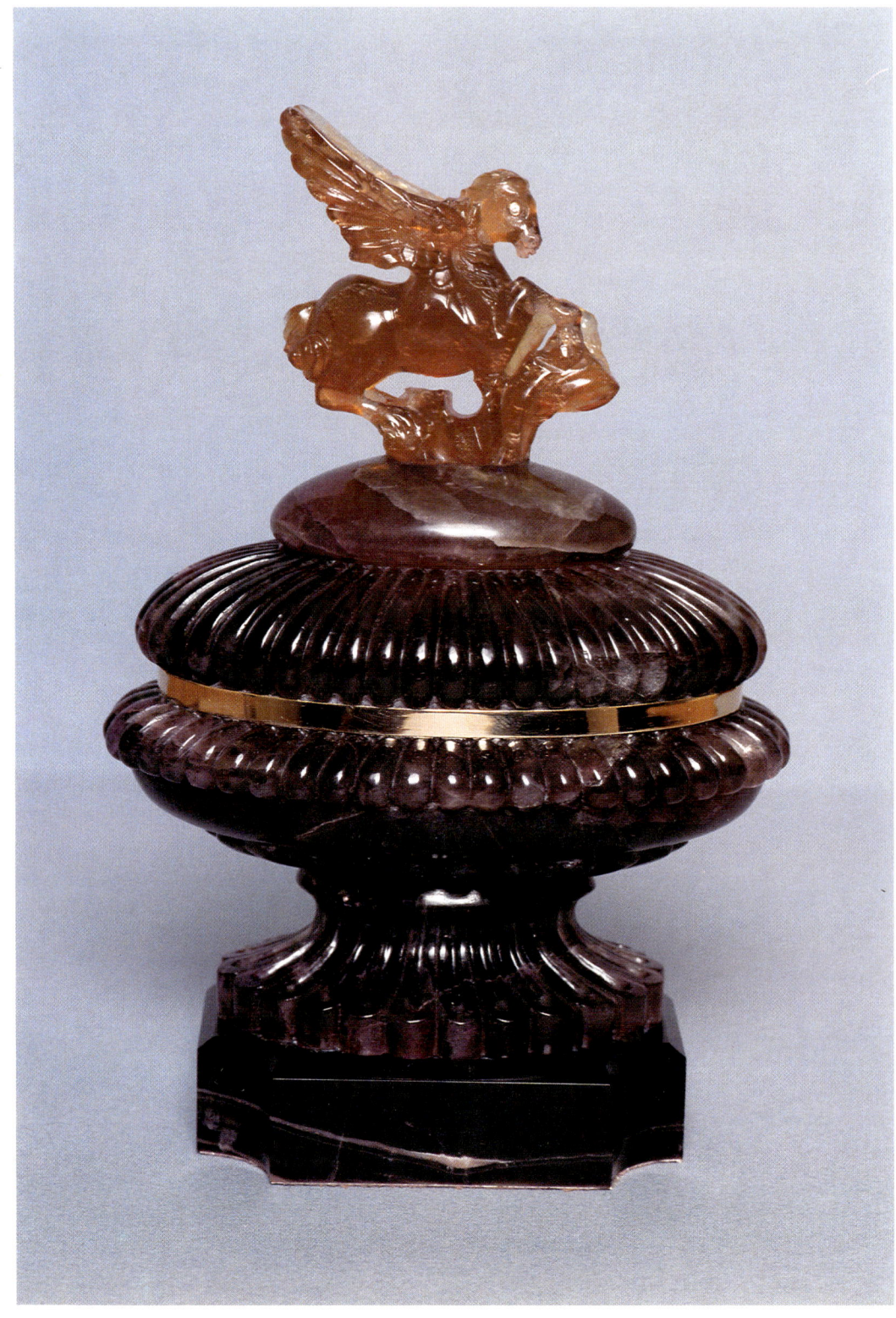

HELMUT WOLF

His works are on display in the world's greatest museums; he creates for royal families: Helmut Wolf's name will endure because of his extraordinary work. He sculpts fine stone for days, weeks, months and sometimes even years.

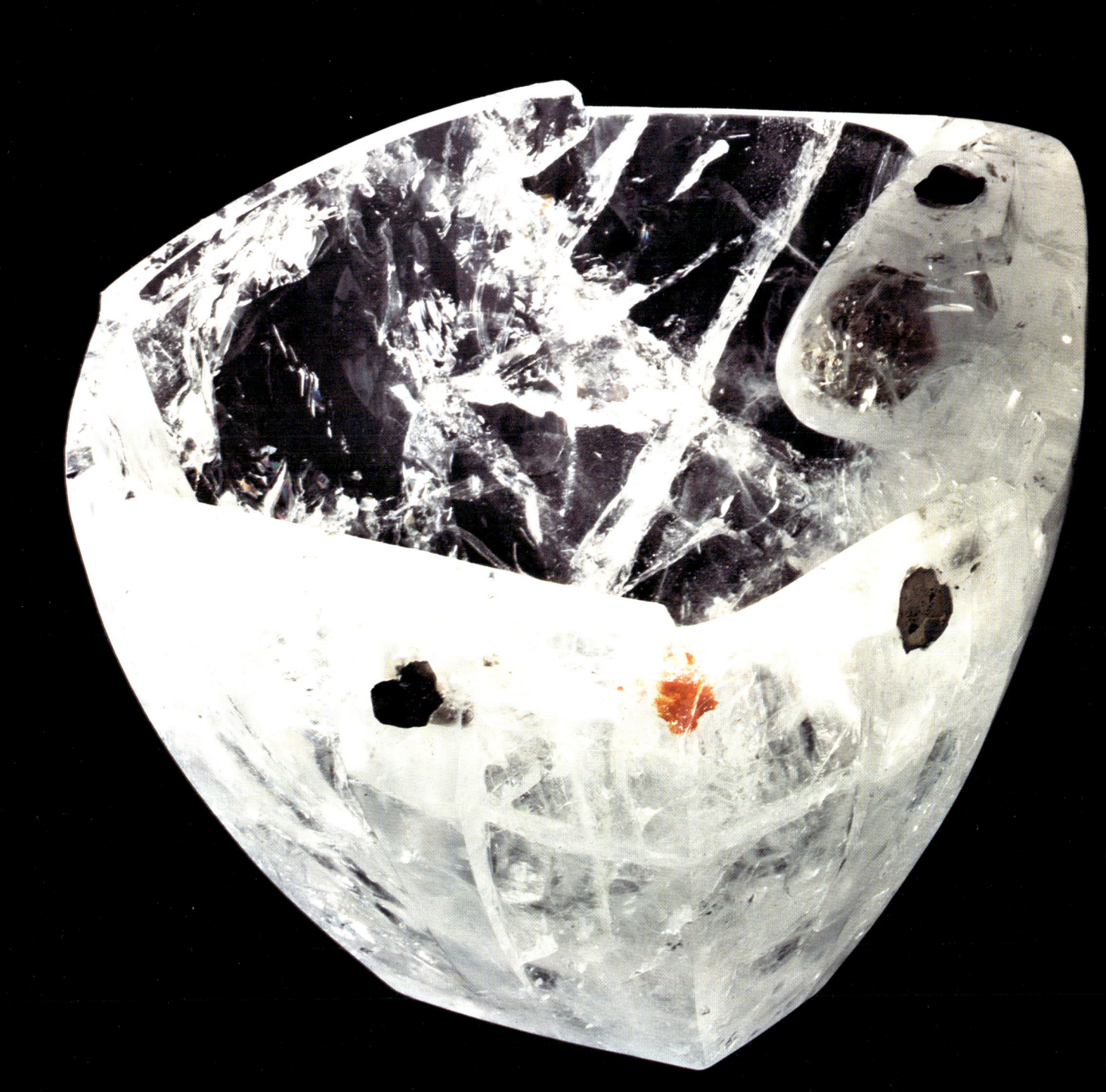

Vase in rock crystal, a rare and unique piece by sculptor Helmut Wolf.

CLAUDE
MAZLOUM

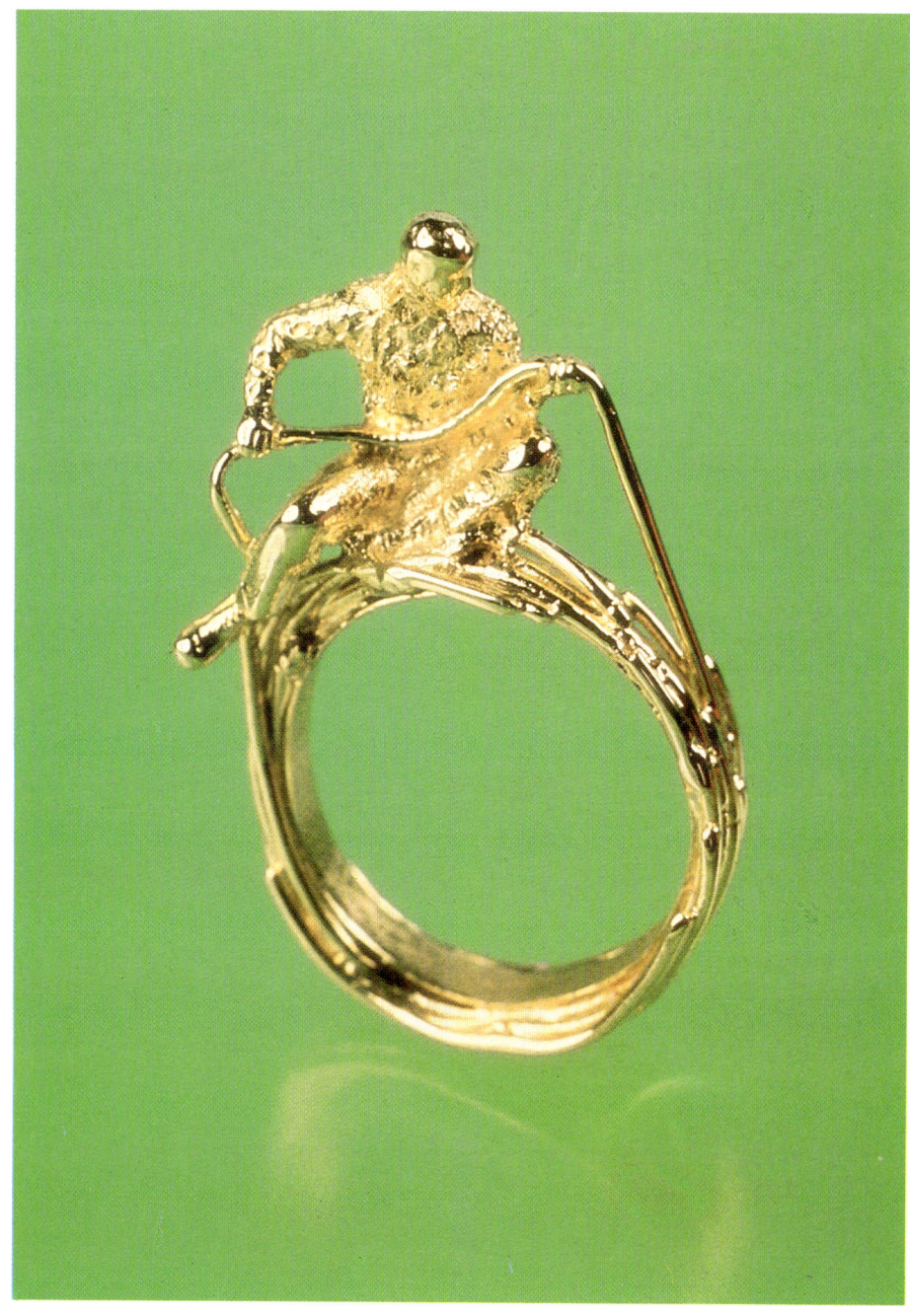

'The Thread of Time', display jewel in sculpted gold; this jewel is part of the prestigious collection of the Wuppertal Historical Museum.

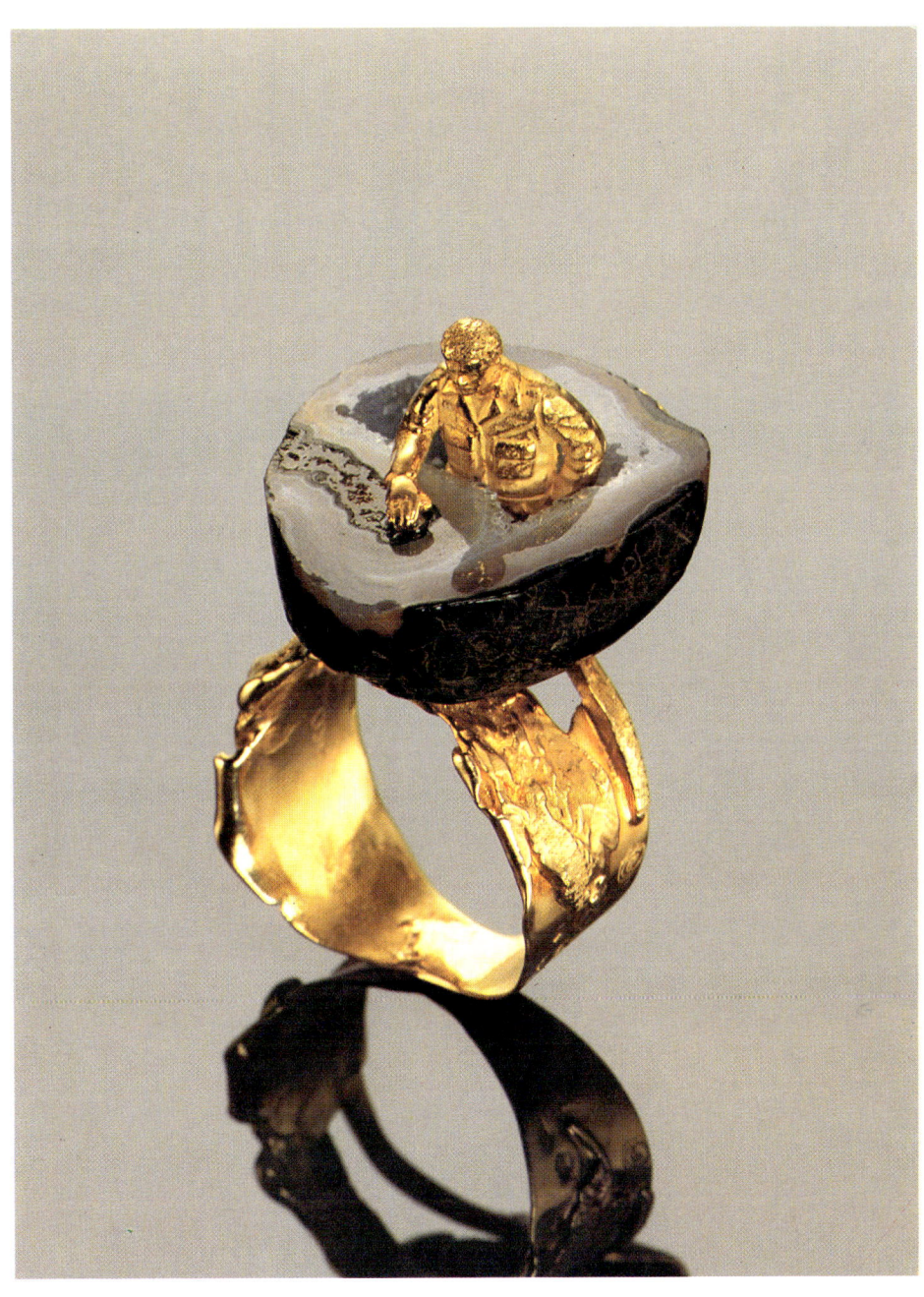

Ring-sculpture in gold and geode entitled 'Man and Stone'. This jewel is on display in the Idar-Oberstein Museum as a symbol of the mysterious rapport that exists between those who search for precious materials and the nature that offers them.

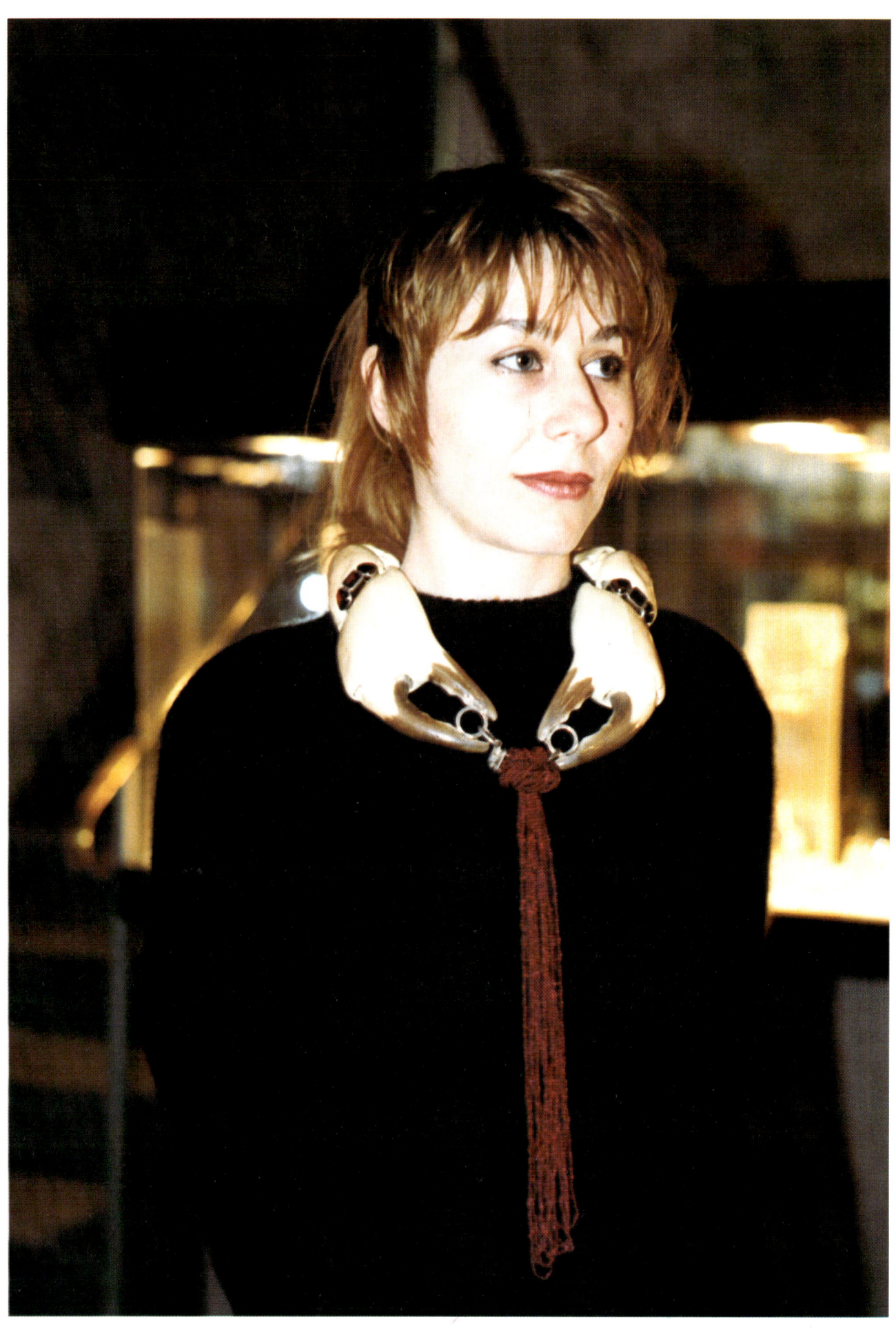

166   *Caroline Portail trying on a necklace by Thierry Vendome, a unique piece in silver and 'sea products'.*

CHAPTER VI

USING UNUSUAL MATERIALS

In collaboration with Caroline Portail

Gold, precious stones, pearls and other rare elements are the principal components of jewels. But there are other materials that are just as beautiful, or that become magnificent with the intervention of the artist and the artisan. Caroline Portail reveals to us the art of transforming a simple item into a sublime jewel.
'In the world of jewellery and precious materials, there is a clear-cut distinction between materials called precious and those that are not. It seems to me that the designation of "precious" is linked to different values. On the one hand, a symbolic value that reflects aesthetics, the subjective and fecund feeling of beauty, and the paradox of something that is both eternal and ephemeral. On the other hand, a social and commercial value linked to the product's rarity, due to its uniqueness, and thus, in the logic of the marketplace, to its price, all the higher according to the rarity of the object or the material. What gives a precious value to a material is the beauty that I see in it, and by beauty I simply mean that this material has the subtle ability to move me.
'In my jewels or objects that are made from both precious and non-precious materials, using contrast or even paradox as a basis for the design is more than just an artifice.
'It is a kind of language, a meaningful form of expression of the creative moment.
'Whatever feelings, will and reflexion I bring to it are set in motion and escape from me in the moment that the object is finished, so that each person may then capture them according to his or her own sensitivity.
'In my creations there is a kind of poetic progression made up of certain resonances: Emotion is often a starting point in my plastic and aesthetic explorations, as it is in the choice of the elements to be used. Nature offers me a profusion of all sorts of elements that are palpably beautiful. In their raw state, they carry within themselves the signs of life, of time, of an existential power that is full of contrasts. Contrast seems to me to be a permanent and inherent characteristic of all life. It is fundamental, for it contains a dynamic.

'In a harmonious form, the contrast of a broken line, of an unexpected, anachronistic element, symbolises one of life's realities. In nature, even in the most structured, the most geometric systems, one finds an element that does not respond to logic, a detail that is anarchic, inexplicable, which stirs up a system that had appeared to be perfect.
'It is this detail that makes the material moving, by emphasising its life and its uniqueness, in revealing the movement, the dynamics that are inextricably linked to it, by betraying a certain kind of masked unreason that subtends reality. The words "moving", "stirring" and "movement" also resonate in emotion.

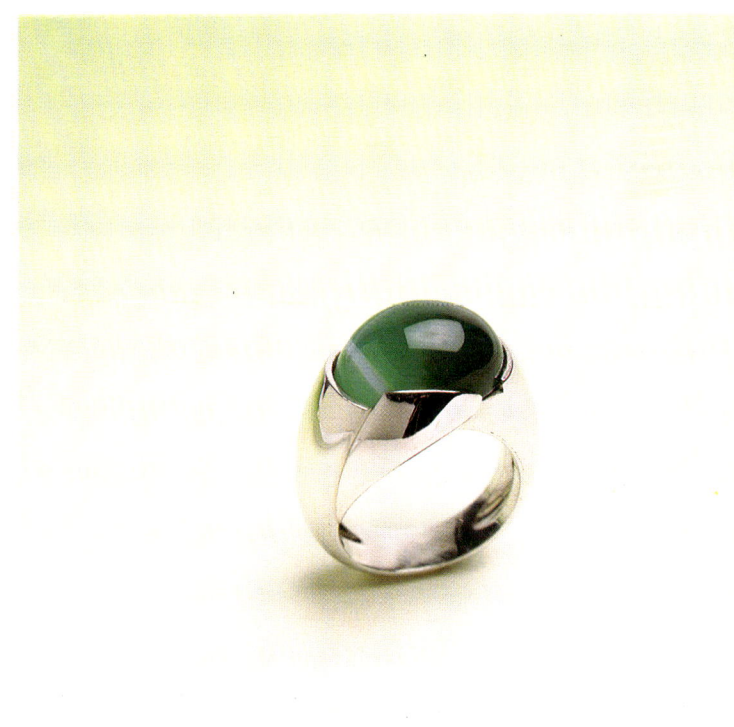

Ring in silver and green agate by Caroline Portail. The value of the ring lies not in the raw materials but in the purity of line.

'The contrast of precious materials and non-precious ones thus symbolises this search for a movement, a dynamic that emerges through the contrast of forms and materials.

'Mixing precious and non-precious materials, as well as associating a raw material with one that is refined, polished, faceted, figured by man, also allows me to create the contrast that will reinforce each person's individuality.

'The jewel thus becomes significant and full of meaning.

'Within all of this there is doubtless an inquiry into the questions of time, of roots and of becoming, a reflexive and possibly mystical dialogue, in which the jewel serves as a vehicle or mirror, transporting the viewer by what Kundera calls the unbearable lightness of being.'

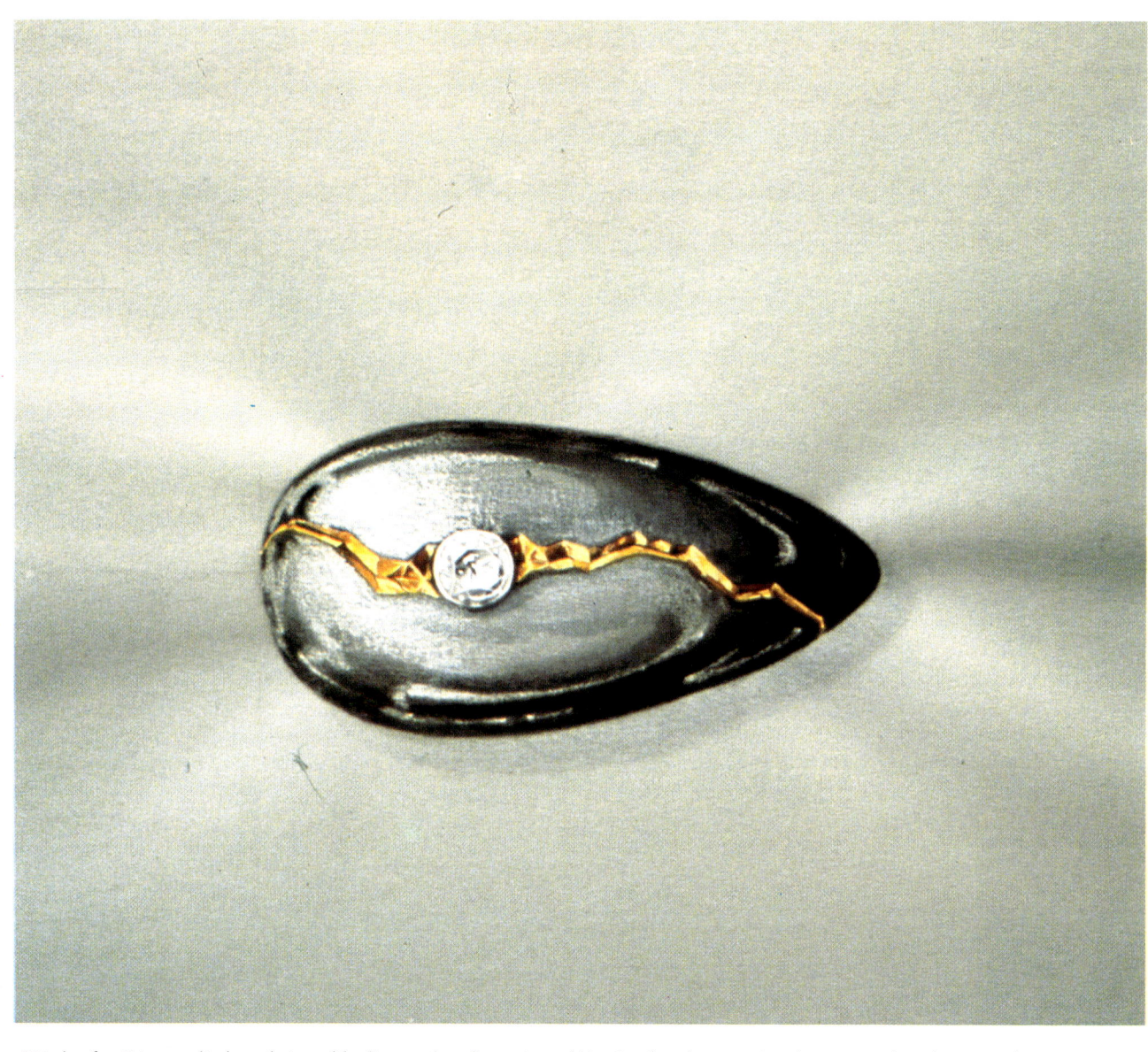

'Birth of a Diamond', brooch in gold, diamond and granite pebble. In this design, Caroline Portail underscores the contrast between the precious stone and the ordinary stone, gold being nothing more than a link between the two.

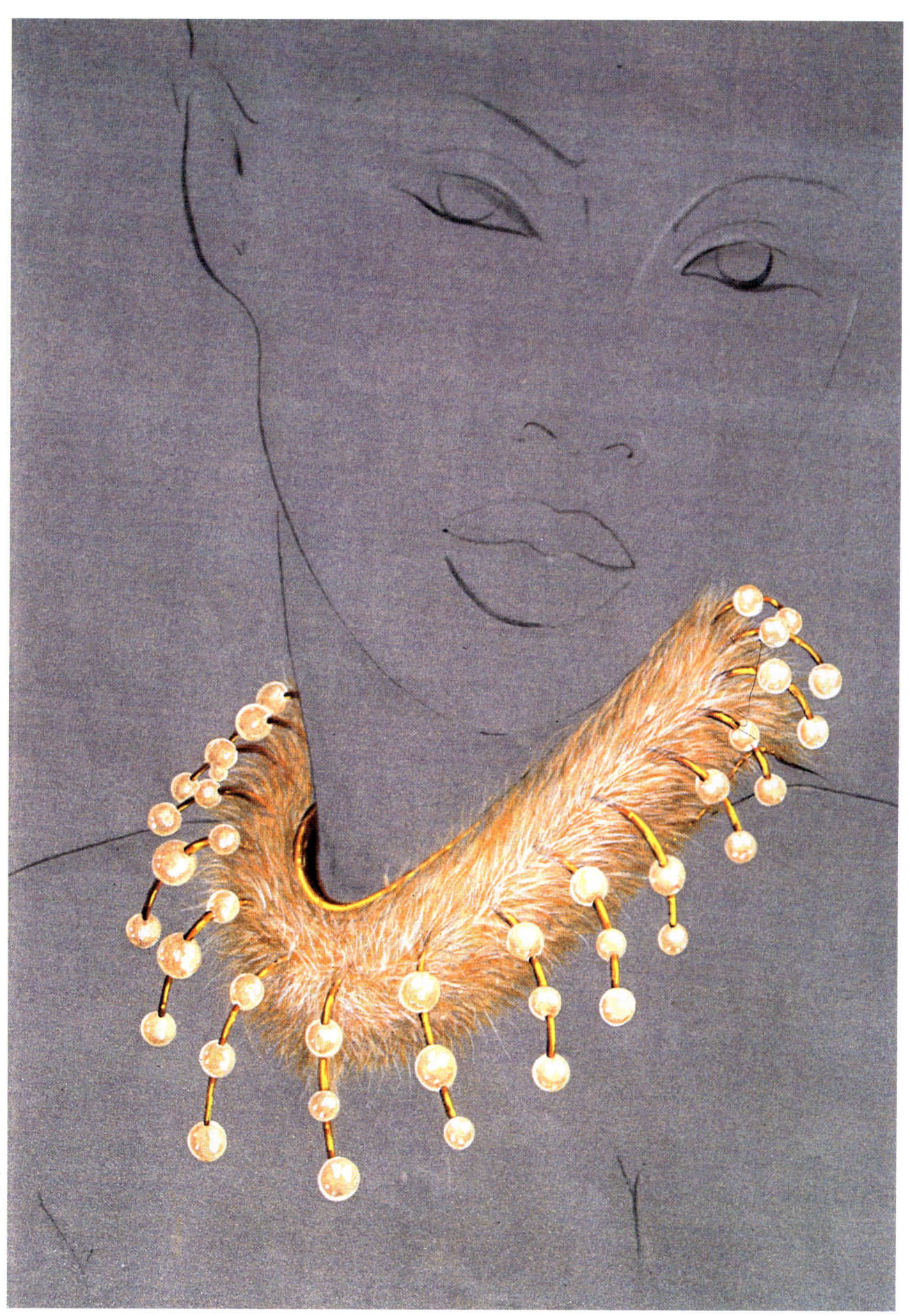

'Pearl Fountain', necklace in gold, pearls and fur by Caroline Portail. Thanks to the gold, which in this case is used simply as a vehicle, the pearls sparkle in the fur to recall the terrestrial and marine origins of this work.

THIERRY VENDOME

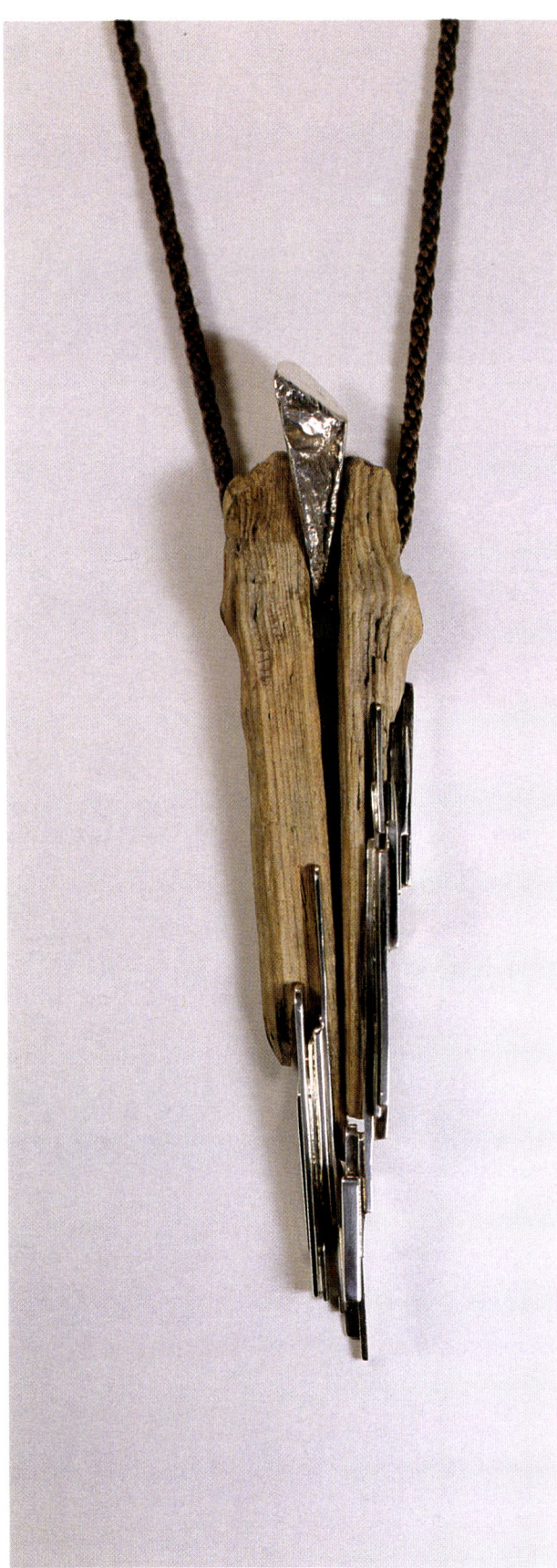

Thierry Vendome expresses his personal point of view to us:

'...In my case, the difficulty is in creating a contemporary line of jewels different from my father's. There are two "poles" in my work: "jewellery" jewels, and jewels made from such natural materials as shells, pebbles or driftwood. These latter have existed for years at the bottom of the sea, being rolled, polished, fashioned by the ebb and flow of the tides, making them into sculptures, the patina of whose wood I wish to set off to advantage by the addition of metal and minerals for their brilliance, enhancing the whole.

'Bits of driftwood carry with them a long marine history. Through my jewels, I manage to reconcile my love for the sea with my love for this region of The Hague, where I experience the freedom brought by untamed nature that forges the wind and the currents.

'The void is often present in my creations, for it delimits the boundary between two worlds, of the couple... It symbolises contact, hope or rending, while giving lightness, elegance and dynamism.

'I conceive my jewels as miniature sculptures and plan them out very thoroughly, later taking certain forms or rings or pendants for my monumental sculptures.

'I am against a certain type of jewel of limited duration, known as ephemerals—that is, objects in paper, cardboard, cotton or plastic. On the contrary, a jewel must have a definite value, in the same way that a sculpture or painting does.

'One must not confine oneself to a single system and use it, but rather one should constantly question it.

'There are different motifs in my creations, due to my state of mind at the moment, whether this be modern, romantic, baroque or sculptural. I care about maintaining a style that is personal, but multi-faceted.

'My jewels in silver are unique, low-priced pieces that give me the freedom to express myself fully without the constraint of an investment that is too great for our times, because art jewels must be available for all budgets.

'In another era, did not Lalique make jewels based on silver, enamel and glass?'

170 *Pendent in 'bois flottés' and silver by Thierry Vendome.*

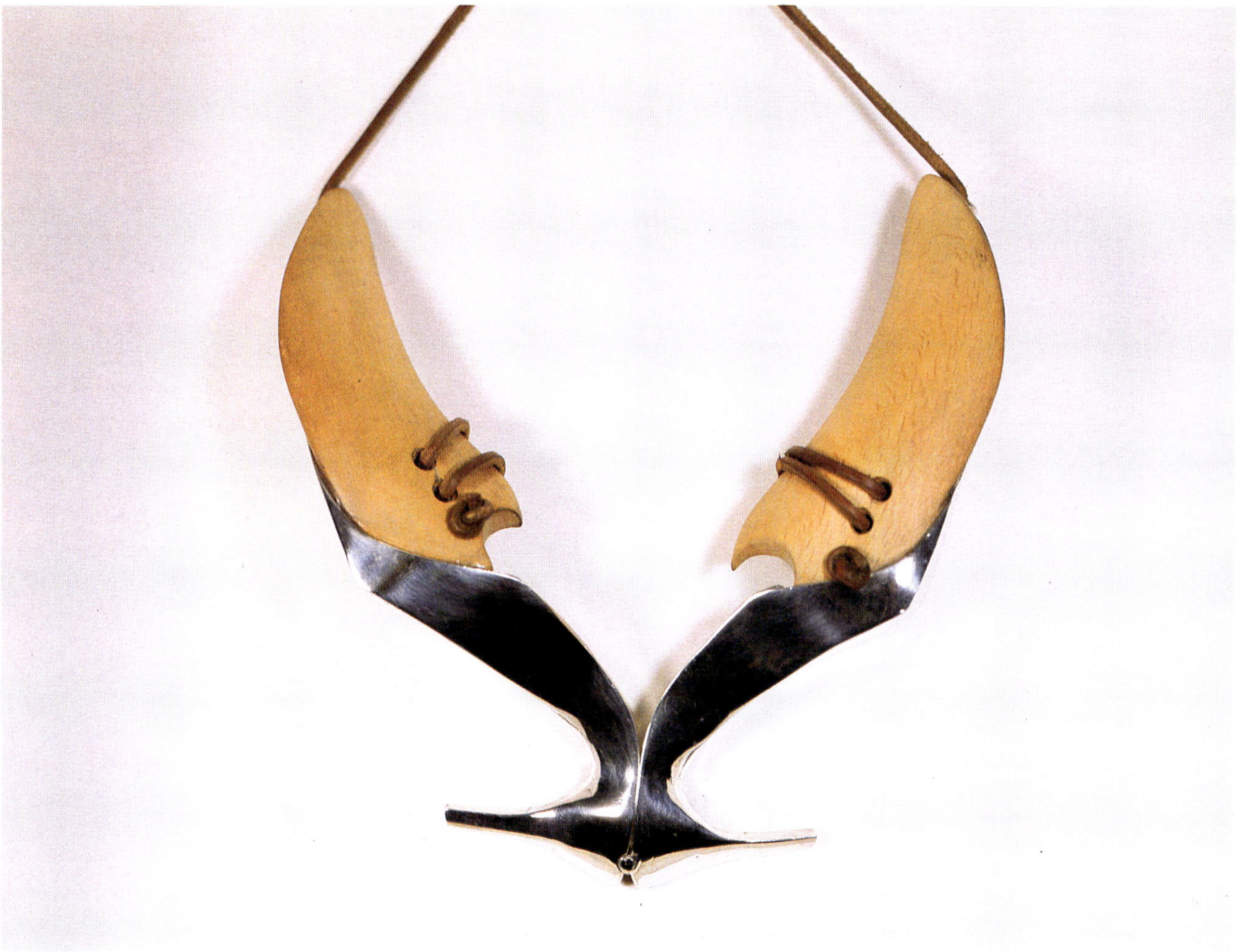

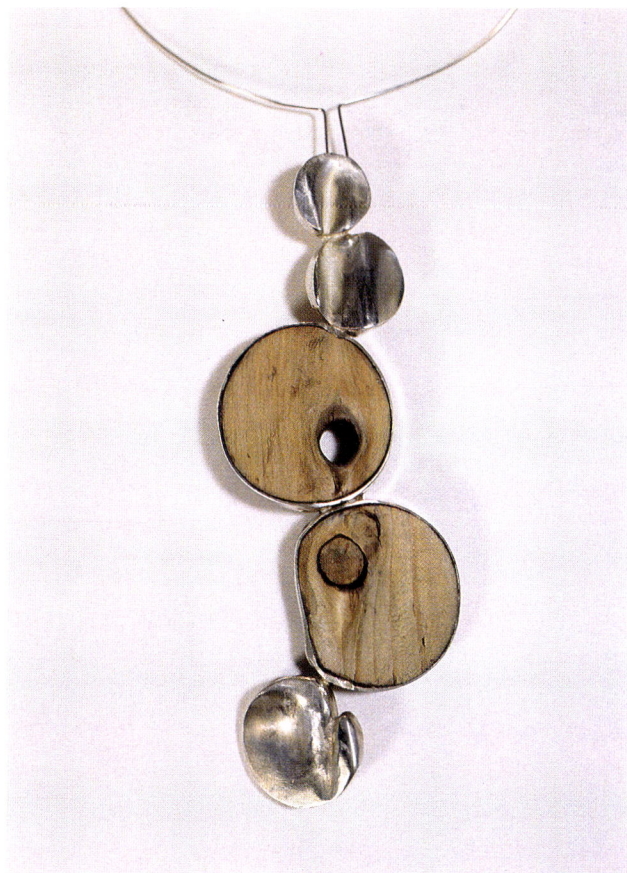

Thierry Vendome's 'bois flottés' mounted in silver.

Beyond the symbolism of duality and the couple — "the void that enters within the couple" — Thierry Vendome's jewels are also heartbeats, dreams, emotions experienced anew, torments, memories or messages.

He draws a strong inspiration from the sea, from objects that are worked, sculpted by the water, the natural sensuality of whose forms and materials touch his sensitivity.

In any case, his jewels do not begin from an abstract concept, or from an idea about the woman who will wear them. Instead, they are conceived as sculptures that are dominated by abstract lines, before becoming wearable jewels. Why wood? For Thierry Vendome, driftwood carries the charm of a very ancient history, the mark of the sea within it.

It is extremely important to him that he fabricate his jewels himself, and the rapidity with which this soft material permits him to work suits him perfectly: Thus, far from spoiling this form that has been so carefully chosen and explored, he preserves its spontaneity with great delicacy.

171

ROBERTO
VIOLA

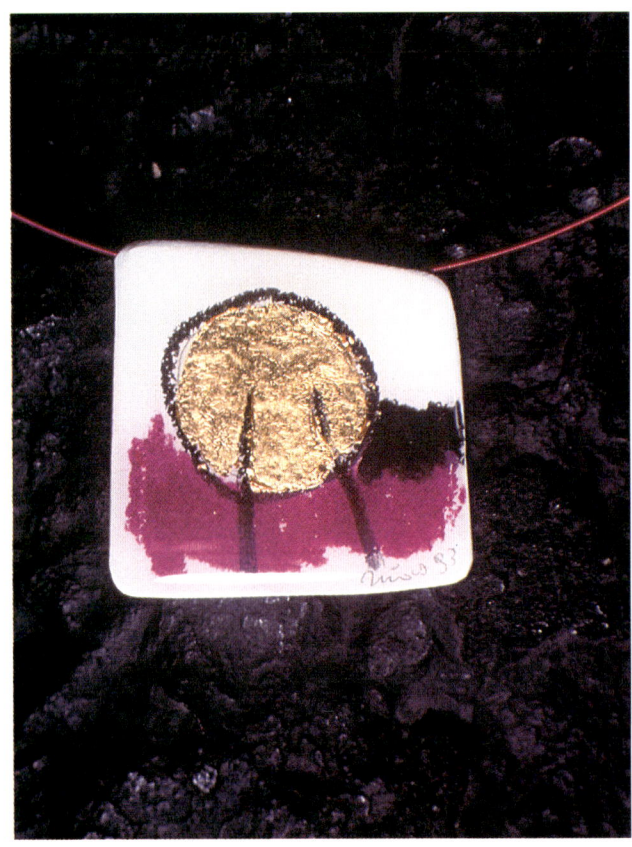 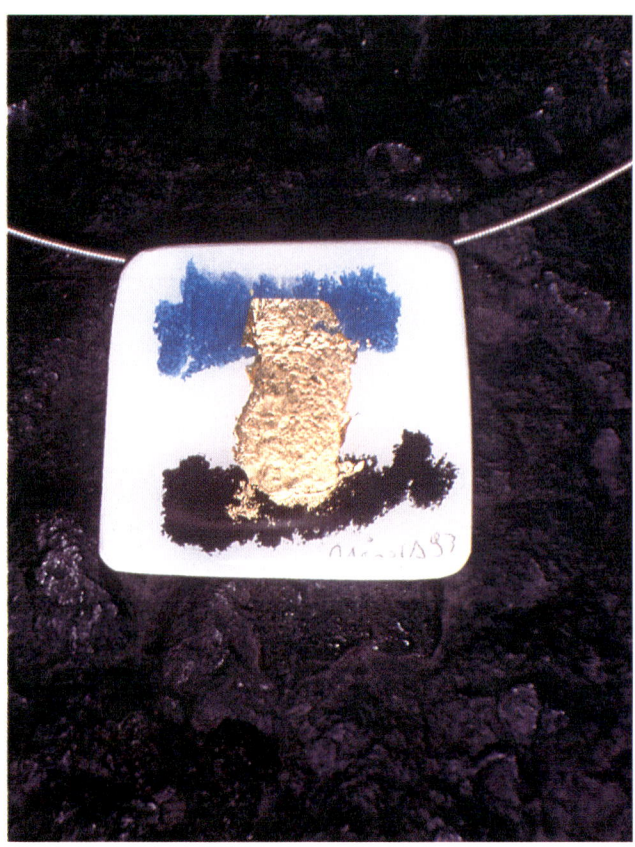

Pendants by architect Roberto Viola. The materials used are plastic, resin, acrylic paints and charcoal. It is clear that jewels of great quality can be made without using precious materials.

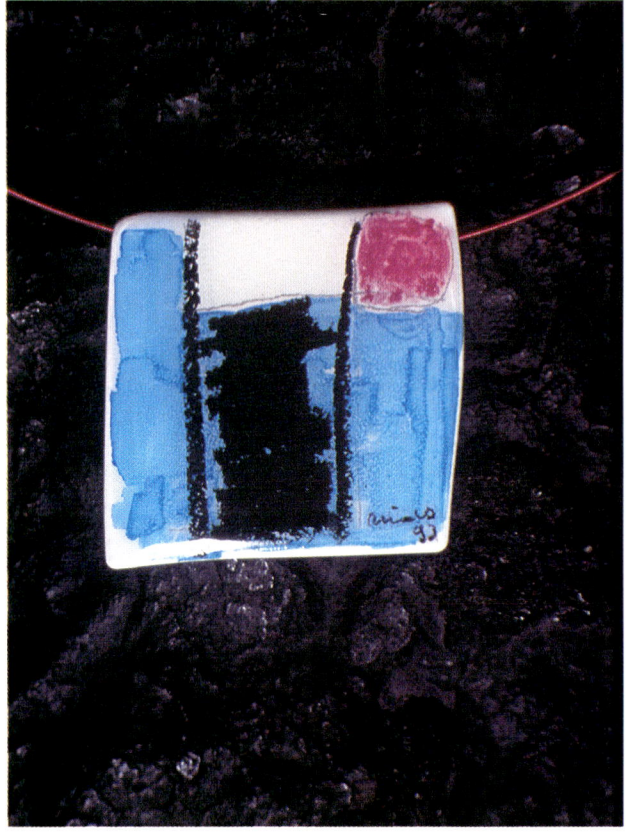 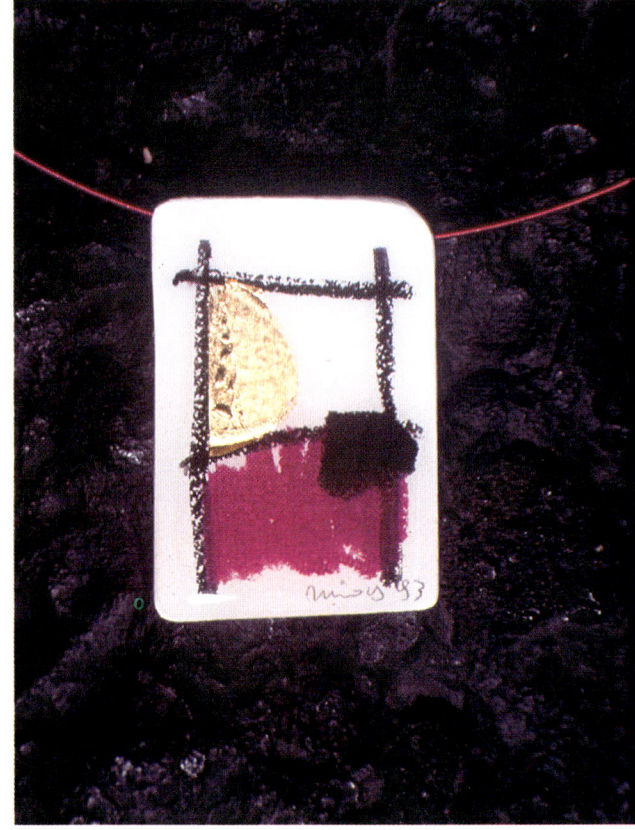

KARLA
MERTENS

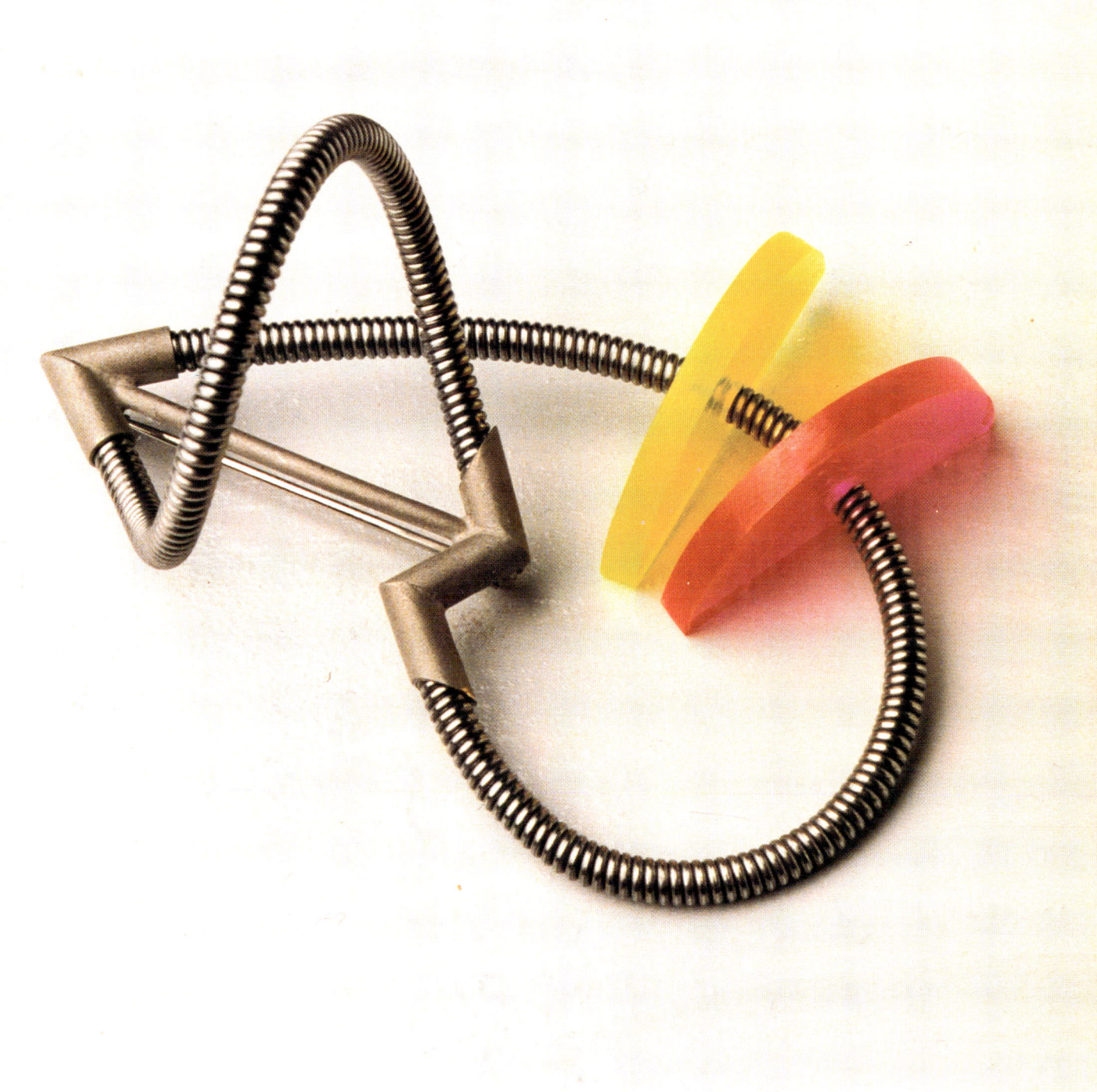

'Spiral Rat' by Karla Mertens. This jewel permits a great deal of movement; the yellow Plexiglas semicircles can be turned around the metal spiral. This piece is made of sanded brass, iron and Liza-plexi.

JACK
TERWEDUWE

Drop-earring in gold, diamonds and feather. The feather is the 'star' in this object. Jack Terweduwe used the precious metal only as a support for the feather, while the diamonds bring brilliance to the work.

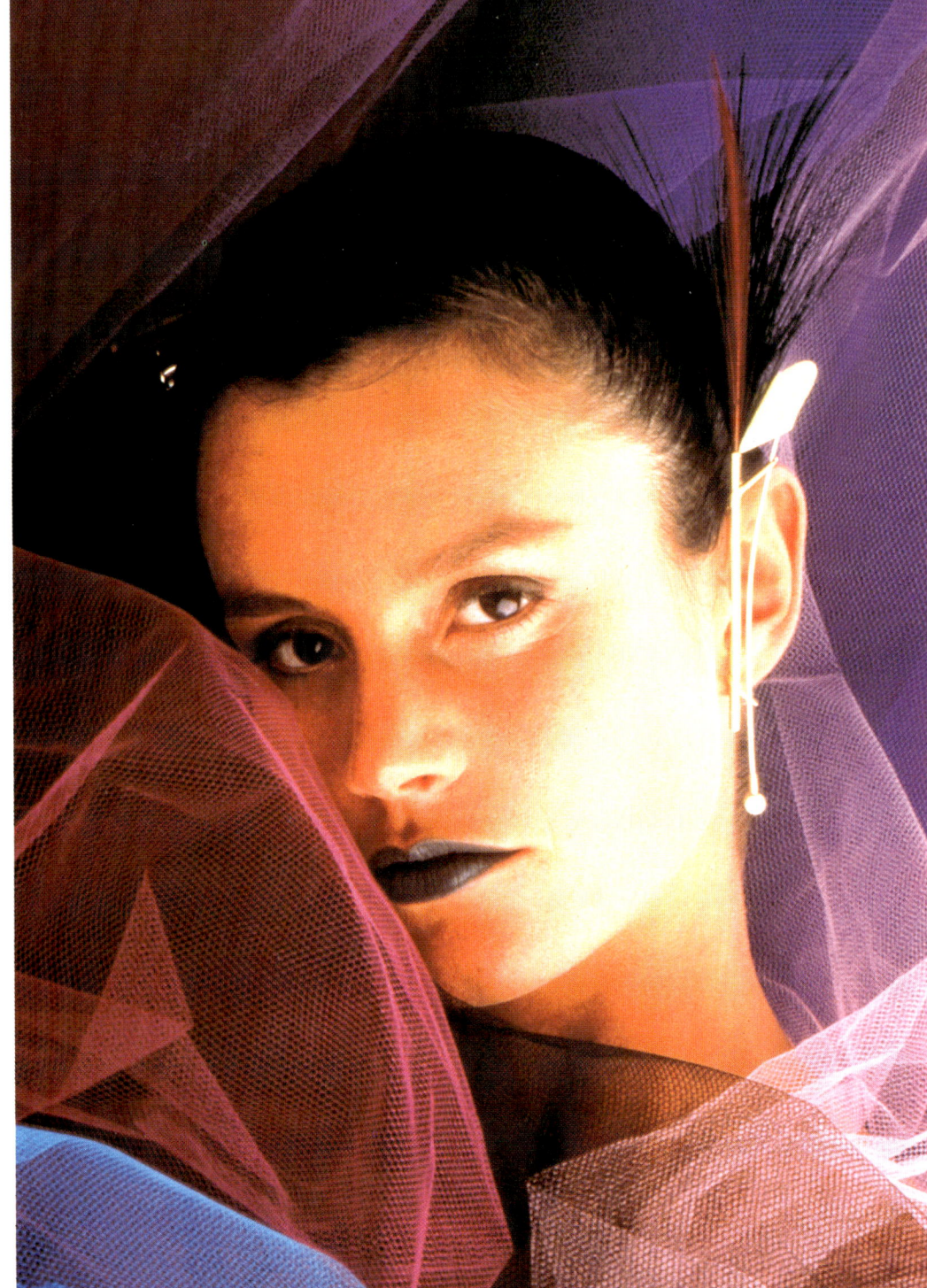

ROXANE
DE SAULE

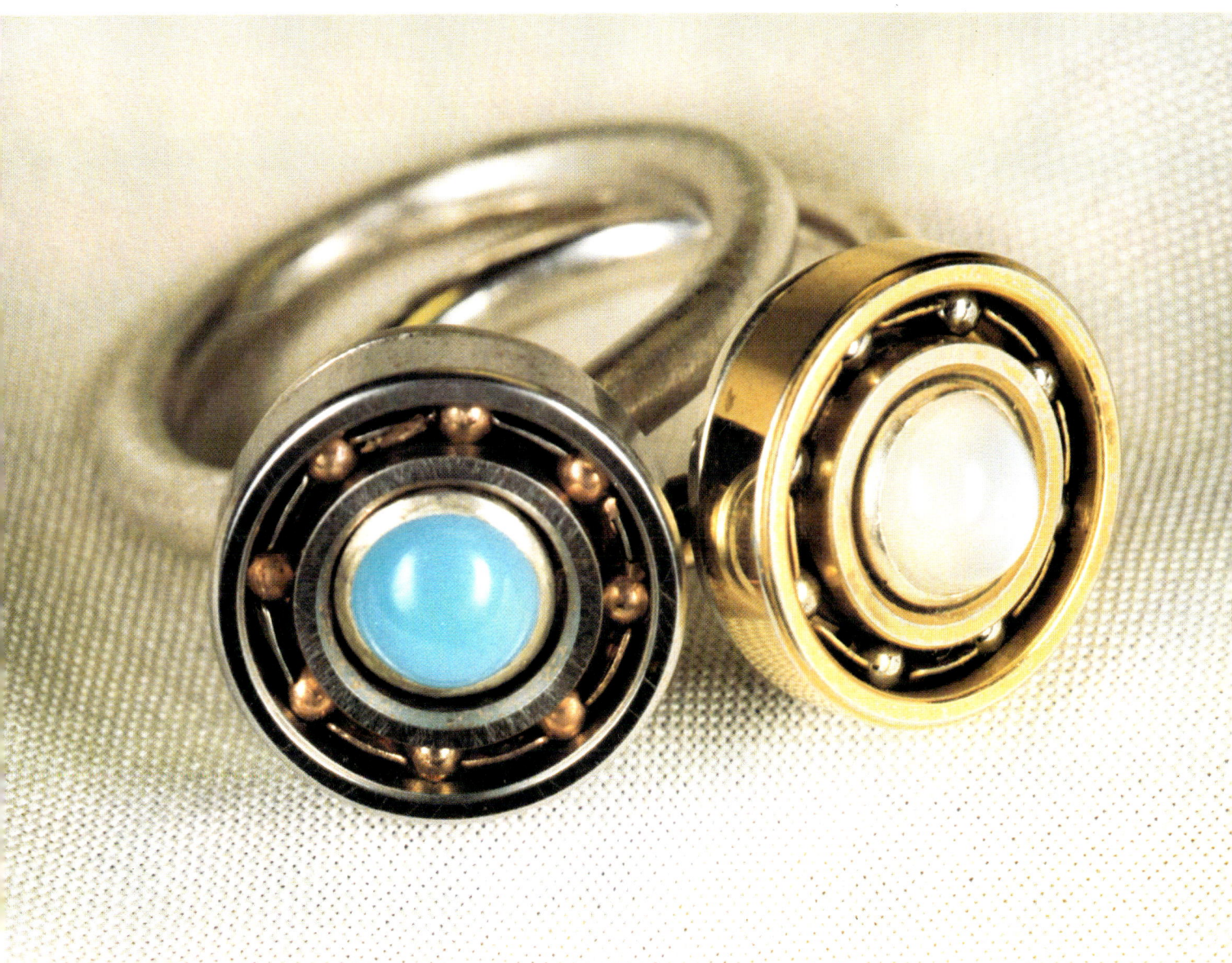

Two rings by Roxane de Saule in silver and ball-bearings with turquoise or moonstone. The contrast between the materials is enhanced by the movement of the stone which, in turning continually, sends out flashes and rays of light.

DANIELLE
GOFFA

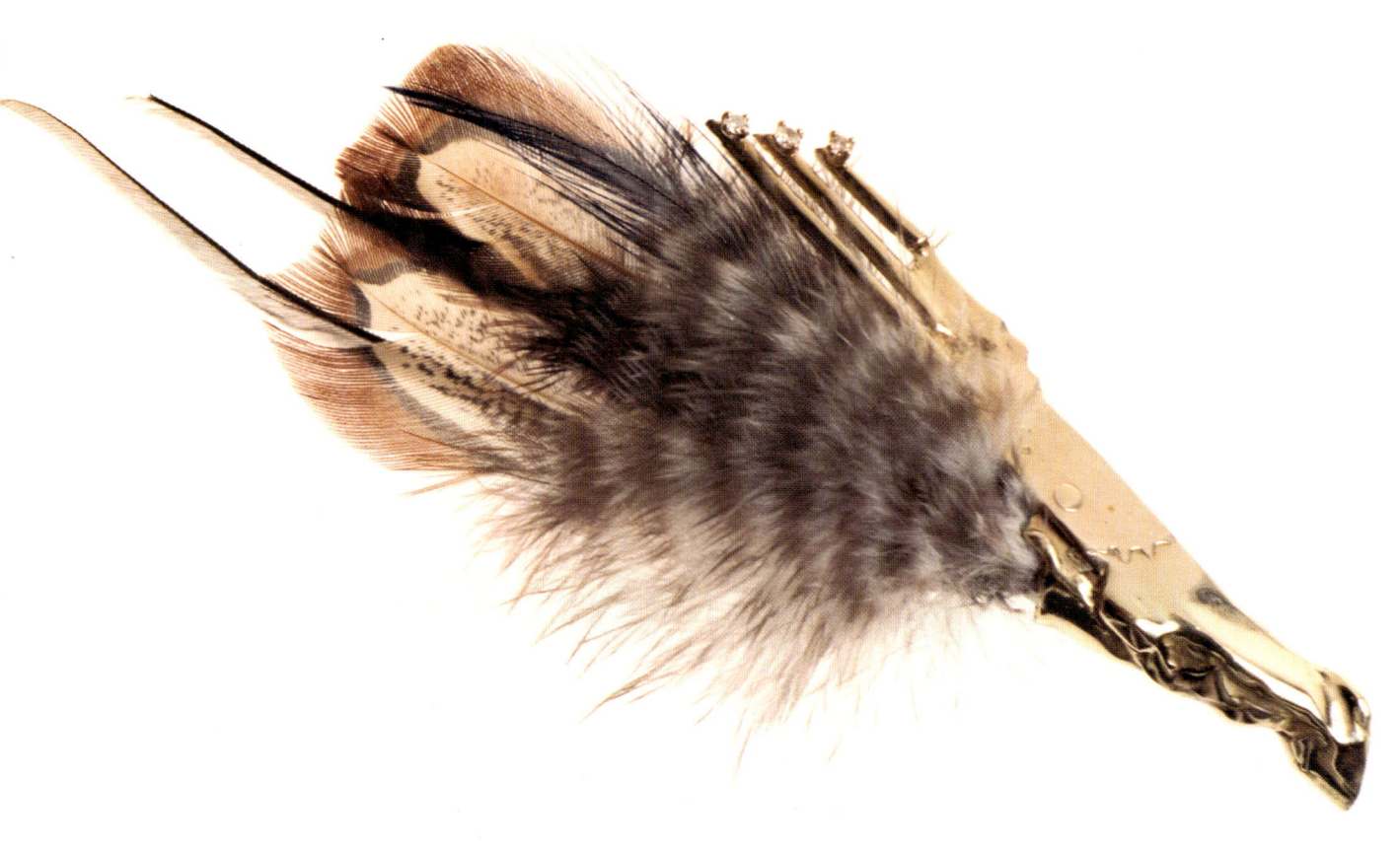

Gold, diamonds and feathers were used by Danielle Goffa to create this brooch of tropical allure.

ELISA
PEUPION

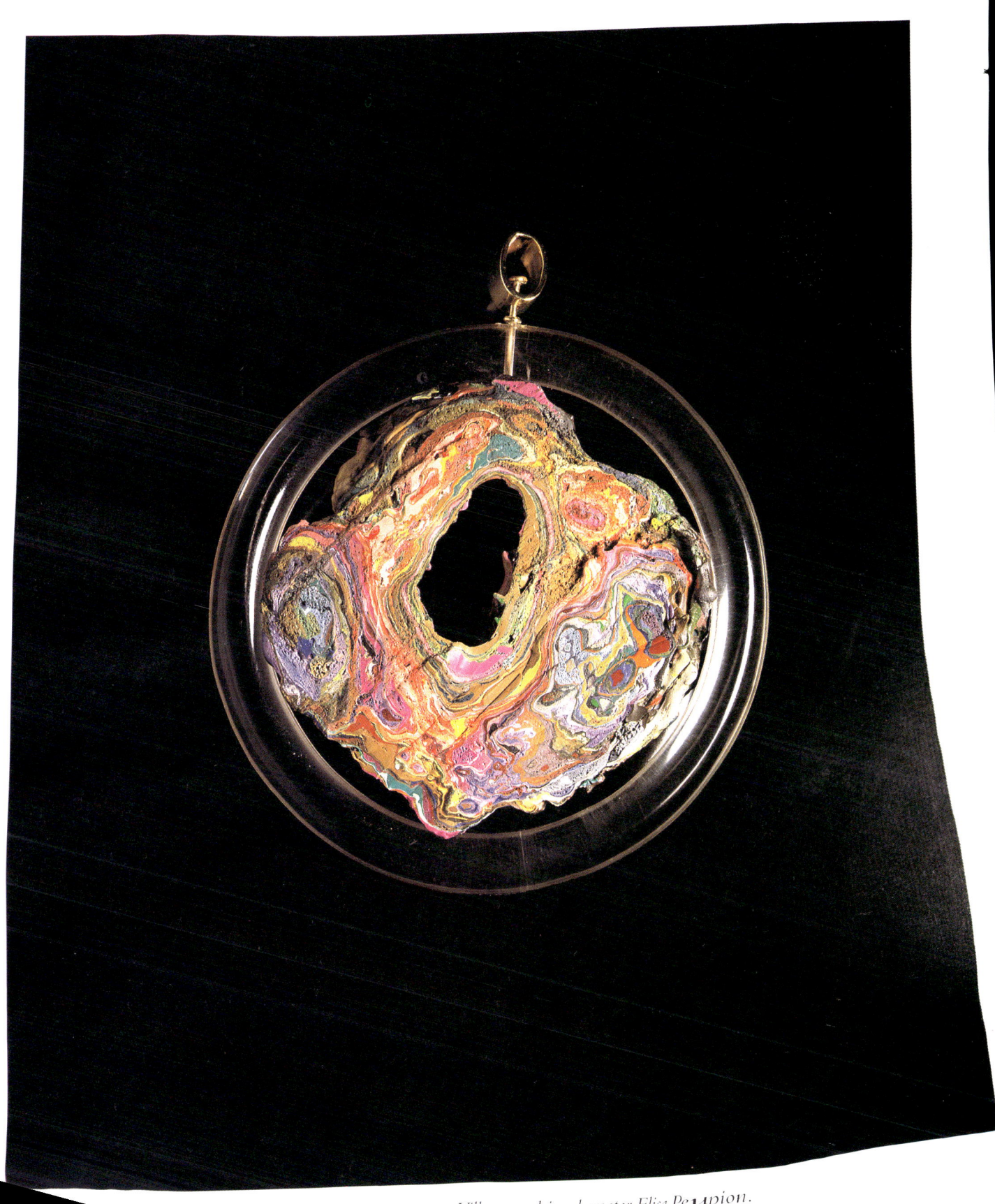

...tant in Plexiglas and acrylic by painter Jacques Villatte and jewel-creator Elisa Peupion.

CARLOS PASTOR '**A**ll materials may be used to make jewels, provided that they can be manipulated in one way or another.'

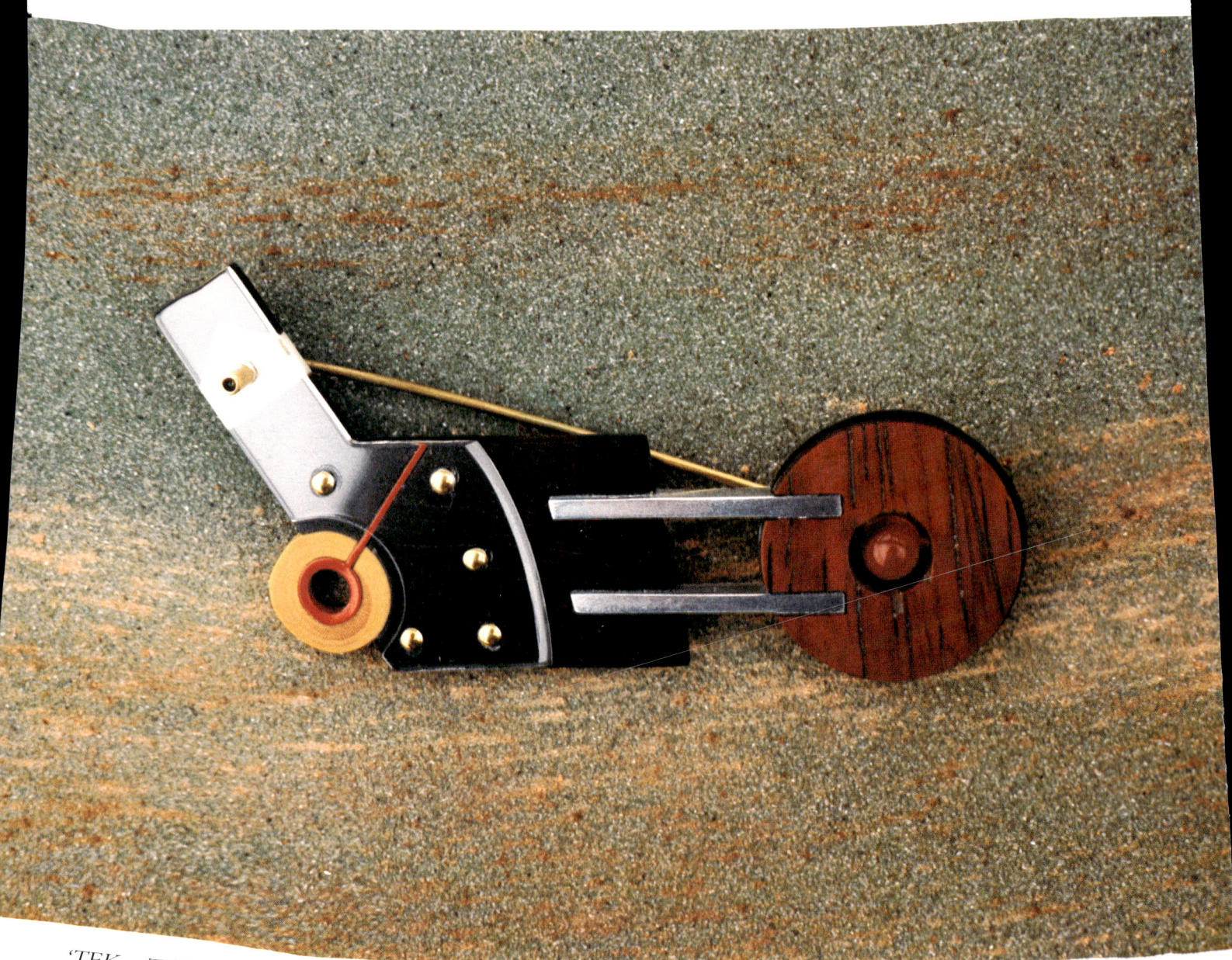

'TEK... TEK...' *brooch* in ebony, rosewood, acrylic, Plexiglas, aluminium, brass and electronic components.

APPENDICES

THE WORLD'S FINEST CREATORS

Nancy ALLERY
Frans Vermissenlan, 1/3
2100 Deurne Belgium

Lena ANTABI
Rua Batatais, 507
CEP 01423-010 São Paulo Brazil

Jean-Marie AUDE
5, Rue Robespierre
94700 Ivry-sur-Seine France

Guy BADOUX
Rue Saint-Pierre, 14
5150 Franiere Belgium

Daniela BAUMGARTNER
3, Rue Paul Dubois
75003 Paris France

Philipp BECKER
Hauptstrasse, 173
6580 Idar-Oberstein 2 Germany

BULGARI
Via Condotti, 10
00187 Rome Italy

Jussara CARACANTE
Al. Minetro Rocha Azevedo, 45-2°
01410-000 São Paulo Brazil

Anna CELLA
Via Torricelli, 30
20136 Milan Italy

Monica CENACCHI
37, Rue de Chaillot
75116 Paris France

Nicola CERRONE
83, Castlereagh Street
2000 Sydney Australia

CHRISTIGUEY
69, Rue de la Gare
7322 Pommeroeul Belgium

Florence CROISIER
12, Avenue Jean Moulin
93100 Montreuil France

DAMIANI
Corso Magenta, 82,
20123 Milan Italy

Philippe DELOISON
39, Avenue Ernest Reyer
75019 Paris France

Rodrigo DIEZ
Sarria, 43
28029 Madrid Spain

Jul B. DIZON
53, Scount Madrinan
Quezon City Philippines

Jean-Pierre DUPORT
5, Rue Victor Hugo
92300 Levallois-Perret France

Michael DÜRNHOLZ
Aachenerstrasse, 5
4700 Eupen France

Christine ESCHER
9, Rue de la Tour
75116 Paris France

Uli GLASER
Theodorstrasse, 41V
2000 Hamburg 50 Germany

Danielle GOFFA
Goudbloemlaan, 7
2980 Halle Zoersel Belgium

Alfredo GROSSO
Via Leonardo da Vinci, 31
39012 Merano Italy

Montserrat GUARDIOLA
Mandri, 9
08022 Barcelona Spain

Asadullah HABIB
Postfach 122302
6580 Idar-Oberstein Germany

Kathy HANUISE
36, Avenue des Bois
7090 Braine Le Comte Belgium

MASHANI
Via Mazzini, 45
15048 Valenza Italy

VINCENT DE JAEGHER
19, Rue Spinhayer
4800 Verviers Belgium

Jean Pierre LALOUX
Rue Neuve, 193
1620 Drocenbos Belgium

Miriam MAMBER
Al Gabriel Montoiro Da Silva 1046
CEP 01442000
Jardim Paulistano Brazil

Thierry MARTIN,
146, Boulevard de Grenelle
75015 Paris France

Claude MAZLOUM
Schupstraat, 9/11 (BP 23/C)
2018 Anvers Belgium

Alfonso MAZZI,
Via San Nazaro, 17B
37129 Verona Italy

Karla MERTENS
Leuvenstraat, 3
3010 Louvain Belgium

Jacques MICHEL
Place, 70
1547 Bievene Belgium

Stefano MICHELANGELI-POLIMENI
Via Bruno Bruni, 65
00189 Rome Italy

Hubert MINNEBO
Cathilleweg, 1
8490 Jabbeke-Stalhille Belgium

MORAGLIONE
Via Sassi, 45
15048 Valenza Italy

Jean MOUCLIER
18, Avenue des Acacias
95160 Montmorency France

Bernd MUNSTEINER
Wiesenstrasse, 10
6581 Stipshausen Germany

Simonne MUYLAERT-HOFMAN
36, Nieuwstraat
9300 Aalst Belgium

Kazuo OGAWA
Minami Aoyama 3, 7, 18
Minato-Ku - Tokyo 107 Japan

Marisa PALLA
Via Giusti, 8
58100 Grosseto Italy

Carlos PASTOR
C/San Vincente De Paul, 19-10°
46019 Valencia Spain

Erwin PAULY
Blumenstrasse, 39
6581 Veitsrodt Germany

Guido PERSICO
Via Dalmazio Birago, 4
20133 Milan Italy

Elisa PEUPION
4, Villa Malakoff
75116 Paris France

Marcello PIZZARI
Via della Cappelletta
della Giustiniana, 24
00123 Rome Italy

Caroline PORTAIL
25, Rue du Chemin Vert
75011 Paris France

Jacques PRADES
308, Silom Road
Bangkok 10500 Thailand

Janine RENARD
Rue Emile Cornez, 8
7387 Angre Belgium

ROBERTA
Via Enrico De Nicola, 2
80059 Torre del Greco Italy

Barbara ROMANO
Via delle Viole, 26
00040 Lavinio Italy

J. P. DE SAEDELEER
Rue du Chêne, 33
5532 Sosoye Belgium

Agahe SAINT GIRONS
49, Rue de Paris
93100 Montreuil France

Roxane de SAULE
6, Rue Mahler
75004 Paris France

Hans SCHINDLER
Postfach 2112
59481 Soest Germany

Hans SCHULLIN
Herrengasse, 3
8010 Graz Austria

Hubert SCHUSTER
Via S. Anna, 10
36051 Creazzo Italy

Paolo SPALLA
Viale Dante, 10 - 15048
Valenza Italy

Georg SPRENG
Hohenstaufenstrasse, 73
7070 Schwab-Gmund Germany

Thérèse SUDRE
89, Avenue de France
59600 Maubeuge France

Jack TERWEDUWE
Martelarenstraat, 3
3200 Aarschot Belgium

Nicole THIEPONT
Berg, 43
9800 Meigem Belgium

Kerina TROICOVICH
Via F.S. Nitti, 11
00191 Rome Italy

Laurence TUFENKDJIAN
B.P. 16-6506
Beirut Lebanon

Krista VANDEVELDE
Hoge Steenweg, 33
1850 Grimbergen Belgium

Pascale VAN HAVRE
Edelinkstraat, 25
2018 Anvers Belgium

Daniel VAN NUFFEL
Singel, 5
2510 Mortsel Belgium

Catherine VAVALEA
10, Rue de Vaucouleurs
75011 Paris France

Jean VENDOME
352, Rue St Honoré
75001 Paris France

Thierry VENDOME
352, Rue St Honoré
75001 Paris France

Roberto VIOLA
Via Santo Stefano, 79
40125 Bologna Italy

Michel WATTEBLED
42, Avenue de la Liberté
1930 Grand-Duchy of Luxemburg

Suzanne WENZ
11, Rue du Bouloi
75001 Paris France

Helmut WOLF
Mühlwiesenstrasse, 20
6581 Kirschweiler Germany

WOO HYUN CHOI
808-5 Yuk Sam Dong Kang Nam
Gu
Seoul Korea

Iain WOOD
14, Rue des Carmes
5000 Namur Belgium

ZARKHANE
59, Achterstraat
9270 Laarne Belgium

Alberto ZORZI
Via Dalmazia, 7/A
35100 Padua Italy

Silvano ZANCHI
Via Vittorio Veneto, 31
63023 Fermo Italy

GALLERIES AND JEWELLERS

AUSTRALIA
-*Contemporary Jewellery Gallery,*
162 A, Queen Street
Woollahra 2025
Sydney

AUSTRIA
-*Galerie Gold Design,*
Fuhrichgrasse, 2
1010 Vienna

-*Galerie El-Avantgarde,*
Altstadt, 2
4020 Linz/Donau

-*Galerie Slavik,*
Himmelpfortgasse, 17
1030 Vienna

-*Galerie V & V,*
Bauermarkt, 19
1010 Vienna

-*Galeries Schullin & Sohne,*
Herrengesse, 3   8010 Graz
Kramergasse, 11   9020 Klagenfurt
Hauptstrasse, 187 9210 Portscaach
Am Korso, 21   9220 Velden
Gasthof Post   6764 Lech

BELGIUM
-*Atelier "Que Van",*
Dumortierlaan, 112
8300 Knokke

-*Christoffel,*
Avenue Louise, 40
1050 Brussels

-*Galerie Badou,*
Place de l'Hotel de Ville, 5
5030 Gembloux

-*Galerie Goussaert*
Kortrijkstraat, 28
8880 Tielt

-*Galerie Muylaert,*
Nieuwstraat, 36

-*Galerie Garance,*
Rue de Namur, 99
1000 Brussels

-*Galerie Embryo,*
Rue de Namur, 49
3000 Leuven

-*Galerie Hertecant,*
Dumortierlaan, 71
8300 Knokke-Heist

-*Galerie Kimbrley,*
Sint Kwintesberg, 19
9000 Ghent

-*Galerie Huis de Koker,*
Markstraat, 15
9550 Herzele

-*Galerie Pools,*
Ooststraat, 7
8800 Roeselaere

-*Galerie Harmagedon,*
Sasboslaan, 7
8540 Bellegem Kortrijk

-*La Maison de la Perle,*
Rue des Drapiers, 2D
1050 Brussels

-*Galerie Nancy Aillery Jewel Design,*
Frans Versmissenlaan, 1/3
2100 Deurne

-*Galerie Sabine Herman,*
Rue Fradier, 86
1050 Brusseles

-*Galerie Christiguey,*
Rue de la Gare, 69
7322 Pommeroeul

-*Galerie J. P. De Saedeleer,*
Place Cardinal Mercier, 17
1300 Wavre

-*Galerie Liehrmann,*
Bouvelard Piercot, 4
4000 Liège

BRAZIL
-*Galerie Natan,*
Rua Visconde de Pirajà, 303 a 309
Rio de Janeiro

FRANCE
-*Myrose Cabrilhac,*
46, Avenue Georges V
75008 Paris

-*Marie Zisswiller,*
61, Rue d'Auteuil
75016 Paris

-*Helene Poree,*
31, Rue Daguerre
75014 Paris

-*Roxane De Saule,*
6, Rue Mahler
75004 Paris

-*Cheret Aam,*
9, Rue Madame
75006 Paris

-*Galerie Pylones,*
57, Rue Saint-Louis en l'Ile
75004 Paris

-*Arthus Bertrand,*
6, Palce Saint Germain des Prés
75006 Paris

-*Look 16,*
16, Rue Vavin
75006 Paris

-*Galerie Franz Litz,*
7, Place Franz Litz
75010 Paris

-*Galerie Didier Clauss,*
26, Rue Pastourelle
75003 Paris

GERMANY
-*Galerie Gerhard,*
Goethplatz, 6
5920 Bad Berleburg

-Galerie Sonnichsen,
Neuer Wall, 44
2000 Hamburg 36

-Galerie Aurum
Oppenheimer Landstrasse, 42
6000 Frankfurt

-Art Curial,
Maximilian Strasse, 10
8000 Munich 2

-Galerie Brohan,
Am Hofgarten Strasse, 41
4000 Düsseldorf 30

-Galerie Cada,
Maximilian Strasse, 13
8000 Munich

-Cardillac Schmuckgalerie,
Waldstrasse, 56
Karlsruhe 1

-Knauth & Hagen Galerie,
Thomas Mann Strasse, 17
5300 Bonn

-Galerie für Schmuck Hilde Leiss,
Grosser Burstah, 38
2000 Hamburg

-Forum für Schmuck und design
E.V.,
Lutticher Strasse, 47
5000 Köln 1

-Galerie Treykorn,
Savignyplatz, 13
1000 Berlin 12

GREAT BRITAIN
-Galerie Hancocks,
29, King Street
Manchester M2 6AF

-Electrum Gallery,
South Molton Street, 21
London W1 YIDD

-Contemporary Applied Arts,
43, Earlham Street, Covent
Garden
London WC 2H 9LD

-Crafts Council Gallery,
12, Waterloo Place
Lower Regent Street
London SW1 4AU

ITALIE
-Fattoadarte 1900-2000,
Galleria Via del Luzzo, 4
40125 Bologna

-Galerie Fallani Best,
Borgo Ognissanti, 15/R
50123 Florence

-Spazio Arte Johnson,
Via Terraggio, 15
20123 Milan

-Galerie Previtali,
Via T. Tasso, 21
24100 Bergamo

-Venice Design Gallery,
Salizada San Samuele, San Marco
3146 Venice

-Bijoux & Pierres,
Via della Penna, 59
00198 Rome

-Galleria d'Arte Ellequadro,
Vico Falamonica, 29R
16123 Genoa

-Galleria Di Nardi,
Via Solferino, 3
20121 Milan

-Il Gioiello per Panarea,
Via Beppe Maria
98050 Panarea

-Argentovivo,
Via Gorani, 8
20123 Milan

JAPAN
-Galerie Better Life,
18-2; Akasaka 3-Chome
Minato-ku
Tokyo

NETHERLANDS
-Galerie Carin Delcourt van
Krimpen,
Eendrachtsweg, 59
3012 Rotterdam

SPAIN
-Galerie Pedro Bueno,
Bergamin, 3
31002 Pamplona

SWEDEN
-Ib Wrange Smychen,
Vastra Strandgatan, 7a
75221 Uppsala

SWITZERLAND
-Schmuckgalerie Rudi Ritter
Marktgasse, 14
9000 St. Gallen

-Schmuck Forum Galerie,
Zollikerstrasse, 12
8008 Zürich

-Galerie Michèle Zeller,
Kramgrasse, 20
3000 Bern 8

-Galerie Monnier,
1, Rue St. Maurice
2001 Neuchatel

USA
-Pennina Design,
18 West Fourth Street
Cincinnati OH

-Helen Drutt Gallery,
1721, Walnut Street,
Philadelphia PA 19103

-Aaron Faber Gallery,
666 Fifth Avenue
New York, NY 10019

-Jewelers'werk Gallery,
2000 Pennsylvania Avenue-
Northwest
Washington DC 20006

-Sheila Nussbaum,
358 Milburn Avenue
NJ 07041 Mill

TRADE PRESS

AUSTRALIA
-*Jeweller Watchmaker & Giftware*, Strawberry Hills.

AUSTRIA
-*Uhren-Juwelen*, Vienna.

BELGIUM
-*Bijoux*, Brussels.
-*Diamant*, Anvers.
-*Kompass*, Brussels.
-*Technica*, Brussels.

BRAZIL
-*Brasil Relogoeiro e Joalheiro*, São-Paulo.
-*Relogios e Joias*, São-Paulo.

CANADA
-*Bijou*, Montréal.
-*Canadian Jeweller*, Toronto.

DENMARK
-*Guldsmedebladet*, Copenhagen.
-*Tid & Syn*, Copenhagen.
-*Ure + Optik*, Silkeborg.

FINLAND
-*Kelloseppa*, Espoo.
-*Kultsaseppien Lehti*, Helsinki.

FRANCE
-*Bijou International*, Paris.
-*Brillance*, Paris.
-*La France Horlogère*, Paris.
-*La Lettre d'Orion*, Paris.
-*Le Bijoutier*, Paris.

GERMANY
-*Aurea*, Ulm/Danube.
-*Diamanberight*, Frankfort.
-*Fz*, Konigsbach-Stein.
-*Gold + Silber Uhren + Schmuck*, Leinfelden-E.
-*Gz European Jeweler*, Stuttgart.
-*Lapis*, Munich.
-*Mineralien Magazin*, Stuttgart.
-*Schmuck Journal*, Constance.
-*Uhren Juwelen Schmuck Ujs*, Bielefeld.
-*Uhren + Schmuck Journal*, Herne.
-*Zeitschrift der Deutschen Gemmologischen Gesellschaft*, Idar-Oberstein.

GREAT BRETAIN
-*British Jeweller & Watch Buyer*, Birmingham.
-*Jeweller*, Herts.
-*Jewellery International*, London.
-*Retail Jeweller*, London.
-*Watchmaker Jeweller & Silversmith*, Kent.

HONG KONG
-*Fashion Accessories*, Hong-Kong.
-*Jewellery News*, Hong-Kong.
-*Jewellery Review*, Hong-Kong.

INDIA
-*Journal House*, Jaipur.
-*Journal of Gem Industry*, Jaipur.
-*Trade Post*, Bombay.
-*Watch Market Review*, Bombay.

ISRAEL
-*Mazal U'Bracha/Adi'Or*, Herzliya.

ITALY
-*Argento*, Rome.
-*Arteregalo*, Milan.
-*Il Mondo dei Gioielli*, Arese (MI).
-*Italia Orafa*, Milan.
-*Italia Orafa International*, Milan.
-*Joy Oro*, Arezzo.

-La Clessidra, Rome.
-L'industria Orafa Italiana, Milan.
-Lombardoro, Milan.
-L'orafo italiano, Milan.
-L'orafo orologiaio, Turin.
-L'orologio, Rome.
-Mida, Rozzano (MI).
-Or, Milan.
-Oro Italia, Florence.
-Orologi e non solo, Rome.
-Orologi Technimedia, Rome.
-Proposte, Milan.
-Techniche nuove, Milan.
-Valenza gioielli, Valenza (AL).
-Vicenza Oro, Vicenza.
-Vogue Gioiello, Milan.

JAPAN
-Horlogical International Correspondance, Tokyo.
-Jewel, Tokyo.
-Les Joyaux, Tokyo.

NETHERLANDS
-Chronos, Amsterdam.
-Edelmetaal, La Haye.
-Euro Juwelier, Amstelveen.

NEW ZELAND
-New Zealand Horlogical Journal, Auckland.

NORWAY
-Gullsmedkunst, Oslo.

PERU
-Silver Crafts Time, Lima.

SOUTH AFRICA
-Diamond News & S.A; Jeweler, Transvaal.

SPAIN
-Arte y Joya, Barcelona.
-Arte y Prestigio, Barcelona.
-Golden Prestige, Barcelona.
-Joyas e Joyeros, Barcelona.
-Oro y Hora, Barcelona.

SWEDEN
-Svensk Guldsmedstigig, Stockholm.
-Svensk Ur-Optik Tidning, Stockholm.

SWITZERLAND
-Brillance, Geneva.
-Europa Star, Geneva.
-Jsh, Lausanne.
-Microtechnic/Agifa, Zürich.
-Précision, Soleure.
-Revue fh, Bienne.

TAIWAN
-Jewellery Circle's Magazine, Taipei.
-Taiwan Jewellery Journal, Taipei.

THAILAND
-Gems & Jewellery, Bangkok.
-Jewelsiam, Bangkok.
-Thailand Jewellery Review, Bangkok.

USA
-Diamond Insight, New York.
-Executive Jeweller, River Ro, Des Grandes Plaines.
-Gems Gemmology, Santa Monica.
-Gifts & Decorative Accessories, New York.
-Jck, Jewellers Circular Keystone, Randor.
-Lapidary Journal, San Diego.
-National Jeweller, New York.
-The Goldsmith, San Francisco.
-Watch & Clock Review, Denver.

Switchgear and Power System Protection

RAVINDRA P. SINGH

Director
Bimla Devi Educational Society's
Group of Institutions
Faridabad, Haryana

PHI Learning Private Limited

Delhi-110092
2014

₹ 325.00

SWITCHGEAR AND POWER SYSTEM PROTECTION
Ravindra P. Singh

ISBN-978-81-203-3660-5

The export rights of this book are vested solely with the publisher.

Third Printing   ...   ...   **November, 2014**

Published by Asoke K. Ghosh, PHI Learning Private Limited, Rimjhim House, 111, Patparganj Industrial Estate, Delhi-110092 and Printed by Raj Press, New Delhi-110012.

MUSEUMS

AUSTRIA
-Österreichisches Museum für Angewandte Kunst,
Stunenring, 5
1010 Vienna

BELGIUM
-Musée du Diamant
de Grobbendonk,
Oude Steenweg, 13a
2280 Grobbendonk

-Provincial Diamant Museum,
Lange Herentalsestrasse, 31-33
2018 Antwerpen

FRANCE
-Musée du Luxembourg,
19, rue de Vaugirard
75015 Paris

-Musée des Arts Décoratifs,
Rue de Rivoli, 107
75001 Paris

-Bibliothèque Forney,
Rue du Figuier, 1
75004 Paris

-Musée d'Art Moderne et d'Art Contemporain,
Promenade des Arts
06300 Nice

GERMANY
-Schumuckmuseum Pforzheim,
Janhstrasse, 42
7530 Pforzheim

-Staedtisches Museum,
Im Prediger
7070 Schwabish Gmund

-Musée des Gemmes d'Idar-Oberstein,
Mainzer Strasse, 34
55713 Idar-Oberstein, 1

-Heimatmuseum Idar-Oberstein,
Haupstrasse, 436
6580 Idar-Oberstein, 1

-Museum für Kunst und Gewerbe,
Steintorplatz, 1
2000 Hamburg

-Collegium Cadoro,
Schumann Street, 15
6200 Wiesbaden

-Museum für Gestaltung,
Bauhausarchiv
Klengelhoferstrasse, 14
1000 Berlin

-Wuppertaler Uhrenmuseum,
Poststrasse, 11
5600 Wuppertal, 1

GREAT BRITAIN
-Goldsmiths' hall,
Forster Lane
London Ec 2v 6 bn

NETHERLANDS
-Stedelijk Museum,
Paulus Potterstraat, 13
1071 Hv Amsterdam

-Museum Het Kruithuis,
Citadellaan, 7
5211 XA S. Hertogenbosch

SPAIN
-Mineral Museum,
Rios Rosas, 23
28000 Madrid

-National Encarving Museum,
Alcalà, 13
28000 Madrid

-National Decorative Arts Museum,
Montalban, 12
28000 Madrid

SWITZERLAND
-Museum Bellerive,
Hoschgasse, 3
8034 Zürich

-Musée des Arts Décoratifs,
Avenue Villamont, 4
1005 Lausanne

-Musée de l'Emaillerie et
de l'Horlogerie,
Route de Malagnou, 15
Geneva

-Gewerbemuseum/Museum
für Gestaltung,
Spalenvorstadt, 2
4051 Bâle

-Museum für Gestaltung,
Ausstellunstrasse, 61
8005 Zürich

USA
-The American Craft Museum,
40 West 53rd Street
New York - NY 10019

-Craft and Folk Art Museum,
5814 Wilshire Boulevard
90036 Los Angeles, CA

-Cooper Hewitt Museum
of Decorative Arts & Design,
Smithsonian Institution
9e, 90th Street
New York - NY 10019

-Metropolitan Museum of Art,
5th Avenue, 82 Street
New York - NY 10019

We must also mention the world's most important museums that display collections of jewels and precious stones: the Louvre Museum in Paris, the British Museum in London, the Victoria and Albert Museum in London, the Natural History Museum of Paris, the Topkapi Museum in Istambul, the National Museum of Florence, the Natural History Museum of New York, the Smithsonian Institution of New York, the Museum of Natural History of New York, the Gold Museum in Bogatà.
... Moscow and the Gold Museum in Bogatà.

PHOTOGRAPHIC CREDITS

- Jürgen ABELER/Wuppertalen Uhrenmuseum: 164
- Philippe ACHER/De Beers: 12, 30, 72, 75, 86, 90
- Alessandra ALIPERTI: 79
- Editions ASCENDANCE: 136
- Louis De BACKER: 148, 149, 151, 152, 153, 154, 155, 157
- Nelly BARIAND: 16, 20, 21, 131, 144
- BARSAMIAN: 38
- BARSAMIAN/MINSART: 28, 29, 143
- Foto Studio BAUMANN: 122
- J. P. BEAUDET: 14, 144
- Guy Van BELLEGHEM: 56
- Jacques BREUER: 22, 23, 137
- BULGARI: 52
- Marcello FAUSTINI: 10, 63
- CASA DAMIANI: Cover
- Diamond Information Centre of Vienna: 24
- Nicola CERRONE: 94
- Chris COLEMONT: 99, 147
- Adriano CORRADINI: 64
- CROCE & UIR: 24
- Guido DAELMENS: 36
- Frédéric DELEUZE: 39
- DEREY MACKER: 58, 59, 60, 61, 141
- Juul DEVENS: 30, 40
- Rodrigo DIEZ: 73
- Jul DIZON: 81
- Studio ENG: 26, 27
- Mauro FERRACUTI: 34, 35
- Romulo FIALDINI: 80
- FOTOTECNICA: 83
- Ferran FREIXA: 62
- Kurt GÄBLER: 74
- Moreno GALLONE: 158
- Giorgio GALVANI: 41
- Marco GIORLEO: 97
- GOFFIN VISUAL ART/HRD/DE BEERS: 104–105
- Hilde D'HAEYRE: 31
- Rony HEIRMAN: 146
- Gerherd HOSSER: 126, 127, 160, 161
- HRD/DE BEERS: 12, 30, 46, 72, 75, 86, 90, 98

- Vincent De JAEGHER: 134, 135
- Studio JOHN: 42
- Willy De LAUWER: 132
- Pol LEEMANS: 77
- Michel LEFRANQ: 89
- Christophe LEPAIRE: 96
- L & D Photographie: 101, 174
- LICHT BLICK FOTO-DESIGN: 116, 119, 120, 121, 123, 125
- R. MANCUSO & L. UGOLINI: 57
- Thierry MARTIN: 93, 145
- Claude MAZLOUM: 11, 53, 166
- Anna MONASTA: 84, 141
- Karla MERTENS: 173
- Simonne MUYLAERT-HOFMAN: 48, 49, 139
- Luciano NICOLINI: 54, 55, 172
- Gabriella NORIS: 6, 65
- Vincenzo PASTORE: 162
- Bertrand PAUL: 87, 91, 92, 133
- Erwin PAULY: 128, 129
- PENTASTUDIO: 37
- Guido PERSICO: 50
- François REYROU: 82
- PHOTOCROM: 2, 3, 4, 43, 70, 71, 158, 159
- PHOTO LAND/WOO HYUN CHOI: 76
- PIEMONTI: 47
- Caroline PORTAIL: 15, 169
- Jacques PRADES: 95
- Trise ROSEN: 66 (1 photo), 68
- Agathe SAINT GIRONS: 46
- Roxane De SAULE: 175
- Uli SCHEIBE: 25
- Maryke SERESIA: 32, 33, 176
- Massimo SORMONTA: 45
- Gerd SPRENG: 51
- TAKAGI: 66 (2 photos), 67, 69
- Antonio TORRES IÑIGO: 178
- J. M. TRONQUET: 177
- Raphaël VENDOME: 17, 18, 19, 130, 170, 171
- Helmut WOLF: 163
- Iain WOOD: 44
- Donald Barry WOODROW: 78
- David ZANARDI: 88
- A. ZANETTI: 84 (1 ...)

EDITOR'S MESSAGE
TO JEWELLERY ARTISTS

As part of our international program, we are planning to complete our collection on books on jewels and precious stones, continuing our on-going collaboration with Claude Mazloum. Our next edition will be a complete, illustrated world survey of creators and artists who make jewels. Later, we will publish a major work of art devoted to the erotic aspect of jewels. If you wish to take part in these projects and be included in one of the two planned works, please send a complete résumé immediately to:

Claude Mazloum
c/o Gremese International
Via Virginia Agnelli, 88
I-00151 Rome, Italy

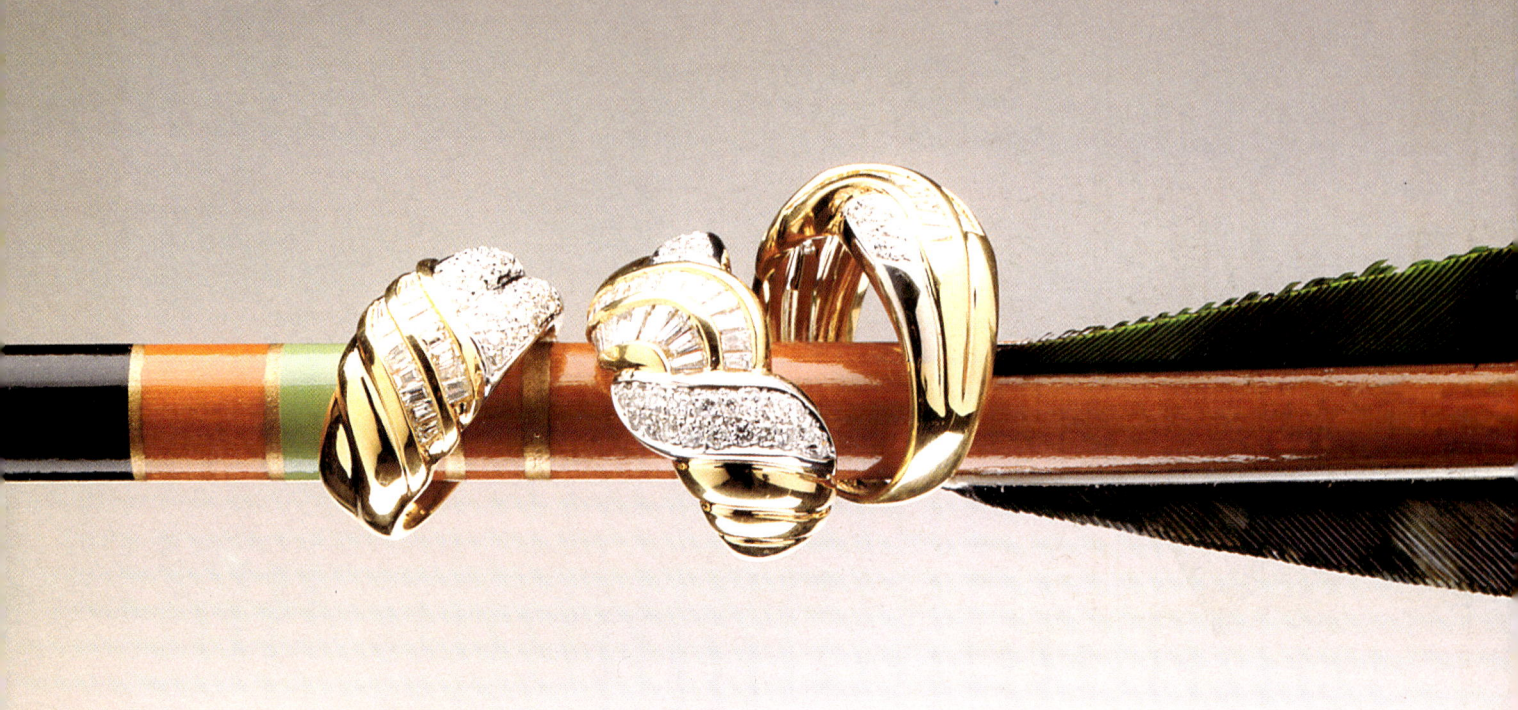